RIVERS
OF
MY
LIFE

ULLA MORRIS-CARTER

Also by Ulla Morris-Carter
I Am a Piano

ISBN: 978-0-692-93691-7

JAMorris Publications
jamorrispublications.com

TABLE OF CONTENTS

ACKNOWLEDGEMENTS

I owe an immense debt of gratitude to many who have helped me in my efforts to put this memoir to paper.

First and foremost, my sincere thanks go to my husband, Bill Carter, who steadily encouraged, patiently listened, occasionally corrected my Germanic English, offered structural suggestions, and gave key support at every phase.

Critical help came from my inspiring teacher, Sylvia Haloran, at the Mountain View-Los Altos Adult Education Center. She listened week after week as we Seniors read, corrected, and tried to sharpen our remembrances. This class consisted of a particularly talented group of writers of various backgrounds and of different nationalities whose camaraderie kept us all to the grindstone.

Extremely valuable advice was given by Sarah Ballard, one of the first female journalists on the staff of Sports Illustrated and a talented writer in her own right, who copy read and corrected a key draft of the manuscript.

Indispensable assistance came, for months and years, from my daughter Julia, who had directly experienced much of the story. Her deep picture research and designer's eye found photos that breathe in layers of life, flowing beyond the words alone.

to
my
three
beautiful
daughters
Maria, Karin, Julia
and to
their children
and those to follow

. . .

Portrait taken in Cairo, Egypt. Early 1960s.

FOREWORD

Memory is life, it is always carried by living people and

therefore it is in permanent evolution.

It is subject to the dialectics of remembrance and amnesia,

unaware of successive deformations . . . .

Memory becomes latent for a long time and

then suddenly revives . . . .

It always belongs to our time.

~ Pierre Nora, French historian

I've never thought of myself as an extraordinary person, but I did live through extraordinary times characterized by war, separations, adventure, risk, resilience, love and loss.

Much to my regret I never kept a diary, never wrote down names of fascinating people and places, never recorded important dates. I write from memory, a memory that may have inadvertently changed the actual facts to fit the story I have replayed in my head and, on occasion, told family and friends.

Winston Churchill once wrote, "Truth is so precious that she should be attended by a bodyguard of lies."

Where do we come from?

Where are we going?

What is the meaning of this life?

That is what every heart is shouting,

what every head is asking as it beats on chaos.

~ Nikos Kazantzakis

Drawing of Ulla by Herr Grulich, a Düsseldorf painter and neighbor of my maternal grandmother, Oma. Grateful for my grandmother's care and sharing of rationed food in the hungry postwar years, he made a drawing of myself and my brother Hans in 1945. I am 11 years old and wearing the gold earrings my father sent me from France in 1943 for my Communion.

Top: *Bridge in Düsseldorf over the frozen river Rhine, December 1946.* **Bottom:** *The Nile River, Egypt 1956.*

RIVERS OF MY LIFE

Nothing has really happened until it has been recorded.

- Virginia Woolf

Two great rivers shaped my life, the Rhine and the Nile. I grew up on the banks of Germany's most important river, the Rhine. The Nile, sometimes called the greatest single stream on earth, became part of my story when I was in my twenties.

Those two mighty rivers, with their rhythm, their power and their beauty have inspired centuries of poetry, tales of the gods, stories of love and death, songs of women and wine.

They are part of me.

People who live near the Rhine are called Rheinländer. They have a reputation for being particularly light-hearted, happy and outgoing compared to the more reserved northern and eastern Germans.

Ulla Morris-Carter

The devastation of WWII changed that characteristic. My hometown, Düsseldorf, suffered heavy bombings, partly because of its location only 40 kilometers away from the armament factories of Friedrich Krupp in Essen. These events forced many difficult changes in my family's life.

In the dark days after WWII, I was unable to ask my mother the questions that would have been important to understanding my family's background. The war and all of its repercussions were not open for discussion, neither in my family nor in society in general. Silence surrounded the subject of the suffering and losses of the German civilian population. I only asked my mother once, many years later when she visited me in Beirut, what her experiences, feelings and opinions of that time had been.

She appeared angry and distressed that I questioned her:
"I was busy raising and supporting two children without a father and trying to protect them from bombardments and the ravages of war," she said.

Her voice made me realize immediately that further talk on this subject was taboo. I never mentioned it again.

Daniel Johnson wrote in the *London Times Literary Supplement* in 2003:
> The reconciliation between victors and vanquished after 1945 depended on a tacit understanding to keep silent about the past.

And that silence continued all through my life. Still suffering from the after-effects of both World War I and World War II, nobody, including my grandparents, touched the subject. Guilt, shame and deep pain seemed to lie beneath this silence.

Now there is nobody left to ask.

People who live near or on the Nile have been called Nile Dwellers. When in 1955 I was offered a job in Cairo, Egypt, I became a Nile dweller myself. Nothing changed my life more than that move from Düsseldorf to Cairo.

Ulla Morris-Carter

From Day One I loved the country, its climate, even the heat and the dust, but particularly the great hospitality of its people.

I experienced them and their special qualities on one of several adventures—among them a Nile journey on a slow boat from Cairo to Aswan in early 1957. More than half a century later I would try to depict some of these peoples and places, and subsequent experiences, from the vantage point of a world that has changed almost beyond recognition.

The richness of life on the Nile was shaped by the power with which the river used to flood the land every year. The construction of the Low Dam at Aswan around 1902 and particularly the completion of the High Dam in 1970 transformed, for the first time, the age-old method of irrigation and the renewal of the fertile soil.

Despite this change, the Nile Festival, celebrated for thousands of years upon the arrival of the flood, continues until today. Even Napoleon Bonaparte was fascinated with Egypt and the Nile. During his Egypt campaign in 1798-99 his scientists discovered the Rosetta Stone, key to deciphering the ancient Egyptian hieroglyphs. Trying to untangle my past has made me remember the Rosetta Stone. No such Rosetta Stone guided my journey from Germany to the Middle East in early 1956. I had no idea what role that decision would play—not only for my future, but also for understanding my earlier years.

Some day my fragmentary memories may be of interest to my children and grandchildren, who, now, in their busy lives, have no time to ask the questions they might later want answered, when it may be too late. They have heard a few tales around the dinner table. But in case they don't remember them, these *Rivers of My Life* stories are my legacy.

Ulla Morris-Carter

Early Düsseldorf days. My father and mother in the garden and home where I grew up.

THE EARLY YEARS
FAMILY AND WWII
GERMANY

Unexploded bomb in the basement after hitting my paternal grandparents, the Kirschbaum's, house.
It went right through the living room. If it had exploded none of us would be here.

FIRST BOMBARDMENT

"Of course it's a full-moon night," I mumbled to myself. "That's when they always come. How else would they know where to drop their bombs?" When the bomb hit our house in Düsseldorf, we huddled in our shelter in the basement. It was the first major bombardment we experienced.

The year was 1940. I was almost seven years old, and my brother was three-and-a-half. The sirens went off at three in the morning. I jumped out of bed, dressed in the dimly-lit room, picked up my little suitcase with emergency supplies and a couple of blankets and started down the corridor toward the basement. I already had plenty of practice. Near-nightly alarms had become the norm. The wailing sound of the sirens frightened me every single time. Our apartment was only dimly lit. All windows had to be darkened or covered with black shades. Lifting one of the shades slightly, I saw again the full moon, brilliant and sinister, illuminating the otherwise black city streets. After a short rain shower, the cobblestones and the city lanterns looked shiny as if polished for a special occasion.

My mother tried to wake my brother. He could sleep through anything. He opened his eyes for a split-second but was asleep again the next. My mother had to carry him to the basement. His 40-pound body was heavy, even heavier in his deep, limp sleep.

We struggled down a narrow wooden staircase to reach the shelter, a recently reinforced former coal and potato basement. The shelter was small, barely big enough

Ulla Morris-Carter

to accommodate the five families that lived in our four-story apartment building. Most of the younger men had already been drafted, including my father. Two families had left the city for safer surroundings. Only one man, not physically fit enough for the army, remained as our sole male protector.

We took our seats on a narrow wooden bench on the left-hand side. In back, a couple of wooden pallets served as beds for the small children. The shelter was cold, a bit humid. The air smelled stale. As soon as everybody was assembled, the last woman locked the heavy iron door by sliding two heavy handles into place.

On the right-hand side of the shelter, an escape hatch had been constructed down low, in case we could not get out into the open via the staircase after a bombardment. By knocking a hole into the thick double wall dividing our house from the one next door, we could, in an emergency, escape into the next building, or into the next one after that, until we found a way out into the street. Right now the hole was closed with easy-to-remove small bricks. A hammer was attached next to it for that purpose.

We sat in silence in our little prison, waiting and listening to the distant sound of the approaching British RAF bombers. I felt cold even though we sat squashed thigh to thigh. The longer I sat still, waiting for the unknown, the colder I felt. This was a creeping cold, the kind that slowly descends into your bones, not a sudden jolt of icy wind. If only I could run around, move my sleepy, cold body into some kind of action, I would feel warm again. I imagined running along a river, flowers in bloom, and bright sunshine warming my cold feet.

How wonderful! Wishful thinking. We remained in our little prison, motionless, a huddled mass of dark shapes.

Suddenly the sirens sounded full alarm, three times, their screeching blare announcing imminent danger. I forgot the cold. All I felt, in my stomach, was terror. If the sound of the wailing sirens had frightened me earlier, it was nothing compared to the danger signaled by the somber, sonorous drone of those approaching squadrons.

In the silence I became aware of breathing patterns of all of us. Short in, long out, in and out, in and out, in rhythm with the awful melody of the approaching bombers. The closer the sound of the planes, the heavier and more laboured our breathing became. We squeezed closer together, shivering and trembling. Closing my ears with my index fingers, I tried to shut out the increasing drone. But the noise grew louder.

Then, a powerful explosion. I held my breath. A second explosion. The floor trembled. The house shook dangerously, but it stood.

When the floor stopped trembling, I planted my feet firmly on it. That made me feel better. Some of the fear in my stomach began to disperse. One or two of our shelter companions prayed. A child cried. Frau Schmidt wrapped her black woolen

Ulla Morris-Carter

shawl tighter and fingered her rosary. My brother was still sleeping. Frau Müsch, on the opposite bench, nervously pulled her grey coat even more tightly around her small, body. Everybody wore only grey or black in those dreary days. Nobody owned a green, red or blue coat.

Normally chatty and lively, Frau Müsch now sat in terrified silence. My mother seemed calm, her right arm around my shoulder, holding me close to her. After another moment of eerie quiet, everybody relaxed, exhaling, breathing deeply and sighing, shoulders dropping with relief. This time we had been spared.

Seconds later, it came like a thunderbolt, a horrendous whizzing sound followed by an earsplitting boom. We all dove to the floor. The house shook in its foundations, perilously swaying from right to left. The lights went out. We all clung to each other in total darkness, darkness that was darker than black.

There was only dust, noise, shock, terror, lack of air and fear of death.

We could hardly breathe. Nobody dared to light the lantern for fear of a gas explosion and fire. Somebody tried to open the heavy iron door. The handles did not move. The door did not budge. It was shut tight. Was it the pressure of the explosion or was it debris on the other side of the door that prevented it from opening?

We coughed and gasped for air. Someone close to the escape hole found the hammer and tried desperately to knock out the thin layer of bricks. It seemed to take an eternity. The first brick fell out. Why was this taking so long? My mother crawled toward my brother at the far end of the shelter. Even he was awake now, crying and pleading to get him out of the dark.

We thought we could breathe no longer. There was no oxygen left in the room. Then, a slight stream of fresh air. It seemed to be coming from the next-door shelter.

Thank God! The escape hole was beginning to open!

There was no panic. Our group of friendly neighbors tried to be brave. The escape hole grew larger by the minute.

An anxious face appeared on the other side:

"Are you alive, are you OK, anybody injured?"

It was our neighbor from the next-door building. Everyone scrambled toward the escape, wanting to get out as fast as possible. Helping hands reached out to pull us through the hole into the neighbor's basement shelter.

The bombardment continued but the sound of the explosions moved farther and farther away. Half an hour later, the sirens sounded the end of the alarm, meaning the bombers had left our airspace. Until now nobody knew what had actually happened to our house. Shaken and with wobbly knees, we finally managed to go upstairs from the neighbor's basement and out into the street. There we realized how lucky we had been.

At the end of our street, buildings were burning, and the sky was fire-red from the phosphorous bombs that had hit some of the houses. Ambulances, their sirens

Ulla Morris-Carter

ominously urgent, began to arrive. One look at our house made clear that it had been hit. The roof was gone, but the outside walls of the house were strangely intact. How was it possible? We stood in the street, shivering in the cool night air.

When we tried to enter our house someone shouted: "Don't enter! You have an unexploded bomb in the basement. Get away! Quick, quick, move on! It might explode any moment."

"Move on" was easier said than done. Where to go? We had nothing but the clothes on our bodies. We started walking away from the burning street, from our house with the unexploded bomb.

My maternal grandparents lived only ten blocks away. My mother decided to try to walk to their house, hoping they had not been hit. The city looked frightening. Disturbed people stood in the street, their eyes glazed over, watching their belongings going up in flames or lying invisible under a heap of rubble. Trees lay like huge bodies in the middle of the road. Several times, large bomb craters blocked our eerie journey.

My little brother straggled along, tired, not understanding why he could not be in his cozy bed. After what seemed to me like hours, we reached my grandparents house. It was still standing in one piece. My mother knocked on the door. It opened. My grandparents stood there, unharmed. They were very, very relieved to see us.

On the next day we learned that an enormous bomb was firmly embedded in our personal coal storage basement, right next to the shelter. The bomb had smashed through the four floors of the building, taking out most of our living room and creating a huge crater.

Only one lonely cabinet remained upright, attached to a wall, complete with books and other objects. It hung there, unreachable.

There was no floor left to walk on.

Left: *My brother Hans and I around this time.* Right: *The hole in the floor from the unexploded bomb.*

Ulla Morris-Carter

The house of my maternal grandparents, Jakob and Emma Liesenfeld, who owned and ran a delicatessen and grocery store on Lorettostrasse in Düsseldorf-Bilk.

Ulla Morris-Carter

In German: Liebe Mutter! Aus Melle sende Ich dir viele Grüsse. Ich bin hier gut angekommen und es gefält mir ganz gut. Wir gehen viel spatzieren in den Welden. Viele Grüsse von diener Ursula. *In English:* Dear Mother! From Melle I send you many greetings. I have arrived well and I like it all right. We take lots of walks in the forest. Many greetings from your Ursula.

Postcard of the safe house, sent by me to my mother written in Gothic script.

SAFE HOUSES IN
THE COUNTRY

The first time away from home alone put me into a state of anxiety. Because of the increasing number of air raids and the dangers of living in the city, my elementary school on Konkordiastrasse had put into place a program that sent children to a safe house in the country, *Landverschickungsheim*. School children would spend a few months there with school instruction.

I have only a fragmentary recollection of my time in Melle, a small town in the district of Osnabrück in Lower Saxony. What I do remember vividly is that I was assigned the upper bunk bed in a room with four children. A terrifying thought to be up there alone.

How was I to find my way to the bathroom in the middle of the night? It seems strange that I remember the room and the bunk bed but not the place itself. The large, hostel-like house, judging by the picture on a postcard I sent to my mother, was surrounded by trees, maybe even a forest. But no other details come into my mind.

Where did we eat? Where did we study? Did we study?

The report card I later discoverd gave no grades, only a remark by a school instructor that grades were not posted for that period of time. My first letters to my mother, hand-written in Gothic script, were not very newsy and not very revealing either. But what can one expect from a seven-year-old who had only just learned to write?

The letters, a miserable attempt to stay connected, were our only means of communication. We could neither phone our parents, nor could they phone us, unless there was a dire emergency.

Ulla Morris-Carter

Letters I wrote in early Gothic script to my mother, **left,** *and father,* **below.**

Here, in translation, are three of my letters:

Dear Mother,

I am very well dear mother. I have mailed the birthday card to grandmother. I am very happy that I am allowed to accompany you to Kapellen. We walk every day in the forest. Greetings from your Ursula. I do not need handkerchiefs.

Dear Father,

We are now in Melle. I like it very much here. For a long time I have been waiting for mail. When the weather is nice we often go walking in the forest. I received a postcard from Aunt Kate. I send you greetings, your Ursula.

An old yellowed report card that survived the war stated that I was in Melle from May 15 to December 18, 1941. I have always thought I was sent away for only a few weeks, not six months.

Why don't I remember my eighth birthday, which fell in the middle of my stay in the country? Why did my mother send me away when I was only seven years old? Why can't I remember more?

Ulla Morris-Carter

My memory is blank, empty, like a dark hole or a desert. Only certain detached images remain. The answer is, of course, that my mother wanted to protect me. But the thought haunts me nonetheless.

In retrospect, the experience of being separated from home and family for that length of time at so young an age seems a great loss.

Städtische Volksschule in – an der – am *Konkordiastr.*

Zeugnis

für *Ursula Kirschbaum*

Schüler in der *I. a* Klasse, *1.* Schuljahr, *1. r. 2.* Halbjahr 19 *40/41*

Leistungsstufen: sehr gut; gut; befriedigend; ausreichend; mangelhaft, ungenügend. Die Beurteilung der Leistungen in den einzelnen Leibesübungen werden mit Punkten 1 bis 9 bewertet. Dabei 1 = ungenügend und 9 = sehr gut.

I. Allgemeine Beurteilung des körperlichen, charakterlichen und geistigen Strebens und des Gesamterfolges: *Ursula war vom 15. Mai – 18. Dez. 1941 ... ...*

My early school report card book, Zeugnisheft, *from Melle, the safe house town to which I was sent.* **Above:** *Cover and inside page of the report book which indicates the dates I was there and away from home, much longer than I had previously thought.* **Right:** *Inscription on inside of the report card book.*

Translation: Through German Parents gave us God our Life. From German Soil He gifts us our Bread. Everything we have comes from the hands of God: Blood and Soil, People and Homeland. Never do we want to let go of these hands. We want to hold tight to the German Homeland and be one with our German People.
Berlin, 18th June, 1935.

Durch deutsche Eltern gab uns Gott das Leben. Vom deutschen Boden schenkt er uns das Brot. So sind Blut und Erde, Volk und Heimat die Hände Gottes, aus denen wir alles haben, was wir sind. Nie wollen wir diese Hände loslassen. Wir wollen festhalten an der deutschen Heimat und eins sein mit unserem deutschen Volke. Berlin, den 18. Juni 1935. Rust.

Ulla Morris-Carter

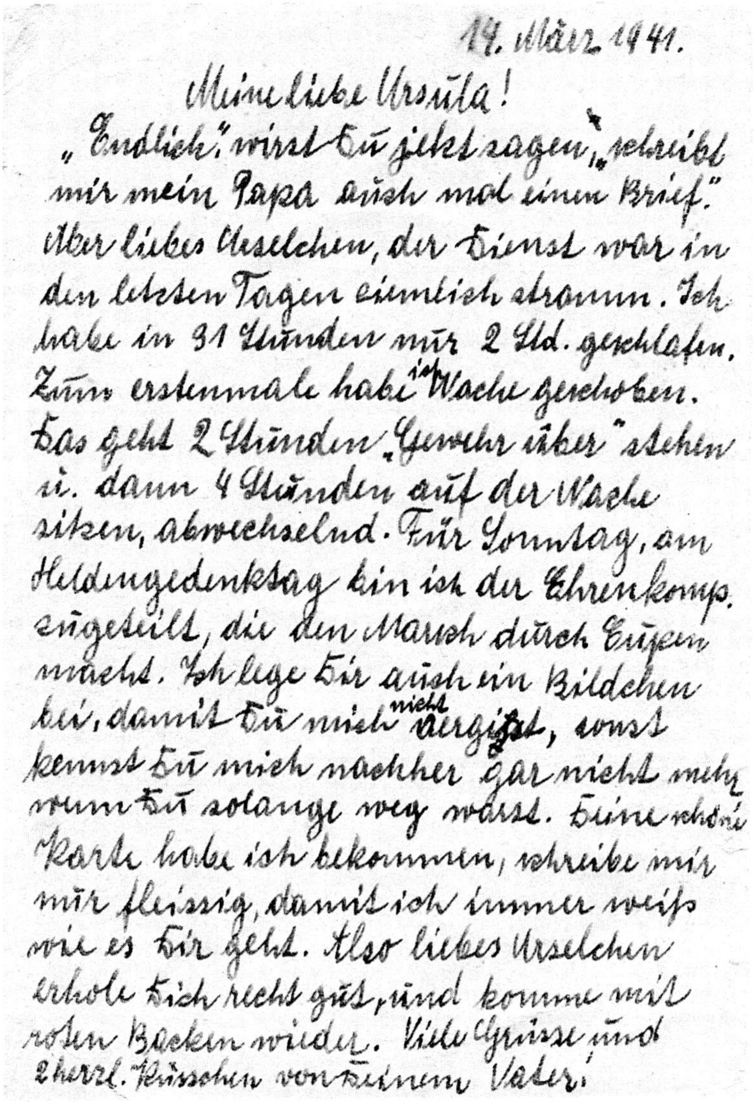

14. März 1941.

Meine liebe Ursula!

[handwritten German letter]

Letter from my father while I was in Melle: March 14, 1941

My dear Ursula!

"Finally," you will say, my Pappa is also writing me a letter." But, dearest Urselchen, my program was extremely demanding during the past few days. During 91 hours I only slept two. For the first time I had to be on guard. That means standing for two hours "shoulder arms," and then four hours sitting while having guard duty. On Sunday, during "Hero's Memorial Day" parade, I have been assigned to the honors company, who will march through Eupen. I am enclosing a little photo, so that you won't forget me altogether. Otherwise you might not recognize me after your long absence. I did receive your beautiful card. Just keep on writing frequently, so that I always know how you are. Now, dearest Urselchen, take good care of yourself, stay healthy and return with pink cheeks. Warmest greetings and two big kisses from your father.

Ulla Morris-Carter

Above: *My father in the army at his typewriter. Possibly the picture sent with the letter.*

Below: F*amily pictures with my father on his first home leave,* Heimat Urblaub, *from the army circa 1941.*
Clockwise from top right: *My father and I. My father Hans and I. My mother Maria, my brother Hans, my father Hanns, and I.*

Ulla Morris-Carter

My parents before marriage. **Left:** *My father, Hanns Kirschbaum.* **Right:** *My mother, Maria Liesenfeld, in 1928.*

My Family

For almost half-an-hour I have been staring intently at an old photograph, a sepia-colored picture of my mother at age 21. That was 87 years ago. It is part of my little family gallery on a wall near my computer.

The woman I knew as my wonderful mother is shown here as a beautiful young lady, her profile distinct, her hair dark and short, her partially exposed bare back decorated by a long string of pearls held together by a knot. I know relatively little about this young woman and feel bereft that there is no longer anybody alive to ask. According to family legend, my mother's mother, my adored grandmother, was so shocked when she saw the photograph with the bare back that she slapped my mother's face.

Next to this picture hangs a second sepia photo, that of my young and handsome father. It looks as if it had been taken recently rather than in 1928, when he was 25. The casual black sweater he is wearing, with white trim around the open-neck, reminds me of artists we might see today in a gallery or on a stage. He is not in suit and tie, the normal attire when one was photographed in days past.

Next to this photo there is yet another nontraditional picture of my father, wearing a dark cap with motorcycle glasses strapped over his forehead. He owned a motorcycle, a BMW I was told, of which he was extremely proud. He would put my mother riding on the seat behind him, much to the consternation of my grandmother, who thought it inappropriate for a young lady to ride on such a vehicle. All the neighborhood children would gather around the motorcycle when the sportive, handsome couple took off on a ride. My mother's older brother also owned a motorcycle, but his bride rode in a sidecar, which my grandmother apparently found less objectionable.

Ulla Morris-Carter

Top left: *My father in his motorcycling outfit.* Bottom left: *My mother and father with his motocycle.*
Bottom: *My parents in their garden.*

It does not surprise me to see my parents in these nontraditional photos. No doubt, everybody believes one's parents are special. I certainly did. But I now know that both were individuals who resisted being forced into a mold.

My father was an artist, a painter and graphic artist, as well as a photographer. I have often wondered whether he took the infamous photo of my mother showing a bare back. Nobody ever said so. My father, at age 23, painted himself in the mirror, a small self-portrait, which luckily survived the war. It is now part of my little gallery. Most of his other paintings have been lost. He loved the poetry of Rainer Maria Rilke, as evidenced by a book my mother presented to him in 1928, a year before they became engaged.

My mother was a gifted musician who had hoped to become a professional concert pianist. She was well on her way when, at age 20, she broke her arm. Her ruptured tendons were irreparable in those days. She continued to play frequently but no longer professionally into the last years of her life.

Ulla Morris-Carter

I remember a tender scene, in 1939, in our small living room. My father was standing behind my mother while she played his favorite song:

Alle Tage ist kein Sonntag: Not every day is Sunday.

Alle Tage ist kein Sonntag, alle Tage gibt's kein Wein,
Aber Du sollst alle Tage recht lieb zu mir sein.
Und wenn ich einst tot bin, sollst Du denken an mich,
Auch am Abend eh Du einschläfst,
Aber weinen sollst Du nicht.

Not every day is Sunday, not every day can you drink wine,
But every day you should much love me and always be mine.
And after I have died, please remember me,
Especially in the evening before you fall asleep, But please do not shed tears.

My parents' engagement announcement, designed by my father:

Düsseldorf. 16. February. 1930. Maria Liesenfeld Hanns Kirschbaum Jr. Verlobte. Lorettostrasse 15. Konkordiastr. 41.

Düsseldorf. February 16th, 1930. 15 Loretto Street, my mother's home. 41 Konkordia Street, my father's home.
Maria Liesenfeld, Hanns Kirschbaum Jr., Engaged.

Ulla Morris-Carter

Multiple Marriages L-R: *My mother Maria, my father Hanns, sister-in-law Käte and my mother's brother Karl married together in a joint, modest ceremony in a small chapel, Stoffeler Kapellchen, near the South Cemetery of Düsseldorf, 1931. Käte was a protestant and could not get married in the Catholic church and my father had already left the church at age 15. The Germans have a special expression for getting married,* **Unter die Haube bringen.** Die Haube *is a bonnet. So literally it means to bring the bride under the bonnet, hence, the white bonnets the women are wearing.*

Liesenfeld Familie *(maternal):* Jakob und Emma Liesenfeld with their five children. **Back row:** *Son Karl Liesenfeld, daughter Johanna Windhoevel, daughter-in-law Liesel married to son Willy Liesenfeld, son-in-law Hanns Kirschbaum.* **Front row:** *Daughter Agnes Liesenfeld, Emma (Oma) Liesenfeld and Jakob (Opa), daughter Maria Kirschbaum. Early 1930s.*

Ulla Morris-Carter

Left: *Me as a young baby.* Top Right: *With my mother.* Bottom Right: *With my father in our garden and the pond he built.*

URSULA ANNEMARIE AGNES KIRSCHBAUM

That's me. On a cool beautiful fall day—it was a Tuesday—I entered this world at 9:30 in the morning. The date was October 26, 1933.

My place of birth was the St. Martins Hospital in Düsseldorf. My proud parents, Maria and Hanns Kirschbaum, later told me that they were delighted to have the little girl that my father, in particular, had wished for.

My mother, the third of five children, was born to Emma and Jakob Liesenfeld. Jakob was an elementary school teacher. Emma ran the delicatessen and grocery store they owned on Lorettostrasse 15 in Düsseldorf-Bilk. They were a musical family. All siblings loved singing, and most played an instrument. When I was born, my parents lived in the ground floor apartment of the four-story Kirschbaum family house on Düsselstrasse 65.

My paternal grandparents, Josefine and Hans Kirschbaum, occupied the third floor of the building, one of the larger apartments with a balcony that looked out over the garden. Our ground floor apartment was small but cozy. It consisted of a bedroom, a

Ulla Morris-Carter

living room, a kitchen, a small bathroom with a toilet and a little sink but no actual bathtub. Baths were taken at a nearby bathhouse. Few of the old buildings had proper bathrooms in those days.

From a small terrace attached to the kitchen, stairs lead into the garden, a place I remember well. The garden, designed by my artistic father, seemed to me like a little paradise filled with flowers and plants of all kinds, with ivy and ferns. As one who had studied art, my father may have remembered the lush Monet gardens in France. A small pond with a fountain in the middle, for which my father himself had poured the cement, was the most fascinating spot. Two ducks, some goldfish and an eel occupied the pond. And there were pigeons, and there were fluffy gray and white rabbits that, when released from their cages, hopped happily around the garden.

I remember playing ball in these lovely surroundings despite the small space. My father, an animal lover, also had a dog, a Great Dane. After I was born and occupied center stage, the dog was so filled with jealousy that my parents had to find a new home for him. He would not let anybody near my crib.

One of my earliest memories of the house on Düsselstrasse is of going to fetch fresh rolls from the bakery across the street in the morning.

"Here are 30 pennies for the rolls."

Brötchen we called them, meaning little breads. My mother put three coins into my small hands. Clutching the money tightly in my fist, I skipped out of our flat, ran through the corridor, then, with all the strength I could muster, opened the heavy wooden entrance door and ran out into the cobblestone street. It was eight o'clock in the morning, and I was thrilled to be allowed to fetch the fresh rolls from the bakery for breakfast with my mother and father. This was a newly acquired responsibility, and I took it very seriously. I was four years old, a light-footed, skinny little thing with slightly curly blond hair and blue eyes.

The bakery was close enough that I was allowed to go by myself. The indescribably delicious aroma of freshly-baked bread emanating from this place of desires is still with me today. No other place fascinated me as much as this bakery.

The owner, Frau Rittershaus, a kind but imposing woman of about 50 years, stood behind the glass counter helping customers. She was a serious person who wore gold-rimmed glasses and a white apron. Her graying hair was pulled back into a chignon. Working fast and efficiently, and not given to a lot of chit-chat like other grown-ups I knew, she counted out crisp rolls or wrapped a loaf of bread and placed them into the baskets or shopping bags the customers handed her.

How I envied her! To be able to live every day surrounded by these delectable items and, in addition, to be engulfed by that mouth-watering aroma. The glass counter was high for me. I had to stand on my tip-toes to look above it. The lower glass shelves of

Ulla Morris-Carter

the counter were filled with luscious-looking pastries, fruit tarts, chocolate cakes, and butter cream cup cakes plus, so it seemed to me, hundreds of different kinds of cookies. Assorted fresh breads were arranged in order on wooden shelves behind Frau Rittershaus, the dark, crusty bread my father loved, the white braided bread, soft and sweet and covered with glistening butter and sesame seeds that we were allowed to eat only on Sundays, and the long brown loaves and square grainy black breads, already thinly sliced.

While waiting my turn, I fantasized that one day I might be Frau Rittershaus and that I could decide which one of the pastries I would choose to eat at any time of the day or night. We had these delicacies only on special occasions. Feeling the now warm coins in my hand, I knew that they were just enough to buy the rolls, nothing else.

A young Ulla.

"Please, Frau Rittershaus, could you give me six rolls?" I asked while handing her the basket I carried on my arm.

I kept wishing I could stand behind the glass counter and count the rolls fresh from the oven. They were oval-shaped and golden brown with a crusty top created by a slit cut through the middle of the dough before they were baked. One day Frau Rittershaus had let me go into the back room, where her husband was baking the bread.

But no time to linger now in this paradise. With my treasure in my basket, I ran home. The carved, wooden entrance door to our apartment building was even harder to open from the outside than from the inside. I could barely reach the bell at the right-hand side of the entrance. Ours was the second one from the bottom. After my mother pressed the buzzer, I threw all my weight against the door, pushing and struggling to keep it open long enough for me to slip through. I ran up three steps to our ground floor apartment. My mother was waiting at the door.

Shortly after my fourth birthday I was told that soon there would be a new baby in our house. When my mother had to leave for the hospital, my father stayed home with me. He was nervously waiting to be called with news from the hospital. As night fell, still no news. Finding me fast asleep, he went to the corner pub, just a few steps away, for a beer. Then, of course, I woke up. Being alone at home did not scare me, because I knew exactly where to look for my father.

On December 29, 1937, in the midst of a cold German winter, I ran, barefoot and clad only in my nightgown, to the corner pub owned by Herr Krevett. A heavy brown

Ulla Morris-Carter

felt curtain with leather trim, hanging in a half-circle inside the door, kept the cold air out when the main door was opened. I remember how difficult it was for me to push aside the curtain to be able to peek through a slit and look for my father. I saw him immediately, my tall handsome father, standing at the bar and drinking a beer.

He didn't seem overly surprised to see me. His strong arms immediately swooped me off the floor and held me tight and warm. In this neighborhood pub everybody knew everybody else. Father took me back home and tucked me into my bed, which was in my parents' bedroom at the foot of their large bed.

Three days later my mother returned home from the hospital with a baby boy in her arms. My new brother, born December 29, 1937, was called Hans, like his father, his grandfather and great-grandfather before him. And he was born the same day as my mother, 30 years earlier, December 29, 1907. In my own memory and by all subsequent accounts, we were a happy family.

KIRSCHBAUM BUSINESS

My father worked with his father, a photographer and the founder of the Kirschbaum *Klischee Anstalt,* an engraving plant located in the same Kirschbaum family building where we lived. Its entrance was just opposite our apartment. Design, photography and engraving of zinc plates for four-color-printing were the mainstay of the family business.

Kirschbaum Männer, *men* L-R: *my father Hanns Kirschbaum, my great grandfather Hans Kirschbaum, and my grandfather Hans Kirschbaum, 1934. If my brother Hans had been born at the time of this picture, there would have been four generations of Hans Kirschbaums.*

Ulla Morris-Carter

My father, who was trained in all three fields, worked mainly as the designer and graphic artist. Apart from him and my grandfather, there were four other employees, among them Herr Wahlmann, a photographer, and Herr Müsch, the excellent retoucheur and graphic artist.

I loved visiting Herr Wahlmann in his tiny darkroom while he was developing film. The room would be dark except for a small red light glowing in the corner. It was a mysterious place, filled with unfamiliar smells and full of secrets, or so I thought. Herr Wahlmann was a sweet man, always with a smile. He was thin, not very tall and fairly pale. I thought all photographers were pale because they spent too much time in a dark room. The most impressive object in the first of the three rooms was the big photo camera that moved along rails on a wooden plank that was three feet high and about nine feet long. The rails reminded me of railroad tracks.

What a place to play! When my father was working with this camera, he would occasionally allow me to participate. He would put me on a chair so that I was the same height as he was and let me look together with him at the object he wanted to photograph, both of us hidden under the large black cloth that he threw over our heads and the camera. What an exciting, mysterious and exotic game this was!

I also recall sitting next to Herr Müsch at his drawing table, while he was working on a delicate retouching project. He was short with wavy dark hair, and he seemed to work with lightning speed, designing, perfecting and retouching the project in front of him.

KRISTALLNACHT

Here is an incident from those early days that survives in my memory.

I had just turned five when I was allowed to spend the night with one of my aunts. Darkness fell as I stood by the window of her home to look down on the street two floors below. At the far end of the street was a small square where we often walked and played.

"Aunt Agnes, please come quickly and look. The square is burning," I shouted excitedly.

My aunt came racing to the window, and together we rushed onto the small balcony to have a better view. Indeed, what looked like a huge bonfire seemed to have engulfed the whole square. We did not know what had happened and watched in silence, fascinated by the flames that were rising higher and higher.

Suddenly there was commotion on a balcony two houses away from us. Shouting and screaming orders to step away were three men in brown uniforms who were struggling to force a black upright piano out onto the small balcony. Without any explanation they shoved, pushed and finally hoisted the piano high enough that it rested precariously on the railing. But not for long. The next thing I remember was seeing the piano fly through the air as if it were a light-weight object and landing with an ear-shattering

Ulla Morris-Carter

crash on the cobblestone street below. The trembling piano wires gave out an eerie sound, one note after another, reminding me of the scales my mother played on the piano when she practiced. Then the strange sounds became quieter, humming slightly like a broken record. The piano seemed to be in the final seconds of life. And then there was silence, total silence.

We stood in stunned silence, staring at thousands of splintered pieces of black wood spread all over our street. The white of the ivory covered keys shone mysteriously and ghostly under the light of the lanterns and the fire. I had no idea what this incident meant. I was five years old. I knew about fires and their danger. That much I understood. My aunt gave me no explanation. If she knew what was happening, she must have thought that I would not be able to understand.

Today I know that this fire was one of many that were set on November 9-10, 1938, during *Kristallnacht*, or, as it is known in English, *The Night of Broken Glass*. All over Germany, Austria and other Nazi-controlled areas, Jewish shops and department stores had their windows smashed and their contents destroyed, supposedly in revenge for the assassination of a German diplomat by a Jew in Paris. Synagogues were set on fire while local fire departments stood by and did nothing. The contents of houses and stores belonging to Jews and hundreds of books that had been banned by the Nazi regime were burning on our little square. Many Jewish men were rounded up and arrested.

It was a preview of what was to come.

War Begins

Shortly after I entered school in 1939, World War II began, an event that I do not recall as anything dramatic. I was almost six, and I was fully occupied with my first experiences in school. Shy as I was, I remember being terribly embarrassed when some of the boys in my first grade class thought it amusing to tease me by changing my family name from *Kirschbaum,* meaning cherry tree, into other fruit tree names, such as *Pflaumenbaum*, plum tree, *Birnbaum*, pear tree, or *Apfelbaum*, apple tree.

I was mortified when they called out, "Apple tree, pear tree, where are you?"

In May 1940, when I was six and a half, the first bombardment occurred in a small neighboring town, Mönchengladbach. There was no industry in Mönchengladbach, no factories that manufactured war-related machinery. We all wondered why it was shelled. Düsseldorf, only a few kilometers away, was not directly hit, but the civilian population was ordered to prepare for possible future bombardments. My home town, Düsseldorf, was a lovely old baroque city on the river Rhine, only a few miles away from the important industrial Ruhr district—the Ruhr is a small river—home to Krupp's major armament manufacturing plants.

Ulla Morris-Carter

Hitler issued this proclamation:

> The firm of Friedrich Krupp, a family enterprise for 132 years, deserves the highest recognition for its incomparable performances in boosting the military power of Germany.
>
> — The Arms of Krupp, *William Manchester.*

Consequently, this region became particularly vulnerable. Nicknamed the "office of the Ruhr district," *der Schreibtisch des Ruhrgebietes,* Düsseldorf was the site of the home offices of the major iron and steel companies. Many top executives of those giant companies lived and worked there. Throughout the war, this part of the Rhineland— Duisburg, Essen, Düsseldorf, Krefeld, Wuppertaland and surrounding cities—were heavily bombed time and again. In one night in June of 1943, during one of many bombardments called the Battle of the Ruhr, hundreds died or were wounded, and in Düsseldorf alone, 140,000 people were left homeless.

Jakob and Emma Liesenfeld family 1939

The Jakob and Emma Liesenfeld Family 1939.

Just before the outbreak of WW2, my maternal family gathered for this farewell photo as son Willie, my mother's brother, and his wife Liesel were returning to Indonesia, where Willie was working for Royal Dutch Shell. They were subsequently on the boat when WW2 broke out. Upon arrival, Willie, (**back row, far right**)*, was interned in Indonesia, and Liesel was sent to Japan with two of the children for the duration of the war. I am,* (**front row, middle**)*, sitting in front of Opa Liesenfeld. My mother Maria, front row,* **far left***, is holding nephew Theo. My father Hanns is standing 2nd from left. Cousin Hänschen is standing far right, next to Tante Agnes, and my brother Hans is middle front on Oma Liesenfeld's lap.*

Ulla Morris-Carter

LIESENFELD FAMILY

My Maternal Grandparents: *Young Emma Schmidt and Jakob Liesenfeld, before their marriage (Oma and Opa).*

My mother Maria, as a young woman.

KIRSCHBAUM FAMILY

My Paternal Grandparents: *Hans & Josephine Kirschbaum (Grosspappa and Grossmama Kirschbaum).*

My father, Hanns, as a young man and young boy.

In Halsenbach, Hunsrück , about 8 years old.

ALWAYS ON THE MOVE

Our gypsy life started right after that first traumatic bombardment. The Hunsrück, a stunningly beautiful region alongside the river Moselle and bordered by the rivers Rhine, Nahe and Saar, had not yet been involved in the bombardments. Relatives of my maternal grandfather, who owned a big farm in Halsenbach in the Hunsrück, offered us, my mother, my brother and me, temporary accomodations.

Our stay was short. One memory remains vivid, a fascinating oven in the center of the village. Built of natural grey stone topped with a rounded dome, it resembled an enormous beehive. The oven would be fired up once a week, always a major event, and was available to all residents. The farmers' wives would meet there, carrying their unbaked bread loaves on wooden trays or in baskets. Large, round or oval-shaped, dark loaves and white braided bread dough for Sundays and holidays would be placed on a big, flat wooden shovel with a long handle. Then the unbaked breads would disappear into the darkness of the mysterious oven center. Heated with wood, it gave delicious, crunchy crusts to all breads baked in it. I always wondered what the inside of the oven looked like, but as soon as all the breads vanished, a little iron door on the outside of the oven was tightly locked. We were never allowed to look inside.

"Too hot," was always the explanation.

Not only bread was baked. For special occasions, the most delectable looking cakes, apple crisps or plum cakes on large metal trays, followed the breads into this mysterious sanctum. One cake in particular attracted my attention, fluffy dough covered with roasted oats, honey and butter. Almonds were no longer available, but living on a farm gave us milk and butter. The smell emanating from that oven filled the whole village

Ulla Morris-Carter

center. It made your mouth water. We children loved hanging around there, hoping to be lucky enough to get a little taste of that freshly baked bread or cake. I remember my aunt standing in the kitchen in the evening of baking day, clutching one of those large dark loaves to her ample chest. With a sharp knife, she cut from the outside, moving expertly toward her chest, slicing a piece of the still warm, crisp bread for everybody's evening meal. There simply was nothing better than a slice of warm, crusty bread with homemade butter.

But the Halsenbach farm was only a temporary stop in our wartime odyssey. We were travelling like refugees, pretending to feel at home wherever we landed. Apart from a minimal amount of clothing and a few school items and exercise books, we traveled with very little.

Next stop: Klein-Ingersheim, a small town in the state of Baden-Wurttemberg on the river Neckar, where we stayed with yet another far-off relative.

The year was 1942.

Finally tired of moving from place to place, my mother took us back to Düsseldorf despite increasingly heavy bombardments there. Again we lived with my maternal grandparents, who had meanwhile re-organized their apartment to accommodate us. But this arrangement did not last long, at least not for me.

A new upheaval arrived.

A wartime handmade birthday card from my artisic father, oven wih straw and flowers.
"Ursula Happiest Wishes for your Birthday, Your Father"

Ulla Morris-Carter

Away From Home Again

1943-1944

Bombers

Black as vermin, crawling in echelon,
Beneath the cloud floor, the bombers come:
The heavy angels, carrying harm in
Their wombs, that ache to be rid of death.
That is the seed that grows for ruin
The iron embryo conceived in fear.

~ Cecil Day-Lewis

The Düsseldorf railroad station was bustling with activity. Mothers and children were nervously running backwards and forwards. From which track would the school train leave?

My mother, like all the other mothers, was holding my hand and pulling me along track No. 5, which appeared to be the track where we should gather. In her other hand she was carrying a suitcase, my suitcase she told me, filled with all the things a 9-year-old might need for the next few weeks or months. Very few fathers were around; they had all been drafted into the army, as was my father, my beloved, *Vati*.

"You will be so glad to be out of the city, just think of how nice it'll be to sleep through the night without the sirens going off and all of us staggering into the shelter." Mutti reassured me, squeezing my hand.

It was May 1943 and, despite the fact that the weather in May was normally pleasant and spring-like, the wind blew through the railroad station with a bite like winter. Mutti seemed nervous. I was worried and fearful but pretended to be happily looking forward to this new adventure.

Ulla Morris-Carter

All my schoolmates were assembled here, some seemingly unperturbed, others clinging to their mothers, panic in their eyes, scared like I was, and obviously not wanting to let go of their mother's hand. Our school on Konkordiastrasse had closed the week before, after two consecutive major *RAF* bombardments on Dortmund, Düsseldorf, Essen, Duisburg and Wuppertal. during the so-called "Battle of the Ruhr." These five cities are located in the Rhine-Ruhr district, the part of North-Rhine Westphalia between the rivers Ruhr and Rhine, where most of the German armaments were manufactured by the Friedrich Krupp factories. Duisburg in particular offered great military targets, because one third of the nation's iron and steel was produced there. Continuous air raids had completely worn out the local population. The principal of my school, Rektor Jäger, had called an emergency meeting of all parents.

"The whole school, grades one through eight, including all teachers, will evacuate to the countryside to a safe place in the Bergische Land, the hill country, only 80 kilometers away. Every child will receive home hospitality in the village of Gross-Ösinghausen."

I really didn't care whether it was 20 or 80 kilometers away from Düsseldorf. All I cared about was that I had to leave home and family again and live with total strangers. Tearful departures from the railroad station, handkerchiefs frantically waving out of the windows of the departing train, sobbing mothers. We children tried to be brave. We didn't want our schoolmates to think we were sissies.

Just two weeks earlier, still in Düsselorf, I had celebrated my First Communion, a major event in the mostly Catholic Rhineland that was usually accompanied by a family celebration. My religious instructions, just before the actual day of the first Communion, had not been disrupted by the war. We prayed to be spared from the intensifying bombardments.

My grandmother sewed and embroidered a special white dress for me for this occasion. Somewhere my family even found a pair of black patent-leather shoes for me. I was immensely proud of my new belongings. Every time the alarm sounded, I packed my little suitcase with these precious items and carried it to the air-raid shelter.

A slight misting on the day of the Communion did not diminish the festive mood of all the participants. My grandparents, my mother and my aunt accompanied me to church. The church felt like a refuge, filled with warm candlelight, incense and music. After Church we returned to my grandparents home, where we again lived temporarily, for a festive meal of cake and coffee. We did not receive any extra food ration cards for this occasion but managed to bake one delicious real butter cake.

Most of all we missed my father, *Vati*, who was serving in France and was unable to join us. One of my grandmothers' gave me a special gift, a gold necklace with a cross attached. I received two other gifts, a new pen with a small leather-bound notebook and two gorgeous blooming hydrangeas. I was so proud.

Ulla Morris-Carter

O. U.,den 29.Maerz 1943.

Meine liebe Ursula.

Zunaechst einmal meine herzlichsten Glueckwuensche zu Deiner hlg. Kommunion. Es hat mir sehr weh getan, dass ich nicht dabei sein konnte. Aber das ist alles zu ueberraschend gekommen. Der Brief von Mutter ist erst Samstag abend hier angekommen, selbst wenn ich dann noch Urlaub bekommen haette, waere ich ja doch zu spaet gekommen. Ich habe aber trotzdem noch gefragt, aber es war nicht moeglich, da erstens mein Leutnant nicht da war und zweitens schon vier Mann auf Urlaub waren. So muessen wir uns eben gedulden bis in etwa vier Wochen. Dann holen wir aber alles nach. Hoffentlich habt Ihr mir noch etwas von den leckeren Sachen verwahrt. Inzwischen schreibst Du mir aber auch sicher mal, wie denn alles gewesen ist, damit ich mir wenigstens ein kleines Bild machen kann von Deinem schoensten Fest Deines Lebens. Ich bin den ganzen Sonntag in Gedanken bei Dir gewesen, vielleicht hast Du es auch ein bischen gespuert. Jetzt warte ich ich schon mit Schmerzen auf einen Brief, wie alles verlaufen ist.

Nun gruesse mir recht herzlich Mutter und Hannes und die beiden Opas und Omas und sei Du recht herzlich gegruesst und gekuesst von Deinem

Vater

In my Communion special white dress and shoes. And the letter my father wrote me at the time.

Translation: D.U., March 29, 1943.

My dear Ursula.

First and foremost my heartfelt congratulations to your first Communion. It pained me a lot that I could not be with you. But the news took me by surprise. The letter from Mother arrived only Saturday evening. Even if I had been able to take a few days off, I would have arrived too late. Nonetheless I asked, but it was not possible, since my Lieutenant was not there, and beyond that four other people were on leave. We just have to be patient until about four weeks from now. We shall then make up for what I missed. I hope you have saved me a piece of that delicious cake. In the meantime, I hope you will write to me to tell me all about what happened, so that I can at least imagine how the most beautiful day of your life proceeded. All Sunday long my thoughts have been with you. Maybe also you felt it. Now I am longingly waiting for a letter to tell me how the whole day went.

Give my love to your Mother and your brother, and also to both grandmothers and both grandfathers. And love and greetings to you and a big kiss from your Father

But the festive mood did not last. The day after my first Communion, the sirens blasted again at 10 p.m. We raced into the basement of my grandparents four-story house. Almost immediately after settling into our little prison, we heard the dreaded sound. Swarms of approaching bombers.

My grandmother, Oma, a very religious woman, instructed us calmly to pray with her. We all did, whispering our prayers. Fear was in the air. We were all breathing heavily. Mrs. Maier, a next-door neigbor, pulled her rosarry out of her small handbag

Ulla Morris-Carter

and mumbled 'Hail Marys.' Other than the sound of a few mumbled prayers, the shelter became eerily silent.

Suddenly we heard the whizzing sound of an approaching bomb. Panic broke out. With ear-shattering noise a bomb hit the wall close to us. Everybody screamed. We huddled together. The walls shook, the lights went out and the floor trembled. The air was so thick with dust that we could hardly breathe.

"Not again," was all I could think.

It had only been a few months since the last bombardment, when the house of my father's parents had been hit, and we had sat trembling in the shelter. Now my other grandparents' house was a target.

Sitting in total darkness, we did not yet know what had happened. All we knew was that the house had been hit. Everybody in the shelter was still alive. My heart was beating up to my throat. It was cold in the basement, but I began to sweat. Mutti held me tight in one arm, and she cuddled my brother in the other. She too was trembling.

But I heard her reassuring voice: "It's ok, we are all still alive."

In the darkness we scrambled for flashlights and lanterns. Nobody dared to light a match for fear of a gas explosion. Slowly the dust began to settle. Breathing became easier. Finally, sirens sounded the end of the bombardment. The bombers had left. My grandfather stood up. He was the first one who dared to climb the still-standing stairs to inspect the upstairs damage.

He shouted to us from up above: "Half of the store is gone."

My grandparents owned and managed a large delicatessen store.

"The bookstore is badly damaged, and all the upstairs apartments are half destroyed."

It became obvious that the house was unlivable.

I thought of my beloved Communion presents and my beautiful dress. There had not been enough time to pack them up before racing into the shelter.

"They are all gone," I said to no one in particular.

But more important was the question: "Where are we going to find a place to live this time?"

In Gross-Ösinghausen, my final destination in the hill country, I was assigned to the Jungmann family. Frau Jungmann, a woman about 32 years of age, with gold-rimmed glasses and short-cut blondish hair, was friendly, matter-of-fact and obviously extremely busy. She told me to call her Aunt, no name attached, just Aunt.

When I arrived there was no time for chit-chat or a warm hug to take away my apprehension. Apart from caring for her two small children, boys aged three and five named Kurt and Bernd, Aunt managed the farm. With two cows, two pigs, chickens, potato and wheat fields and a large vegetable garden, the farm was relatively modest in size. But there was more to this household. Aunt also owned and ran the small

Ulla Morris-Carter

village grocery shop. Finally I was introduced to Grandfather, the only other person I encountered in the house. I was told that he was the forest ranger. He made his rounds every morning with two large hunting dogs, basset hounds named Oskar and Sigi. The dogs scared me. Entering the house through the main door, the grocery store was located on the left. On the right was the village pub. It took me a while to understand that Jungmanns' was not only a farm, but a small village establishment as well, now managed and run by two people, Aunt and Grandfather.

All farm hands and helpers had been drafted to fight in the war. Aunt's husband, Fritz Jungmann, was also fighting somewhere on the front lines. Aunt had two photos of her husband displayed on a shelf in the kitchen. Fritz Jungmann looked so very young, a smooth face without lines, not like a tough, seasoned soldier. Aunt never talked about him. I did not know where he was fighting. In the late afternoon Grandfather tended the village pub, but unless there was something to celebrate, a rare occasion, traffic was slow. After all, what was there to sell other than the occasional corn Schnaps or a rare beer?

Nobody fussed much over me. Aunt didn't have time, and Grandfather was a solemn, somewhat withdrawn man. I never found out what happened to his wife. Nobody ever mentioned her. I was assigned a very small room on the second floor where the bedrooms of Aunt and the children were also located. I felt lonely and isolated in my room, a room that was oddly shaped, almost triangular. There was just enough space for a bed, a little dresser with a chair and a closet. To undress I had to squeeze myself into the narrow space between my bed and the dresser. But I had no time to feel homesick, except at night after Aunt had closed my door. Nobody cared much about my little soul. To Aunt and Grandfather I was a pair of hands, and there was a lot of work to be done.

In the morning, before leaving for my new school in the nearby town of Hilgen, a half-hour, two-kilometer-walk, rain or shine, I had to wash the wooden kitchen floor and then eat breakfast. Breakfast was what I hated most of all. I had to drink fresh cow's milk, still warm from the cows that Grandfather or Aunt had just milked. My mother had told me I gave up drinking milk at age three. But now I sat here, warm milk or milk soup in front of me, ready to gag just smelling it. I was not allowed to leave the house without finishing my breakfast.

Watching the kitchen clock ticking away on the wall behind the large wooden table, I was afraid to be late for school. Pinching and holding my nose I tried to force down this horrid breakfast. Then it was time to face the elements. It was hard going in the winter. I, like most of my schoolmates, lacked a good, waterproof pair of shoes. By the time I arrived at school, my feet were wet and cold. If we were lucky, the heating system worked, which allowed us to dry our socks and shoes underneath the radiators.

Judging by the only photograph from that time, I was a skinny girl with short blond hair. What actually happened during class in the school in Hilgen, what we studied and

Ulla Morris-Carter

learned, I hardly recall. At that point in my life everything else was more important than school and grades.

At the Jungmann house I learned fast what was required. As time passed, I became better acquainted with Aunt. She turned out to be a pleasant lady, organized and directed, and actually quite warm. She meant well, but was simply overwhelmed by the tasks at hand. After school there was rarely time to play, unless I was in charge of the little boys. The youngest one, Kurt, a cute boy with blond curly hair, tended to throw temper tantrums.

Three o'clock was potato-peeling time. Every afternoon my job was to peel potatoes, one bucket three quarters full. We ate potatoes every day for lunch, and every night for dinner. Everybody plus the dogs ate peeled potatoes. I stared at the bucket in disbelief. Three-quarters full seemed never-ending. It was a nightmare. I even dreamed I was suffocating in a mountain of potatoes. But after a while I got the hang of it. In fact, I was actually proud of my work as the fastest nine-year old potato-peeler. And, I learned how to milk a cow, though I couldn't quite manage to finish it, because my hands weren't strong enough. I learned how to dig potatoes. I learned how to make hay and to clean out the pigsty.

Ah, but cleaning out the pig sty was not exactly fun. One day I neglected to close the wooden gate properly. The big old sow immediately spotted my mistake and knew how to take advantage of the situation. Pigs are smart. She turned around, raced toward the gate, and in doing so ran right between my thin legs, planting me firmly on her back and carrying me along with her. Not for long, though. Racing out through the main door of the stable, I couldn't hang on any longer and with one fell swoop she dumped me right in the middle of the dung heap. Aunt appeared quickly when she heard me screaming at the top of my lungs. She grabbed me by the collar. Holding me, like a cat, as far away from her as possible, she deposited me on a bale of straw.

We had no bathroom on the farm, only an outhouse with a little heart carved out of the green door. Baths were taken on Saturdays in the washroom, when a fire was lit under the big kettle and everybody, one after the other, took a bath in a big zinc bathtub placed in the middle of the washroom.

For the time being, I was banished from the house, perched on a bale of straw, dripping wet and not exactly smelling like a rose, waiting for my bathwater to be hot and ready. This washroom was also used when, with the help of neighbors, a pig or a goat was slaughtered, which happened once while I was there. A permit was needed to slaughter, and the owner of the slaughtered animal had to give up the greater part of meat and sausages that were yielded. We all had food ration cards.

Not all was hardship. When the cherry season arrived, I was allowed to pick them, the most delicious cherries I had ever seen or tasted. They were of the Rainier variety, plump, shiny red and yellow. Sitting in the cherry tree, I forgot the potatoes, the cows'

Ulla Morris-Carter

milk and the pigsty. For a short while I rested and dreamed, until I was called back to duty. While picking cherries and placing them into a basket, I ate and ate until I felt sick.

The Phone Call

Because we had the pub at the house, we were also the proud owners of a public phone. It was one of the few phones in the village. The phone was installed on the wall of a small, narrow phone cabin in the corridor between the pub and the store. It was furnished with a dark red velvet-covered bench. The phone was not used much, only in emergencies.

One day, Aunt emerged from the cabin, crying, her eyes red with tears behind her gold-rimmed glasses. She had to remove them to wipe off her tears. She didn't say anything, just motioned me into the cabin.

My mother was on the line, something extremely rare, her voice faint, compressed, far away, barely audible:

"It's Vati, Vati is dead, killed in France," she whispered.

Silence.

"I want you to come home, I need you here with me. Frau Jungmann will help you get to the station and catch a train."

My mother was crying now and then she hung up, or so I remember. She probably said much more, probably something reassuring and gentle, but I did not hear her anymore. And I do not remember. I was not sure that I really grasped the message. The full impact of the news was not reaching me.

Did I even comprehend what it meant to be dead? All I understood was that my father, my beloved Vati, was not coming home anymore.

I had seen him two months earlier after a long absence, when he was on home leave for one week from his post in France. He was such a handsome man, tall and good-looking, an artist with an artist's soul, who hated the war and the military.

He arrived home in early December, 1943, but had to return to Brittany where he was stationed before the Christmas holidays. My mother and my brother were living with my grandparents in temporary housing, after the bombardment of our, and then their, houses. When my father was on home leave, I had been allowed to leave school before Christmas break that year to return to Düsseldorf to be with my family.

What a happy, glorious week at home that was, despite the cramped quarters!

My grandparents' temporary apartment was not spacious, but the joy of the reunion for a short few days made all of us forget our separations and hardships.

Happy times always pass too quickly. These memories flooded my young head as I sat by myself on the train to Düsseldorf, three days later.

Ulla Morris-Carter

My father on what was probably his last home visit, in December 1943.
L-R: A cousin, my brother Hans, my father in uniform, my mother, me.

I had to change trains in Opladen, and worried that I would miss the station. But I succeeded in finding the connecting train. Two hours later I arrived in Düsseldorf. My mother stood on the platform, the same one that I had departed from ten months ago. "A few weeks" Rektor Jäger had said then, not ten months, with more to come.

Mutti looked pale and thinner than I remembered her. She had wrapped her dark coat tightly around her. February was always cold and breezy. She swept me off my feet and folded me into her arms, holding me tight while she quietly sobbed.

We did not speak. This was the saddest day I had known in my ten years of life.

Back at my grandparents' apartment, my grandmother and Mutti told me the details. Three days earlier, the doorbell had rung. My grandmother answered the door and a stranger holding a large yellow envelope greeted her politely. Before he could deliver his message, my mother appeared from another room.

She took one look at the stranger and gave a loud scream:

"No, no, don't tell me why you are here! I already know!" My mother shouted.

My grandmother opened the envelope with shaking hands, pulling out the official military death notice, while the messenger of the tragic news stood at the door, quietly uttering condolences.

My father had been killed five weeks earlier, but the news had only now reached us. We would never know what actually happened. The war with France was already over. My father had belonged to the occupation forces. He was with the military police and might have been on a special intelligence mission. The letter said he was accidentally

Ulla Morris-Carter

killed. A priest had found my father lying in a ditch, but he was declared dead by the time they reached the hospital. The heavy, hand-knitted personal sweater, which my father had worn under his uniform on that cold winter day in January, showed a sharp, clean cut that made us believe he had been stabbed. His sweater and his wedding ring were returned to my mother.

We shall never know what really happened.

Two weeks later I was back in Gross-Ösinghausen. I had to finish the elementary school year, fourth grade, in the school in Hilgen. The next year I was supposed to be in a *Gymnasium*, high school. The closest high school for the Gross-Ösinghausen district was located in Burscheid. But Burscheid was five kilometers away. My mother decided that a five-kilometer, one-hour walk each way, rain or shine, would be too long and too dangerous. No public transportation existed.

I had no idea if or where I would be able to attend school in the fall of 1944. Would my mother be able find a still-functioning school in a safe area, and a place for me to live?

Hanns Kirſchbaum
Uffz. der Feldgendarmerie
geb. 15. Febr. 1903, geſt. 2. Jan. 1944

Hanns Kirschbaum
Sargeant, Military Police.
Born February 15, 1903. Died
January 2, 1944

Above: *The official death announcement distributed by the church in Düsseldorf at my father's memorial service.*
Right: *My father's original grave. Later the Americans relocated all German graves into a large war cementary in Ploudaniel-Lesneven, Brittany.*
(More in later chapter: 'Finding My Father's Grave.')

Ulla Morris-Carter

THE WEATHER

Today: Partly cloudy and warmer, with moderate to fresh winds

Temperatures Yesterday. Max. 67. Min. 51

Detailed Report on Page 23

Herald

N

Vol. CIV No. 35,632

Copyright, 1944,
New York Tribune Inc.

Invasion On,
As Planes an
Montgomery

Allies Across Tiber on Heels Of Routed Foe

Planes Hammer at Nazis Jamming Highways to North; Tanks Follow Up

Enemy May Delay Stand for 150 Miles

500 U. S. Bombers Blast Rail Lines to Cut Off Flow of Reinforcements

By The Associated Press

ROME, June 5.—Allied armor and motorized infantry roared through Rome today, crossed the River Tiber and proceeded with the task of destroying two battered German armies fleeing north.

Allied fighter-bombers spearheaded the pursuit, jamming escape highways with burning enemy transport and littering fields with dead or wounded Nazis.

The enemy was tired, disorganized and bewildered by the slashing character of the Allied assault, which in twenty-five days had inflicted a major catastrophe on German forces in Italy and liberated Rome almost without damage to the historic city.

Aerial forces including 500 American heavy bombers blasted railyards at five points in northern Italy between Venice and Rimini along which the Germans might attempt to move reinforcements and equipment to bolster their bent-

Hitler Loses Standing As a Vegetarian, Too

From the Herald Tribune Bureau
Copyright, 1944, New York Tribune Inc.

LONDON, June 5. — Adolf Hitler has lost his standing as a vegetarian, according to Leslie Severs, newly elected secretary of the London Vegetarian Society.

"Our information," Severs said today, "shows that for some time Hitler has lived on liver extract."

"As for Mussolini," he added, "he may have taken up vegetarianism on doctor's orders because of stomach trouble, but we don't regard him as a vegetarian, either."

Insurance Held Subject to U. S. Anti-Trust Law

Supreme Court Rules It Is Interstate Trade, Upsets 75-Year-Old Precedent

From the Herald Tribune Bureau

WASHINGTON, June 5.—The Supreme Court, upsetting a seventy-five-year-old decision, ruled today in a 4-to-3 opinion that the insurance business may constitute interstate commerce and is, therefore, subject to Federal regulation under anti-trust provisions of the Sherman act and under the national labor relations act.

The decision in the anti-trust case was reached on a government appeal from an action by the Federal District Court for Northern Georgia dismissing Federal anti-trust proceedings against 196 stock fire insurance companies

'Tough' Fight Ahead Is Seen By Roosevelt

President Says Capture of Rome Finds Allies Poised for New Blows

Hails Victory With: 'One Up, Two to Go'

Says Italy Will Get Help, but Cannot Hope for a Militaristic Empire

By Bert Andrews

WASHINGTON, June 5.—The capture of Rome was hailed tonight by President Roosevelt with the exultant exclamation that it is now "one up and two to go," as far as the Axis capitals of Italy, Germany and Japan are concerned, but with a sobering warning that "it will be tough and it will be costly" before Berlin and Tokyo are also conquered.

Then, in another of the cryptic invasion hints that have kept the Germans tantalized, the President, in words that were carried over all American networks and to the rest of the world, laconically remarked that the Italian triumph is only a foretaste of more blows to be struck by the United Nations.

"Our victory comes at an excellent time, while our Allied forces are poised for another strike at western Europe and while armies of other Nazi soldiers nervously

YORK

Tribune

EXTRA
LATE CITY EDITION

DAY, JUNE 6, 1944

- THREE - CENTS -
In New York City

llies Land in France
Ships Blast Coast;
eads the Advance

Battle Raging Over 75-Mile Coastal Area

Attack on Europe Follows Air Campaign to Pave Way for Land Forces

Invasion Centers In Seine Estuary

Air-Borne Troops Drop After 'Terrific' Rain of Shells and Bombs

By The Associated Press

SUPREME HEADQUARTERS, ALLIED EXPEDITIONARY FORCE, Tuesday, June 6. — American, British and Canadian troops landed in northern France this morning, launching the greatest overseas military operation in history with word from their supreme commander, General Dwight D. Eisenhower, that "we will accept nothing except full victory" over the German masters of the Continent.

Text of the communique:

"Under the command of General Eisenhower Allied naval forces, supported by strong air forces, began landing Al-

My brother Hans and I around the end of war.

Even the Pilots' Faces were Visible

Last Evacuation and End of the War Memories of an 11-year-old

What a gloriously happy day, the day after Christmas, 1944. My mother and my almost 7-year-old brother had come to visit me in Andernach over the holidays. A reunion with my family, whom I had missed so much for the five months since my arrival here, was the greatest gift I could receive.

Andernach, a mid-sized city located on the Rhine River between Cologne and Koblenz, had been my home since August. I had been sent to my great aunt Hedwig, my grandmother's sister, and her husband, great uncle Paul, to attend the still functioning school in Andernach. That was my first meeting with my great aunt and great uncle. My grandmother was one of 17 siblings. It was a huge family, many of whom I had not gotten to know yet.

War was still raging all over Germany. Düsseldorf continued to suffer merciless bombardments. But Andernach seemed relatively quiet. It was considered "a safe city." Unlike Düsseldorf, located close to the armament factories of Krupp, the small garden city of Andernach was declared a military hospital city, not to be bombed. Or so we believed. Every available large hall, every hotel, gym or ballroom was converted into a hospital to accommodate the daily increasing number of wounded German soldiers returning from the front lines. A huge, highly visible red cross on white background decorated all those temporary hospital roofs now.

But wars are unpredictable. Suddenly Andernach suffered the same fate as other cities, a major bombardment. The alarm sounded three times at three in the afternoon, the highest air raid warning.

Ulla Morris-Carter

An old wine map of the Rhine river showing Andernach, where I stayed with one of my grandmother's younger sisters, Tante (Aunt) Hedwig and her husband Onkel (Uncle) Paul during my 3rd evacuation from Düsseldorf.

We didn't have an air raid shelter in the two-story family house. We didn't need one, we thought.

When the first distant droning noise of the American Air Force bombers came closer, and the sound of a nearby bomb explosion shattered our optimism and confidence, we rushed into the un-reinforced basement. There was no other place to go.

Unlike the shelters I had known in Düsseldorf, this one was just a normal storage basement, not built to withstand bombing. The ear-piercing whistle of the incoming bombs still resonates in my ears. Without reinforced walls, ceilings and protective iron doors, we felt completely exposed.

Suddenly, a terrifying explosion, worse, it seemed to me, than any of the ones I had experienced before. No doubt, this one had landed on our house. We all hit the floor, huddling close together, with our arms over our heads to protect ourselves from falling debris. I heard the sharp sound of shattering glass. Fruit and jams stored in glass jars on wooden shelves crashed to the cement floor. The cloud of dust filling the whole basement was so thick that at first we couldn't see each other despite the fact that the basement's small windows had turned into open gaping holes. It was only 3:30 in the afternoon, but the basement was dark.

After what seemed like an eternity, the dust slowly subsided. Coughing and sneezing and gasping for air, we sat up, looking around to see whether we were all still alive. All had miraculously survived, unhurt.

A big collective sigh of relief. Though badly shaken and covered with dust and debris, we stared in surprise at a mountain of precious potatoes that surrounded us.

Where did they come from? In the far corner we noticed the large wooden potato storage crate damaged by the explosion. Luckily, our winter supply of potatoes had survived. Not so the house. What was left of it was no longer habitable. There was only half a roof and half a house.

The next morning, two days after Christmas, a cold December day, I found myself huddled on the open back of a small wood-burning truck, sitting among as many

Ulla Morris-Carter

belongings as could possibly be crammed into the relatively small truck bed. The wood burner, a large kettle that needed to be fed frequently with wood chips and took up the biggest part of the truck bed, made the truck run. There was no gasoline for anybody except the army. At least the wood burner gave out some heat for me to stay warm. But most important, we had a means of transportation, which many others did not.

My Aunt Hedwig, Uncle Paul and I, just turned 11, were leaving Andernach. Also with us, crammed into the front part of the truck, were my mother and my brother, their hope for a few quiet days dashed by yesterday's bombardment. Aunt Hedwig, in her late 50s, was a statuesque lady with thick wavy grayish hair pulled away from her face. She was loving but decisive, unlike uncle Paul who was gentle but quite impractical.

Finding ourselves homeless, Uncle Paul and Aunt Hedwig had decided to pack up what could be rescued and take us all to the volcanic quarries Uncle Paul had leased and managed for many years. A bumpy two-hour drive from Andernach, this lava mine was located near the imposing Benedictine Abbey of Maria Laach on the banks of Laacher See in a region known as the *Eifel.* The deposits had been formed when an active volcano erupted nearly 10,000 years ago, showering its ashes over this beautiful region and forming lava hills of differing colorations, black, red and mustard-yellow. The black porous lava was mined for building airstrips and roads, the red was used for, among other things, the top layer of clay tennis courts.

My mother and brother had not intended to be in Andernach for more than a few days. But now they found themselves stuck in the quarry with no return transportation in sight. They had arrived by train, which now, after the bombardment of Andernach, was no longer operational. My mother worried about her elderly parents alone in Düsseldorf. She worried about the job she had recently taken following the news that my father had been killed in France. After a few nervous days in the quarry my mother found out that a furniture truck was leaving from the Abbey of Maria Laach, traveling towards Cologne and Düsseldorf, willing to take her, my little brother and a few other stranded passengers.

It was early January, 1945, bitter cold, and the passengers had to travel on the open truck bed. Communications were erratic at best. One could only hope for an occasional telephone call to come through. Therefore it took almost two weeks for the news to reach us that my mother and brother had indeed arrived in Düsseldorf, but both seriously ill. My mother had contracted pneumonia and apparently almost died, having wrapped my brother into her only coat when he complained about being too cold on the open truck. My mother had nothing except a thin blanket, the only one my aunt could spare, to keep her warm for the journey.

Our new home in the volcanic quarry, the black quarry, consisted of three barracks, formerly used by the mineworkers for their lunch break or for shelter during bad

Ulla Morris-Carter

weather. Now the barracks were unused. All the miners had been drafted into the war. The barracks, each about 12 feet by 12 feet, were not connected to each other. There was no running water and no electricity. Water had to be carried from the nearest village, Wassenach, a 15-minute walk downhill from our primitive abode. A metal drum strapped to a small wooden wagon served as our water carrier.

Winter brought snow, and according to my aunt, melted snow or rainwater, which we collected in buckets, were particularly soft and excellent for bathing and washing hair. There was neither a bathroom nor a toilet. We had an outhouse about 50 yards away from the barracks. Baths were taken in a metal tub in the kitchen. When darkness fell—it came early in January in northern Germany—we used lanterns and sometimes candles if they were available. What used to be a little office when the quarries were being mined, became our living room.

The most important item in it was a wood stove in the corner. The wooden walls behind it were covered with metal sheeting to prevent them from catching fire. There was an old desk with many drawers that took up most of the space, a swiveling wooden office chair with arms, which my uncle usually occupied, a small couch covered with striped red and beige cotton material, and a couple of straight chairs. A bookshelf attached to the wall above the desk held papers and photographs.

Even now I can see as clearly as then, in the framed photo, the handsome face of Horst, my aunt and uncle's 22-year-old son, a fighter pilot, shot down and killed over England. The photo showed him in his pilot's uniform, young and so good-looking. A second son, Werner, was missing in action, and a third one was still somewhere on the front lines. Two daughters worked as nurses in hospitals.

The office chair was my most coveted item. I loved it, and my uncle often let me sit in it. Since I had no playmates, I would pretend to be a sales person, allowed to use the old receipts for the sale of lava. Selling bathroom equipment, toilets and wash basins—I don't remember why, maybe because we lacked that kind of facility—could occupy me for hours.

"How many toilets can you ship out today?" my uncle would ask. "I need 10 urgently."

The next door barrack was our bedroom, which the three of us shared. Most of the space was taken up by a large bed, marble-covered night tables on either side, and a narrow couch at the foot of the double bed, my bed. I can still feel the cold creeping into my bones when I think about that unheated room. We warmed bricks on the wood stove or in the kitchen oven, wrapped them into towels to pre-warm our damp, cold beds.

A short walk outside around the living room and the bedroom led to the kitchen, the most uncomfortable and coldest of the barracks. Its roof, made of corrugated metal, was slightly rusty. Frequently, before the old kitchen stove was fired up in the morning,

Ulla Morris-Carter

the room was so cold that the water, kept there in a basin for washing face and hands, was frozen over. De-icing was the next task.

If I complained about feeling cold, my aunt, a loving but no-nonsense lady, occasionally sent me barefoot out into the snow.

"Dr. Kneipp," she would lecture me "says it's great for your circulation and generally good for your health to walk barefoot in the snow. Your feet will be warm in no time."

Once we were more or less settled, another attempt was made to get me into school, my fourth school that year. The village school was still functioning. Bernd, a local boy my age, was recruited to accompany me on my first day. It had snowed heavily the day before, and not knowing exactly where the dirt road to our barracks ran, we walked straight across the white open fields.

Suddenly, we heard the well-known droning sound of approaching planes. Out of clear blue sky, whizzing noisily and dangerously low overhead, a group of American dive bombers appeared. We knew they were American, because we could see their insignia.

Even the pilot's faces were visible.

Bernd and I threw ourselves face down into the snow—no bush, no tree, no place to hide. We both wore dark-blue warm-up suits, *Trainingsanzüge*, and were doubtless visible, two lonely little figures in the open snow-blanketed landscape. We were terrified and cold. The planes swooped down low over our heads, the splitting screams of diving wings resounding in our ears.

Then, as fast as they had appeared, they climbed back into the sky. Gone within seconds. We found out later that there was a secret airstrip near us, where, it was said, the German Military Intelligence Service stored important documents in an underground bunker.

It was January, 1945. Everyone knew, even I, that the war was lost. But before the end, living alone on top of that hill, surrounded by darkness and sometimes a star-lit sky at night, we witnessed the launching of the V2. The latest and most feared German weapon, it traced an orange-reddish line into the night sky, resembling a two-colored rainbow. This V2, *Vergeltungswaffe 2* or Vengeance Weapon 2, was a short-range ballistic missile that traveled faster than sound. Developed by Wernher von Braun, it was being used against England.

To make matters worse, my almost 60-year-old uncle was drafted into the army in February, 1945. The German army was making a last stand against the approaching American army of General Eisenhower at the West Wall, the *Siegfried Line*. Men as old as my uncle, and boys as young as 15, were being drafted and sent to the front.

Aunt Hedwig and I remained alone in the barracks to survive a harsh winter. One day she asked me to accompany her to the kitchen to prepare our dinner. I was hungry

Ulla Morris-Carter

enough that I did not complain at having to trade the cozy little living room for the freezing kitchen barrack. The two of us, carrying a lantern, walked through the snow to the kitchen barrack,

"Let's make a sauce," she said.

"Out of what?" I asked incredulously, knowing we had neither meat nor oil nor butter.

I knew that sauce always came together with a roast. Aunt Hedwig cheerfully continued to instruct me:

"First, start the fire, then heat the heavy iron pot."

Luckily we had dry wood in the kitchen corner to build a fire in the big kitchen stove. The largest of the two holes in the stove top, surrounded by iron rings to adjust to the size of the pot, was exactly the right size for our pot. I had never before paid much attention to this matter.

"A spoonful of flour is left in the green jar on the top shelf. It will be just enough to make our sauce. Put it into the pot, then stir continuously until it begins to turn brown. And don't forget to reheat the potatoes we boiled yesterday."

At this point I was wondering whether I would ever consider becoming a cook. I certainly was not convinced that this procedure would produce anything edible. But after pouring the flour into the pot, I continued to stir it as if my life depended on it. I did not want to be responsible for ruining the last spoon of flour. The kitchen barrack was beginning to warm up. I felt much better. Warmth is the most important first step to happiness, as I had already learned from babysitting. A baby needs to be cuddled and kept warm to stay alive and content. The flour finally was beginning to change color, from white to beige to light brown.

"Now add some water, slowly, a bit at a time. Continue to stir until the sauce thickens, then add a little salt."

Aunt Hedwig's instructions did not allow for complaints. The contents of the pot looked more like mud for mud pies we used to make as children in years past after a heavy rainstorm. Aunt Hedwig, looking at my miserable expression, made another attempt to convince me of the success of the dinner sauce.

"This sauce will taste just great over our boiled potatoes," she announced in her convincingly loud voice.

We returned to the living room barrack, carrying our lanterns and our delicious dinner of potatoes and home-made gravy. When one is hungry, almost everything tastes alright.

One day in early spring a friend borrowed my uncle's truck. I was allowed to come along for the ride, sitting on the open truck bed. It was a sunny day. Life didn't seem so bad after all. I was enjoying the first signs of spring, blooming bushes and some spring

Ulla Morris-Carter

flowers along the side of the road. As we drove on the dirt road, I suddenly heard the by now familiar sound of approaching aircraft. I looked up and saw, right above my head, what appeared to be the same low-flying American dive bombers I had encountered in January. Their drone still lingers in my ears, fear and terror in my stomach.

"Not again," I thought.

Desperately, wildly, I pounded as hard as I could, on the roof of the truck cab to alert the driver to stop. But the truck made so much noise on the bumpy and pot-holed dirt road that the driver didn't hear me. Heavy dust enveloped the truck.

Could the driver even see the low-flying bombers?

I kept pounding and screaming with as much force as I could muster.

The bombers, with ear-splitting sound, were diving lower and lower over my head. I could see the pilot's faces. I was sure that at any moment now they would shoot or bomb us. Our truck just kept lumbering slowly down the hill. Finally, in desperation, I jumped off the truck into some bushes beside the road.

"Saved," I mumbled to myself, breathing a sigh of relief, hiding motionless.

Thick, lush-green branches surrounded me like a protective cover. Only after I tried to move, did I realize that I had landed in a large cluster of wild blackberries, thorny, prickly and outright painful. My bare legs and hands were already bleeding. I had no idea how to get myself out of this disaster zone. Forgotten were the dive bombers, which by now had disappeared. My full attention was now devoted to the painful extraction from the blackberry thicket.

Slowly, one by one, I removed the thorny, stinging branches that had attached themselves to my skin and to my clothing. Just when my head emerged from the blackberry thicket, I saw the truck driver appear, on foot. He was running breathlessly up the hill, toward me. Having finally heard and recognized the dive bombers, he had immediately stopped the car. Not finding me on the back of his truck, he was now in search of his lost passenger.

Was I ever happy to see him! Probably he was just as relieved to see me.

In March, 1945, a major storm ripped the tarpaper off our roof, causing it to rain into our living room. Aunt Hedwig, no longer very agile, sent me up the ladder to repair it. Holding a small bucket of tar and a roll of tarpaper I was standing on the low, flat roof, when I suddenly saw a German Army truck stop at the bottom of our hill. They had run out of gas, it seemed, but there was none to be found in our region. At this point we all understood, even I, that the German Army was in retreat, exhausted, hungry and defeated.

But this was the first time that I had set eyes on the dissolving Army. The soldiers came running up the hill, begging for civilian clothing, anything to replace their uniforms. They were the first group of many that would pass through our relatively

Ulla Morris-Carter

isolated area, far from the cities and 15 minutes away from the nearest village. All they desperately wanted was to go home and not end up in a prisoner-of-war camp. We knew that many didn't make it. The war was lost, but it wasn't over yet. My aunt gave them as much as she could spare of my uncle's clothes, but we didn't have a lot to give here in our primitive living quarters. And food was very scarce. All we had to offer were a few potatoes.

One of the soldiers gave me his army bicycle. It was too big for me, but I was in seventh heaven. I had never owned a bicycle. The soldiers wanted to rid themselves of anything that connected them to the military. Another, who accepted a pair of my uncle's shoes gave me his army boots in return. The size wasn't right, but a little cotton filled the extra inches, and they kept my feet warm and dry. Until then I had been wearing shoes homemade out of discarded rubber tires. One soldier even produced a small box of margarine.

"Don't you want to keep it?" I asked incredulously.

Why would someone give away food when he is hungry?

"It has military markings," he said. "We have to get away quickly. We can't carry it, and we don't have any bread to eat it with."

It was heartbreaking to see the soldiers disappear into the forest into an unknown future, trying to get away from the advancing American troops. I often wondered how many, if any, made it home.

I thought of my father who had been killed in France in early1944.

What did he have to go through? Had anybody come to his rescue when he might have needed help?

In the early morning hours, coming from the nearby village still shrouded in silence, more retreating soldiers kept asking for clothes and food. But we had nothing more to give. One soldier was determined to hide in a 10 foot high stack of straw near our barracks, but my aunt insisted that he would get us all killed if he were discovered.

Suddenly, Uncle Paul returned. I do not remember how he made it home, but there he stood, in front of us, just days ahead of the arrival of the American troops. News traveled by mouth, and the village gossip around the water well in Wassenach warned us of the imminent arrival of the allied troops. Wassenach was just a few miles west of the town of Remagen, which had the only functioning bridge left across the river Rhine, a bridge 400 yards long with three spans.

One of the last desperate commands given the retreating German troops was to blow up the bridge at Remagen. The German army had wired the bridge with demolition cables to be activated as soon as the American troops attempted to cross it. The Americans, delighted to find a functioning bridge, suspected that crossing the bridge might be dangerous, and frantically tried to cut every demolition wire they could find.

Ulla Morris-Carter

Their first infantry platoon began to cross the bridge. When they had almost reached the east bank, a huge charge went off. Others followed. The bridge shook and was damaged, yes, but it did not collapse.

Time Magazine on March 19, 1945 called it "A Moment for History":

Suddenly [General] Hoge's men realized that they had forced a fantastic break in the fortunes of war. They had seized a Rhine bridge intact. It was a moment for history. German prisoners ruefully reported that the deadline for blowing the bridge had been 4 p.m.—ten minutes after the Americans burst into Remagen. It was also a moment of historic ironies. Remagen's bridge had spanned the years between World Wars I and II. Completed in 1918 . . . its seizure occurred nine years to the day after Hitler had brazenly violated the Versailles and Locarno Treaties.

Time continued:

Dog-weary troops heard the electrifying words: 'We got a bridge.' One order flashed through: get across and get set. That night tanks by the score, trucks by the hundreds headed for the bridge. Next day they came by the hundreds and thousands.

Later we learned that Hitler gave orders to have the German officers who had been charged with blowing up the bridge, executed.

We lived in terror of what might happen to us. Would the Americans take revenge on the civilian population? We knew that the American troops were more disciplined than the Russian troops, but that was little comfort considering that they were still our enemies. Nazi propaganda had succeeded in making the prospect of military defeat a terrifying vision.

My uncle ordered the family to gather all valuables, cameras, watches, jewelry, pack it into a large, covered casserole and bury it in the quarry. My bicycle and the box of margarine with the military markings had to be buried as well, he said. I was devastated to think of giving up my newly acquired bicycle.

While my uncle and aunt, in their 50's and 60's, not exactly the most agile or fit couple, were digging a hole into the loose sand of the quarry, I had to stand guard in the road to make sure nobody was coming who could see what we were doing. Frightened, I kept running backwards and forwards for fear of missing somebody.

Finally my aunt signaled that the hole was deep enough to bury all our valuables. Hurriedly, I carried the heavy casserole containing our jewellery deep into the quarry. I loaded other boxes on my bicycle. We covered everything well. The last item, the bicycle, disappeared under a layer of porous lava, and we were pleased with our task. We buried everything of value except our field glasses, which we felt were vital to our existence in the hills. When we needed water, I would go down to the village, pulling a little wagon with the empty water barrel, fill it up at the village pump and return with the full barrel to the bottom of our hill. There I waited for my uncle or aunt to come

Ulla Morris-Carter

down to help me push the now heavy barrel uphill. They would use the field glasses to watch my progress.

When the Americans arrived, we saw them first through our field glasses when I was transporting water. The Americans established an army post at the bottom of our hill and were using their field glasses to watch for fleeing German soldiers or other unrest. When they spotted my aunt with her field glasses, they jumped into a jeep, raced up the hill, confiscated our field glasses, surrounded our barracks and put us under house arrest, all in a matter of minutes.

It happened so fast we hardly had time to react, nor did we have time to get a good look at our occupiers, who locked the door and surrounded our barracks. After we had overcome the initial shock of being locked up for more than an hour inside the barrack, I thought it was time to try to make a move. My aunt and uncle agreed. After all, what could a child of 11 possibly do?

I knocked timidly on the door, which one of the soldiers opened a crack, just enough to look inside the room. I stared into the dark eyes and the face of a black soldier. I had never before seen a black man. I was startled. But after a moment of hesitation I simply pushed the door open and ran out. The soldier chased me.

When we arrived at the outhouse, he got the message. He smiled, pointed to the little heart in the green door and waited for me to come out, then accompanied me back to the barrack. We couldn't communicate. I spoke only a few words of school English that I had learned in the first three months in the school in Andernach, and he spoke no German.

The American soldiers seemed so young, younger and healthier than the German soldiers I had seen fleeing. They were good-looking fellows in clean and crisp uniforms, and they appeared to be continuously eating or chewing something. Lucky them, I thought, They have enough to eat, when all we exist on are potatoes and a bread spread made out of egg powder that we used if and when we could get bread with our ration cards. At that point I had never heard of or seen chewing gum. Later, one of the American soldiers offered me an orange, the first orange I had ever seen, plus a piece of chocolate and chewing gum.

My aunt, standing by my side, whispered, barely audibly:

"You are not going to accept these from our enemy!"

So I didn't.

A few days later an American Army truck arrived at the barracks. The driver pointed to the volcanic quarry indicating that they needed material for road building. The house arrest had been somewhat relaxed, as the soldiers came to understand our primitive living conditions. My uncle accompanied the captain to the quarry and pointed to an area where the best lava material could be found.

Ulla Morris-Carter

But the captain insisted that he preferred to take material from the other side of the quarry.

"My father has a similar business. I know something about mining," he said in broken German with English thrown in.

He brought in his men and they began digging exactly where we had buried our goods. It took them only a few minutes until the handle of the bicycle appeared, then the margarine, then the casserole with our precious items. That did not go over well. One of the soldiers started racing around on my bike, blew a tire and finally loaded it on top of the lava material. They took all the other goods, including the casserole, and our house arrest was tightened.

In the middle of all this commotion my aunt and uncle's two daughters, both in their twenties, beautiful and blond, returned from their hospital duty. Luckily, my uncle had meanwhile acquired another wooden shack in preparation for just such an event, knowing that nobody could live in the family house in Andernach. His daughters were to occupy the new room. Of course, the daughters were also put under house arrest. My aunt rightly worried about her daughters after one of the soldiers made advances toward the younger one.

A problem was that we could barely communicate with each other. We were in different rooms, and no room connected to another. We were not allowed out, except to go to our outhouse. My aunt, a resolute and determined lady, told the soldiers that she needed to see the commander or whoever was in charge. She didn't wait for an answer. She simply marched herself down the hill to the command post and demanded to see the "boss." Whatever she said in her poor English or whom she spoke to, I don't know, but she was obviously successful, because she returned triumphant, and the guards were removed.

Our lives normalized as much as living in barracks beside a lava quarry can be called "normal." But we appreciated the fact that we were better off than many people in the large cities. We had a roof over our heads, and we lived near farmers and peasants who occasionally were willing to trade a few eggs or a pound of butter against a set of bed sheets or silverware. But we didn't have much left to trade.

Communication with my family in Düsseldorf had broken down completely. The war ended. I have no recollection of May 8, 1945, the day Germany officially surrendered. There were no celebrations in my surroundings. Maybe some relief that the nightly bombardments would stop, but the pain and the wounds that the war had inflicted on all of us were too overwhelming to even think about anything resembling a celebration. There was nothing but unbelievable chaos. My aunt and uncle had lost two sons, with a third still missing in action. I had lost my father and two cousins. Two uncles

Ulla Morris-Carter

were in prisoner-of-war-camps in Russia and Indonesia. The war was over, indeed, but that knowledge made me suddenly, desperately, homesick. I desired nothing more than to go home to my mother, my younger brother and my grandparents. The last I could remember, my mother and brother were living with my grandparents in Düsseldorf, having found a small apartment after both their houses had been bombed. But I knew little about their present whereabouts, how they had survived the last weeks of the war, or whether indeed they were still living in the same small apartment on Neusserstrasse.

Nonetheless, I was determined to make my way home. I had been away, off and on, for more than four years, a very long time for a little girl. There were no trains, no buses, no public transportation of any kind. The only way to travel was with the Occupation Army.

I packed a small suitcase and told my aunt and uncle that I was going home. They were stunned by my sudden decision. They were not prepared to let me leave alone, but they soon realized that I was determined to go. So we negotiated.

Finally, Aunt Hedwig extracted a promise from the American Army captain with whom we had become acquainted during our house arrest, that the army would take me on one of their trucks as far as the border with the British Occupation Forces. From there I was to hitch a ride with the British Forces to Düsseldorf, my hometown, which was under British control.

So I traveled first with the American Army, who deposited me some 30 miles north at the first British checkpoint, north of Bonn. I was not at all worried. I was convinced that someone would offer me a ride to Düsseldorf. And indeed, I quickly found a British Army truck willing to take an 11-year-old girl with that small suitcase. One of the soldiers even gave me a ride close to Neusserstrasse, my final destination. I hardly recognized it after 11 months away. Parts of the street had simply disappeared or were just a heap of rubble.

Now I began to worry for the first time. Would I find my mother and grandmother? Would they be home? Would they be alive?

My worries did not last long. I soon discovered the three old chestnut trees in front of my grandparents' apartment building. The branches of the largest, I remembered, grew almost into their bedroom. If the trees were standing, I convinced myself, so must be the house. I ran the last 50 yards and found the house just as I remembered it. A few bullet or shrapnel holes added new decoration to the outside wall, but I hardly noticed. I bounded up the old worn-down wooden stairs to the second floor, right into the arms of my mother, who had come to the door when she heard the noise on the staircase.

I was home again!

Ulla Morris-Carter

RUBBLE AND LILACS

"Enjoy the war—the peace is going to be terrible."

This sentence appeared on a wall in Berlin. Whoever the author, the graffiti was not far from the truth. On May 8, 1945, Germany surrendered unconditionally and ceased to exist as a state. Germans referred to the date as 'Zero Hour', die Stunde Null.

What did Zero Hour mean?

Was it the hour between 'Past' and 'Future?'

Or was it the hour of a new beginning?

It was not clear. But Zero Hour became a historical expression that referred specifically to the end of the Nazi regime.

The weeks and months before Germany capitulated were some of the hardest and most terrifying for the German population. Heavy bombardments of the cities, combined with Hitler's hysterical orders to fight to the very end, and to the last man, resulted in unbelievable loss of human life.

Forty million people across Europe were dead. They had died in battle or lay buried under the rubble of their homes, they were murdered or had died in concentration camps. Europe was a heap of rubble, physically, emotionally, morally and politically.

May 8 was a beautiful, sunny spring day. But how to enjoy the sunshine when one is surrounded by misery, the loss of loved ones, and grinding hunger?

The German writer, Erich Kästner, noted:

> Nature does not pay the least bit of attention to our lost war nor to the long since threatened demise of western civilization, *Abendland*. Soon lilacs will

Ulla Morris-Carter

bloom again out of the rubble . . . . Birds will sing their song, and spring will hasten the sprouting of blossoms that will appear between the cracks of the remaining walls . . . . Nature doesn't care about history. It rebuilds without thinking about it.[1]

Germany had no communications of any kind, no mail, no telephones, no newspapers. We had no way of knowing what happened in the next town a few kilometers away. People wrote messages on the walls of ruins where they had lived, hoping that whoever might be looking for them would know at least that they were alive. There was little electricity and little water. Most utility lines had been destroyed. We found a hand water pump on the corner of our street near our apartment that was still working. All the neighbors, equipped with buckets and containers, lined up and waited patiently for their turn to pump water.

Without anybody in charge, and the Allied Forces not yet in full command, life was chaotic. Only in the countryside could one find near normal conditions, although villages were overcrowded with refugees from the eastern zone fleeing the Russians, and city dwellers searching for places to live. Whoever was connected to electric lines and had a radio could hear our admired Nobel-Prize-winning author, Thomas Mann, speaking from American exile:

> German Listeners:
> What a bitter experience to see the world rejoice over the defeat and over the most painful humiliation of ones own country.
> I maintain, however, that despite this, there is a tremendous possibility: namely Germany's return to humanity. It is hard and sad that Germany did not have the strength to accomplish this by herself . . .

The two-room apartment of my grandparents on Neusserstrasse was too small for all of us, but at least we had a roof over our heads. Looking at my miserable wardrobe of faded dresses, my grandmother decided that I needed a new summer dress. It didn't take her long to come up with an idea. I remember her bending over the sewing machine creating a dress for me.

But what she made was no ordinary dress. The Nazi flag, which every household had been obliged to own and to display during the Hitler regime, was no longer of any use to her. Despite orders to hand over flags and other Hitler memorabilia to the Occupation Forces, my grandmother detached the swastika, burned it in the kitchen

---

1. In 1933 Nazi supporters started a campaign to "rid" Germany of "un-German" books. Kästner's books, considered "pieces of dirt," were among those. Unlike other condemned writers, Kästner refused to leave Germany during WWII. But he suffered for it. During a rainy night in May 1933, students set fire to huge numbers of undesirable books on the Berlin Opera Square and in other cities. Kästner watched in awe as his books were being burned and consumed by the flames.

Ulla Morris-Carter

stove, and, miraculously, produced a beautiful outfit. Our flag dress had a particularly juicy red color. My grandmother, Oma, then decorated the dress with leftover pieces of blue material, a blue stripe at the bottom, another at the waist and blue trimming around the puffed sleeves.

I just loved that dress and thought it was the most exquisite thing I had ever owned.

Stores had little, if anything, to sell. People had money, but money wouldn't buy anything. We had ration cards. For the average German, the most pressing concern in the summer of 1945 and in the spring of 1946 was food. The official ration per person per day was 1500 calories. But in the summer of 1945 those numbers quickly declined to 1300. Finally the daily ration for a normal consumer in the British zone dropped to 1,042 calories a day, and even fewer in the French zone. Only miners and men employed in heavy industry received extra rations. A ration card, however, did not guarantee that the allotted amounts were available. Early every morning long lines formed in front of stores. One could never be certain that there was enough ration card food available that day.

Most people's modest reserves had been exhausted. The last pieces of china or silverware had long since been traded for butter or flour. We had nothing left to bargain with. My mother traveled by bicycle to the countryside to find whatever food items a farmer might be willing to sell. 1945/46 turned out to be an extremely cold winter, adding to the misery of a hungry population existing in shacks or in ruined and drafty buildings, often barely protected from the elements.

On one of my mother's excursions to Düsseldorf's harbor, she had made the acquaintance of the captain of a large cargo ship that had anchored there for the night. His motor barge pulled four or five barges loaded to the brim with coal from the mines in the neighboring Ruhr district. The captain would deliver his precious cargo to cities along the Rhine such as Cologne, Bonn and Koblenz.

As winter came on, the captain and his wife motioned to my mother to return after dark so that they could give her a few small bags of coal. My mother understood that she would have to smuggle the coal out of the harbor. She bicycled to the harbor after dark and crawled under the barbed wire fence that ran along the banks of the Rhine. The barge captain then filled three small sacks with coal, a dangerous undertaking for the captain as well as for my mother. The occupation forces considered this "stealing." Military police arrested everybody they found smuggling or trading on the black market. Such petty crimes were the order of the day.

Today it is hard to imagine my lovely and dignified mother, who had been a pianist, crawling under the barbed wire fence to smuggle coal. However, in those postwar years, everything was unusual.

Ulla Morris-Carter

If we thought that this first post-war winter was terrible, we didn't yet know that the winter of 1946/47 would be even worse. In December and January, 1947, it was cold enough for the fast-flowing Rhine to freeze over, something that has never happened again in my lifetime. The daily temperature was minus 20-30°C, minus 22°F. I remember crossing the Rhine on foot from Düsseldorf to Oberkassel, a small town on the opposite side of the river, climbing over high ice floes. Because of the bitter cold winter, some people risked their lives by jumping onto slow-moving open coal trains, quickly filling a few sacks with coal, throwing them off the train to a waiting family member, then jumping hurredly off the train.

The archbishop of Cologne, Cardinal Josef Frings, announced from the pulpit that he did not consider such maneuvers a sin. This, he declared, was not stealing. Quickly a new verb entered the dictionary: "*fringsen*". *Fringsen* was ok, the good Rhineland Christians repeated, the archbishop had said it was not stealing.

At the Potsdam Conference from July 16 to August 2, 1945, the 'Big Three', U.S. President Harry Truman, British Prime Minister Winston Churchill, later replaced by Clement Atlee, and Soviet Premier Joseph Stalin, discussed postwar arrangements for Europe.

Many of these ended in unworkable compromises. The Allies had previously agreed to partition Germany into three zones of occupation: A large Soviet Zone in the East, a British Zone in the Northwest and an American Zone in the Southwest. The fourth Zone, the French Zone, was established later, after France was also recognized as a victorious power. The Saarland, on the border with France, would return to French administration. The zones were to be governed by distinguished military officers. The most famous among them was the American general, Lucius Clay, whose name now graces a beautiful street in Berlin, Clay Allee. The city of Berlin itself was treated separately and was partitioned into four sectors, British, American, French and Soviet.

Düsseldorf was located in the British zone. British efforts to prevent starvation in their zone stretched their own economy enormously at a time when English civilians still lived on ration cards. The preferred zone was the American zone, where well-fed American soldiers would at times part with a piece of chocolate or a fruit for the thin, hungry children.

Fraternization at first was strictly forbidden, but as the months went by, restrictions were loosened. And German Fräuleins did not object to the advances of the GIs in return for a pair of silk stockings or a package of cigarettes. However, German men resented the women's willingness to consort with U.S. soldiers and were frustrated over their own inability to compete with them. There were even a few incidents of Germans attacking American soldiers, unheard of earlier.

Ulla Morris-Carter

I did not fully understand the political decisions of those days. I just knew that we had to adhere strictly to the orders and regulations handed out by the Occupation Forces. They left no doubt that they were the conquerors and Germany the defeated nation. U.S. President Truman, in August 1945, had issued a directive to the Joint Chiefs of Staff. This document had been in the making since April, 1945.

It read:

> It should be brought home to the Germans that Germany's ruthless warfare and the fanatical Nazi resistance have destroyed the German economy and made chaos and suffering inevitable and that Germans cannot escape responsibility for what they have brought upon themselves.
>
> Germany will not be occupied for the purpose of liberation but as a defeated enemy nation . . . .The principal Allied objective is to prevent Germany from ever again becoming a threat to the peace of the world.

Nor did General Dwight D. Eisenhower mince words when he addressed the German people by radio on August 6, 1945:

> The coming months are going to be hard for you. You will just have to be tough—there is no alternative. Every sign indicates a severe shortage of food, fuel, housing and transport. There will be no coal available for heating homes this winter. To meet your basic requirements in the next few months, you will have to go into the woods and cut your own firewood. A third priority is the provision of living accommodations.
>
> As far as the weather allows, damaged properties must be repaired to offer as much protection as possible. You will have to collect scrap material over the widest possible area and gather dead wood in the forests. These are your problems.
>
> Your courts of law and schools will be open as soon as they are purged of Nazi influence.

In July 1945, a small newspaper, the *Aachener Nachrichten,* was granted the first license to publish a thin three or four-page edition, subject to pre-publication censorship by the Occupation Forces. Such media were heavily conditioned by the political developments in the country. Paper itself was in very short supply. We had neither paper bags for groceries, nor, for that matter, toilet paper. My grandfather sat at our only table and carefully cut that flimsy newspaper into little squares. He then spiked them on a piece of wire and hung them in the tiny toilet room. Our toilet was not inside the apartment, but 10 steps downstairs on a landing between the first and second floors.

Most news reached us by word of mouth. Once, we heard a rumor that a soap factory had been broken into and lots of soap was scattered in the street. Off we raced to grab as much as we could carry. The soap, a gray-colored, dull-looking square, resembled

Ulla Morris-Carter

a small brick. It did not foam and was called "swim soap," *Schwimmseife,* because it floated on the surface of water. Another rumor told of a warehouse full of barrels of cooking oil. My grandmother, Oma, dispatched my grandfather, Opa, to get some oil for the family. Opa was a short, portly type of a man, an elementary school teacher by profession, who also occasionally played the church organ, good-hearted, but not too practical. Opa did not return from his expedition until two or three hours later.

"Jakob, Jakob, *um Gottes Willen,*" for God's sake, I heard Oma shriek from the front door.

Oma hardly ever raised her voice, so I immediately knew that something was wrong. Opa stood in the doorway, looking dejected and disheveled. His suit, the only one he still owned, was soaked in oil and his bucket was, guess what, empty. The oil in the warehouse had flowed freely and non-stop out of a large barrel, he explained. People were pushing and shoving for fear of missing out on this precious golden liquid. When it was Opa's turn, somebody pushed him, he slipped on the oil-soaked floor, fell, and of course, lost his place at the spigot. Instead of fighting back, he just left, discouraged and embarrassed, and walked home, carrying an empty bucket.

Despite hunger and fatigue, the so-called bucket brigades of rubble women, *Trümmerfrauen,* became a familiar sight. Bucket after bucket of rubble would be passed from one woman to the next, standing in the ruins of what once were lovely homes. Since most able-bodied working-age men were either in prison camps or in the few remaining factories, the task of clearing the mountains of rubble fell almost entirely to women. All of us, children included, had to participate in the clean-up efforts, collecting and cleaning bricks from the rubble and searching for metal pieces and other reusable materials.

Sometime in 1946, my mother, my brother and I managed to move back into our original apartment, after some temporary repairs had been made. Primitive as it was, with boarded up windows, we were delighted to move back into a place of our own. But we had to give up two of the three rooms. A three-person family like ours was allowed only one room. Throughout Germany the need for housing was desperate, particularly with a steady stream of refugees and displaced persons from the eastern part of Germany flooding into the West.

One of my clear memories of that time was playing in the ruins. My new girl friend, who lived around the corner, had the same first name as I, Ursula. She was called Uschi and I was called Ursel. We had few, if any games or other means to entertain ourselves. There were no ice skates, no roller skates, no bicycles. We had to invent our games. The house next to ours had been heavily bombed and was partly burned out. A shell of its former self, it stood there like a skeleton. But there was nothing more exciting and, at the same time, mysterious and terrifying than to play in the ruins. Hide and go seek,

Ulla Morris-Carter

our favorite game, meant looking for corners and dark corridors in what used to be the basement of our neighbors' house. Excited and scared, we could not resist searching for new hiding places in the furthest corners.

Our parents had warned us: "Please, do not go deep into the ruins, it's dangerous! Debris might come crushing down on you."

We understood their concern, but we knew that nobody had time to check out our hiding places for safety. The ruins beckoned day after day. Occasionally we would find something that once upon a time might have belonged to the people who lived there, a metal cup, a small bucket or a basket that had somehow survived the bombing. It scared us to imagine that people might have died where we were now playing.

"Who do you think this spoon belonged to?" Uschi asked me.

"If it belonged to a girl, what do you think her name was?"

We played this guessing game for hours. Uschi and I invented stories, sat on the cold basement stairs and shivered, either from the cool late-afternoon breeze or from fear. The ruins kept us in their grip.

In the fall of 1945, schools began to re-open. I had been out of school for a whole year. Now, two months short of my twelfth birthday, I was to enter the first grade of the *Gymnasium,* called the *Sexta.* German *Gymnasiums* counted classes in Latin language: *Sexta, Quinta, Quarta,* etc. My school, the *Helene Lange Schule,* had been damaged during an air raid. The outside walls were pockmarked with bullet and shrapnel holes. Wooden boards covered the windows, walls were in need of paint, and there was no heat. But it was a start.

Former U.S. President Herbert Hoover had been dispatched to Europe by President Truman to direct the first of several relief missions. Hoover spoke about a world threat "more destructive than armies", hunger and starvation, striking much of Europe and Asia, and particularly affecting children in Germany.

He said, "Civilization marches forward upon the feet of healthy children."

Consequently he started a massive school lunch program that fed millions of German children. I was one of them. For me at age 12, the school lunch program was by far the best part of going to school. We received a warm meal, mostly soup, made from American-supplied soup powder. We ate pea soup, bread soup or lentil soup, it didn't matter what kind, when you're hungry everything tastes good. All students in our school had kitchen duty for a few days once a month, a task for which we volunteered eagerly and gladly. The soup was cooked in enormous kettles. We fired up the big kettles with wood or briquettes, and then stirred the heavy liquid with huge wooden spoons until the soup bubbled and formed a crust on the side of the kettle wall. We then carried a pot of soup into each classroom, which was distributed to the individual students. Students were required to bring their own tin cups and spoons.

Ulla Morris-Carter

Kitchen duty allowed us to be in a warm room. In the winter it meant defrosting our ice-cold feet and frozen toes. Best of all, before cleaning the big kettles after lunch, we were allowed to scrape off the crust that had formed on the upper part inside the kettle. It was a most delicious treat. I can still remember the taste of that crunchy crust. For me it was a treat every bit as good as a chocolate chip cookie or candy.

Due to lack of classroom space, we alternated between morning and afternoon classes, one week from 8 am to 12:30 pm, the next week from 1:30 pm to 6 pm. When not in school, I was in charge of our small household and looking after my brother, four years younger than I.

My mother tried to keep her children and herself alive by working at first in a small bank that reopened in Düsseldorf-Hamm. A few months later she decided to try to re-start the family business that my father and his father had established in 1925. It had run until the war disrupted their business. Design, photography and the making of zinc plates, *Klischees, clichés,* for four-color printing were the mainstay of the *Kirschbaum GmbH,* named after my father and grandfather. Not a technician, my mother borrowed the equivalent of $500 from a bank and re-started the business after two of the former technical employees returned home from the war.

My mother was a courageous woman, like so many other women who took over when men were not around to help or support them. Germany's very authoritarian society had changed tremendously during and after the war. Women now took on leadership roles when required, they worked in factories, they drove tractors and trucks, and managed jobs that only men used to do.

Deliveries of agricultural goods to the cities were sporadic. Food shortages in all the zones were the biggest source of misery, although the situation was slightly better in the American Zone. Returning German soldiers trickled in from Allied internment camps, or from prisoner-of-war camps in Russia and Siberia, where they had barely survived horrendously harsh conditions. Now they confronted not only ill health and hunger, but traumatic flashbacks of the horrors of war. Nobody seemed to pay much attention to the deep-seated, terrible pain, physical and psychological, that the war had inflicted on so many.

Unlike today, when society speaks openly about war-inflicted post-traumatic stress disorder, post-war Germany lived by stiff upper lip, ones pain buried in the darkest corners of the human soul. Men were not supposed to cry. Men were not supposed to be weak. Men were not supposed to show emotions. Many returned home and sat in silence, emotionless, as if wrapped in ice. Many spent nights walking around or screaming in nightmares. Thus another major problem presented itself, the soldiers' re-adjustment to family life, often in extremely cramped surroundings. In addition they had to face the fact that their wives, in many cases, had taken over the reins of the family. Where did that leave fathers who had been used to making all major decisions?

Ulla Morris-Carter

Erich Kästner published several poems after the war, while also writing for the just reopened *Literary Cabaret* in Munich.

He described the return of a prisoner of war in 1947:

Das ist die Heimkehr dritter Klasse
Ganz ohne Lorbeer und Hurra.
Die Luft ist still. Der Tod macht Kasse.
Du suchst Dein Haus. Dein Haus ist nicht mehr da.
Du suchst Dein Kind. Man hat es begraben.
Du suchst die Frau. Die Frau ist fort.
Du kommst, und niemand will Dich haben.
Du stehst im Nichts. Das Nirgends ist Dein Ort.

English Translation: (by Ulla Morris-Carter)

This is the third-class return
Without any laurels or hurray.
The air is still. Death has taken its due.
You try to find your house—
The house is not there any more.
You look for your child—it has been buried.
You look for your wife—the wife is gone.
You come home but no one wants you.
You stand in a void—nowhere is your place now.

Similarly, in 1946, a young German writer, Wolfgang Borchert, wrote a touching and disturbing play, which described the despair of a whole generation surviving years of war and captivity. It was called 'The Man Outside', *Draussen vor der Tür*. [2]

My uncle Karl and Aunt Kate managed my grandparents' grocery store. Sometime in 1946, a German prisoner of war entered the store. He was a tall and lanky fellow, clad in rags, his hair shorn off, wearing ill-fitting self-made rubber sandals. No more than one hundred pounds covered his 6'3" frame.

"Look at that poor guy, obviously another POW returning home," my aunt whispered into her husband's ear.

My uncle agreed: "Do we have another piece of bread to spare?" he asked his wife.

The POW looked so hungry. My aunt ran to find a slice of bread and was about to hand it to him, when he spoke: "You don't recognize me," he said haltingly, embarrassed and bewildered, looking around the store.

He was squinting, obviously unable to see well. The moment my aunt and uncle heard his voice, they realized with horror that this POW was their brother-in-law, Heinz. He was married to uncle Karl's and my mother's sister, Agnes.

---

2. *Borchert died in 1947 at the age of 26 from wounds and malaria he contracted as a soldier.*

Ulla Morris-Carter

"Is it possible, is that you, Heinz?" Aunt Kate cried. "We didn't even know whether you were alive or dead. Thank God, thank God, you are alive!"

Aunt Kate sobbed, her voice trembling while tears of joy streamed down her face. They fell into each other's arms. Uncle Karl and Aunt Kate struggled to recover from the shock of not having recognized their brother-in-law. He had once worn glasses, but they had long since disappeared.

Nobody had heard from him while he was in a Soviet POW camp. His wife, my Aunt Agnes, was still living in Tirol, to where she had evacuated with their five-year-old daughter after their apartment in Düsseldorf was bombed and completely burnt out in 1943. They had been unable to return to Düsseldorf due to lack of transportation and, more important, lack of housing.

Uncle Karl and Aunt Kate immediately sent their 12-year-old son, my cousin Karl-Theo, to fetch my mother. We still didn't have telephone service. My mother had always been close to Uncle Heinz and Aunt Agnes. Breathless, my mother arrived, overjoyed to see uncle Heinz alive, though he was obviously not well. A small family council tried to deal with the problems at hand. Many questions had to be resolved quickly.

"Where can Uncle Heinz get quick medical help? Where can he find a place to live?" asked Uncle Karl.

It was obvious that Uncle Heinz was in urgent need of medical attention. He perspired heavily, he was shivering and shaking, and he could barely stand up or walk. He had used his last bit of energy and strength to make it this far. Fortunately, our family physician, Dr. Hecker, was still alive and had his practice nearby. He came as fast as his feet would carry him.

"He must get to a hospital as soon as possible, if we can find a bed for him."

Dr. Hecker was all business now, checking Uncle Heinz's pulse, heartbeat and lungs. Dr. Hecker looked worried. He suspected tuberculosis, which was confirmed once Uncle Heinz was in the hospital.

Meanwhile, my mother told one of our renters that we needed his room for our sick relative. We prepared the small room near the kitchen for Uncle Heinz once he was released from the hospital. TB is contagious and his care required serious precautions. With my mother working fulltime to re-establish the business, I was put in charge of my uncle. Dishes and silverware needed to be sterilized, bedding changed and washed daily, without a washing machine. I do not remember exactly how long this arrangement lasted but long enough for my still vivid memory of the seemingly endless daily laundry.

Always there was the ever-present hunger. One night our neighbors appeared close to a divorce over a slice of bread, judging by their shrill, unpleasant dispute. We were forced to live so close to each other that we could not avoid hearing their shouts, insults and screams. It emerged that when the family was asleep, the husband apparently took a slice of bread that wasn't part of his ration. Only one slice per person per day was

Ulla Morris-Carter

available. The husband allegedly had eaten a slice of bread that belonged to one of the other family members. Even the available bread was terrible, often wet and heavy.

The Occupation Forces, seeing the unbelievable hunger and cold in the winter of 1946, had delivered some bread flour to Germany. But it was not regular flour, it was corn flour, something the Germans had never heard of. American corn was not known in Germany. German corn, called *Mais*, is very different from American corn and was considered only suitable as chicken feed. Indeed, German *Mais* is neither sweet nor tender. The Germans felt that being supplied "chicken feed" by the Occupation Forces was adding insult to injury. The confusion, mostly due to translation problems, was eventually straightened out. German *Maisbrot*, corn bread, became more acceptable, though it was definitely not a delicacy.

Another food item, until then unknown for human consumption, was horsemeat. We felt fortunate if we could find it in the butcher shop. Whether smoked or pan-fried like steaks, we considered it a delicacy.

Denazification

Denazification was a high priority for the Allied Forces. But the sheer number of people to be *denazified* was overwhelming. The Nazi Party had 12 million members and many more sympathizers, plus a huge number of *muss-Nazis,* the must-be Nazi's, those who had to join the party to keep a job or simply survive under the Hitler dictatorship. The method of *denazification,* particularly in the American zone, was harsh and often unjust. It brought more chaos than cleansing.

As a first step, all public officials were removed from their jobs without either salary or pension, and no chance of re-employment. This procedure was followed by a decision to have everybody, meaning those not yet otherwise *denazified,* fill out a questionnaire, the famous *Fragebogen*, with no fewer than 131 questions.

Allied offices were flooded with completed questionnaires, most of them accompanied by supporting letters written by former bosses, friends and relatives, declaring the person in question had never held Nazi Party membership, and was known as a decent, "clean" person.

These supporting letters became known as *Persilscheine*. The word *Persil* referred to a brand of detergent similar to Tide. It meant that whoever had a *Persilschein* had an affidavit of good and clean character. I remember shouting matches over *Persilscheine*, when one of our neighbors declared that Herr Beyer, another neighbor, was not eligible, because he had belonged to the Nazi Party. Fights broke out in front of us.

The Allies did not have enough staff or knowledge to unravel the past actions of so many. Therefore, denazification turned out to be a much more demanding job than they had anticipated. It proved impossible to carry out successfully. Amid constant political

Ulla Morris-Carter

shifts emanating from Washington, London and Paris, many of the most wanted Nazis managed to escape either to the Middle East or to Latin America.

In the end the Allies tried and failed to reform the civil service. Denazification was not as successful as the Allies had hoped.

Relaxed Moments

Not all was gloom and doom. There were relaxed moments when the world did not appear as dark and desperate as it had been for so long.

One of my great aunts, the younger sister of my grandmother, years ago had joined the Catholic order *Vom Armen Kinde Jesus*, 'The Sisters of the Poor Child Jesus', located in Neuss, across the Rhine from Düsseldorf. When inducted into the order, she was given a new name, 'Sister Leonilla Maria'. She quickly became a prominent person in the convent, a decisive lady, statuesque in her black and white habit. In her fifties she was appointed Mother Superior, and as such she was also in charge of the orphanage attached to the convent.

Not long after armistice, Sister Leonilla Maria called for a family reunion. We all rallied. She was a lady of authority, and nobody dared to say no to her invitations.

For us it was a difficult journey by tram and train and on foot, to arrive at the convent early in the morning. Nobody in our family owned a car at that point. Quite a few family members were missing. My father had been killed in France in 1944. One cousin, a pilot, had been shot down and killed over England, two younger cousins were dead and one was missing in action. One uncle was still in a Soviet prisoner-of-war camp. Another, my mother's brother Willy, who had been working for Royal Dutch Shell in Sumatra, Indonesia, when the war broke out in 1939, was still in an internment camp. Although liberated by now, he was unable to find transportation back to Germany. His Wife Liesel and two of their three children had been deported from Sumatra to Japan, where they had spent the next six years. They now experienced the same problem, no transportation back to their home country.

The convent day started with 8 am mass, followed by breakfast at long tables set up for the family in the auditorium. Some of the orphans performed a short play for us.

What I remember best, however, was my visit to the nursery. In post-war Germany quite a few illegitimate babies, born to German women from American, British or French soldiers, were left on the doorstep of the nunnery. Sister Leonilla had organized the orphans into small families of eight children each, headed by one 'mother' plus a helper or teacher. I thought the babies were the most adorable creatures ever, particularly the 'chocolate-colored' ones, as I called the children born to German women, fathered by black soldiers. As mentioned earlier, I had never seen a black person until the U.S. army occupied Germany.

Ulla Morris-Carter

With food in short supply even before the end of the war, the ever-resourceful Sister Leonilla Maria had learned to drive a truck around the countryside to gather food for her orphans. Donning a steel helmet over her habit, she begged farmers for potatoes, butter and eggs. She never failed to return with a load of food.

Nothing fascinated post-war Germans more than theater and music. Germany had always considered itself a country of culture, *Kulturstaat.* People were hungry for something to take away the troubling thoughts of daily survival. Few, if any, concert halls or theaters had remained intact. Yet the first rehearsal of the Berlin Philharmonic Orchestra was held in May, 1945, only two and a half weeks after Germany's unconditional surrender. There were no announcements, no transportation, no posters to inform the public. There was only word of mouth. Musicians walked or rode bicycles, even transporting their cellos and basses on bicycles to the ruined hall of the former Philharmonic. Concerts started in the late afternoon to give people enough time to return home before the 11 pm curfew.

Ruth Andreas Friedrich wrote in her book *Battleground Berlin* about the first post-war concert:

> The violins are playing. Playing Tchaikovky's Fourth Symphony with jubilant pizzicati.
> "That something like this is still possible," stammers a man next to me . . . .
> We don't see the ruins. Forgotten are the Nazis, the lost war and the occupation forces. Suddenly everything else has become secondary. Only what the violins are playing is of importance.
>
> *– Ruth Andreas Friedrich: <u>Battleground Berlin</u>, 1990* [3]

Whenever people had the chance to see a movie, listen to a concert, or view a theater performance, they arrived in great numbers. Full of amazing enthusiasm, they were delighted to have a chance to spend their *Reichsmark,* which didn't buy much else anyway. Some performances took place in living rooms. *Theater in a Room,* one of the actors called his personal theater. Fifty people were all his living room would hold, but come they did, climbing badly-lit stairs without complaint.

In the winter, performers on stage felt the cold as much as the living room listeners or theater-goers, who frequently wrapped themselves in blankets they had brought along. I vividly remember watching my first theater performance with the actors Gustav Gründgens and Marianne Hoppe, later highly acclaimed artists.

---

3. *Leo Borchard, the conductor of the first concert, was born in Moscow to German parents. He had conducted the Berlin Philharmonic in 1933, but was declared politically unreliable and was banned by the Nazi regime in 1935. However, he stayed in Berlin and was a resistance activist. He became one of the tragedies and paradoxes of the peace that followed war. While accepting a ride by a British general after a concert on August 23, 1945, the general's British driver misinterpreted an American sentry's hand signal to stop. The sentry fired one shot at the car, killing Leo Borchard.*

Ulla Morris-Carter

Disagreements occurred frequently between the artists who had fled the country and those who had stayed. Whose life was more difficult? Who suffered more? Most disputes centered on the question of guilt, particularly collective guilt, which would preoccupy the new Germany for decades.

HÄNSCHEN

I heard my mother scream shortly after the phone rang:

"No, no—please, it can't be true. It can't be possible." Her voice trailed off.

"What happened?"

I had run to the phone to find out. My mother was hardly able to speak.

"Your cousin Hans, our beloved Hänschen," she cried, "he was killed an hour ago. It is too terrible for words. It exploded."

She had to sit down, holding on to the edge of the table. Her face had lost all color. She looked as if she might collapse.

"What exploded?" I asked, terrified by the sight of my mother.

"A piece of ammunition exploded. Nobody knew that live ammunition was still hidden in the rusty anti-aircraft gun."

My mother got up from the chair, too distraught to discuss this traumatic news any further.

"I must go immediately and be with his mother, Aunt Johanna," my mother said, already halfway out the door.

One year older than I, Hans, age 13, was my favorite cousin. He lived with his parents Johanna and Theo Windhövel in Düsseldorf-Hamm, a rural suburb of Düsseldorf. Hans' older brother, Karl-Heinz, was missing in action somewhere in Serbia. Hans' mother, my aunt Johanna, was my mother's older sister.

Apparently Hans had joined his friends to play on the abandoned anti-aircraft gun, which they used as a merry-go-round. All the neighborhood children participated. Even I had once played on it together with Hans.

When it started to rain on that fateful day, all the children ran home, except for Hans. He decided to have one round all by himself. And that's when it happened. Apparently an old piece of ammunition suddenly came to life and exploded, two months after the war had ended.It ripped my cousin to pieces.

The adults of the family would only whisper to each other about the tragedy. It was an accident too horrendous, too horrible, too devastating to be discussed in detail. I overheard my mother whispering, confiding to my aunt that they found only one shoe with Hans' foot inside. Little else could be identified. We children were not supposed to know the gruesome details.

Ulla Morris-Carter

The tributes at his funeral services indicated that he, beloved by all, did not die unprepared. A few weeks before the tragic accident, he attended evening prayers in the nearby church every day without being asked or accompanied.

Did he have a premonition? And why was he alone when the accident happened?

Everybody among our family and friends had had losses and trauma. But for my young cousin to be killed shortly after the war had ended seemed truly unacceptable. How was his mother to survive the loss of a second child to an unbelievably dreadful tragedy?

My cousin Hänschen's death notice.

Twelve years before his death, his sister Hannelore had died at age five. She had enjoyed a wonderful Christmas eve at her home in Düsseldorf-Hamm. Her father had lovingly created a present she had so much wished for, a doll's house, hand-crafted out of cigar boxes. The doll's house consisted of five rooms and a kitchen, plus a school classroom with benches, desks and a blackboard. In the living room stood a beautiful wood-carved angel carrying a small candle.

Following the cozy Christmas mood her parents had created on Christmas eve, Hannelore wanted to do the same. Tip-toeing to the downstairs kitchen at six the next morning, she put a footstool on top of a chair so that she was tall enough to reach the ledge where the kitchen matches were kept. Having retrieved the matches, she then proceeded to light the candle held by the little angel standing in the new doll's house.

My aunt and uncle were still asleep upstairs. While leaning over the angel, Hannelore's long, blond, wavy hair caught fire. Her terrified six-year-old brother pulled the burning Hannelore up the stairs to the parents' bedroom, by which time she was completely engulfed in flames. She died at noon on Christmas day.

My distraught aunt and uncle lost three of their four children—their missing-in-action oldest son never returned from Serbia, where he had last been stationed as a 19-year-old soldier. I have often wondered how parents who suffered such unbelievably tragic losses could continue to live and stay sane.

CURRENCY REFORM: END OF THE REICHSMARK

1947 was a year of changes. Some among the Western Allied occupation forces seemed more interested in re-education than in punishment, but the main thrust remained one of penalties, vengeance and future deterrence. The British and the

American zones formed the 'Bizone', which meant that planning for production and general administration were streamlined throughout both zones.

In Washington and London, sympathy for Stalin and the Soviet Union quickly gave way to fear and suspicion of the Soviets. President Truman announced the Truman Doctrine, through which the United States sent financial aide to Greece and Turkey, two countries threatened by the Soviet Union.

U.S. Secretary of State George C. Marshall, in a speech at Harvard University in June, 1947, announced the Marshall Plan, the European Recovery Plan, ERP. Marshall stressed that America could help Europe to recover, and that such assistance would contribute to preserving peace and democracy.

In fact, Marshall invited the Soviet Union to join in the program. But after short negotiations the Soviet participants withdrew and intensified their purge of all democratic elements in the zone they controlled. Under the Marshall Plan, twelve West European countries received about $12.5 billion in grants and loans between 1948 and 1951.

At the famous Foreign Ministers' conference in London in 1948, the four Occupation Powers could not reach an agreement on Germany's political and economic future. Political tensions between the western powers and the Soviet Union grew steadily worse, which was manifested in the formation of two separate German states in 1949.

But before the formation of separate German states, East and West, currency reform took place in the Western zones. In June 1948, the Office of Military Government for Germany, United States, OMGUS, issued a statement:

> Currency reform in Germany is necessary in order to withdraw excess money from circulation, to eliminate the black market and to produce an incentive to produce . . .
> The abundance of money does not provide an incentive to work, as people have been reluctant to work merely in order to obtain more money with which nothing could be bought.

German Economic Director, Ludwig Erhard, later to become Chancellor of the German Federal Republic, worked closely with the Allied Forces to plan the introduction of a new currency. It was to be called the *Deutsche Mark*. The new currency had been printed in secret in the United States, and secretly it arrived in Frankfurt as part of an operation code-named 'Bird Dog'. The Deutsche Mark, I was told, invalidated the *Reichsmark*. The Reichsmark would be worth little or nothing.

I had a savings account, containing 350 Reichsmark, which I considered an absolute fortune. I had saved it over years from pocket money or gifts from my grandparents and aunts. I could not understand that my money would not be worth much in the future. My mother insisted that I take my precious little red savings book and retrieve

Ulla Morris-Carter

all my money from the bank. The savings book had gold lettering on the cover, and my name was beautifully printed on the first page. It was a document like no other I owned. Rarely had it been taken out of the box where we stored important documents. Inside the booklet, a bank employee had carefully listed the many small sums I had deposited over the years.

The bank employee reached into the drawer next to his desk, took out what looked like a mountain of money, counted them, and then handed me a pile of Reichsmark. I was afraid to carry that much cash in my wallet, so I carefully placed it in my handbag, which I clutched so tightly under my arm that my arm went numb. I didn't walk but raced around our part of town fearing there would be nothing left to buy. I looked at every store. Was there nothing special anywhere that would be worth my fortune?

People and stores had hoarded anything of value in order to trade it on the black market, which meant the stores had hardly anything to sell. On the black market one pound of cherries—it was early June when the cherries were at their best—could be had for 100 Reichsmark. A watch would cost as much as 7,000 or 8,000 Reichsmark.

When I finally reached the handicraft store of Frau Beckmann, I saw a few balls of yarn inside the store window.

"Ah," I mumbled to myself, "finally something that I can use. I'll knit a sweater. Oma will help me."

I put my money on the glass counter and asked Frau Beckmann how many balls of yarn I could buy for my fortune. She looked at me carefully, realizing that I did not understand that 350 Reichsmark were worth practically nothing.

She finally put a ball of white cotton yarn on the counter and said gently:

"This will be enough for a pair of socks."

"But I need more, much more" I answered. "I want to knit a sweater, a sweater made out of soft wool, maybe red or blue. My grandmother will help me with the design."

"I am sorry, but your money won't buy more than one ball of white cotton yarn."

Too distressed to answer, I left the store almost in tears, unable to understand why my whole fortune of 350 Reichsmark could not buy more than one miserable ball of white cotton yarn.

On June 19, 1948, a Saturday, the Americans, the British and the French Occupation Forces announced the currency reform for Sunday, June 20. The Reichsmark would be invalidated, and the Deutschmark introduced as the only currency. Every citizen was allowed to exchange 60 Reichsmark for 60 Deutschmark, of which 40 Deutschmark would be paid immediately and the remaining 20 within 60 days. It meant that every citizen started with the same amount of money.

Suddenly the stores were filled with food items and goods that many of us had only been able to dream about. Bakeries displayed cakes and breads. Butter, eggs and meat appeared in abundance. There were stockings, dresses, suits and material of many colors and qualities in one store, and bicycles and roller skates in another. The only problem for many of us was that we did not have much money to spend.

Nonetheless, on the day after the currency reform, with our new Deutschmarks in hand, my mother asked my brother and me:

"What would you like to eat? What are you craving the most? You can each choose one special item."

I didn't have to think long to make a decision. I knew what I wanted. It had been on my mind for a long time.

Finally that dream would come true: "Steak tartar for me with a slice of fresh dark bread."

My mother was astonished to hear my choice. And probably a little concerned as to how my stomach, unused to such heavy foods after three years of a low-fat and often near starvation diet, would handle it.

But a promise was a promise, and she did not object or deter me. I do not remember what my mother and my brother chose.

I recall fixing and mixing my steak tartar, sitting in the one room that we were allowed to live in, the room with the bay windows that used to be our living room overlooking Düsselstrasse. My first task was to cut onions into tiny pieces, which posed an immediate problem. My brother hated the smell of onions. Since we had to share our kitchen with the other renters, who now occupied it, I accomplished this task by disappearing in the small toilet room and cutting the onions on the toilet seat. Returning to our room, I continued with the preparations. I added salt, pepper, mustard, capers and an egg yolk. What a pleasure it gave me to put together this gourmet concoction with all the items we had not seen in years. My mouth was watering. I could already taste it in my mouth. It felt like eating a forbidden fruit. Finally, the steak tartar looked perfect, ready to be devoured. I ravenously ate, the whole portion in one go. It was an unbelievable feast. Before long I started to feel unwell and finally very sick. Needless to say, I had a very bad night, one I will never forget. It was thirty years before I could look again at steak tartar, or hamburger meat for that matter.

Berlin Air Lift / Operation Candy Bombers

Another extremely serious political crisis developed in June, 1948. The Soviet government, which did not allow any participation in the currency reform in their zone of occupation, used the currency reform as an excuse to blockade the whole city Berlin. When the Deutschmark was introduced in the Western sectors of Berlin, the Soviet military forces closed off all rail, road and water traffic to and from the West. The more than two million inhabitants of the American, British and French sectors of

Ulla Morris-Carter

Berlin were dependent on food supplies from the West. Electricity was cut immediately. American General Clay's answer to this action was clear and forceful:

> . . . this is one of the most ruthless efforts in modern times to use mass star-
> vation for political coercion.

The real reason for this action was that the Soviet government wanted to force the Allies out of Berlin and introduce Communist rule over the whole region. Therefore, it became very important to maintain Western presence and to show Western will to guarantee democracy. General Clay decided to supply Berlin by air, a highly risky decision. He consulted with the head of the American Air Force, General Lemay, in Frankfurt:

Clay: "Do you have planes that can transport coal?"

Lemay: "Transport what?"

Clay: "Coal."

Lemay: "I cannot hear you very well. It sounds as if you are asking for planes that can transport coal?"

Clay: "Exactly, that's what I mean."

Lemay: "The Air Force transports anything."

So began the Berlin Air Lift, *Die Luftbrücke*. Everything people needed to survive, milk, meat, fruits and vegetables, medical supplies, coal and fuel, were flown into the city. The beginning of the Air Lift was chaotic and dangerous, but after a few weeks the operation was running fairly smoothly.

> Every two minutes a plane arrives from West Germany, loaded with food
> for West Berlin! The sound of the engines can be heard constantly in the air,
> and is the most beautiful music to our ears. One could stand for hours on
> the *Tempelhof* elevated station platform and watch the silver birds landing
> and taking off.
>
> *-Ph. Davison, Berlin Blockade*

When Lt. Gail Halvorsen, a pilot and amateur filmmaker, decided to observe and film the landing of the numerous Air Lift planes arriving at Tempelhof, he encountered a group of children, watching and waiting patiently for the landing. Seeing all the big-eyed children, some looking hungry, he wanted to give them something. But he found only two sticks of Wrigleys chewing gum in his pockets. What to do?

"I'll give you these sticks of chewing gum, if you can divide them and manage not to fight over them. I'll fly into Berlin again tomorrow, and I will bring more, plus some chocolates. I'll drop them here."

The children were thrilled. Many were too young ever to have seen or tasted chocolates, and certainly not chewing gum.

One child asked: "How will we know that it's you flying over?"

Ulla Morris-Carter

"I will wiggle my wings," he answered.

The next day Lt. Halvorsen flew, as promised, into Tempelhof, equipped with chocolate bars attached to handkerchief parachutes. Having learned about the air-drop, many of the other C-54 pilots, joined in the new adventure.

The Air Base Commander was not happy when he found out. But U.S. General Tunner thought that it was a great gesture for a victorious nation. Lt. Halvorsen became the best known pilot of the Berlin Airlift with his *Operation Little Vittles,* which was also sometimes called *Operation Candy Bombers.*

It was eleven months before Stalin relented and reopened the roads and rail into Berlin. On May 12, 1949, the blockade ended. The Allies had flown 782,000 metric tons of coal, 374,000 tons of food, 8,000 tons of newsprint and much more in 275,000 flights. Sadly, 27 planes had crashed and 74 pilots had died during operation Berlin Air Lift. What was left of the cooperation among the four victorious countries, America, England, France and the Soviet Union, came to a complete end after the Berlin Blockade. The aims of the Soviet Union had been clearly exposed, as Winston Churchill had already warned in his famous 1946 Iron Curtain speech:

> From Stettin in the Baltic to Trieste in the Adriatic an 'iron curtain' descended across the continent. We do not know what is going on behind . . .

My brother Hans and I around the end of the war.

Ulla Morris-Carter

FIRST ADVENTURES
POST-WAR

George C. Marshall, Secretary of State in U.S. President Truman's administration, gave the commencement address at Harvard University in 1947.

Realizing that many of the wartorn nations of Europe had not only suffered terrible human losses, but were also confronted with a major economic crisis, he proposed a plan. He called for "the American assistance in restoring the economic infrastructure of Europe." His was an ambitious plan, aimed at reducing the hardships in Western Europe—the hunger, homelessness, and unemployment.

Among the Occupation Forces, Britain and France warmly welcomed the plan, but the Soviet Union opposed it, seeing it as an attempt to exert American influence in post-war Europe. Despite bitter Soviet opposition, the plan, officially named the "European Recovery Program", *ERP*, but commonly known as the Marshall Plan, was established. The total expenditure of the four-year Marshall Plan, which particularly focused on the rebuilding of the iron, steel and power industries, amounted to more than $12 billion. It went into effect in 1948, almost at the same time as the German currency reform, which introduced the Deutschmark and helped fight inflation.

By 1949 the German economy and our lives in general were slowly beginning to improve. A German government had been formed following the first democratic elections in West Germany, the Basic Law[1], *das Grundgesetz,* had been approved, and Konrad Adenauer was the new chancellor. The German Bundestag selected Bonn, a

---

1. *The Basic Law is the constitution of the Federal Republic of Germany signed by the Western Allies.*

Ulla Morris-Carter

rather quiet and unexciting city, as West Germany's new capital. Almost at the same time, in 1949, East Germany established the *German Democratic Republic*, GDR, in the Soviet Zone. But, if we thought life would be smooth sailing from here on, we could not have been more mistaken. The Cold War between East and West began to escalate, and the Korean War started when North Korea attacked South Korea in June, 1950. Ironically, the Korean War decisively affected West Germany's economic future. Germany was not allowed to produce armaments, but German iron and steel and industrial products, precisely the things Germany was permitted to produce, were much in demand.

This was the political and human background of my teenage years.

VILLA HÜGEL—"CALL ME KRUPP"

The alarm rang at 6:30 a.m. I jumped out of bed, immediately awake and excited. It was Sunday—a Sunday in the summer of 1949. Opening the curtains in my small bedroom, I could just see the early morning sun appearing over the wild cherry tree in our not very organized garden. Nobody had had enough time to think about planting—our first priority had been to remove all the rubble, the bricks and debris that still cluttered what once had been attractive flowerbeds. My father, the painter and artist, had always lovingly tended the garden, but he was no longer with us. His grave, probably equally untended, was somewhere in Brittany, France. Our garden was a sad reminder of the war that had partially destroyed our house—a war that had come to an end four years earlier. But at this moment I was not thinking about war, or my father's death or of gardening.

"Ah, fantastic," I said to myself.

A sunny Sunday, just what I had hoped for. I dressed quickly, ran into the kitchen to prepare coffee, a new luxury since the currency reform of 1948—then made a few sandwiches for my Sunday outing. My canvas bag was standing ready near the door, containing sweaters and a windbreaker. One never knew what the weather would be like once we arrived at the lake. Karin, my best school friend, would be here any minute to pick me up. We had to run to catch the tram that would take us to the Düsseldorf railroad station. On Sunday mornings the trams did not run frequently, so we couldn't afford to miss one.

We caught the train to Essen-Villa Hügel—a one-hour ride from Düsseldorf. Then a 10-minute walk from the Essen-Villa Hügel railroad station, mostly downhill, through a gorgeous stand of oak and beech trees. It was almost 10 a.m. when we reached our destination.

In front of us stretched the beautiful Lake Baldeney, bathed in glistening sunlight, not a ripple in sight. Perfect for a Sunday trip. For a short while one could forget the

Ulla Morris-Carter

bombed-out cities and ruined factories, the soot and the dust of rebuilding. Surrounded by trees and large areas of green, it was as peaceful a place as one could imagine.

On the banks of Lake Baldeney stood a run-down wooden shack, badly in need of a coat of paint. A rusty padlock secured its creaky doors. It seemed oddly out of place in this glorious surrounding. But this unattractive shack held our most precious belonging, an old double kayak, a canvas touring kayak which the Germans called a *Faltboot*, folding kayak.

Our unbelievable luck in being the recipients of this most precious object was based on one of those tragic war stories. It had belonged to someone who did not return from the war, the young son of family friends. His parents had no interest in the kayak and simply gave it away, to us, to Karin and me. War memories were often too painful to be discussed, and objects belonging to those killed too upsetting to look at.

For Karin and me this kayak was a gift from heaven. Our families were struggling to stay alive, to rebuild and forget. We owned little, no bicycles, no roller skates, no ice skates. The kayak made us feel rich. We had already spent several Sundays repairing the neglected boat, fixing rips and leaks. Seaworthy at last, it would have its first outing on Lake Baldeney. Would our patches hold?

"What do we do if the boat takes on water?" I asked Karin.

"I have no idea. I have never repaired a kayak, nor have I ever been in one."

I was hardly more experienced, although I knew the basics, having been included on a few short kayak trips with my cousin. At least both Karin and I could swim well. Swimming had been part of our school curriculum. Now we encouraged each other, took a deep breath, gave a brief blessing and gently pushed the boat into the lake.

We watched intently as the kayak floated into the calm greenish waters and then bounced happily ashore in the wake of a passing boat.

"Bravo, fantastic!" we both shouted.

Beaming from one ear to the other, we slapped each other's shoulders and decided we had obviously done a good job. Paddles in hand, we eased into the boat and began to move. Almost instantly we found our rhythm as if we had practiced for weeks. Awed by the beauty that surrounded us, and filled with a sense of wonder, we moved in silence.

Karin was a lovely girl, age 15 or 16, with white-blonde hair and skin that looked like Meissen porcelain. Too much sun did not agree with her. In 1949, there was no such thing as sunscreen. Our outings had to be carefully timed, so Karin didn't get sunburned and blistered, as had happened three weeks earlier. But Germany is not California, and sunshine was never guaranteed.

Some kayakers we saw regularly baptized us "the black and the white captains", because I wore mostly a black T-shirt, sitting in the back of the boat and steering, and Karin, in front, always wore white. We paddled along the shore of the lake until we reached the place where the river Ruhr, a tributary to the Rhine, entered Lake Baldeney.

Ulla Morris-Carter

Kayaking on Lake Baldeney, near Villa Hügel. Karin in front, and I am in the back.

We picnicked when we could find a place to tie up and to sit comfortably in the grass. Even if the kayak was a little creaky, we felt as if we had won the lottery.

Was there anything better in life than a day in a kayak on Lake Baldeney?

During WWII, the Ruhr district had been one of the most heavily bombed regions in Germany. The city of Essen—indeed the entire Ruhr district—was dominated by the Friedrich Krupp steel and armament industries. As the nation's biggest steel producer and the manufacturer of all the major armaments for Hitler's war, the Krupp industrial plants and worker towns around the area had been high on the Allies' list for carpet bombing. Since precision bombing did not exist, surrounding cities, including my hometown, were frequently unintended targets and suffered major losses and destruction.

The Krupp family, with fortunes made from steel and armaments, resided in Villa Hügel atop the hill overlooking Lake Baldeney. It was often referred to as a castle. The Krupp dynasty dated back to the 16th century. It had been Europe's richest and most prominent family. Emperors and kings, politicians and heads of state and businessmen from all over the world had been guests in Villa Hügel. The history of Krupp and the history of Germany were inextricably linked. Alfried Krupp von Bohlen und Halbach, the head of the Krupp industries during WWII, had been an ardent supporter of Hitler and the Nazi Party. After the war ended in 1945, the American Occupying Forces confiscated the Krupp Villa Hügel, arrested Alfried Krupp von Bohlen und Halbach, the last of the Krupp brothers to reside in it, and locked him up in Landsberg prison.

Ulla Morris-Carter

In captivity, it is said, a guard politely asked him how he would like to be addressed: Herr Alfried, Herr von Bohlen und Halbach, or Herr Krupp?

"Call me Krupp. I am here because of that name. This cell is my share of the great Krupp inheritance."

During the Nuremberg Trials in 1948 Alfried Krupp was sentenced to 12 years' imprisonment for crimes against humanity and abuse of slave labor. But he served only a few years. He was released in 1951 by the U.S. High Commissioner for Germany on "political grounds". The Krupp's estate was later restored to him.

When paddling around Lake Baldeney, Karin and I could easily spot Villa Hügel atop the hill. Accustomed to cramped surroundings in Düsseldorf, we stared longingly at the imposing Villa. It was easily visible, even from far away. Partially obscured by surrounding shrubbery, the villa's white walls shone through the pine and cypress trees. How mysterious it looked, like a forbidden fairytale castle waiting to be explored. Alas, we were not allowed to even come close to it. Had we been told that it had 269 rooms, some as big as a concert hall, we would simply not have believed it.

Today Villa Hügel is a center for internationally famed exhibitions and cultural events, organized by *The Alfried Krupp von Bohlen und Halbach Stiftung,* Foundation.

Scouts—Sweden & Rome

At age 15 in 1949, I did not participate in the sorts of proms and similar activities important to American teenagers. Such fun events simply did not exist. However, looking around to find something to take my mind off the dreary surroundings, I discovered that a few people my age and older were becoming involved with an organization new to me, the German Scouts. Until then I had never heard of Boy Scouts or Girl Scouts.

Whatever I could find out about this international organization sounded truly exciting. We were all looking for something, anything, to help us out of the post-war depression that surrounded us on a daily basis. The German Scouts had to be affiliated with a church or religious organization to make them acceptable to a Germany that had suffered from an overdose of organized youth groups, such as the Hitler Youth. Uniforms, in particular, were frowned on. But the Scouts had worn uniforms ever since their establishment in 1922 by the British Lord Baden Powell.

Baptized a Catholic, and disregarding complaints from family and friends, I joined the St. Georges Girl Scouts, *Die Sankt Georgs Pfadfinderinnen,* established in Germany in 1947. (A similar organization existed for Protestant Girl Scouts). Although we wanted to be just like our British and American counterparts, our first project was the slow and delicate process of convincing parents and winning over skeptical, gruff, older Germans.

Ulla Morris-Carter

Leading (**middle**) *a group of Girl Scouts, with our home made flag.*

Tying knots for earning badges could wait. We had more important things to do. We sewed our own flag, made out of a white bed sheet, with the blue cloverleaf—the Girl Scouts symbol, as the centerpiece, embroidered by hand. We sewed and created whatever parts of our uniform we could make ourselves.

Nothing ready-made was available in Germany in those early days, and in any case few of us had money to spare. We marched in church processions, proudly carrying our home-made flag and wearing our uniform, dark blue skirts, light blue shirts, dark blue ties and dark blue berets.

SWEDISH JAMBOREE

In late 1949 came a huge surprise, an invitation to an International Scout Jamboree in Sweden. Only a few German Scouts, including myself, were invited to participate. In 1949 hardly any German traveled outside of Germany. To be invited to Sweden and to stay with Swedish Girl Scouts was unbelivable! I was in seventh heaven, the envy of my friends. Seeing Stockholm, a city still whole and beautiful, without bombed-out ruins and skeletons of houses, was an unanticipated bonus. My specific memories of that trip are few, apart from escaping old confines, but I experienced an inner delight. The thrill of exploring new places would remain with me throughout all my life.

The Girl Scout who invited me, my so-called home hospitality—Karin was was

Left: *Camp at the Swedish Jamboree.* **Right:** *With our fearless leaders, I am second from left.*

Ulla Morris-Carter

her name —was older than I, probably in her twenties. A beautiful blonde, Karin was one of the Swedish Girl Scout leaders. She lived by herself, and I was her houseguest for three or four days.

To be part of this worldwide gathering of international youths was a brief, but unforgettable experience. Seeing Stockholm, a city still whole and in tact without bombed-out ruins and skeletons of houses, was an unanticipated bonus. My specific memories of that trip are few, apart from escaping old confines, but I experienced an inner delight. The thrill of exploring new places would remain with me throughout all my life.

ROME

A scant year later, in 1950, another major Scouting experience fell into my lap. As Catholic Girl Scouts we observed religious affairs and holidays. Pope Pius XII had proclaimed this as a Holy Year of pilgrimage to Rome:

> *Those who hate God, may they see his light.*
> *May social justice spread around the globe to your families, to ensure that hunger disappears . . . .*
> *Always remember that pilgrimage should not be a secular excursion, but motivated by pious ideals.*

The tradition goes back to the year 1300 AD. The Holy Year, or Jubilee, is supposed to be a year of joy and a year of remission and universal pardon. Originally occurring every 100 years, the intervals were shortened over the centuries to 50 and then to 25 years. Roman Catholic pilgrims from every corner of the world journeyed to Rome. And we, the Catholic Girl Scouts, did not want to be left out. About 25 Girl Scouts from our region of North-Rhine Westphalia took the train to Rome. It seemed to us an epic journey. We walked along the ancient Appian Way, were overwhelmed by the sight of the Coliseum and the Roman Forum, visited the Catacombs of the early Christians and saw more churches than I care to remember.

Left: *Waiting to attend an audience with the Pope at St. Peter's Cathedral.* **Right:** *Mass with Pope Pius.*

Ulla Morris-Carter

Finally, we stood in St. Peters Square, in front of us the Basilica St. Peter with its magnificent dome, *il cuppolone,* the Italians call it. Awed by the sheer size of the huge square and marble columns by Bernini, we entered St. Peter's Basilica. Names like Donato Bramante, Michelangelo, Carlo Maderno, Giotto and hundreds more swirled around our heads. Then, sitting quietly in a side chapel toward the end of the day, we could feel the spiritual embrace of this sacred place.

Our journey continued. By train we traveled the short distance to Castel Gandolfo, the summer residence of the Pope, where we had been promised an audience with Pius XII. Perched high above the lake of Albano, *Lago di Albano,* Castel Gandolfo was a historic town with near perfect climate. It was a relief to be in a slightly cooler place after the hot days in Rome. We gathered in the inner courtyard of the Pope's residence and waited quietly for His Holiness to appear on the balcony. We did not have to wait long. Pope Pius, clad in his white robes, looking regal and refined, stood on the balcony and gave us his blessings.

He specifically greeted our group of Girl Scouts:

> *May peace enter the heart of your families.*
> *May all those be strong who have to suffer because of justice and persecution.*

That experience left a deep spiritual impact on all of us. Early the next morning, on our last day in Rome, we attended a farewell mass at St. Peters Basilica.

Our return train journey, unfortunately, allowed only a brief stop in Assisi, the birthplace of St. Francis, Patron Saint of Italy and founder of the Franciscan order. An impressive medieval town with its splendid 13th century *Basilica di San Francesco,* with its Roman Ruins, ancient cobblestone roads and sacred shrines, Assisi required much more time to explore than our allotted two hours.

A long train trip lay ahead of us; and eternal Rome was behind us, but the memories of this glorious city with its history of more than 2000 years did not fade.

Rome remains indelible in my memory.

Left: *On the train returning from Rome.* Middle: *Hitchhiking to Austria on the* Velveta *truck.* Right:. *An unforgettable summer of hiking and mountain climbing with the Girl Scouts and with friends.*

Ulla Morris-Carter

RHEINLÄNDER
OR NILE DWELLER

Ever since I had the chance to travel to beautiful Sweden in 1949, visiting Stockholm—a city untouched by the horrors of war, where wide-open boulevards showed an abundance of blooming flowers instead of ruined houses—I dreamed of leaving Germany for a less stressful and more peaceful place.

My Girl Scout journey to Rome by train a year later in 1950, only added to my yearning to explore the world beyond Germany. But this desire of a 15-year-old remained a dream for a few years to come.

We still lived in cramped quarters in Düsseldorf at that time. For lack of housing, my mother had offered one of our three rooms to her newly hired technical manager, a 30-year-old bachelor, who had the qualifications and master's degree to run a business such as the one re-established by my mother. A redhead, with freckle-covered white skin, the new technical manager turned out to be a hard worker—a person my mother needed. I called him Mr. B.

From the first meeting I disliked him, but understood that my mother's choices to hire a first-class technician were limited. Too many men had never returned from the war, and for my mother to find someone with the required qualifications, was certainly not an easy matter.

When she suddenly had to be hospitalized with a ruptured retina, and with the possibility of remaining blind, I realized that I was now in charge of our small household, which included my 12-year-old brother Hans and Mr. B. A ruptured retina—in the 1950s, was extremely hard, if not impossible, to repair.

Ulla Morris-Carter

By chance, we found out that the prominent Professor Custodis, had developed a procedure that would allow the welding of a ruptured retina—a completely new and rather difficult operation. Some years earlier, he had treated my mother for a different eye problem. Luckily, he worked and operated at times in a nearby well-known clinic in Düsseldorf. He called me in for a meeting to make sure that I, a 15-year-old, understood the seriousness of this situation.

"This operation requires your mother to lie totally still on her back in the hospital for approximately four to six weeks following the procedure. You need to realize that she will not be back home quickly to look after home and business," he said matter-of-factly.

No further comment. Professor Custodis was a man of facts and few words. I understood exactly what he meant.

Upon entering the hospital for this, her third operation, my mother told me:

"I may remain blind and you must be able to stand on your own feet. Once you can fend for yourself, you may do whatever you desire."

1951 happened to be a particularly hot summer. The eye operation turned out to be successful, but only if my mother would be able to strictly follow doctor's instructions of lying completely still for almost six weeks in the hospital. Fortunately a tram stop near our apartment allowed me to travel to the hospital to visit my mother almost daily. It was a painful and difficult time, mostly of course for my mother, but also for me. Seeing my poor mother, day after day, in the same room, the same bed, patiently enduring the heat and her understandable worries and concerns about being away from home and business, brought back the realization that the war continued to have consequences for our family.

My mother, who never complained about her sore back—she had developed back sores from lying still, in the same spot, for too long—was totally aware of the fact that possible blindness would be worse than all of these discomforts. Professor Custodis, very frank and open, had told my mother that she might remain blind on this operated eye, with her other eye already very weak.

I am not sure that I truly understood the seriousness of this situation and its possible repercussions, namely losing the only supporter of our little family. Who would run her business? Who would pay for school fees and food? Her modest widow's pension certainly was not enough.

One day my Aunt Käte arrived with a rather large basket filled with red currents from her garden:

"Make jelly out of these berries!" she ordered, without giving me more detailed instructions. "Your mother loves red current jelly."

I stared at this basket, immediately feeling overwhelmed with anxiety and

Ulla Morris-Carter

apprehension. How was I ever to make jelly out of this huge amount of lovely looking fruit? Was it more than 20 pounds? I had never cooked jelly before, although I loved spreading it on my *Brötchen*, small rolls, in the morning. I felt totally overwhelmed by this task, which I was responsible for in addition to all the other obligations I had acquired that summer.

It seems strange that up to this day I remember the worry of that day over a simple matter of having to make jelly. Why were other people lucky enough to just enjoy a hot summer day while I had to make jelly?

First the red, sweet berries, still warm from the sun, had to be washed, then stripped off their delicate stems. The next step was cooking them in a large pot, followed by putting the now soft berries through a cheesecloth-lined collander extracting all the juice as there was no machinery available. Finally, after collecting and re-heating the juice, adding sugar, lemon juice and pectin, the juice began to thicken. According to instructions, I had learned that the jelly was supposed to be ready when it would stick to a cool spoon. I tried, and, miracles over miracles, the hot and thickened jelly stuck to the spoon.

What a relief! After tasting the delicious syrupy mass, the jelly seemed ready be pored into sterilized glasses to cool down. At that moment I threw off my apron, left the hot kitchen and ran into our little garden for a breath of fresh air. I swore to myself that I would never cook jelly again. And I didn't.

While my mother was in the hospital, Mr. B. had become a real nuisance. He frequently walked into my room, unannounced and without knocking, whether I was in a state of dress or undress. My embarrassment quickly turned to anger and outrage. With my brother sleeping next-door, I hardly dared to raise my voice. This was not a subject for open discussion. Once I dared and managed to shove Mr. B. out of my room and locked the door—something I had never done before. We never locked any door in our house.

After my mother's return, I didn't dare to breach the subject. She was still feeling weak and appeared overwhelmed by work and family. Who was I to add to her dilemma?

It wasn't until almost a year later that I finally confronted my mother: "Either he leaves, or I leave."

The subject of sex in those days was not open for discussion—certainly not with one's mother. Hurt, angry and feeling unprotected, I left our house and found refuge at a friend's house, without contacting my mother. Needless to say, the friend understood my problem, but also my mother's dilemma. Concerned about my mother, she contacted her after three days to tell her about my whereabouts. Mr. B. remained in the business, but had to find another place to live. Was I ever relieved to have him out of my sight.

Ulla Morris-Carter

Following this incident, my brother, at a very young age and still in school, interned with two companies similar to ours, to learn the ropes of the business. He had a very creative mind and an understanding beyond his age of what was at stake. Still only 18, he joined the *Kirschbaum Klischeeanstalt,* the Kirschbaum business, to help my mother.

Because of our family's problems, I left high school in 1951 and started working as a trainee at an Iron and Steel company, called *Eikomag,* located in Düsseldorf-Benrath. In addition to a full-time job, I was required to attend a vocational school twice a week, taking classes in shorthand, German and English, typing, bookkeeping, export and import, plus evening classes in technical English. Evenings at home required house keeping, while my mother often worked late to keep and to improve the Kirschbaum business. These were busy days. At the end of 1953 having passed all vocational school exams, I was a full-fledged secretary, and as such, was occasionally asked to work for the top director of Eikomag—a job I considered a great honor at my age.

But Germany was still in post-war mode. Thousands of German soldiers still lingered in Soviet Prisoner-of-War camps. These POWs, approximately 10,000 surviving Germans, were not released until German Chancellor Konrad Adenauer's remarkable first trip to Moscow in 1955—a trip highly charged with emotions. The negotiations lasted six days.

Adenauer, in his memoirs, mentioned an amusing detail: "A great deal of alcohol was consumed," with the Soviet hosts insisting on serving Vodka for all occasions.

To prevent intoxication, Adenauer's assistant, Hans Globke, gave every member of the German delegation a large drink of olive oil before every reception. Neither Adenauer nor Globke ever explained or confirmed that it worked.

In 1953, I was invited by my cousin Theo, to a party at his Kayak and Rowing Club on the river Rhine. I was thrilled to be asked. Kayaking was one of my long-time favorite sports, ever since my friend Karin and I had started kayaking on the Baldeney Lake two years ago. Looking out of the Kayak Club window that evening, with the Rhine waters sparkling and glittering under a gorgeous full moon, I felt happy to be alive. Forgotten, at least for a while, were the hardships of the past, and I just enjoyed being young. My cousin introduced me to a handsome young friend by the name of Elmar, who came to be my first boyfriend. Owning a double kayak, Elmar introduced me to more serious kayaking on the fast-flowing and sometimes difficult-to-maneuver Rhine river and beyond.

In the 1950s we traveled by train with our folding kayak, *Faltboot,* to Lake Lugano in Switzerland and to the Wolfgangsee, Lake Wolgang, in Austria. Some exciting wildwater rafting adventures on scenic rivers, running through spectacular mountainous country, added to this great experience.

Ulla Morris-Carter

Kayaking with my first boyfriend Elma.

However, these wonderful summer adventures did not diminish my desire to leave Germany. My mother and my brother were working very hard and successfully to make the Kirschbaum Klischeeanstalt into what later became the much larger company called *Kirschbaum Laserscan.*

In the Spring of 1955 my employer Eikomag dispatched me to Hanover for a week to work at the International Trade Fair, a yearly event in the Northern German city of Hanover. Because of my course in technical English, I could now discuss technical problems with our international visitors. I was excited to travel by train to Hanover and to escape for a few days from the daily routine of my job as a secretary. I had not chosen to work in this field. But my mother's serious eye problems had prompted an unwelcome change of plans.

Upon my return from Hanover I broke the news to my mother. The Egyptian representative of Eikomag, had offered me a job in Cairo, Egypt. Business communications between Egypt and Germany had at times been difficult, mainly due to language problems. Mr. Abbas Hussein, the owner, a middle-aged Egyptian businessman, seemed convinced that I was the perfect answer to his problems. I was flattered to be asked, but my interest went beyond that. I had long hoped to find a way to leave Germany for a while, not an easy task in the 1950s when Germans were still unwelcome in many parts of the world. But here appeared the answer to my prayers.

Ulla Morris-Carter

My mother was flabbergasted, to say the least, when I told her about my plan to move to Cairo, When the news finally sank in, she assumed that I would come to my senses and forget about this outrageous idea.

After all, how does one even get to Egypt? What language do they speak there? What kind of a person was Mr. Abbas Hussein? Where would I live?

She would have to meet him, she said.

That was of course not possible—he had already left Germany. My contract and the ticket to Cairo would be brought to me by a German businessman, I said, trying to convince my mother of the seriousness of my intentions.

After a few days with no mention of Egypt my mother finally countered:

"In any case, no decent German girl goes to the Orient."

And with that remark she considered the subject closed.

A few weeks passed, during which I waited anxiously for further news from Egypt. Mr. Becker, a German businessman, finally called. He had just returned from Cairo, my contract and return ticket in hand.

Could I meet him in Bielefeld, he asked?

Like my mother, he did not sound too enthusiastic about the idea of a young German *Fräulein*, 21 years of age, traveling alone to the Arab world. To make matters worse, a second German businessman who lived in Beirut, a client of Mr. Abbas and his Egyptian company, visited my mother without my knowledge. He insisted that under no circumstances was she to allow me to depart for Egypt.

"I would break her neck, if she were my daughter, rather than let her go to Cairo," he apparently told my mother.

But my mind was made up. At the age of 21 I was legally an adult and could make my own decisions, I thought. Nothing, not even my dear mother, who had done so much for my younger brother and for me, would deter me from leaving.

It was then, when she was most vulnerable, that I reminded her of the promise: "You can do whatever you want to do, once I know that you can survive on your own."

She nodded sadly:

"Yes, you are right. I did promise, and I never want to hold you back, though this particular request is a hard one to swallow. But I will never go back on my promise, because you fulfilled your part of the deal. Now it's my turn."

She turned away, and I knew she was crying.

Ulla Morris-Carter

DÜSSELDORF-BENRATH
Kappeler Str. 51 · Postschließfach 35
den

Unsere Zeichen
PA/Br/S.

Betreff:

Fräulein Ursula K i r s c h b a u m , geboren am 26. Oktober 1933,
wurde im Anschluß an die vor der Industrie- und Handelskammer zu
Düsseldorf "mit gutem Erfolg" bestandene Prüfung ab 1. April 1953
weiterhin als Kontoristin und Stenotypistin beschäftigt.

Nach erfolgreichem Einsatz im Offertbüro unseres Stahlbau-Betriebes
wurde Fräulein Kirschbaum in die Verkaufsabteilung für das Inlands-,
vorwiegend aber für das Auslandsgeschäft unserer Baumaschinenfabrik,
übernommen. Dortselbst wurde sie mit den vorkommenden kaufmännischen
Arbeiten betraut, und infolge ihrer Sprachkenntnisse konnten wir ihr
die anfallende englische Korrespondenz einschließlich Übersetzungen
übertragen, die sie nach Angaben selbständig erledigte. Im Rahmen
ihrer Tätigkeit erwarb sie sich gute Kenntnisse und Erfahrungen auch
in der bankmäßigen Abwicklung von Exportgeschäften sowie in der Be-
arbeitung von Transporten in das Ausland.

Vertretungsweise als Direktionssekretärin eingesetzt, erledigte
Fräulein Kirschbaum auch die ihr in dieser Tätigkeit übertragenen
Aufgaben stets zur vollsten Zufriedenheit der Geschäftsleitung.

Durch ihr aufgeschlossenes und zuvorkommendes Wesen, verbunden mit
der Freude an den ihr übertragenen Aufgaben, war sie allen Vorge-
setzten und Arbeitskollegen gegenüber eine angenehme Mitarbeiterin,
die stets im Interesse unseres Unternehmens einsatzbereit war.

Fräulein Kirschbaum scheidet am heutigen Tage freiwillig und auf
eigenen Wunsch aus unseren Diensten, und es begleiten sie unsere
besten Wünsche für ihren ferneren Lebensweg.

Düsseldorf-Benrath, den 31. Januar 1956

E I K O M A G
Eisenkonstruktionen und Maschinenfabrik
Aktiengesellschaft

Above: *Letter of evaluation and departure from Eikomag, after I quit to leave for my new position in Egypt. Partial translation of the Eikomag letter of evaluation at the time of my departure for Egypt:*

Miss Ursula Kirschbaum, after having successfully passed all exams at the Chamber of Commerce, was employed by Eikomag since 1953. She worked in all departments from sales to Import and Export, as well as Secretary to the director. Because of her excellent knowledge of English, she was trusted to correspond directly with our foreign clients.

Her courteous and open-minded character, and the joy with which she completed all her tasks, made her a pleasure to work with.

She is leaving us of her own volition, and our best wishes accompany her for her future.

Düsseldorf-Benrath, January 31, 1956.

A portrait photo of me from around this time.

Ulla Morris-Carter

Le Cai

Postcard of the Great Pyramids, from my early days in Cairo.

Les quatre Pyramides - The four Pyramids

THE EGYPT YEARS

POSTE ITALIANE

LIRE 5 REPVBBLICA ITALIANA

10-11 26-11 1956

Frau
Maria Kirschbaum,
Norfer str. 38,
Düsseldorf,
Germany .

Translation: I have already arrived in Naples, and I have to tell you that I feel terrific. *S.S. Esperia* is a wonderful ship, and thank God, at this time of year it is not overcrowded. In case you cannot reach Mr. Steinhauer, please, don't worry. It doesn't matter. Everything is in order. Your Ursel

Postcard that I sent to my mother from Milan, of the S.S. Esperia, *the ship I traveled on to Egypt,*

Traveling to Egypt

"No Decent German Girl Goes to the Orient"

You may give (your children) your love, but not your thoughts.
You may house their bodies but not their souls,
For their souls dwell in the house of tomorrow,
which you cannot visit,
Not even in your dreams.
You may strive to be like them,
but seek not to make them like you.

-Khalil Gibran, Lebanese poet

On a cold, gray and rainy February day in 1956, typical Düsseldorf weather, my uncle Heinz, husband of my mother's sister Agnes, accompanied me to the railroad station, where I boarded a train bound for Milan, Italy. There I was to pick up some business documents for Mr. Abbas Hussein before proceeding to Cairo.

My mother, much too upset to accompany me, remained at home. She knew that a trip to Cairo in 1956 meant that I might be away for two years or more. Uncle Heinz, who had been a prisoner of war in Russia for two incredibly hard years, where his 6'3" frame was reduced to 104 lbs, was more sympathetic to my desire to leave Germany. He himself would leave, he said, if only he could.

I did not want to admit, even to myself that I was a little scared to travel this big new world all by myself. At that time I had only been out of Germany for the short Girl Scout adventures to Sweden in 1949 and Rome in 1950. The huge Milan railroad station had many more tracks than I had ever seen in German stations. I felt lost, not speaking a word of Italian. For the first time I wondered whether this whole trip made

Ulla Morris-Carter

sense. But my doubts didn't linger. A taxi took me to the modest hotel where the Milan company had booked a room for me. Walking out of the hotel, I suddenly found myself in a big square. There, in the golden light of the setting sun, stood *Il Duomo,* magnificent in its illuminated splendor. I had not even thought about sightseeing. I had been too preoccupied with travel preparations. But here I was, standing in awe of one of the great sights of Europe. I had a hard time extracting myself from this beautiful spot when darkness fell, and I had to return to my hotel.

Early the next morning I was on my way by taxi to collect the documents for Mr. Abbas Hussein. Then off by train to Genoa, Italy, where I was to board the *S.S. Esperia,* bound for Alexandria, Egyt. In Genoa I was to meet up with Soraya Farid, of Egyptian-German origin, two years older than I, whom I had met at Eikomag some weeks ago. She was an industrial photographer, and while photographing at Eikomag, she had mentioned in passing that she was returning to Egypt on the same ship I was booked on. The president of Eikomag, Director Schaf, had tried to convince Soraya to bring me to my senses and talk me out of going to Egypt. The company would gladly send me to England for a while, if I desperately wanted to get out of Germany.

"But Egypt, quite impossible," remarked Director Schaf.

Soraya, however, was on my side. Like many Egyptians, she spoke several languages, was curious about everything, and loved to explore the world. She encouraged me to travel with her to Egypt.

"You will love Cairo," she said, "the hospitality of the people, the history of ancient Egypt, the weather, the bazaar . . ."

I needed no convincing. But when I reached the quay in Genoa, there was no Soraya. I boarded the ship and inspected the cabin Soraya and I were to share with two other women. She wasn't there either. Nervous, I went back on deck. People were saying their tearful goodbyes, others were lugging huge steamer trunks on board, still others happily waving and embarking on what promised to be a joyous journey. The sound of the ship's horn rang out, inviting passengers to board as soon as possible. Still no Soraya. When the horn sounded its last three warnings before departure, reminding relatives and friends to disembark immediately, I saw a figure in the distance, carrying what looked like two big floor lamps, one under each arm. She was trying to run as best she could with this bulky load. It was Soraya. Breathless, she managed to board seconds before the sailors pulled up the gangway.

We had a wonderful journey until day three.

Suddenly, a huge winter storm swept across the Mediterranean, with ferocious winds and huge waves. *S.S. Esperia* rolled mercilessly in the heavy waters, giving us a roller coaster ride. White foam capped the normally greenish waters, at times obscuring its color completely and making the ocean appear completely white against the dark gray sky. Most passengers were seasick. Soraya and I, however, enjoyed the full attention of the stewards who had befriended us on the first day. They brought meals to our cabin in addition to some extras from the first class menu. In fact, in the lower quarters we were better off than the first class passengers upstairs. At the bottom of the ship the wave motion was less harsh. On day four the storm subsided, and the balmy Mediterranean temperatures hinted that we were approaching our destination.

The *S.S. Esperia* docked in Alexandria in the afternoon. The sky was overcast, but the temperatures were mild, in the 60s. Soraya's parents were waiting on the quay for her to disembark. I moved slowly toward the exit and disembarked hesitantly, turning my attention toward the heavy figure of Mr. Abbas, whom I recognized immediately. He was in his fifties, stocky, balding, well dressed. His dark, intense and almost bulging eyes dominated his face.

Mr. Abbas greeted me in English: "Welcome to Egypt," his baritone voice boomed at me.

He quickly followed with the Arabic greeting, "Ahlan wa sahlan!" *welcome*, and presented me with a welcoming gift, actually two gifts, a small box and a larger one.

"You can open them in the hotel. We shall overnight in Alexandria and travel tomorrow to Cairo by car. The desert road to Cairo takes three to four hours. We would arrive too late if we leave now," he told me matter-of-factly.

"Make sure you call us as soon as you are settled in Cairo," Soraya shouted over the noisy greetings and shrieks of passengers and relatives who likely hadn't seen each other in years.

"You have my address and telephone number,"

Soraya reminded me, as she and her parents departed almost instantly. There goes the only person I know in Egypt, my only support, I thought to myself. And here I stood on the quay, a 22-year-old German girl, politely conversing with an Egyptian man, more than double her age, her new employer, whom she had met only once.

"What do I know about him?" I asked myself.

Nothing, except that he is a businessman who represents Eikomag in Egypt.

I suddenly remembered the German-Lebanese businessman who visited my mother before I departed.

"Mr. Abbas is not trustworthy, he is not honest," he had warned my mother. "You must prevent your daughter from going to Cairo."

Egyptian porters appeared and took care of my luggage, two large suitcases, while Mr. Abbas ushered me into the back seat of his car, driven by a chauffeur. The hotel in Alexandria was more elaborate than any I had ever seen before. I was intimidated. Mr. Abbas guided me toward the elevator.

"I don't have a key yet," I said.

Ulla Morris-Carter

"You don't need a key. We have a suite."

Without further comment he moved on. Did he say "we" or had I misunderstood him? I looked at him questioningly.

"Come on now, we are on the third floor," he said as he moved toward the elevator, holding my arm and guiding me along.

He had caught me totally by surprise. I was so stunned I could neither speak nor move. I stood there in the middle of the elaborate lobby as if frozen.. He turned and again said everything was just fine and not to worry. I did not move, refusing to follow him to the third floor. One suite for the two of us could only mean one thing.

"I am waiting for a key to my room," I announced coldly.

I had gathered myself together now and was not about to be intimidated by a man obviously accustomed to having his orders followed without questions.

"Alright then, if you insist," he relented. "We'll get a second room. We'll meet for dinner in an hour."

The reception clerk handed me a key for my single room.

I was shaken. What a beginning! I had to remind myself that I had somehow always managed to get through difficult situations. I had survived bombs and occupation and cold and hunger. But this was different. A woman of the world I was not. I was scared. I sat on my bed, holding my head. What would be the next surprise? How would I handle myself?

It was time to prepare for dinner. What to wear? I did not own elegant clothes of the kind I had seen ladies in the lobby wearing. My gray-blue suit would have to do. It was my only suit, and I was proud of it. It fit me well and matched the color of my eyes.

I have no recollection of how the dinner proceeded. I was preoccupied with the uncertainties of my situation. Going upstairs after dinner, Mr. Abbas insisted on accompanying me to my room. He was carrying the two boxes, my welcoming presents, as yet unopened.

"You must open them now. I hope you like what's inside."

He settled down in one of my chairs and watched with obvious delight when I opened the small red box first. I was not prepared for what I saw, a gold watch set in diamonds displayed on a red velvet stand. The watch face itself had a gold cover which, when closed, made the watch look like a bracelet with diamonds. Luxury goods were not part of my post-war German life, and definitely not gold watches with diamonds. Beautiful as this piece of jewelry was, I wished I didn't have to deal with it. I really didn't want it. It was too ostentatious, too expensive, too outrageous. What to do?

I had to thank him, of course, which I did as best I could, all the while pointing out that this was definitely too extravagant a present for someone like me and that I could not possibly accept it. He ignored my excuses.

Ulla Morris-Carter

"Now please open the other box," he said while handing me the larger one with a smile. This game was becoming terribly embarrassing.

If I had been in shock over the first present, the second one took the prize. Beautifully wrapped in perfumed paper was a floor-length white silk négligée, split down the middle. My face turned red. He suggested I try it on. I was not amused.

How dare he treat me like this? I thought.

"I feel very tired and really need some rest now," I ventured, fearing he might make further advances. But he got up, wished me a good night and departed, reminding me to be ready by 9 a.m.

We left after breakfast, driving on the only road that in early 1956, connected Alexandria and Cairo, the so-called Cairo-Alex desert road. We did not speak much. I was totally absorbed and fascinated by my very first experience of desert. The road, a narrow strip of asphalt, resembled a gray ribbon running through a flat patch of brownish-beige sand. No trees, hardly any elevations, an occasional dusty village of mud brick houses with narrow alleyways. The air was dusty, the sky overcast. It was winter in Egypt. The trip of approximately 140 miles took four hours.

Approaching Cairo the scenery changed. In 1956, Cairo was a relatively "small" city of about three million people (vs. todays's almost 15 million.) The city's suburbs were green with lush gardens surrounding elegant villas. Big squares sparkled with fountains and statues. Despite the fact that Cairo is a desert city, its vegetation, all manner of trees and exotic plants, gave the impression of a little paradise. After a short rainfall in January, the flame trees were in bloom, the bougainvillea, the jacaranda and oleander overwhelmed me with their intense colors, and the sycamore, the eucalyptus and the banyan trees looked freshly washed.

However, approaching the center of Cairo, the city took on a more desert-like, sand color look. Crowds of people moved slowly along the sidewalks on either side of the bustling streets as if pushed by an invisible force. Crossing streets on foot appeared life threatening and next to impossible. The roads were filled with donkey carts, horn-blowing automobiles, dilapidated, battered taxis and streetcars and buses. The buses and streetcars were packed with passengers, clinging outside the doors like bunches of grapes. I feared for their lives. Some of the buses leaned so far toward the pavement that it looked as if their entry steps might scrape the ground. But Cairo, in 1956, four years after King Farouk had been deposed and with President Nasser now head of state, this ancient metropolis still showed much of the grandeur of the British Empire in wide avenues, fountains and parks.

Finally we reached the Nile, its legendary green waters flowing quietly at a steady pace, much slower than the river Rhine of my hometown. Graceful *feluccas*, the shape of their sails unchanged since the Pharoahs, sailed calmly in its current. They transported

Ulla Morris-Carter

people, or they were loaded with pottery and goods of all kinds. This life-sustaining river travels 4,160 miles from its central African source, at three and a half miles per hour, to the Mediterranean Sea. Once every year, for thousands of years, this miraculous artery has fertilized the parched lands of the Nile Valley, flooding the low-lying areas, soaking the ground and depositing a rich layer of silt. White egrets and blue herons stood silently on the banks of the river.

I was in awe of this vast river of which Napoleon Bonaparte, the first from the west to conquer Egypt, is said to have written:

"In Egypt, the Nile, the spirit of good, and the desert, the spirit of evil, are ever present."

We crossed the Nile on one of Cairo's bridges, the Great Gezirah Bridge, to arrive at Mr. Abbas' home. At this time of year, early February, the Nile, was barely audible, flowing quietly towards its Delta at the Mediterranean Sea. Here, near the Gezirah Bridge, two islands split the Nile into two arms, which make this powerful river seem smaller than it really is.

Mr. Abbas' villa, located in Gizah, was a large, two-story house, surrounded by a lush garden. Having just arrived from still impoverished post-war Germany, I was impressed by the luxury that surrounded me as I took in the gilded furniture in the spacious high-ceilinged main room, the salon, that seemed to be the center of the house. The walls were painted in light blue and covered with either paintings or wall hangings. The many members of the extended family who apparently lived in this villa, appeared almost instantly from of all corners of the house as we arrived.

Mr. Abbas' wife, Mrs. Hussein, a short, heavy-set lady with a kind face and pale complexion, almost white in comparison to that of her husband, was clad in a long black robe with a black scarf thrown loosely over her hair. Mr. and Mrs. Abas's children, their spouses and grandchildren followed. Their sheer numbers amazed me, but they gave me the warmest and friendliest of receptions.

Some spoke English, some only Arabic, but all welcomed me with the legendary Arab hospitality.

"Ahlan wa sahlan," said Mrs. Hussein, who spoke no English.

She greeted me with a smile and a weak handshake.

Mr. Abbas sat down in a special chair, a gilded Louis XIV piece, reserved for him, in the middle of the room. Everybody else gathered around him in a circle. He made sure all paid attention. They addressed him as Abbas Bey—a Bey ranks just below a Pasha, I learned. The titles date back to the Ottoman Empire. A rapid dialogue in Arabic followed, which I did not understand. Abbas Bey snapped his fingers, and a male servant dressed in a red-and-white striped Galabiya, a long kaftan, typical Egyptian wear, appeared with a tray of small cups of tea. Delicious mint tea, heavily sweetened, was

Ulla Morris-Carter

served all around. I sat stiffly on my straight chair and had no idea what was expected of me. Mr. Abbas did not linger long. He rose suddenly and announced that he would take me now to the apartment where I was to stay.

"You are new to Cairo and cannot live by yourself. It does not become a young foreign woman."

"But I want to find a room for myself," I explained.

"You will live in my apartment and can search later for a place of your own after you have acclimatized yourself and have learned your way around Cairo," he announced, leaving no room for counterargument.

I followed him as he walked me to a somewhat drab-looking building, not far from the house, where he either owned or rented an apartment. He explained that this was his apartment, a place where he could withdraw when the commotion and noise in the big family house was too much for him.

Two pleasant-looking young girls, dark-skinned and smiling, no older than 12 and 14, opened the door. They helped carry my suitcases and immediately began unpacking.

"I will do this myself, please," I pleaded, to no avail.

They did not speak English, and they were trained to do everything. I was distressed. I carried only a few items other than clothes, a photograph of my family, a special candle, a small vase, a present from my best friend, a book of poetry by Rilke, letter writing paper and other small mementos, all of them precious to me.

The room was simple. It had a bed, a nightstand, a chair and small desk, a chest of drawers and a big closet that took up most of the space. A balcony, accessible from every room of the apartment overlooked a busy, dusty street filled with handcarts, donkey carts and cars honking loudly for no reason that I could determine. A steady stream of people, some carrying groceries and vegetables, others just strolling and chatting, crowded the sidewalk.

"I will pick you up for dinner in an hour." Mr. Abbas announced.

I did not know whether that meant dinner with the family or dinner with him alone. I did not have to wait long. He returned, and as I had feared, it was dinner with him alone in a restaurant. Abbas Bey displayed a healthy appetite. He was a big man and obviously loved food. He made a few verbal advances but was otherwise pleasant and even businesslike when he told me about his office and the plans he had for me. The office needed to be refurbished, he said, and I was to choose new furniture.

Was this part of a secretary's job? I wondered.

The servant girls, Zeinab and Leila, were still awake when we returned. They helped Mr. Abbas out of his coat and seemed ready at a moment's notice to jump into action to serve their master.

"Where is Mrs. Hussein?" I enquired.

"She remained in the family house to be with her children and grandchildren."

Ulla Morris-Carter

There was nobody to ask, nobody to explain some of what appeared to me to be strange habits. Mrs. Hussein, Mr. Abbas explained, frequently stayed in the family house while he, needing rest and quiet surroundings, spent the night at the apartment.

While I was unpacking and organizing my belongings, he, ever so quietly and unexpectedly, entered my room from the balcony. Suddenly this figure, appearing out of the dark, stood in the middle of my room.

I almost shrieked: "You scared me, please don't do that again."

My demeanor was so off-putting, my voice so cold and uninviting that whatever his intentions may have been, he apologized and left.

Abbas Bey drove me to the office the next morning. It was located in an old-fashioned four-story building in the center of Cairo, close to *Midan al-Tahrir,* Liberation Square, one of Cairo's landmarks. In its better days the building must have been an apartment building, but now it seemed to house mostly offices for a variety of professionals.

A creaky elevator took us to the second floor. We entered a foyer, which led to a large high-ceilinged room. It was crowded with people, some young, some middle-aged, some older, but all busily working away at their desks. Attached to this spacious room was a smaller one, separated by a heavy wooden door, my office. Mr. Abbas' office, next to mine, was the largest of the rooms. A door with panels of corrugated glass, separated his office from mine.

Mr. Abbas introduced me to some of his employees: Mr. Odsi, the first one I met, a black-haired medium-sized man in his mid-to-late-thirties, seemed to occupy a special role in this office. He was, as I found out quickly, closer to Mr. Abbas than any of the other employees. Mr. Odsi looked me over critically and appeared somewhat puzzled, something I did not understand until later. Unlike other Egyptians I had met, he was light-skinned which made his black eyes stand out in even greater contrast. Other employees, all seated in the big room, were introduced as accountants, export managers and bookkeepers. My head was spinning trying to take in strange names such as Mohammed, Mahmoud, Ali, Talal, Hassan, etc.

Of great comfort to me was the fact that Mr. Odsi spoke exquisite English. He spoke it with a distinct British accent. From the moment I set eyes on him, Mr. Odsi seemed gentle and trustworthy. He was to take care of my papers and work visa for Egypt, Mr. Abbas said, and I was to give him my passport for that reason. For safety reasons it was to be kept in the office safe.

My office looked like most other offices I had been in. A plain room, it had a desk with drawers on either side, a small typewriter table with a vintage typewriter, a bookshelf and a couple of chairs. The view out the tall, old-fashioned two-paneled window was of Tahrir Square with its perpetual traffic, noise, motion and movement. The job itself turned out to be a very busy one. Visitors were going and coming to

Ulla Morris-Carter

discuss major contracts for government and private companies. Much of this I could not understand unless the foreign visitors were conducting their business in English. At that point I could take dictation in both German and English shorthand, and I wrote in both languages. Mr. Abbas hovered over me at all times, hardly ever leaving me out of his sight.

Sadly, I had not heard from Soraya. I asked Mr. Abbas whether I could phone or visit her. He did not take kindly to this idea:

"Her family does not have the best reputation. You must not get involved with these kinds of people."

To say that I was taken aback would be an understatement.

"But she is my friend," I ventured, "I met her in Germany in the firm you are representing, and I traveled with her."

"You do not know Cairo. I have made inquiries about her family. Under no circumstances are you to continue this contact. It does not become you! And it does not reflect well on my reputation."

My heart sank. Soraya was the only person I knew in Cairo, and I was not about to give up on her. I must try to contact her. To make a telephone call I had to go through the office operator. And the Egyptian telephone system was a long way from state-of-the-art. Often one had to dial and re-dial repeatedly. I waited for Mr. Abbas to leave his office, then asked the operator to connect me to Soraya's number.

"No answer," I was told repeatedly after a number of attempts.

Mr. Abbas still rarely let me out of his sight. Every wish was fulfilled, except for one, to venture out on my own. He took me to the office in the morning. Evenings we went out to dinner. Seldom did we eat with his family in the family house. Usually dinner was with him alone or with his friends.

One evening, this time with the whole family, we drove to the *Auberge des Pyramides*, located on the road leading to the three great Pyramids of Gizah. In 1956, the Auberge des Pyramides was the most glamorous and expensive restaurant and nightclub in Cairo. With its glittering decorations and exotic furnishings, heavy carpets and seductive lighting, it resembled a place out of *Thousand-and-One Nights*.

No sooner were we seated at a specially reserved table to accommodate our large group, then a bottle of whisky and a bottle of cognac appeared. Even more surprising was the fact that some members of his family drank alcohol. I had already observed that Mr. Abbas drank, whereas his wife and daughters did not touch it. But his son and some of his sons-in-law had no problem with it.

The family had mentioned a number of times that they thought I was too thin and needed fattening up to be more attractive. Not having been allowed out by myself to

Ulla Morris-Carter

walk around Cairo, and not having had any exercise, something I was used to and missed terribly, I had already added a few pounds to my normally slender body. Again, big meals were ordered all around. Next to my plate I suddenly noticed a little box.

Was that yet another present? More jewelry maybe? I was desperate. What to do? I glanced at Mrs. Hussein, who appeared calm and poised, while I was filled with fear and anxiety.

"On the occasion of your upcoming Easter, a little Easter present," Mr. Abbas announced to all gathered at the long table.

I was not accustomed to receiving presents for Easter, and, after all, Easter was a Christian holiday. Easter for me meant colored eggs and a delicious Easter cake in the shape of a lamb, for which we had a special cake pan. The cake sat on a bed of green Jello to resemble grass. The little red box remained untouched, sitting next to my plate, accusingly staring at me. I was determined to ignore it while all the family, and particularly Mrs. Hussein, were present and observing me. I would open it later at home. When I finally did, I discovered a beautiful golden chain bracelet, precious stones dangling from its many links.

Meanwhile exotic-looking belly dancers appeared, their beautiful almond-shaped eyes flirting with the men. When the dancers moved, throwing out their hips, the bells on their ankles sounded in rhythm with the castanets they were clicking with their fingers. The skin of their heavily perfumed bodies looked as smooth as velvet, their bellies were not covered with veils, and their moves were as seductive as anything I had ever seen. I was envious of their gorgeous looks, their beautiful arms and manicured hands and, above all, their flowing veils. In a society where touching or even holding hands in public between a young man and a woman was out of the question, these exotic creatures took on special importance.

My efforts to contact Soraya failed. I had been in Cairo now for more than a month and had not met anybody other than Mr. Abbas's family and his friends. I felt isolated and lonely. Working and eating was all I did. There were no outings, no hikes, no sports, no girlfriends.

Once I tried to leave the office on my own, ostensibly to go to the pharmacy to buy personal items. Mr. Abbas was out of the office. One of the employees, Ahmed, an elderly man with kind eyes, stopped me:

"It's too dangerous for you to go out alone, you don't know your way around," he said, looking anxiously at me, his eyes practically begging me to follow his advice to stay put. I could not understand why. After all, the whole of Cairo was on its feet, and there was no danger that I could detect. I decided to defy Ahmed, marching out on my own.

The next day Ahmed was not in the office.

Mr. Odsi pulled me aside and said:

"We must talk when Mr. Abbas is away the next time. There are some things you need to know."

That same afternoon Mr. Abbas left the office for a business meeting. Mr. Odsi entered my office immediately.

"I wrote the contract that Mr. Becker delivered to you in Germany, and, therefore, I feel somehow responsible for you. I am Mr. Abbas' confidant and know a lot about him. I am a Christian, like you, not a Moslem. Mr. Abbas must never know that we are having this conversation. I might lose my job, just as Ahmed lost his yesterday. Abbas Bay fired him because he was supposed to prevent you from going out alone. He did not obey orders. Abbas Bay can be ruthless. When I wrote the contract I expected someone very different from you to arrive in Cairo. Unlike those who came before you, you are a trained secretary, but at the same time you are young and ignorant about many things in this country. Your two predecessors were women looking for adventure. Mr. Abbas imported them for his pleasure, but hardly for real work. This is not a good place for you in the long run. We'll talk again."

He left my office as abruptly as he had entered it, without any further explanation. When I passed him a little later at his desk, he didn't even seem to notice me.

In March, 1956, Mr. Becker from Bielefeld visited Cairo on business. He asked me out to dinner. Mr. Abbas was not pleased but could hardly refuse to let me meet a German compatriot with whom he was also connected through business and who had carried my documents to get to Cairo. Mr. Becker was a charming man in his thirties, blond and fairly tall. His interest in me seemed to go beyond the fact that we were both German and spoke the same language.

He inquired in detail how my stay was progressing. How did I feel in Cairo all by myself? Endless questions. He either knew or sensed that I had encountered a few problems, a subject I definitely did not want to share with him. I had defied everybody before leaving, including his advice, and I was not about to admit that I was disturbed and distressed by some of the things that had happened.

"Would you not consider returning to Germany?" he enquired casually.

"Out of the question. I have a contract for a year and I can't just leave. I have only been here for two months."

"I could give you a job in my company in Bielefeld. You wouldn't have to return to Düsseldorf immediately, if that is embarrassing to you. Why don't you think it over? I hope to have dinner with you again tomorrow."

Mr. Becker was in and out of the office during the next two days working with Mr. Abbas on a government contract. He assumed that I was free to leave when my workday was over to join him for drinks and dinner. Mr. Abbas, overhearing our conversation, made it known that he had other plans for me that evening.

Ulla Morris-Carter

Mr. Becker, politely but firmly insisted on taking me out because he would be leaving the next morning. Mr. Abbas had no choice but to let me go. Mr. Becker took me to the bar of the Semiramis Hotel, the first time I had seen the elegant and famous old hotel on the Corniche, the road that runs alongside the Nile. We had cocktails on the roof garden that overlooked the river. The view was breathtakingly beautiful. Mr. Becker told me that we would be joined by an Egyptian friend of his who, he thought, I would enjoy meeting.

The friend, Talal was his name, turned out to be the chief of the Cairo Tourism Police, a cordial, serious man in his early fifties, I guessed. We spent an hour with fascinating conversation about Cairo, the latest exhibits in the museum and the new exciting excavations in Upper Egypt. I was totally intrigued by all that I heard and learned about Cairo. At the same time I was reminded of how isolated I had been for more than two months, a period devoid of news and ideas.

"I want to make sure that you know where you can find help or advice should you ever need it," Talal remarked casually. "We really want our visitors and tourists to be happy in our great city," he said reassuringly and gave me a big smile. "It takes time to get to know Cairo. Just call me any time. A friend of Mr. Becker's will always be my friend as well."

He had a warm demeanor, almost fatherly, and it didn't escape me that also he seemed to know something that I didn't. When Talal departed, he handed me his card with telephone numbers. Mr. Becker, now more insistent than the day before, tried to persuade me to reconsider my stay in Cairo.

"You could return with me. It's easy to arrange for a ticket for you. I really do not like to see you in Mr. Abbas' office."

I was adamant, unrelenting: "No, I cannot leave now. I have a contract and he paid for my ticket to Egypt. I must stay here."

He didn't realize that by taking me to the Semiramis Hotel he had shown me a side of Cairo that made me want to know more about this fascinating city, regardless of my problems. Obviously disappointed, he departed, but promised to return to Cairo.

Meanwhile my situation at the apartment in Gizah became more distressing. I felt like a bird in a golden cage: I was imprisoned. I had no privacy. Mr. Abbas entered my room whenever he wanted to. He never left me alone. If I locked my door he entered my room from the balcony that surrounded the whole apartment. Because of the warm temperatures I often left the balcony door open at night. No longer. I began to lock that door as well, with the result that I had to sleep in a hot stuffy room without fresh air, if I could sleep at all. I was beginning to be terrified. Nights were filled with frightening thoughts of dramatic escape. But how? I didn't even have my passport. It was locked in the office safe.

Ulla Morris-Carter

Mr. Abbas made aggressive advances, which a few times ended up in bitter verbal exchanges. I had to use force to keep him away from me. Not an easy matter. He was a large, strong man. Once, in despair, I hit him.

"Ursula," he cried, "you have a hard heart. You are like iron. How can you do this to me? Here I am your father, your mother, your lover."

Then, more threatening: "Eventually I will get you where I want you, I am convinced."

Then almost begging: "I can't live without you. How can I soften your heart?"

We often worked late. Indeed there was a lot of work to be done. When we came home his wife was either asleep, or, more often, not in the apartment, but had remained in the big family house. For reasons I did not understand at first, she seemed to support him in all his endeavors. Mr. Odsi explained to me that she came into this marriage with a lot of money, most of which he had used or was spending freely. Not wanting to be shoved aside or divorced, a fairly easy matter in Cairo in those days when women had few rights, she obliged him in every way.

When Mr. Abbas suggested I accompany him to Saudi Arabia on a business trip, Mrs. Hussein concurred. But Mr. Odsi immediately warned me:

"Under no circumstances can you travel with him to Saudi Arabia. You will never return. He wants to present you to one of his business partners in exchange for more contracts. Saudi Arabia is a country without laws and without any rights for women. Use any excuse you can think of, but DON'T go."

What to do? Maybe I could be sick. Maybe I would have to attend church on Sunday.

We had a very unpleasant fight. He finally relented and went alone to Saudi Arabia, but he made sure I could not venture out by myself. He drove me to the villa of his brother-in-law, who owned a farm in the desert. His brother-in-law conducted agricultural trial projects, hoping to "make the desert bloom" through irrigation and new farming inventions. And there I was, miles away from civilization, somewhere in the middle of nowhere. Running away in the desert was not advisable. I didn't even know where I was. The brother-in-law and his family treated me like a long lost child, they spoiled me and could not have been kinder, except that I was again kept under guard.

Mr. Abbas returned after four days and took me back to Cairo. Mr. Odsi appeared in my office presenting me with four pages of a work visa application to be signed by me, all in Arabic, of course.

"You must refuse to sign these papers. Demand a full translation," he said ominously. "This is not a visa application. These are marriage papers! Mr. Abbas intends to make you his second wife, which would solve the problem of the work visa at the same time. You would become an Egyptian. It's easy in Egypt. All he has to do is to announce to

Ulla Morris-Carter

his wife: 'I divorce you, I divorce you, I divorce you.' Three times, and he'll be free to take on another wife."

"Could you repeat this, please, Mr. Odsi, I don't think I understood."

"Oh yes, you heard correctly, marriage papers. I can only warn you, but I am unable help you. You must think of a way out of here. Mr. Abbas is becoming very impatient."

The next day two German businessmen, employed by a German pump manufacturing company with offices in Cairo, visited Mr. Abbas. Their firm was building the first drinking-water pumps for Egyptian villages, a huge government contract. Mr. Lepique and Mr. Wieland, both engineers, seemed startled to find a 22-year-old German girl in Mr. Abbas' office. I understood their surprise, because I knew that not many single foreign women lived and worked in Cairo at that time.

"How did you land here?" asked Mr. Lepique.

"I worked for a German company in Düsseldorf, a company that Mr. Abbas represents, and he offered me a job and sent me a ticket."

We made polite conversation in German until Mr. Abbas was ready to receive them. I thought that they were rather inquisitive. Mr. Abbas and the two Germans had obviously known each other prior to this visit, judging by the way they greeted each other without further introduction. I did not participate in their business meeting.

On the way out Mr. Wieland dropped his calling card discreetly into one of my open desk drawers. The two Germans did not linger or talk to me again. They left immediately.

When I had a moment to look at the card, I found a message on the back:

"Please, call us immediately."

Immediately was underlined. I was puzzled but also pleased that two men from my home country took an interest in me. I could not telephone right away, I had to wait for an opportunity to arise.

A few days later Mr. Abbas was in a meeting. I rushed out of the building to a public phone that I had recently discovered not far from the office. Mr. Lepique answered the phone:

"Where are you? We have been trying for days to phone you in the office without any luck. We even had our wives try to reach you. What is happening over there? We are worried about you."

I was astonished but realized quickly that the office telephone operator had instructions not to relay any phone calls to me. That explained Soraya's silence, as well as the silence of a number of other *Esperia* passengers, who had promised to be in touch with me.

"We have made enquiries at the German Embassy, but you are not registered there. You must know that Mr. Wieland, unbeknownst to Mr. Abbas, speaks fluent Arabic. He

Ulla Morris-Carter

was born in Haifa (then Palestine, now Israel). He overheard a conversation between Mr. Abbas and one of his employees. Mr. Abbas was scolding him for letting you converse with us. He obviously wants to isolate you. You must go to the Embassy at once and register. We have heard of other foreign women just disappearing. Who would even know that you exist here?"

"I cannot go to the embassy right now, I am really busy," I lied to Mr. Lepique.

How could I reveal to him how terrified I was that Mr. Abbas might find out that I was in touch with his German clients. Abbas was a powerful man with many connections, and I knew he would find me, no matter where I was. And most important, I did not have my passport. Mr. Lepique, I could tell, realized that I was scared.

"We could meet you and may be we can help," he said reassuringly.

"I will call you back when I have more time," was all I managed to answer, my voice barely audible.

I could not possibly tell them over the phone of my dilemma, nor did I want to admit defeat.

"We can offer you a job in our office. Just try to leave as soon as possible and meet us," Mr. Lepique's voice had taken on a more urgent tone.

"I'll call back as soon as I can." I hung up.

I raced back to the office, my head reeling with all I had heard. Fearing that Mr. Abbas might have discovered my absence, I tried to regain my composure and took a deep breath before entering. I was definitely losing my coolheadedness. Thank God, Mr. Abbas was still in the meeting. I breathed a deep sigh of relief.

Mr. Odsi seemed to be waiting for me: "Another trip to Saudi Arabia is in the making. Under no circumstances should you accompany him. Find any excuse you can think of to stay behind. Still, you need to leave this place. Abbas is very angry and his patience with you is running out. Find a way out of here while he is in Saudi Arabia. I will help as much as I can afford to help."

Easier said than done. My head was spinning, and a bad headache did not help. I was afraid I might collapse and crumble under the pressure and uncertainty surrounding me. Mr. Abbas took me home in the early evening, asking me to help him organize a few gifts and documents for Saudi Arabia.

"I acquired 100 yards of the finest sharkskin cloth for my friends in Riadh. I want you to help me cut it up into pieces big enough for suits. I have to make a few presents."

Dutifully, I obliged. Equipped with scissors and tape measure I stood in front of my bed where we had spread the soft, silky material in off-white and light gray. The cloth felt luxurious and cool to my skin. Temperatures in April were already reaching 95˚ degrees Fahrenheit. Abbas stood behind me and watched. He inched his big body closer to mine, and I could feel his breath on my neck. I pretended not to notice.

Ulla Morris-Carter

"Stay calm," I told myself.

Just as I was cutting into this exquisite cloth, holding the material in one hand and scissors in the other, he grabbed me from behind, his strong arms clutching my body with the force of an iron clamp, his trousers open, rubbing up against me. I dropped everything, wrestled myself out of his clasp and, surprised by strength I didn't know I had, swung around and kicked him hard. I couldn't believe that I did it.

He tumbled backwards, momentarily shocked and dazed. But not for long! He raised himself off the floor, and without any hesitation, unloaded his full fury upon me, his dark eyes filled with hatred and scorn. I stood there, frozen, aghast, frightened, and disgusted. And ashamed. How would I ever be able to look him again in the face? How could I ever sit across from him and not be ashamed? I felt humiliated, abused, and dirtied.

In his rage he shouted and screamed: "I will eventually get you where I want you. How can you do this to me?"

He abruptly opened the door and ran out of the room, slamming the door shut behind him. It took me a while to regain my composure. At the same time I knew that I had to do something. I had to act fast. But I couldn't think clearly and didn't know what the act should be.

Suddenly I spotted one of my suitcases in the corner of the room. Of course, that was it. Why hadn't I thought about it before? I had to pack up some of my belongings as fast as possible and get out of here. I threw some of my clothes and a few of my treasured items into the suitcase, whatever came to hand, paying no attention to folding or sorting.

Within minutes the suitcase was full. I grabbed it, ran out of the apartment, down the stairs and into the street, where I quickly hailed a taxi.

"To Garden City, please," I told the driver, who spoke no English, but seemed to know where Garden City was.

He nodded, *"Ayua, ayua,* yes, yes."

Obviously he wanted to reassure me that he could find the place I was looking for, Soraya Farid's home. We stopped in front of a large, imposing apartment building on Kasr el Aali Street near the Nile Corniche. Soraya had described it to me while we were traveling.

"Our apartment is on the ground floor with a large garden full of jasmine and orange trees," she had told me on the boat.

Now I stood in front of this imposing, four-floored sandstone building whose balconies were filled with flowerpots of blooming geraniums and oleander. I had never been there before.

I rang the bell. Nobody answered.

"Of course, nobody is home," I thought.

Ulla Morris-Carter

I had expected nothing else. At this point I hardly cared. Actually I had tried, a few days ago, to call Soraya from the recently discovered public phone, but I was told that the Farids were out of town. I had not had another chance to escape the office to telephone, or to leave the office without repercussions.

The *bawab,* the concierge, at the Farid's house, a friendly Egyptian in a long black and grey striped robe and white turban, helped me with the heavy suitcase and seemed to understand that I wanted to leave the luggage with the Farid family, despite their absence. I thanked him and ran to the waiting taxi that took me back to the office.

Thank God, Mr. Odsi was still in the office. I was most relieved to see him:

"I need my passport. Please, please, can you get it out of the safe for me?" I begged. "I must get out of here tomorrow when Mr. Abbas travels to Saudi Arabia. I cannot possibly stay another day. I am going crazy."

Odsi nodded knowingly. He understood immediately that I had now reached the point of no return, that I was in trouble and had to make a fast decision.

"I have started to prepare the letter for you that we discussed yesterday. You can send it to Mr. Abbas or leave it behind. Let's review it and make a few copies. It'll help to protect you should he try to find you and pursue you, which I am afraid he might do. We have only limited time. He just called and will be here within the hour."

When Mr. Abbas returned to the office, he did not speak to me. For my part, I could not even look at him without repulsion. Silently we headed back to the apartment and had dinner with his wife, who seemed to be expecting us. I was completely unnerved. I could hardly eat. I had the feeling that he brought his wife along that evening because he realized he had gone too far. All I cared about was finding a way to leave this house.

But where to go? Where would I be able to find an apartment or a room that I could afford? Which part of Cairo was safe or suitable for me? I knew nothing. After two months in Cairo, I was still ignorant about this city, its intricate structure and its workings. Soraya and family were out of town. No use trying to go to her house. There was nobody else in Cairo that I could contact, except, maybe, the two German businessmen. But I did not feel comfortable trying to tell these strangers my story over the phone. I was too embarrassed.

Next I had to find my second suitcase which Zeinab and Leila had stored away somewhere. Many items that I wanted to take with me still had to be packed. I was prepared to leave a few things behind if necessary, but I also had to consider the fact that I had little money at my disposal. I had so far earned two month's pay, but half of each was being paid into my personal bank account in Germany. Now I needed at least enough money to pay for a room in a hotel or a guesthouse.

As soon as we finished our dinner I went back to my room. Mr. Abbas followed me shortly thereafter.

"Aren't you ashamed of yourself entering my room while Mrs. Hussein is sleeping next-door? Please, leave me alone."

"Don't worry about Mrs. Hussein. She is fast asleep. I sometimes help her sleep by putting some sleep powder in her soup."

I was too taken aback to speak for a moment. What else might he be capable of, I wondered.

"Get out of my room! And don't try to enter it again!"

I had never spoken to him that way. I knew I was at the end of my nerves. Abbas, to my surprise, left the room without further attempt at reconciliation. I was desperate now to find my second suitcase. Because Mr. and Mrs. Abass' bedroom in the apartment was very close to mine, I was worried that they might wake up as I was prowling around in search of my luggage. I decided to run a bath, opening the water taps as far as possible. I deliberately left the bathroom door open to drown out any sounds. There was a storage space above the bathroom door, which I hoped might be the hiding place of my trunk. Carefully and quietly I placed a chair underneath the attic vent, but, as I had feared, it was not tall enough.

Where was the footstool that I had seen somewhere? Tiptoeing through the apartment I finally located the footstool, placed it carefully on top of the chair and made my first attempt. Climbing up was not too difficult, but reaching into the storage space was a different matter. One had to be an acrobat to reach inside.

Eventually, around midnight, I managed to pull my suitcase out of this relatively small space. I climbed down quietly, tightly holding this unwieldy piece of luggage, trying not to drop it nor break my leg.

Rapidly I threw in anything that would fit. I left such items, as photographs, paper and pen, bathrobe and slippers in their usual places and hid the trunk inside the wardrobe. As I locked the wardrobe with its key, I suddenly remembered the running water. I raced to the bathroom. Just in time. The tub was filled to the brim, only an inch away from overflowing.

A sleepless night followed. At breakfast Mr. Abbas reminded me to be ready to leave for the airport at two p.m. But first we had to pass by the office to take care of a few last-minute items.

"I am not feeling all too well. I am afraid I have a migraine coming on," I lamented as we reached the office.

"I have a terrible headache and can hardly bear to open my eyes. I need to lie down for a moment."

I lay down on the couch in my office, took two aspirins and covered my eyes with my hands. I no longer had to pretend to be sick, because I was indeed feeling as if I were falling apart. I was exhausted from lack of sleep. My body was aching and my

Ulla Morris-Carter

head was spinning. I lay there completely still, wishing this was all a bad dream that would disappear as soon as I woke up.

Mr. Abbas entered my office where I was still stretched out on the couch:

"There has been a change of plans. I just received a telegram from my business friend in Ryadh. He has decided to come to Cairo instead of us flying there. We shall pick him up at four p.m. at the airport and then take him out to dinner. I hope you are feeling better by then."

Now I was feeling worse. How would I ever get out of here? I didn't move and I didn't answer. I thought I was going to be sick. Mr. Abbas was tending to some business matters in his own office when Mr. Odsi entered my office. Seeing me lying there, he quietly handed me the letter that we had discussed and he had meanwhile edited. He left without saying a word.

"Time to depart for the airport," Mr. Abbas announced, sticking his head into my office. "I suppose you are feeling better by now after your rest."

"No, no, I feel worse. I can't open my eyes, the light hurts too much. You probably never had a migraine. Maybe you don't understand," I whispered and tried to describe all the symptoms of a migraine, which, in reality, I had never experienced.

Five more minutes of discussion, during which I assured him that, no doubt, I would be fine and ready to go out to dinner when he returned from the airport. The minute he left, I jumped up and ran out of the office to the public phone nearby.

"Please, please, dear God" I prayed, "let Talal be in his office. I need him, I need him urgently."

With shaky hands I dialed Talal's direct number at the office of the Cairo Tourist Police. This time luck was on my side. He answered and knew immediately who I was.

"I need your help, I am in deep trouble. I am leaving Mr. Abbas' house, right now. Can you possibly pick me up on Sharia Hamadan? "

Talal did not ask any questions.

"I'll pick you up, but not in front of Mr. Abbas' home. You will find me around the corner in a red Opel."

A taxi took me back to the apartment. Thank God Mrs. Hussein was not there. But Zeinab and Leila were. I felt sorry for them and had great sympathy since I found out two weeks earlier that Mr. Abbas had beaten Zeinab since learning she had let me leave the apartment without his permission. But now I was only focused on finding the fastest way out of this place. I grabbed whatever I could carry in addition to the hidden suitcase, which I pulled out of the clothes closet.

At first Zeinab and Leila were helping me, assuming I was flying with Mr. Abbas to Saudi Arabia. But they suddenly realized that I was taking more than one normally needs for a one-week journey. They tried to stop me. I hustled past them, suitcase in one hand, a bag over my shoulder and a bathrobe over my arm. They were so shocked and frightened that, for a short moment, they stood still as I pushed past them. Loaded down as I was, I could not move very fast. The bathrobe slipped off my arm, the suitcase was too heavy to lift more than an inch off the ground and dragged behind me.

But I made it around the corner where—I could hardly believe it—Talal was sitting in his red car waiting patiently. He jumped out when he saw me, helped me with the luggage and into the car, and drove off.

We had not spoken a word so far. I had climbed into the back seat and lay flat on the floor. I was so terror-stricken and afraid that someone might recognize me that I never even lifted my head off the floor. Talal tried to calm me down, realizing that I was close to a breakdown. Indeed, at that moment I was in such a state of nerves that I could hardly converse intelligently.

"I'll take you to a small, inexpensive guesthouse. It's not very elegant, but Abbas will never suspect you're there. I know Abbas and his tastes. We'll deposit your luggage at the guest house, and then I'll invite you to my club, where we can talk."

"Oh no, I am not going anywhere," I protested. "He might find me. He's so powerful and has so many connections."

"My club is safe. It's a hunting club. Abbas is not a member and he has never set foot into it."

Talal had to use all of his persuasive powers to convince me that I would be protected. He was such a caring, kind and serious person that finally I had to believe him.

An hour later we were settled in a quiet corner of his elegant, relatively small private club. He wanted to know my story, though he already seemed to be fairly well informed about Mr. Abbas. His main concern was my future. He knew I wanted to stay in Cairo, but was astonished to hear that I had already had a job offer from the German company.

"I would like to be of assistance to you if and when possible. But I have a busy job and a wife and children. However, always remember that you can call on me whenever you need me."

He accompanied me to the little guesthouse, located right in busy downtown Cairo. I never saw Talal again but I will remember him forever for what he did for me in those desperate days. He had no ulterior motive, there was nothing in it for him except wanting to help a stranded young foreigner who had landed in the wrong place in Cairo.

Ulla Morris-Carter

Ursula Kirschbaum   Cairo, the 4th April, 1956

Mr. Abbas El-Sayed Hussein
Sharia Hamadan
GUIZA
CAIRO.

Sir,

You will no doubt be astonished to know that since the first day of my
arrival I have been thoroughly studying the situation not as it
existed but also with sight on the future   As a result of all such
deep thinking and exchange of thoughts with those intimate friends
whom I know both in Germany and in Egypt I have found it advisable to
leave your firm and your home without delay as to save myself the
trouble of running into risky situations.

I admit that all the members of your family have been kind to me but
you will appreciate that such kindness and generosity must not be on
account of my personal liberty and future happiness or only to satisfy
your illicit wishes. I am willing to put you on oath that until the
time of my departure you were inducing me to be your mistress,
sometimes gently and sometimes by warning and stressing that your
honourable wife is agreeable to your shameful deeds   I do not want to
relate here all what you wanted to practice with me which matter I
will never tell when I am back to my home country as this will reflect
badly on the Egyptians whom I have known as gentle and honest always
proving to be generous supporters to the foreigners. I really feel
ashamed when I remember that my employer has been weeping and crying
both in my private chamber and in the car saying "Ursula you have a
hard heart," which matter has made all my friends laugh and mock upon
this type of business men. You have always been telling me that
businessmen often keep mistresses but I must tell you that men of
integrety who care for their reputation never think of doing that.

I must say that I have made all that is in my power to change your
ideas for another stressing on the fact that I have been engaged as
your secretary and that I have one whom I love in Germany and will
marry immedeately I am back   Needless to say that I have been
suffering considerably from the feeling that both the members of your
family as well as those of the staff and all those who know you well
think that I am leading with you an unlawful life.

With the above in mind I would request you to leave me in peace
treating this matter as finally settled. However, if on the other
hand you feel you must do otherwise, I will find no other alternative
but to put you in a great trouble as I have in hand documentary
evidence that fully protects my interests.

Before coming to an end I would say that all the gifts that you have
presented to me are entirely at your disposal and will be sent to you
through one of my friends.

With my best regards to all members of the family,

Above: *The letter Mr. Odsi wrote on my behalf to Mr. Abbas on my
departure.* Right: *Portrait photo from my early Cairo days.*

Ulla Morris-Carter

Le Caire - View of the Citadel

Le Caire - Sphynx and Pyramids

Postcards from my early Cairo days, of the Citadel, **above,** *and the Sphinx,* **below.**

CAIRO

1956

He who does not know Cairo,
does not know the grandeur of Islam.

- David Roberts

On my first morning of "freedom" in Cairo in April 1956 I woke up in a small room full of sunshine and light. I did not jump out of bed, something I would normally have done when awakened by the light of what seemed to be a perfect day, brilliantly clear and warm. Rather, my tired body got heavier and sank deeper and deeper into the pillows and blankets of my bed.

My room in the small guesthouse was on the top floor of an ancient building in the center of Cairo. The ceiling was slanted, and painted white. Faded reproductions of two tasteless paintings covered the wall across from my bed. The thin, flowery curtains, their colors bleached by the strong sun, did not prevent the heat from penetrating my new, uninspiring home. But the smallness of the room made me feel protected, and cozy as if being embraced by the warmth of strong arms. I lay there asking myself how I ended up in this somewhat rundown place.

What to do next? I did not want to get up, let alone face the outside world. I felt vulnerable and alone in this exotic and bustling city. How was I to survive in Cairo by myself? Where to start looking for a place to live? Money was a major issue. I had so far earned only two months' pay, half of which was sent directly to my German bank account. I was not feeling hungry. No need to go down for breakfast. Barely moving,

Ulla Morris-Carter

covers over my head, I lay there until I heard the muezine call for midday prayers from the nearby mosque. Already noon! I felt that I was close to a nervous breakdown. My body seemed paralyzed, my brain incapable of clear thought.

How was I to make any decision? Another hour passed, or maybe two. I had to break out of this nightmarish cycle of fear and confusion. But how? There was nobody to ask, nobody to talk to.

By early afternoon, still feeling shaky, I reluctantly moved myself out from under the covers. I took a shower, dressed slowly and went downstairs in search of a public telephone. Luckily, I spotted one at the entrance to the guesthouse. What a relief! I didn't have to venture into the street. I called Soraya. She was still out of town, a female voice told me, but she would be back the next day. Gathering as much courage as I could muster, I called Mr. Lepique at KSB, Klein, Schanzlin & Becker.

"Where are you? When can we meet? How about right now?" He seemed delighted to hear from me.

"Mr. Wieland and I have been waiting for your call. We want you to work for us. What do you think? We really need some help quickly."

They know nothing about me, I thought. What do they expect of me? But I really couldn't worry about that right now. Their offer was an opportunity not to be missed. The future already looked brighter. The fact that I was already in Cairo, and they didn't have to import me from Germany undoubtedly played a role. But I didn't feel like starting a new adventure before I had recovered from the last one. I needed a little quiet time. I told Mr. Lepique that I would call the next morning for an interview.

Suddenly I felt hungry. Where was the nearest restaurant? I hardly dared risk more than a few steps from my guesthouse for fear of being detected. Was Mr. Abbas already looking for me? Had he filed a missing person report with the police? Had he sent out his son to find me? Had he alerted some of his friends to look for me? He could easily find out whether I had left the country.

I was being paranoid. I had to overcome this fear if I wanted to live and work in Cairo. So I took a deep breath, straightened my body and walked into the bustling street. Around the corner I found a small cafe. A strong Arabic coffee, *ahwa baladi*, and a sandwich of warm Arabic bread with yoghurt and *kofta*, ground spicy meatballs, helped me feel a lot better. After my mid-afternoon meal I went back to my room and spent the rest of the day in recovery mode. All the energy I had gathered had suddenly disappeared. In its place I felt nothing but total exhaustion and fatigue, my body limp and heavy, my mind muddled. I threw myself onto my bed. Sleep was all I wanted.

How could I put an end to this nightmare? I kept telling myself this was just a bad dream. Maybe I would wake up to a new and normal day. But what was normal? I couldn't sleep, My mind was racing. Question after unanswerable question crowded my

Ulla Morris-Carter

thoughts. Am I doing the right thing in going to work for KSB? Where am I going to live? What am I going to tell my mother? Was Mr. Abbas hot on my heels? One thing was clear. I did not want to return to Germany right now. The sun was setting when I fell into a deep, dreamless sleep, sleep that gave me peace for a while.

Waking up the following morning, I knew it was time to face the real world. Reluctantly, I climbed out of bed, showered and dressed. Slowly I made my way to KSB for the interview. The city was still quiet at this early hour. The morning air felt fresh and cool and calming. I had enough time to stop for a coffee before reaching my destination. KSB's office was on the fourth floor of a fairly modern building on 26th of July Street, a broad avenue named after the 1952 revolution in Egypt that ousted King Farouk, who abdicated on July 26. The office suite consisted of four large rooms, one each occupied by Mr. Lepique and Mr. Wieland, a third to be occupied by the secretary, who Mr. Lepique indicated, he hoped would be me.

From the foyer one entered directly into the secretary's office, a bright, airy room with a balcony. A corner of the room was furnished with comfortable bamboo chairs and was reserved for visitors. The furniture was simple and office-like. A desk with telephone and typewriter and a filing cabinet completed the decor. The fourth room, with kitchen attached, was headquarters for Mohamed, the KSB messenger. A slight, friendly man, not overly tall, always with a big smile on his face, Mohamed was, compliments of KSB, just learning how to read and write Arabic. Nobody, including Mohamed himself, knew his exact age, but we assumed he was in his early-to mid-thirties. Mohamed made delicious Arabic coffee and sweet mint tea, important for meetings or visits that could not possibly proceed without that ritual.

Mr. Lepique, whose name was French but who was born in Germany, was a slender man with elegant features, blondish hair,, blue eyes and in his late thirties. He had a doctoral degree in engineering. Mr. Wieland, more robust, also an engineer, was born in Haifa, which in 1922 had become part of mandated Palestine and would later become one of Israel's larger cities. He grew up speaking German and Arabic, a most useful background for his present job in the Arab world. Later I noticed that Mr. Wieland, when engaged in business discussions, never revealed his fluency in Arabic.

Mr. Lepique and Mr. Wieland received me as if I were an old friend. They had already prepared a contract for me. Briefly, they checked my credentials, prior work experience and resume.

Could I start tomorrow, they asked?

I begged an extra day or two, wanting to experience my newly gained freedom and look for a place to live. They suggested the Pension Swiss, a modestly priced lodging house owned and run by a Swiss lady. It catered to foreigners in particular and was conveniently located in walking distance from the office. I signed the KSB contract, went off to Pension Swiss and rented a pleasant spacious room.

That afternoon, I took a taxi to Rue Kasr el Aali in Garden City near the Nile Corniche. As the taxi slowed down because of heavy traffic, beggars thrust their dirty hands into the open window on my side of the car and mumbled something in Arabic.

The taxi driver yelled at them: "*Yalla, Yalla!*, go away!"

The sudden onslaught frightened me. I had a lot to learn before I would be comfortable in my new hometown. The taxi stopped in front of the Farids' house in Garden City. Their sandstone-colored house opened onto a beautiful garden, still looking fresh in April when the temperature in Cairo was nearly perfect. The Farids welcomed me with open arms as if I belonged to the family. I was overjoyed to see Soraya again, my young, attractive friend and travel companion whom I had not seen since we parted in Alexandria two months earlier. We sat down and talked and talked. My adventures began to seem more distant, as if they belonged to someone else.

Was it really just a couple of days ago that I had been in such a panic? Hard to believe.

Soraya spoke fluent German. Her mother was a German who met her Egyptian husband while he was studying chemistry in Hamburg. The whole family was equally at home in German, Arabic, English and French. I gladly accepted their invitation to stay for dinner. Surrounded by the warm hospitality of the Farids, I was feeling better by the minute. I would come to understand that this familial warmth was an important aspect of Egyptian life.

On day three, another beautiful day, I wandered around the downtown part of Cairo. In the narrow alleys houses seemed to be bunched together untidily on both sides of the street. What a noisy, turbulent and cosmopolitan city this was. One moment I walked along wide avenues lined with fairly modern buildings and shops, the next, I found myself in narrow, filthy little courtyards, crowded with cute, incredibly dirty children, jumping around or squatting on mud floors.

Maybe it was my newness to this city or my foreign looks that attracted beggars and street vendors. Black-robed women, holding up their babies, their eyes ringed by flies, pulled at my skirt. Men in long white robes like nightgowns, their sandals flapping as they passed, stared at me. The gulf between rich and poor was wide and deep, even though they existed side by side. For me the contrast between those splendid villas surrounded by lush gardens, and the nearby suffocating slums where little sunlight entered, was incomprehensible.

The largest city of the Arab world, Cairo, is called alternately the Jewel of the Orient, the City of the Thousand Minarets and the Triumphant City. It lies at the center of all routes leading to and from three continents, Asia, Africa and Europe. My first

Ulla Morris-Carter

impressions did not exactly reveal a Jewel of the Orient, but then I had not yet seen any of the Islamic, Coptic, Christian or Jewish monuments, which make Cairo such a diverse and fascinating city to visit. It seemed next to impossible for a Westerner without any experience of the Middle East, to understand, even superficially, the workings and mystique of this place. A predominantly Sunni-Moslem city, Cairo was also home to Christians, Copts, Greek-Orthodox and the few remaining Jews, who had not fled persecution after the establishment of Israel in 1948.

I had not known that Islam was the world's second largest religion after Christianity. I did not know that the Moslem calendar year has 354 days and 12 months, that the month always starts with the new moon, hence the continuous change of Moslem holidays. Before my experiences at Mr. Abbas' house I had not known that a Moslem could legally have more than one wife, though, in fact, most Egyptians practiced monogamy. And I had not understood this society's conservative views on women. At this moment, however, I had more important things to do than to contemplate the problems and splendors of Egypt. I had to organize my life and move into Pension Swiss.

KSB was a well-known pump manufacturing company, headquartered in Frankenthal, Germany, with a very busy Middle Eastern office. I had to learn a new subject and a new vocabulary about three different types of pumps: centrifugal, rotary and piston, as well as the output of each. Apart from Mr. Lepique and Mr. Wieland, I discovered that KSB employed a third German engineer, Mr. Wechsler, who was based in Alexandria. He, too, spoke Arabic. The company had just landed a huge contract from the Egyptian government to supply Egyptian villages with drinking water pumps. I worked in both German and English, and occasionally in French, although I was not fluent in French.

We started at 7:30 a.m. and worked till 1:30 or 2 p.m., followed by a long break in the afternoon. We restarted at 5 p.m. and worked until either 8 or 9 p.m., in line with the working hours of many Egyptian businesses. We had no air-conditioning in those days. When the temperatures hit 115 degrees, I knew that summer was upon us and was glad we started so early in the morning. With every inch the sun rose the heat increased. Some days were so hot the sweat ran down my bare legs and glued me to the leather-covered chair. Cars turned into ovens, their steering wheels too hot to touch. Most Egyptians took a siesta after lunch during the hottest part of the day. I learned to appreciate this pattern and followed their example, particularly when we ate a late dinner in a cool garden restaurant until midnight or beyond. How wonderful to be able to enjoy fresh cool night air and the greenery of the gardens.

Living alone as a young, foreign woman in Cairo was not easy. There were few unattached foreign females around Cairo in those days, and most of those worked in bars and nightclubs. Egyptian men considered themselves irresistible and saw foreign women

Ulla Morris-Carter

as available and fair game. They assumed that Western free spirit and lack of morals had long since corrupted its women. I had already learned to wear modest clothing, such as dresses with sleeves. Shorts and short skirts were absolutely taboo, unless one enjoyed having ones bottom pinched. I was often followed by young Egyptian men, whistling as they moved past me, and never failing to touch me lightly on the arm or shoulder as if by mistake. There was no way to disguise the fact that I was a foreigner I was blond and blue-eyed and looked very German, or so I thought. Young Egyptian women were never allowed to go out with a young man unless chaperoned.

After a few unpleasant encounters, it became obvious that while I would have loved to have my own apartment, it would not be the best solution. Under these circumstances the idea of living with a family sounded appealing. After a couple of months at Pension Swiss, I found a room with the Attalahs, an Egyptian-Lebanese family in Heliopolis, an ancient city in the Nile Delta, about six miles away from Cairo. Heliopolis was renowned as the center of sun worship: Sun God Ra was its deity.

The Atallah family lived in a sand-colored house on 10 Sharia Sesostris. It was a gracious building with more terraces than rooms, surrounded by a flower-filled garden in full bloom and a few fruit trees. The house was cool and spacious. My room, a corner room at the end of the first floor, was a perfect solution.

Importantly, Heliopolis was connected to Cairo by Metro. Most mornings this clean, fast, modern electric train whisked me off to the office. Both Mr. Lepique and Mr. Wieland also lived with their wives and children in Heliopolis and they picked me up whenever possible.

Mr. Atallah was a most gentle person of about 75. He seemed much older than Madame Atallah, a vivacious lady, whom I guessed to be in her fifties. Mr. Atallah had lost almost all of his eyesight to glaucoma and spent most of his waking hours sitting on the cool veranda, listening to the radio.

The best part of my residence here was the Atallah's daughter, Huguette. Three years older than I, she was a very attractive young woman with dark olive skin, dark eyes and a good sense of humor. She had been educated in the British School in Cairo, and, when not otherwise busy, gave piano lessons to young students. We became friends instantly. Huguette helped me a lot by showing me around and introducing me to her friends and acquaintances, mainly Egyptians. They were a sophisticated group, fluent in two or three languages. The business language in Egypt was mostly English, but both French and English were spoken in social circles. All members of the Attalah family were fluent in both languages, but being of Lebanese origin, they preferred French, the language commonly used in their native land.

Within walking distance from my new home I discovered the Heliopolis Sporting Club with its beautiful gardens. Its lively group of members included the later famous

Above: *One of many envelopes of letters I sent to my mother in Düsseldorf from Cairo. My mother kept the envelopes, but unfortunately not the letters.* Top Right: *Mr. and Madame Atallah at the house.* Bottom Right: *Hugette and I in the garden.*

actor Omar Sharif. He already had a reputation as an Egyptian actor, but in those days he was not yet the international film star he later became. Just married to the beautiful Egyptian actress, Fatem Hamama, Omar frequented the Sporting Club mainly as an internationally known bridge player. But he occasionally joined our group for a movie or a get-together. We were all in our twenties, and some members of our group had been his school or university friends.

Among other amenities, the Heliopolis Sporting Club had tennis courts and a swimming pool where I could swim unhindered. I often had lunch there, or rested in the shade during my long lunch break, or visited with my new friends, or took my first tennis lessons.

Life was beginning to be fun again!

So far I had not encountered Mr. Abbas, or anyone of his family. Shortly after my escape, however, he had called Soraya Farid's family three times, then appeared at their door, demanding they tell him where I was.

"You know where she is, don't deny it! She must be with you. You are the only people she knows in Cairo."

The Farids denied knowing anything about me, and Soraya was traveling again and couldn't be asked. In a more mellow tone, he apparently begged them to tell me that he wanted me back, promising to leave me alone.

Then, more urgently: "Please, let her come back to me. I need her and will do anything she wants."

The Farids repeatedly tried to convince him that they knew nothing of my whereabouts and couldn't help him in any way. Mr. Abbas finally left. I never heard

Ulla Morris-Carter

from him again. Only once, months later, I ran into his son in the downtown streets of Cairo. My heart almost stopped beating for a moment, but he just gave me a friendly hello and went on his way.

THE SUEZ CRISIS OF 1956

While I was struggling to get my feet on the ground, the world around me did not stand still. The incredibly volatile Middle East showed signs again of coming upheavals. I was rather apolitical in those days, much too busy with personal matters in my first hot Cairo summer. But one could feel the tension rising along with the temperature. Mr. Atallah, politically astute, gently hinted that I needed to be better informed, because he was convinced that crisis was upon us. He became my mentor. Thanks to his patient explanations, I began to learn some of Egypt's political history, but I also learned that Middle Eastern complexities are hard to grasp. I am young and I want to enjoy life, I thought to myself. Who needs to hear of conflict and trouble ahead?

Because of his limitesd eye sight, Mr. Attalah could not read my face. He could not see that I wanted to escape from these dark thoughts, run out to the Sporting Club and meet friends. But I stood politely next to his chair on the terrace when he explained that Egyptian fedayeen, units trained and equipped by Egypt who infiltrated the Israeli-Egyptian border at Gaza, had launched incursions into Israeli territor; and Israel had responded with raids into Egypt. I was not alarmed, nor did I find the subject particularly interesting. But he tried patiently to explain the past so that I would understand the importance of what the future might hold.

After the overthrow of King Farouk in 1952, Gamal Abdel Nasser had emerged as a leader. In June 1956, he had been elected Egypt's first president, receiving 99% of the vote. The Arab nations having recently gained full independence from the colonial empires of Great Britain and France, wanted to assert their rights and power. Egypt sought foreign aid to build the Aswan Dam in Upper Egypt to supply cheap electricity and to regulate irrigation in the Nile valley. The United States, Great Britain and the International Bank for Reconstruction agreed to provide a loan for that purpose. But Nasser also wanted military aid, and the U.S. turned him down. Angered, Nasser turned to the Soviet Union for military help. That greatly worried the U.S. and particularly Israel. Informed of Egypt's $200 million purchase of Soviet-made arms from Czechoslovakia, the powerful U.S. Secretary of State, John Foster Dulles, suddenly withdrew the Aswan Dam loan. Endorsing this punitive action, Britain withdrew its loan as well. The embittered Nasser responded quickly and furiously.

All this was going on in the summer of 1956, when I had been in Egypt for about six months. With increasing urgency, Mr. Atallah explained that more trouble lay ahead. As usual, he was right.

Ulla Morris-Carter

On July 26, 1956, Egypt blockaded the Gulf of Aqaba, Israel's only outlet to the Red Sea and the Suez Canal. Then President Nasser, during his annual three-hour-long address in Alexandria, suddenly announced the nationalization of the British-run Suez Canal. The Egyptian crowds cheered wildly, particularly when Nasser added that the Canal was now closed to Israeli shipping. And he imposed martial law.

These bold acts would not go unpunished. British as well as French ships traveled the Suez Canal, the vital trade route to the east, with great frequency. Consequently, these two nations had direct business interests in the canal. The British government owned 44% of all shares of the Suez Canal Company, and private French investors owned part of the remaining 56%. Thus provoked, Britain and France froze all Egyptian assets. In an effort to settle the dispute, a 22-nation conference on the Suez Canal crisis convened in London in August 1956. When the conference failed, the inevitable happened. Losing control of their centuries-old empires, Britain and France, along with Israel, planned an attack on Egypt to regain control of the Canal. Recently declassified documents reveal that Britain, France and Israel held a secret meeting in Sèvres, France, in October, 1956, during which it was decided that a) Israel would attack Egypt and seize the Canal; and b) Britain and France would then demand that both Israel and Egypt withdraw from the Canal zone, which Egypt was expected to refuse to do.

Three days after my birthday, on October 29, 1956, I was working in the office on a particularly complicated translation when Mohamed burst in, screaming and shouting:

"The war has started! The war has started! Israeli forces have attacked Egypt, supported by French and British troops."

Mohamed was the only one in the office who had a radio. He listened to it all day when not otherwise occupied. He spoke in Arabic, of course, but I understood enough to realize the importance of his message. We all jumped out of our chairs, stunned, despite the fact that the news was not a total surprise. Mr. Wieland, fluent in Arabic, was able to understand the fast-moving news report, ran into Mohamed's kitchen to listen to the little transistor radio. I ran to the window and looked down into the normally busy streets. Suddenly the traffic seemed to have stopped. Cairo's usual turmoil and uproar had died. Wherever someone with a radio appeared, clusters of people huddled around and listened intently.

Mr. Wieland appeared from the kitchen, grim-faced:

"The news is not good. Israeli troops have invaded the Sinai Peninsula and are racing toward Suez. Britain and France are giving air cover to the Israeli troops who have overrun Egyptian resistance. Foreigners will be in danger, particularly British and French citizens. But often nobody asks questions of nationality. We Germans are not directly involved in the war, but we are foreigners and we are Westerners and we look it. Once the mob gets going there will be no way to escape."

Ulla Morris-Carter

"But how are we going to get out of the center of Cairo and drive home?" asked a worried-looking Mr. Lepique, "and what are we going to do to protect the office?"

Mr. Wieland's response was immediate:

"Barricade the office entrance door with all the available office furniture we can move! We'll depart through the servant's entrance."

He was afraid that the Cairo mob might try to break into the office of a foreign company. He had seen it happen before. We worked as hard and as quickly as possible. More dramatic news of the invading Israeli forces, supported by France and Britain, came over the radio. We needed to leave the downtown area of Cairo sooner rather than later, to avoid a possible confrontation with an Egyptian mob. Mohamed was to stay and try to protect the office, if possible.

We joined nervous Egyptians and frantic foreigners hurrying home. The streets were packed with cars, everybody trying to escape the center of Cairo at the same time. Understandably the most worried were the numerous British and French. But all Europeans felt threatened. With tension increasing by the hour, would a mob distinguish between German, French and British citizens? Not likely.

As soon as we arrived at our respective homes, the phone rang to alert us that various embassies were beginning immediate evacuations. Because all sea and airports were closed, the Germans were to be evacuated by Nile Cruise boats, which would slowly make their way up the Nile toward the Sudan, from where the evacuees were to be flown out to Germany. I politely refused the German Embassy offer to join the lemming rush out of Cairo, despite the urging of my two bosses to leave Cairo and accompany them and their families as they headed toward the evacuation center the next morning. Under normal circumstances I would have loved to take this trip up the Nile, passing Luxor and Aswan, but these circumstances were not normal.

Germans were to report to a school gym that had been rapidly prepared to accommodate the huge number of German citizens to be evacuated. To help with their children, I accompanied the Lepique and Wieland families to the gathering place. It was already overcrowded with evacuees, all waiting to embark on the next available Nile boat. They were allowed to carry only hand luggage, plus food and water for 24 hours. The idea of sleeping on the floor of the gym, surrounded by crying babies, bewildered children and stressed out adults, until a space on a boat became available, did not appeal to me. I was alone, with no responsibility other than for myself. One look at the crowd of evacuees was enough to convince me I would be better off right where I intended to stay, namely in Heliopolis, protected by a local family that had become my family.

The Lepiques and Wielands, I found out later, finally left on the so-called Nile evacuation cruise 24 hours after their arrival at the gathering place. For five days they traveled on an overcrowded boat that took them up the Nile towards Luxor, but before they reached the Sudan, the Suez War was over.

Ulla Morris-Carter

Meanwhile, I was determined to make the best of a bad situation. With no bosses around and the office closed, I decided to treat this period as a holiday. That, however, would not work out exactly the way as I had hoped.

I remember those beautiful, balmy late October and early November days in 1956 when the temperature was just perfect after the grueling heat of the summer months. I remember the intense and almost overpowering perfume of the jasmine that seemed to be ever-present in the garden town of Heliopolis. The jacaranda trees were showing off their most intensely colored blue blossoms. It was hard to believe there was a war going on.

On day two of the war I decided to take a walk around the neighborhood in Heliopolis. I had never had enough time to just look at houses, admire the gardens or the architecture. I sneaked out of the house knowing that Madame Atallah would never have let me go had she known that I was going to stroll around the neighborhood. The streets were eerily quiet. Most people stayed home and listened to the radio so as not to miss a word of the terrifying approach of the Israeli army.

Our neighbor's garden was particularly attractive. I went back home to pick up my camera, hoping to photograph some of the most beautiful flowers. When I returned three soldiers were standing in front of the garden. They grabbed me, guns at the ready.

Without any explanation they marched me in the direction of the Sporting Club, one soldier on my left, one soldier on my right, one walking behind me with his gun at my back. I could feel the gun barrel through my light summer dress. I had no idea what in my demeanor or my looks appeared dangerous. But my choices were limited. Run away from them? Where to? Escape seemed hopeless.

I marched silently along, distressed that I was unable to converse with them. We arrived at the Heliopolis Sporting Club, which overnight had been transformed into Military Headquarters. Egyptian soldiers were posted at every corner and as far as the eye could see. I was taken to a small room that I recognized as a storage room close to the office of the club's manager. The soldiers shoved me in, closed the door and locked it with a key. My heart was pounding. Looking around, I found one lonely chair in the corner. The rest of the room contained mainly shelves with papers and books, all in Arabic.

"No help to me," I mumbled.

I hadn't the slightest idea why I had been arrested. Nobody had asked for my passport, nobody had asked which nationality I was. I had not seen or spoken to anybody. Someone must come and explain. But when?

One hour passed. Two hours passed. The little room was getting hot. There was little air. The small window did not open. I was thirsty. I knocked on the door, hoping someone would hear me. Maybe no one knew I was in there. I kept knocking: Nothing. More knocking: Nothing. I was not desperate, I was not panicky, just baffled and

Ulla Morris-Carter

annoyed. And I was bored. The situation was tense, but I had decided to stay calm, polite and patient. I was a foreigner.

But after three hours I had had enough. I started pounding the door angrily and ever more loudly. After quite a while I finally heard footsteps approaching. A key turned in the lock. A face appeared in the door, looking at me, obviously surprised and puzzled. The man looked vaguely familiar. A flash of recognition came over his face as well.

"What are you doing here?" he asked in perfect English.

"That's what I am asking you," I exploded. "I have been here for almost four hours without water, without bathroom, without any explanation."

I was furious. My liberator turned out to be the club manager, now in uniform.

"I was brought here by three soldiers with a gun at my back."

"I know you from the Club, aren't you a member?" the manager finally said after a long pause. "But you are German, from what I remember."

"Yes, of course I am German, what else would I be?" I thought that I still looked as German as they come. "Nobody ever inquired about my nationality."

The manager hurried out of the room, returning quickly with a glass of fresh, cool lemonade.

"I am sorry for the inconvenience, but I was told you were British or French. There is a war going on, as you know. Any foreigner in the street is suspicious. The soldiers might have thought you were a spy. And I see you carried a camera. Not a wise idea. Go home now, and stay off the streets."

He shook hands, and I was dismissed, released from prison.

I left hurriedly, walking alone through silent and deserted streets. When I finally reached the Atallah house, Madame Atallah greeted me like a long lost child, hugging me tightly while scolding me for having left the house without telling her. I had been gone for most of the day, and she was understandably worried.

When the first air raid siren sounded a little later, I was immediately transported back into World War II. I closed my eyes in disbelief and blocked my ears with my fingers. I couldn't believe that this was happening to me of all people, I, who had left Germany to escape from the wounds and after-effects of the war and its hardships. Deciding to stay in Cairo rather than evacuate, I had no idea that French and British aircraft would start shelling Port Said and particularly Heliopolis, where the civilian airport and some military air strips were located. Heliopolis airport was a prime target. Fuel tanks and planes were bombed and exploded. The sky turned a dark orange-red. The air filled with smoke.

I ran out of the house, much to the consternation of Madame Atallah. She was hysterically gesticulating from the front door for me to come back inside. But I felt claustrophobic inside. I was remembering being trapped in the air raid basement shelter

Ulla Morris-Carter

of our house in Düsseldorf, when the bomb hit in 1941. I had to remind myself that this was not WWII, but a serious Middle Eastern crisis.

By November 5, Israel had occupied Gaza and most of the huge Sinai Peninsula, including Sharm-al-Shaikh at the Gulf of Aqaba. The next day French and British parachute troops took the city of Port Said on the Suez Canal. Intense international pressure, particularly from the U.S.and the Soviet Union, and intervention by the U.N. General Assembly, finally resulted in a cease-fire on November 7. France and Britain began withdrawing their forces from Egypt by the end of November, but Israeli troops did not leave completely until March of the following year.

Short as this war was, its repercussions were far-reaching. The British and French were condemned by many, their reputation badly damaged. Nasser, on the other hand, even though he had lost the war, emerged greatly strengthened, his reputation enhanced, particularly in the Arab world, where he was celebrated as the hero of nationalism who had dared to fight the British colonial empire.

That particular November had, in fact, been one of the most turbulent months in modern world history. Not only was the Middle East in uproar. Fears of another world war arose when, after attempts to crush the Hungarian revolt against Soviet domination had failed, the Soviet Union invaded Hungary.

Against a background of these and other crucial international developments, the American presidential elections took place. President Eisenhower was re-elected, defeating the Democratic candidate, Adlai Stevenson.

Ulla Morris-Carter

Made in GERMANY

Fräulein Krause in Ägypten

Fräulein Krause ging vor wenigen Monaten am Rhein spazieren. Sie war eine von Hunderttausenden junger Stenotypistinnen in der Bundesrepublik. Heute ist sie Sekretärin im Kairoer Verbindungsbüro einer deutschen Firma. Kairo bietet der jungen Deutschen ein vielseitiges und abwechslungsreiches Leben: Kinos, der vornehme „Ghezireh Sporting Club", herrliche Schwimmbäder, groß angelegte Tennis-, Hockey- und Fußballplätze locken zum Besuch. Während wir unseren Schnupfen pflegen, badet Fräulein Krause mitten im ägyptischen „Winter" im Roten Meer. Immer mehr deutsche Ingenieure, Kaufleute, Ärzte, Spezialisten und Industriefachleute lassen sich in Ägypten nieder. Sie sind gern gesehen im Land des Nils.

Die deutschen Importwaren mit dem Wertsiegel „Made in Germany" begegnen einem auf Schritt und Tritt. Das ist nicht bedingt durch die politische Situation, sondern das ist der Rührigkeit deutscher Unternehmer und Beamter im Nahen Osten zu verdanken. „Alemani" (Deutsch), und „Made in Germany" ist im Nahen Osten der Qualitätsbegriff Nummer eins.

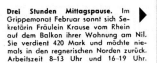

Drei Stunden Mittagspause. Im Grippemonat Februar sonnt sich Sekretärin Fräulein Krause vom Rhein auf dem Balkon ihrer Wohnung am Nil. Sie verdient 420 Mark und möchte niemals in den regnerischen Norden zurück. Arbeitszeit 8-13 Uhr und 16-19 Uhr.

Soraya wrote this short article which appeared in the German weekly magazine Deutsche Illustrierte, *February 1957, featuring the life of a young German woman living and working in Egypt. She changed my name to 'Fräulein Krause'.*

Miss Krause in Egypt

Only a few months ago Fraulein Krause was walking along the banks of the river Rhine. She was one of thousands of typists in the German Federal Republic. Today she is the secretary in the office of the representative of a German company. Cairo offers the young German a varied and very interesting life: movies, the elegant Ghezireh Sporting Club and fantastic swimming pools; and the beautifully maintained tennis, hockey and soccer fields are also most inviting. While we are suffering from colds and sniffles, Fraulein Krause swims in the Red Sea in the middle of the "Egyptian winter."

More and more German engineers, businessmen, medical doctors and industrial specialists are settling in Egypt. They are most welcome in the land of the Nile. German imports, displaying the "made in Germany" seal that guarantees quality, can be seen everywhere. This is not due to the political situation, but mainly thanks to the enormous efforts of the German business community. "Alemani" (German) and "Made in Germany" are considered number one quality products in the Middle East.

Three hours lunch break *(caption to the left)* In February, when we suffer from flue and colds, Fraulein Krause takes a sunbath on the balcony of her apartment on the Nile. She earns DM 420 and never wants to return to the rainy North. Her office hours are from 8-13 hours and from 16-19 hours.

Ulla Morris-Carter

146

Brilliant WaterWays
and Deserts

That exquisite corridor of tinted mountains and
radiant water . . . here and nowhere else, is the
vestibule between the Levant and the Tropics.

- E.M. Forster, describing the Gulf of Suez

How could I, in the grey and cold days of Düsseldorf, ever have imagined experiencing anything as exotic and exciting as a journey to the Red Sea? When I arrived in Egypt in 1956, I had never heard of the Red Sea except in the context of the Bible story of the escape of the Israelites from ancient Egypt.

But shortly after I joined KSB, Mr. Wieland, one of the two German engineers, invited me to join him, his wife and their two young children on an excursion to the Red Sea. Its shore runs from the Gulf of Suez to the Sudanese border. A reddish-colored mountain range, jutting out close to the waters, probably inspired earlier generations to call this the *Mare Rostrum* or Red Sea, or maybe it was the color of the water at sundown.

This was also my first visit to the Suez Canal, which connects the Mediterranean to the Red Sea. Opened in 1869, the Canal was narrow, only 60 yards wide then, cutting right through the desert. Seen from a distance, ships appeared to be passing through sand rather than water. A prime international trade route, the Canal allows transportation between Europe and Asia without navigating all the way around Africa. Little did I know in the spring of 1956 that a few months later a major war would break out over control and passage of the Suez Canal.

Ulla Morris-Carter

We traveled in Mr. Wieland's Volkswagen Beetle along the Cairo-Suez road. Amazingly, we could all fit comfortably into what we now consider a small car, Mr and Mrs. Wieland, their two children and I, plus luggage. The asphalt highway was considered a main thoroughfare, making travel to Suez easy. But continuing to Ain Soukhna, the hot springs, our destination, turned out to be more challenging.

We traveled south on sandy roads, with not a soul in sight. When darkness fell, we set up camp on a deserted, strip of sand at the water's edge. Only three hours' drive from Cairo, it was heavenly. I slept outdoors under stars that were brighter, more numerous and more brilliant than any I had ever seen. Camping was not new to me. I had gone camping in Germany in my Girl Scout days, but never in a spot so silent, unspoiled and fascinating as this coastline, far from the bustling, noisy city.

The waters of the Red Sea were not red. They were brilliant blue-turquoise. Its underwater life was teeming with fish of gorgeous colors and designs. We discovered mysterious, almost fairytale-like coral reefs, surrounded by hundreds of brilliantly colored fishes, species I had never before seen. The fantastic coral reefs stretched far out and deep into the water, forming lagoons, caves and small hills that made me feel I was wandering in a well-designed garden. We swam, snorkeled and explored the clear waters, then rested during the hot part of the day in the shade of our tents. At night, before going to sleep, we would rinse our salty and sunburned faces with a small amount of the sweet water we had carried with us. Nobody had ever heard of protective sun lotion. Nivea cream was as close as we could come.

Days went by without our seeing another human being. The coast guard, a handsome Nubian soldier riding a camel, would pass occasionally in the evening to check on us. He was our only contact with the outside world. Late in the afternoon we took long walks along the reddish mountain chain, whose reflection in the water at sunset made the water appear red.

After my initial excursion to the Red Sea with the Wielands, I returned with a group of Heliopolis friends. Huguette was part of this well-equipped group of mostly young men that regularly went harpoon fishing. It included Toni Shusha, a stocky, strong fellow whom I knew from the Heliopolis Sporting Club; Bubi Bishai, a young doctor and his wife Mona; Ibrahim, our archeologist friend and Samir, Hueguette's fiancé. All expert fishermen, they kept warm for hours in the water by wearing wool sweaters. No fisherwoman myself, I had the task of guiding a small rowboat to wherever one of the fishermen needed to load a fish he had just caught. Much to my distress the fish would be squirming and squiggling around my feet, with no way to escape. But we never failed to have a delicious fish dinner at night. We carried everything we needed— water for drinking and for rinsing the salt off of our burnt faces at the end of the day, food, tents and clothing.

Ulla Morris-Carter

Above: *Camping at the Red Sea.* **Right:** *Hugette, Ibrahim,me and a fishernman friend with the day's catch.*

Once, during a sudden sandstorm, we lost all our fresh vegetables: cucumbers, carrots and potatoes. The strong wind simply carried our precious food into the unknown. Toni pulled an icebox behind his car, a large, bulky trailer he had constructed, cold enough to hold the fish he and his companions had caught for about three days. Upon our return to Heliopolis, Toni's family would invite us all to a fabulous fish dinner.

These were unforgettable days on the empty shores of the Red Sea—a place that is now a major tourist attraction from Suez all the way south to Hurghada and beyond. Luxury hotels, offering special fishing expeditions, plus lots of sun-seeking tourists, have tremendously changed the previously almost meditative, isolated Red Sea coast forever.

Ulla Morris-Carter

EXCURSIONS INTO THE DESERT

As much as the desert itself, it was the attraction of the unknown that intrigued me. Its shimmering sands and the total silence in which only the wind played, gave me a sense of freedom that had seemed unattainable in post-war Germany.

One beautiful summer Sunday morning, I was invited to go horseback riding in the desert with Mahmoud, my Heliopolis Sporting Club friend, and his group. We gathered at 5:30 a.m. at the foot of the Pyramids of Giza at the western edge of Cairo, about six miles from downtown. The sun was just coming up, but the air still held the chill of early dawn. The horses were waiting for us near the Cheops Pyramid, built by King Khufu around 2650 BC. It is considered to be the only survivor among the Seven Wonders of the Ancient World.

I had never been on a horse before. But watching my friends ride in the wide-open desert made it look easy. My friends gave me some basic instructions. Two hours later they decided that I was ready for a short ride on my own.

Under a crystaline blue sky, my first trial ride was easy enough. I gained confidence and was eager to take a second ride. After a short distance I realized, with horror, that my horse enjoyed his freedom in the desert as much as I did, probably even more. He knew instinctively that I was not in control and took off like a flash, seemingly flying through the air, racing through endless stretches of beautiful desert. I was unable to stop him. My friends thought I was having a great time and doing extremely well. In reality I was hanging on for dear life.

Then they realized that I needed help. Racing after me, they tried to get in front of my horse to stop him. Easier said than done. We covered a few miles before one of my friends managed to block my horse from continuing into the endless, open desert.

Amazingly, I wasn't thrown off, and though shaken, I was still in one piece and actually found my adventure quite exciting.

A delicious breakfast was then served in a desert tent near the step pyramid of Saqqara, supposedly the oldest monumental structure made of stone anywhere in the world. Tall and handsome *sufragis*, waiters, mostly of Nubian origin, clad in white galabiyas, their heads covered by brilliantly white turbans that contrasted with their deep-dark complexion, waited for us to arrive. They had coffee and tea ready, and served freshly baked croissants, hot *baladi*, pita, bread with yoghurt mixed with fresh mint leaves, and jucy sliced oranges. For a girl fresh out of war-torn Germany, such delicacies and adventures were beyond belief. The oranges made me remember the first one I had ever seen, offered to me by an American soldier eleven years earlier. I could still hear my great aunt whispering into my ear on that cold April day in 1945, "You are not accepting this orange from our enemies."

However, on that Sunday morning in 1956, sitting at the foot of the Saqqara pyramid, I had no desire to linger on thoughts of war. Saqqara, originally built 4,700

Ulla Morris-Carter

Above: On a camel touring the pyrmids with friends. I am on the far left. Top right: My first adventures on a horse. Bottom right: On our way to Dahshour. L-R: Ibrahim, Hugette and Samir.

years ago for King Djoser of the third dynasty, was located at the great metropolis of Memphis of the Old Kingdom. The desert surroundings overwhelmed me. I felt as if the desert had cast a spell over me. A slight breeze helped to provide an almost perfect temperature, making me wish I could lie in the warm sand and listen to the silence.

Among my fondest memories of those Cairo days of 1956 and 1957 are the excursions with Hugette Atallah, the daughter of my landlord. Accompanied by Samir, Hugette's fiance, a tall, handsome blue-eyed Egyptian, and his archaeologist friend Ibrahim, we ventured to less traveled spots, such as the Pyramids of Dahshour. Twenty miles south of the well-known Giza Pyramids, Dahshour was an important cemetery of the vast necropolis of the old capital of Memphis.

Hardly a tourist attraction in the fifties, it was only reachable by jeep or on horseback. King Snefu, who ruled 2680-2565 BC, chose to build his royal tomb here because it was close to Memphis. What today is called the "Bent Pyramid" was a first, misconceived attempt to built a pyramid. The builders had started it at an angle that would have resulted in a pyramid much too high. So they stopped building.

Years later, the construction was finished by simply changing the angle of the pyramid at the top, which resulted in the strange shape we see today. The pyramid was never used: a new, smaller pyramid was built as a tomb for King Snefu.

Ibrahim pointed to an entry hole about 20 meters above ground on the outside wall of the Bent Pyramid.

Ulla Morris-Carter

"Let's try and crawl inside," he suggested.

We eagerly agreed. Maybe we would find a hidden treasure!

Climbing up to the entrance was the easy part. More problematic was making ourselves small enough to fit through the entry hole. Ducking down as far as possible, we managed to venture inside. Lying flat on our bellies, we crawled along a wooden ladder, which had been placed over the loose soil on the floor of the narrow passage, deeper and deeper into the pyramid. The passage was no wider than one yard and no higher than a yard and a half. The further we went inside, the hotter it became. Our flashlights guided us along until we felt we could no longer breathe. We had hoped to find the opening to a chamber, but there didn't seem to be one. We had no choice but to turn back. Not an easy matter, considering the fact that there was hardly enough space to turn around. But we were young and flexible. Emerging from our expedition, covered in dust and debris, we gratefully greeted the sun and fresh air, and breathed a sigh of relief.

Our archaeologist friend Ibrahim surprised me one day with the news that he had been able to arrange for me to travel to an excavation some 50 miles outside of Cairo. The group of two archeologists and their three assistants used camels to reach the site. They also prepared a camel for me. I had ridden camels before, but then I was comfortably seated on a tourist saddle and helped by an Egyptian guide. This expedition, I soon discovered, was going to be different.

Bedouins, the nomadic desert-dwelling Arab ethnic group, use camels for everything, for traveling from one place to another, for carrying small and large loads, and for providing milk. These animals are well-suited to life in the desert. They can go up to eight days without water. On long-distance journeys an unladen camel is able to run as fast as 35-40 miles per hour. The Bedouins love their camels and look after them the way we look after our children. They call their camels "Ata Allah," or "God's Gift."

I was instructed to sit cross-legged and as far forward as possible on a small saddle and to hold on tightly once the camel started to run. Camels love traveling in groups, I was told. At the onset of our expedition they marched slowly, one after the other, keeping a specific distance between them. Getting used to the gait of my camel took a while, but I soon became comfortable with the rocking motion that sometimes make people feel sea-sick. Once out in the open desert, however, the animals picked up speed.

Was I now in a camel race? I felt as if I were flying through the air. Hanging on for dear life, I grabbed my camel's neck. To say that I was in an uncomfortable position would be an understatement, but I did not want to complain for fear of holding up this expedition. After all, I was an invited guest who actually had no business being with this group. Egyptian hospitality is legendary, though, and Ibrahim's colleagues, out of friendship for him, were honoring one of his rare requests, a request to bring along a foreign girl.

Ulla Morris-Carter

Although the camels were running much faster than I could have ever imagined, it took four hours with only a short break to arrive at our destination. We were to overnight in tents set up on a permanent basis by the working group. I remember little about the actual archeological site or about the overnight. My thoughts dwelled on the return trip the next morning. I was suffering from the worst muscle aches I had ever experienced. I was so stiff that I could scarcely move. The very thought of sitting another four hours on a camel made me feel ill. I wondered if I would even be able to get up on my camel. To mount my crouched camel, I needed to hold onto the wooden tree with my left hand, then place the left knee into the saddle. As soon as my camel felt the weight, it began to rise, allowing me to swing my right leg over and into place. With help, and a good sense of humor by all concerned, I was soon in the saddle. The ride home was painful, but the pleasure of having been allowed to participate in the expedition let me quickly forget the short-lived discomfort.

Never to be forgotten was the eternal desert landscape, scorched by the sun, its glistening rocks polished by occasional rain and incessant wind.

The Step Pyramid at Saqqara, built for King Djoser about 4700 years ago, is considered to be the oldest of Egypt's 97 pyramids. It is a part of the great necropolis of Memphis of the Old Kingdom, which was excavated 1924-26.

Ulla Morris-Carter

Photos from my Nile trip.
Above: *Deckhard on the ship, passing a port town on the Nile.*
Below: *Feluccas, classic egyptian river transport boats, with pottery.*

NILE TRIP: FROM MY DIARY, 1957

All its wealth comes from the blessed river that moves through it with the dignity of a caliph. Regular as sun and moon, it rises and falls again. The hour comes when all the springs of the world must pay their tribute to the king of rivers, which Providence has lifted high above all others; then the waters rise and quit their bed, and flood the plains, depositing upon them their fertile mud . . . . But then, in its wisdom, the river re-enters the bounds appointed by fate, so that those who live there may collect the treasure it has confided to Mother Earth.

~Amr ibn el As, seventh century Arab commander, whose Islamic Army conquered Egypt.

Heavy fog hung over the river on that chilly morning in February when I arrived at the banks of the Nile.

Mr. Lepique and Mr. Wieland had kindly driven me to the harbor at seven a.m. Walking along the quai through the cloudy and misty morning air, I could barely make out a white, middle-sized yacht. As I moved closer, the words *S.S. Sudan* became visible.

"This is my ship!" I shouted excitedly to Mr. Lepique and Mr. Wieland.

I would be a passenger on *S.S. Sudan* together with 62 mostly middle-aged, well-to-do Egyptians. We would spend the next 14 days on what promised to be an extraordinary journey up the Nile. We would see its temples and valleys, experience its peoples and its villages without the usual number of noisy, pushing and shoving tourists.

One after-effect of the Suez War of October 1956 had been the strict application of travel restrictions for all Egyptians. No exit visas were issued. No Egyptian citizen was allowed to leave the country. And no tourist was inclined to visit a country where tensions were still running high. Wealthy Egyptians, used to traveling to European watering holes, had no place to escape. Consequently an Egyptian travel agency had come up with the idea of a luxury Nile cruise.

Ulla Morris-Carter

Top: *The S.S. Sudan.* **Bottom left:** *Our happy dinner group. L–R: Barbara, Paul Lipshitz, me and Dr. Bubi Bishai and his wife Mona.* **Bottm right:** *In a horse-drawn carriage in Assiout.*

The manager of the travel agency offered me the last available ticket, at a much reduced rate, for a single cabin without bath that nobody had wanted. My finances were not in great shape, but this was too good an opportunity to pass up. I decided to join the Egyptian group and experience the mysteries of the river Nile—this fabled waterway that for almost ten millennia had served as the lifeline of the world's oldest civilization.

I could hardly believe that only one year had passed since my arrival in Alexandria. And what a year it had been! Now it felt as if I had won the lottery, being allowed to luxuriate for two glorious weeks on a small cruise ship that would slowly make its way from Cairo to Luxor and Aswan in Upper Egypt.

I was thrilled to find out that among my travel companions would be Barbara, slightly older than I, who was the secretary to the Canadian Ambassador and the young ship's doctor, Dr. Bishai, and his charming wife Mona—a couple I knew from the Heliopolis Sporting Club and had previously been camping with at the Red Sea. We four young passengers quickly became

Ulla Morris-Carter

well acquainted and joined together for meals and other activities.

On the day of our departure, the morning fog lifted quickly. By noon the sun was shining brightly, lifting everyone's spirits after a week of unusually cool and rainy weather in Cairo. Over the next few days, we would visit Assiout, one of the wealthiest cities in Egypt, as well as Baliana—the site of the Temple of Abydos—and Nag Hamadi. At Denderah we visited one of the best preserved and most important sites, the Temple of Hathor. Finally, 6 days after setting sail, we were approaching Luxor, the destination I had dreamed about.

Directly across from our landing place stood the Winter Palace, Luxor's most beautiful and best-known hotel. The hotel garden was a paradise, filled with palm trees and exotic plants in every imaginable color. Spacious enough to accommodate 300 people, the hotel, absent its usual tourist throngs, was practically empty and looked dead. But at the bar we met, by chance, a few of those hardy Europeans and Americans, who had long made it a habit to spend the winter in Upper Egypt, willing to brave the political hazards because they loved Luxor so much.

After dinner we hired a horse-drawn carriage to pay a short night visit to the temple of Karnak. Built more than 5,000 years ago, it was one of the most imposing and most impressive temples imaginable. An astonishing row of ram-headed sphinxes led into the unbelievably glorious temple, which looked even more magnificent in the light of a full moon. Reflected on the stones, it was a kind of light I had never seen before I came to Egypt.

There was so much to see at Karnak: the Great temple of Amon, the Obelisk of Queen Hatshepsut, the Granite Scara of Amenophis III, on and on. The largest of Karnak's three main areas was dedicated to Amon. Within this magnificent temple lies Hypostyle Hall, consisting of 134 massive

Rams statues at the entrance of the Temple of Karnak.

Ulla Morris-Carter

columns, 23 meters high. The outer court, built later, showed the huge granite colossi of Ramses II. These incredible statues, carved out of black or red granite, depicting the old Egyptian king, made us look and feel like dwarfs. Even the smallest detail was beautifully sculpted. I was simply overwhelmed. To experience this mysterious ancient world in total silence made me feel connected to the Gods.

The following day we set out to visit Mr. Habashi, a wise man who reputedly knew everything one ever wanted to learn about Luxor. In a horse-drawn carriage we traveled leisurely through dusty narrow alleys to the old quarter where the people of Luxor live and shop. One of our purposes was to buy the materials we would need to create our costumes for a "Pharaoh's Masked Ball," taking place the next night on our boat.

Shopping in Egypt takes time and a lot of patience. One doesn't just walk into a store, choose, buy and walk out. No, you start with a cup of tea, which arrives the minute you enter. Then, after finding the object of desire, you start the bargaining process. You negotiate. Then you leave the store, pretending not to want to buy anything at the stated price. You return only after the salesman, who has run after you, has assured you that he will give you the best price possible, which is about half or less of what he originally asked.

This elaborate process was abbreviated for us during our visit because of the shortage of tourists. Under the tent-like canopy of the store we bought, for just a few Egyptian piasters, a yellow nightgown to be worn by our doctor, Bubie Bishai,

who was to appear the next night as sun god "RA" followed by his three goddesses: his wife Mona, Barbara and me.

On the way back we discovered a great palm tree, whose leaves seemed just the right size to perfect our costumes for the Pharaonic Masked Ball. We created headdresses of paper according to the old reliefs, which we studied carefully.

Well . . . blonde Barbara and I were not exactly pharaonic-looking types. But once our blond hair had disappeared under a black headdress, green eye shadow had been applied and *kohl*, black Egyptian eyeliner, had made our eyes appear almond-shaped, we thought we looked the part. Most impressive were our long earrings and necklaces plus the scarves draped around our hips over our long black skirts.

When we three sandal-footed goddesses, carrying long palm leaves, appeared on stage marching behind Bubie Bishai— our sun God RA— the whole ship broke out in laughter and applause. We moved very slowly and in measured steps. If you have ever studied a relief you would have noticed, no doubt, that the body is always

Bubie Bishai as Sun God Ra and his three Goddesses; L-R: Barbara, Mona, Bubie and myself.

Ulla Morris-Carter

In my Egyptian goddess costume.

shown frontally, but the face in profile. We tried to copy this exactly—not an easy matter. And yes, we won the first prize.

Early the next morning we sailed across the Nile to the City of the Dead, the ancient Thebes. The Nile, dark green, flowed gently with hardly a ripple. Symbolism is such an important part of Egyptian culture: We had just left the city of the living, Luxor, on the east bank of the Nile, where the sun rises and where the temples honoring the living Gods were built. And we were crossing over to the opposite bank, the west side of the Nile, where Thebes, The City of the Dead, lay silhouetted against the dramatic sky. Tombs and mortuary temples bear out the belief that it was here that the Pharaohs ruled after death.

Reaching the western bank, we continued our journey by donkey. Amid great laughter we all finally managed to get on a donkey, our legs dangling backward and forwards, as we made our way to a small village. A bus waited for us in the village. After a 45-minute bus ride we reached Bilan el Muluk, site of the royal tombs of Tutanchamun, Ramses VI, Sethos and Amenophis III. Not a sprig of green anywhere, only relatively high, light-colored limestone hills and mountains.

The 60 ft high Colossi of Memnon. Symbol of Thebes and the Valley of the Kings.

Ulla Morris-Carter

Deep within these mountains lay the royal tombs, deliberately concealed under earth and piles of stones. Because of the dry heat, they were amazingly well preserved. I could hardly believe the beauty of the wall paintings—the harmony and splendor, the incredible colors and bold designs that had lasted almost 5,000 years.

Eager to see as many sites as possible in one day, we set off to Dar el Bahree, some of us on the bus, while I joined those who hiked over the mountain—a 45-minute trek. The sun now really burned our skin, but the majestic views were well worth it: the whole Valley of the Kings, the Nile Valley, the temples of Karnak and Luxor east side of the river, as well as of the Colossi of Memnon on the Thebes side. Dar el Bahree was unforgettable. Terraces led up to a shrine, cut out of solid rock, with an almost vertical sand-colored cliff as the background.

The temple itself, built by Hatshepsut, the powerful half-sister, wife and co-regent of Thutmosis III, was dedicated to God Amun. Finally, we approached the Colossi of Memnon. Symbol of Thebes and the Valley of the Kings, the two colossi sit enthroned in solitude. They are of such enormous size—I really couldn't call them beautiful—that they simply overwhelmed us. The sandstone southern

Faluccas docked at the shore.

Ulla Morris-Carter

colossos, depicting Amenophis II, was the best preserved: total height including the fallen crown, was over 60 feet. The legs alone up to the knee exceeded 18 feet, and one foot measured 10 feet. The northern colossos, less well preserved, looked about the same, except for two small additions—on Amenophis' right stood the small figure of his wife Teje, and on his left was his mother, Mutenweje.

At the end of an exhausting but fascinating day, we returned to the ship and departed immediately for Aswan, where we arrived at 8:30 the next morning. Often called the "Gem of Egypt," at Aswan the Nile is at its most beautiful and mightiest. Here its waters are truly green and crystal clear. Hundreds of small, rocky islands lie in the middle of the river, which gracefully weaves in and around them—some inhabited, others not. The banks on both sides are covered with a vast variety of flowers, such as the bright yellow sunflowers and hundreds of other species in gorgeous colors.

Upon arrival, we immediately boarded a felucca, moored near our landing place, and set sail to visit Elephantine Island, one of the most ancient sites in Egypt. As far back as one can remember, Aswan was called "Yebu" or "Elephant Land." It is very unlikely that Elephants roamed here, but it is possible that elephant tusks were traded there. And Aswan was, and still is, famous for its granite: pink, red, blue and black. Many world-wide known cities, i.e. Rome, Paris, London and New York proudly display tall obelisks made of Aswan granite.

Huge granite blocks for sculpting of some of Egypt's colossal statues would be floated downstream, during the yearly floods, to Thebes, Abydos, Memphis and even Saqqara. Elephantine Island was a spectacular place to visit. We could wander among the Nubian villages and enjoy the great botanical gardens, filled with lush exotic flowers and plants.

An interesting side excursion was a tour around the island where the fabulously wealthy Agha Khan III had built a house to spend his winters. The spiritual leader of the Moslem Ismailis had chosen Aswan because of the pleasant winter climate. We could not visit the island itself, but admired that beautiful white villa, built directly on the water's edge. In 1957, the year we visited Aswan, the Agha Khan would die. A Mausoleum, housing his remains, was later built above his residence on this island. The Begum, his last, very young, beautiful and devoted wife, apparently—so the story goes—placed a red rose on his grave every day of the year. If she was not present, a gardener would fulfill this task. And if Egypt's roses were not in bloom, a red rose would daily be flown in from Europe.

One more incredible experience awaited us: a visit to the Aswan Dam, three miles south of Aswan (not to be confused with the High Dam which would be constructed between 1960-1970). The older Aswan Dam was built by the British and completed in 1902. This dam and the barrages at Assiout were the principal means of storing irrigation water for the Nile Valley before the High Dam of Aswan was constructed.

The territory around the Aswan Dam had been declared a military zone because of the Suez crisis. Photography was strictly

Ulla Morris-Carter

forbidden: cameras had to be handed over to military personnel. The Dam, though a most imposing and majestic structure, seemed to fit itself beautifully into its natural surroundings.

Later that day we were invited to tea by a couple that had traveled with us for part of the trip. They not only owned a whole island, but also the most unbelievable villa, built right into the rocks, with huge terraces and a wonderful park. There were tennis courts and a gorgeous swimming pool, eight bedrooms and four bathrooms. I was speechless. And this dream house was only occupied for two or three months in the winter.

Never before had I seen anything like it. The neighboring island—it turned out—was the property of the Aga Khan with that stunning white villa, I already described.

And the Begum was the bridge partner of our fellow travelers.

It was already dark when we left at 7:30 pm. There can't be any clearer sky with more stars than the night sky of Aswan. The full moon appeared like a huge dark yellow ball on this star-studded sky. Our felucca sailed quietly through the darkness, barely audible, weaving around the many small islands. An intense stillness settled over the desert and the river, interrupted briefly by the Aswan muezzins calling for prayer from their minarets.

When we reached our "home away from home"—our ship—some of our group went straight to dinner. But a few of us continued to sail around in the felucca, savoring one last hour of this unforgettable trip on the Nile, which we sadly knew would shortly be ending.

Deckhands on the S.S. Sudan.

Ulla Morris-Carter

The next morning I took a swim in the Nile in February. Emerging from the icy waters, I felt terrific, refreshed and full of energy. This was our last day and night on the ship. Every minute was precious. We reveled in the beauty, and I actually drank the water of the Nile, crystal clear and clean, hoping for the fulfillment of the proverb that "those who drink the waters of the Nile will return to the Nile."

Sailing around the lake behind the dam, we saw the foundations for the new "High Dam of Aswan," whose future construction would—amidst great uproar—eventually submerge parts of Nubia and thousands of years of historic monuments.

With heavy heart we returned to the ship and packed our bags. At the station our train was already waiting, and by 10:00 am the next day we arrived in Cairo, the starting point of this absolutely unique and exquisite journey.

Back in Cairo I was invited by some of my fellow-travellors to some of the most spectacular homes. This trip had provided me an entrée into a world of Cairo that I would otherwise never have known.

Right: *1957 Tourist Map of Nile Valley.*

Ulla Morris-Carter

In my new Beirut bathing suit.

First Home Leave

Returning to Düsseldorf
via Beirut-Turkey

1957

After almost two years in Cairo, in late September 1957, my first home leave was on the calendar. Heading home to Düsseldorf, I planned to stop briefly in Beirut, one of the exotic cities I had read about and longed to see.

While I was completing some freelance work for Mr. von Richthofen, the German Middle East representative of the pharmaceutical company Bayer, Leverkusen, he offered me the use of his apartment in Beirut.

"I will be out of the country. Please make yourself at home in my place as long as it suits you," he told me.

I gladly accepted the offer since, for one thing, I did not have vast financial resources at my disposal.

Until that point my travels had all been by train, ship or car, but now I was to have my first international flight adventure. At 23 I felt like a sophisticated world traveler. Hiding my inexperience, I pretended to be totally at ease as I settled into my Middle East Airlines seat for the relatively short flight to Beirut.

Seated at the window, I had my first look at the vast metropolis of Cairo from the air. I gazed down on the turquoise, shimmering Mediterranean Sea with boats and ships like tiny dots bobbing up and down. Soon all this disappeared leaving nothing but bright blue sky. Two hours later we touched down in Beirut.

A taxi whisked me through teeming streets to the upscale section of Hamra, where I found Herr von Richthofen's apartment on the second floor of a large corner building. His housekeeper, a middle-aged lady, greeted me with a warm smile. We conversed in French. My French wasn't perfect, but it was good enough for polite small talk. The

Ulla Morris-Carter

apartment was divided into two parts. The part nearest the entrance was Herr von Richthofen's flat. The second part at the back of the building was occupied by Herr von Richthofen's German colleague, Peter Böhme, who represented the Agfa Film company, a division of Bayer, Leverkusen.

I had assumed that he would be out of town as well, but much to my surprise Peter soon knocked on the door of my room. He introduced himself, looked me over and volunteered to help me find specific sights or shops. Cosmopolitan Beirut, with its wide open economy, offered all the desirable things one could not find in Egypt. I set out immediately.

It was hot and extremely humid. The temperature was lower than Cairo in summer, but the high humidity prompted me to buy something hard to find in Cairo, a bathing suit. It was thrilling to walk up and down Hamra Street looking at French, German or Italian fashions, dainty lingerie, perfumes and international newspapers. Sightseeing would have to wait.

When I returned, Peter Böhme was waiting for me.

"May I invite you to dinner tonight, if you don't have other plans," he asked politely.

I had no plans whatever, nor did I know anybody in Beirut. I accepted with pleasure. Peter was a slender 30 year-old, good-looking with bright blue eyes and brown hair. He chose an open-air fish restaurant for dinner. He was charming, and I enjoyed his company. After dinner it was off to the *Cave du Roi,* Beirut's best-known nightclub, where, as I learned, a famous bartender named Aldo, reigned like a king.

Peter and I danced, laughed, had a good time and quickly abandoned the German formalities of "Herr Böhme" and "Fraeulein Kirschbaum."

A beach outing with Peter and then some sightseeing occupied my second and last day in Beirut. Driving me to the airport the next morning, Peter made me promise to stop in Beirut on the way back from Germany.

Before continuing to Germany, I had arranged to stop in Istanbul for two days, my first visit to Turkey. Istanbul, what a city!

The only city in the world that straddles two continents: the old part of the city in Europe and its modern part across the Bosporus in Asia. I took a room in a small hotel in the heart of the historical center, near the famous sights. As a two-day tourist, I had no time to waste.

No other city has so magnificent a location as Istanbul, with its hills and water side by side, and its seaways connecting Europe and Asia, the Black Sea with the Mediterranean, I managed to visit the Topkapi Palace, the Hagia Sophia, the Grand Bazaar and the beautiful 17th century Blue Mosque. I sat for a long time in the Blue Mosque in the early morning, enjoying the peaceful atmosphere and the light that shone through the

Ulla Morris-Carter

windows. This was one of few times I had visited a city where I knew nobody and where I traveled completely alone. I felt a little lonely and wished I could share my experiences with a sympathetic friend. Upon leaving Istanbul I promised myself to travel with a companion the next time around.

When I arrived in Düsseldorf, my mother and my brother greeted me at the airport.

What a joyous reunion with my family! My mother's eyesight unfortunately had not improved, but strong as she had always been, she did not complain, just showed her love and her happiness to see her daughter again.

My brother, on the other hand, appeared to have changed a great deal. He looked so much more grown-up and mature, having taken on an increasing amount of responsibility in the Kirschbaum family business. My mother and my brother had become close business partners, despite my brother's young age of barely 20.

After we arrived at my mother's apartment, she handed me two telegrams. Both from Peter in Beirut.

The contents startled me: "Miss you terribly, afraid I have fallen in love with you, Peter."

The text of the second telegram was similar, full of declarations of love and emphasis on "your unforgettably beautiful blue eyes."

Alone in the bedroom, I could feel myself blushing. I was excited but also confused. Peter was certainly attractive and charming, but these telegrams overwhelmed me at a moment when all my emotions were geared toward my family, whom I hadn't seen in almost two years. Calm down, I told myself. You are jet-lagged and need time to sort out your feelings. I will deal with this tomorrow. Now it's family time.

Two hectic weeks followed, seeing family and friends. I kept debating whether to stop again in Beirut. Though flattered by Peter's telegrams, I didn't know him well enough to be irresistibly drawn to him. However, after yet another telegram from Peter full of more loving declarations and compliments, I decided to stop and see him on my way back to Cairo.

Those days in Beirut turned out to be much too short. We sat up half the night talking about our past, our hopes for the future, our lives. Peter told me of his traumatic WWII experiences. He had been drafted at the age of 16 and while serving on the Russian front toward the end of the war had seen a friend blown to pieces next to him

On my first visit to Beirut.

Ulla Morris-Carter

in a foxhole. Peter was covered in his friend's blood and bits of his body. The horror of the experience was etched into his mind. He still had nightmares filled with bullets, flares and the screams of the wounded.

Because of my own war experiences, I was convinced that I could help him overcome these problems. Why I had thought I was the one to help him, I cannot explain today.

Parting was painful. We had now started on a path toward our future together, except we would not be together. We lived in two different countries. Though Peter traveled occasionally to Cairo on business, I needed an exit visa each time I wanted to leave Egypt. And air travel was expensive. Ignoring these obstacles, Peter proposed that we be engaged and even gave me a gold ring with a blue stone that his mother had worn. The future looked wonderful.

On one of Peter's visits to Cairo he introduced me to a German wartime friend. Andy Elten was a Cairo-based correspondent for the well-known German publication *Süddeutsche Zeitung*. He had recently married a beautiful Egyptian Coptic girl, named Isis. They were a splendid looking pair and they occupied an elegant apartment on the 7th floor of a modern building, overlooking the Nile.

Having borrowed Andy's car for a day, Peter and I returned to his apartment the next day to return car and car keys. Andy and a visiting journalist friend were just leaving his apartment, and the four of us rode down together in a dimly-lit elevator. Andy introduced his friend as Joe Alex Morris, Middle East correspondent for the *New York Herald Tribune*. We parted company quickly because Peter had a plane to catch for his return to Beirut.

As a result of this visit, I became less convinced that I could help Peter. We had long discussions about his anxieties. Nor was I sure any longer that we were made for each other. More important, gossip traveled quickly and easilly from Beirut to Cairo. Peter, I was told, had been seen dining a number of times with an attractive Lufthansa stewardess. And Andy's wife Isis, always direct and outspoken, did not try to hide her negative opinion of Peter.

"You must definitely not consider marriage to Peter. Yes, he is Andy's good friend, but he is not right for you."

After a few more cross-border sightings of Peter and the stewardess, I decided to travel to Lebanon to clarify the situation. I hated living with uncertainty. Obtaining an exit visa was fairly easy this time, unusual in Cairo's bureaucracy, and I flew to Beirut. Peter did not know I was about to descend on him.

Arriving, I found armed soldiers behind sand-bagged fortifications right outside the terminal, and no taxi in sight. I was unaware that Lebanon was approaching yet another crisis. The underlying cause of the 1958 tension was the instability of Lebanon's

Christian-Muslim political coalition under the twin pressures of the Cold War and approaching Lebanese presidential elections.

I wondered what to do. My flight companions had all been picked up by private cars. Luckily, a polite Lebanese man had stopped his car and jumped out to help me.

"May I give you a lift into town?"

Was I ever glad!

"Yes, if it's not too much trouble for you", I said. "I would be most grateful. I have to go to Rue Hamra."

"No problem. I live not far from there. I am sorry for the inconvenience, but trouble is brewing again in Beirut."

He sounded discouraged.

Half an hour later he dropped me off in front of Peter's apartment building. The streets were relatively empty and quiet. The evening curfew was approaching. I rang Peter's doorbell and waited anxiously. My heart was pounding so hard, I was afraid it could be heard by passersby. I had prepared for the possibility of his not being at home. In my overnight bag I carried a letter explaining my intention to cancel our engagement and to return the ring.

After what seemed like an eternity I heard footsteps approaching. When the door finally opened, there stood, not the housekeeper whom I had expected, but Peter. He froze seeing me on his doorstep and was momentarily speechless.

Obviously unprepared, he nonetheless managed to greet me politely, if not warmly and excused himself to make a telephone call.

Aha, I said to myself. He has to cancel his date for tonight. This assumption turned out to be correct, as he later admitted. We had a long and painful conversation. Breaking up is never easy. I left early the next morning for my flight back to Cairo.

A harbinger of later events in my life, I barely managed to leave Beirut before it was engulfed in conflict. Short-lived as this conflict was, it nonetheless required almost 15,000 U.S. troops, ordered by President Eisenhower, to take control of Beirut's airport and to oversee an orderly presidential election. This intervention helped stabilize Lebanon, at least for a few years. As for my love affair, it was finished. I was not heartbroken, just pained and deeply saddened by what was a mistake on both our parts.

Ulla Morris-Carter

One lonely road sign directing us to St. Catherine's.

A Journey to
the Sinai

1958

Richard Weber, a German friend, called one Friday afternoon, his voice upbeat and excited.

"We are planning a trip, an adventure actually," he announced without any introduction. "I hope you will join us."

"Who is "we" and where are you planning to go?"

"We are my parents, my sister, her fiancé and three other German friends. We are trying to obtain military permits to travel to the Sinai, more precisely to the St. Catherine's Monastery in the Sinai Desert."

"To the Sinai Desert?" I repeated almost breathlessly.

Alone, the name Sinai Desert brought up images of Lawrence of Arabia and the wide-open desert I had come to love.

"Fantastic, "I replied. "Count me in."

I had always enjoyed spontaneous and mysterious trips. I agreed without hesitation. My employers would let me leave for a week. I had only heard the name of the St. Catherine's Monastery, but I knew that the Sinai was on the other side of the Suez Canal, bordering the Red Sea. And I also knew that we needed a permit to travel through territory under Egyptian Military control. I had lived in Cairo now for two years. After my calamitous beginnings in this ancient city teeming with close to 14 million people, I had settled in Heliopolis, a suburb of Cairo.

Life in the "Orient," as my mother called it, was exciting for a German girl just turned 24. I loved the muezzin's call to prayer from thousands of minarets despite its waking me up at 6 a.m. every morning. Yes, I missed my family, but I had no desire to return to Germany in the near future. This was my new life, adventurous, different and

Ulla Morris-Carter

exciting, even if occasionally problematic for an unmarried German girl living alone in Cairo. Never before had I been welcomed so warmly despite the fact that I had no social status, nor any other status for that matter.

Struggling with the Egyptian bureaucracy, Richard eventually secured the military permits for all nine of us.

On April 17, 1958 at five a.m., it was a Thursday, we left Heliopolis in two cars. One was a VW Beetle, carrying the three Germans, none of whom I had met before. The other, a Ford 100, a small truck known to be desert-proof and used extensively by oil companies drilling in the Sinai, carried the rest of us. Richard, the driver, and his parents sat in the cabin. His sister, her fiancé and I sat in the open truck bed, outfitted with air mattresses and cushions to soften the impact of potholes.

Our Ford 100 also carried all the food for five days for nine people, water for the trip and gasoline for two cars. Apart from water, St. Catherine's Monastery could not offer anything to the occasional visitor. On the contrary, one was supposed to bring extra food to leave for the small number of Greek Orthodox monks living at the monastery.

But most important, an experienced traveler advised us:

"Bring a bottle of Johnny Walker Whiskey, or better yet, two, for Father Nikoforus, the guardian of the most ancient and most important icons and old texts of the Bible stored at the monastery. Otherwise you may never be able to see any of them."

We learned that the Sinai monastery holds the most important collection of Byzantine icons in the world. Its remoteness had shielded its treasures from conflicts and wars that destroyed other centers of important Christian art.

Richard Weber, his brother-in-law and sister, myself (with pillow), and Richard's father.

Ulla Morris-Carter

The first leg, 80 miles from Cairo to Suez, proceeded without incident. Pith helmets protected us three "open-air-passengers" from the already intense sun. At Suez there was a one-hour delay as our military permits were checked and double-checked. Finally on our way again, we had to wait for a ferry that took us across the Suez Canal to Asia. Another control station.

At last we were on the 100 mile desert road to Abu Zenima. The first part of the road was still partially asphalted and reasonably drivable. Soon that became a sand road with only occasional tire tracks to show us the way.

Suddenly, the sky darkened. By midday the sun had almost disappeared. The desert's sharp clarity vanished. The air was oppressive and hot. We had trouble breathing. There was a strange smell in the air that I could not identify. My first thought was that a rainstorm was approaching, maybe a thunderstorm. But this was Egypt, not Europe. It almost never rained in Egypt in April. What little rain there was tended to come in January. The sun was obscured. Gloom settled over us. My cotton shirt clung to my body. The thermometer read 104° F.

"A Khamseen is approaching," somebody shouted from the VW.

The Khamseen is a hot southwesterly wind blowing from the Sahara. I had already experienced a Khamseen in Cairo and knew that it derived its name from the Arabic word meaning fifty, because its winds blow for about 50 days, mostly in April and May.

Minutes later the roaring storm hit us. Hot, biting, brownish sand filled the air. There seemed to be no air left to breathe. The inside of my nose burned. My skin felt as if thousands of needles were implanted in it. Sand was in my eyes even though my eyelids were shut tight. Sand between my teeth. Sand in my hair. Sand in every pore of my body. We could see no further than 6 feet. The horizon had disappeared.

Huddling behind our truck we tried to cover our heads with our arms. There was no shelter in this open desert. Within minutes our cars were banked in three feet of sand. For half an hour the storm beat down relentlessly.

Finally the whirling sand started to abate. The frightening roar stopped. Eerie calm settled over the desert. The sudden silence was strange, unnerving. Covered in half an inch of dust and sand, we could hardly recognize each other. Colors were no longer distinguishable, our clothes were pure tan.

Now came the tough task of digging out. A sand dune had formed along one side of each car. We heaved shovels, mats and other equipment. Our worst fear was that the motors might be sanded. Digging up the tires as much as possible, we let some air out of them.

Richard started the motor. The truck moved a few feet, then stalled. Nobody spoke. We dared not complain. Silently we returned to digging the tires out of the sand. Some of us prayed. How long would we be stuck in this vast, empty desert? Not a comforting thought.

Ulla Morris-Carter

Digging the Ford out of the sand after the Khamseen.

The motor started again, and this time it did not die. Then both motors were humming, and the cars were moving again. We breathed a collective sigh of relief. But we had lost two precious hours.

By one pm we reached Abu Zenima, three hours later than anticipated. A miners' town in years past, Abu Zenima had once been famous for its copper and turquoise deposits. Now it was nothing but a small, impoverished settlement located directly on the Red Sea. Its current claim to fame was a hardly recognizable gas station, consisting of a single gas pump behind a rusty Nissen hut, a last fragment of civilization before we entered the desert. It was also the only place to pump gas for the rest of our journey.

Left and Right: *Curious villagers and Bedouins on our way to Abu Zenima.*

Ulla Morris-Carter

A lovely cool breeze greeted us. Somewhat elevated above the turquoise waters of the Red Sea, framed by tall mountains behind and opposite the Red Sea, Abu Zenima looked like an ideal place to rest. But time was of the essence. Road signs stopped here. From now on it was finding our way by tire tracks, most of which had been wiped out by the sandstorm. The temperature rose rapidly as we inched along. A hot mistral was blowing from the south through this stony landscape. Still, the views were spectacular. Huge groups of palm trees, monkey-bread-trees and pine trees enlivened the otherwise monotonous views. Camels and dromedary ran freely in front of our cars. The mountain range seemed to grow higher and higher.

Our next stop would be Wadi Feiran[1], only 40 miles from Abu Zenima. For this short distance we needed four and a half hours, including losing our way, a detour of seven miles. After five more times stuck in the sand we were experts at digging out. It was 5:30 p.m. when an unbelievably beautiful sight greeted us: huge dark-green palm trees that felt like a jungle.

It was the oasis of the Wadi Feiran and it offered the most important thing on earth. Water. Dried out by the wind and the sand, I was never more appreciative of the delicious, cool, clean liquid that bubbled up from the well in the center of the oasis. The Greek Orthodox monks of St. Catherine's Monastery must have felt the same when they created a lush garden in this oasis, a garden shaded by a gorgeous arbor of vines.

All of us wanted to stay for a while in the shade of this little paradise and refresh ourselves. And we did, but for only an hour, because another 35 miles of travel lay ahead of us. The scenery was breathtaking. A harsh and waterless landscape, out of which grew jagged, reddish-brown-hued mountains reaching toward the late-afternoon sky.

1. Wadi Feran, Sinai's largest Wadi is a valley that contains one of its most archeologically important stretches and its most lush oasis. It was here that Moses struck a rock with his staff bringing forth a spring so his people could drink. It is also the fabled oasis where the Hebrews camped and battled the Amelecites.

Ulla Morris-Carter

The light of the setting sun turned everything around us into a sea of gold. Minutes later the sun disappeared below the horizon. Suddenly the air was remarkably cool.

The Sinai can be scorching hot during the day but can turn numbingly cold at night. Darkness fell quickly in this mountainous part. We watched the sky turn velvety dark-blue and then blacker than black, with the most brilliant display of stars I had ever seen.

A brilliant full moon received us when we finally reached the monastery. The monastery lies at 4,900 feet surrounded by mountains that reach nearly 9,000 feet. We hardly dared to move for fear that the sound of our shoes hitting the gravely ground would disturb the exquisite silence surrounding us. Beyond the monastery's four walls loomed the mountains.

Grateful for the light of the moon, we searched for an entrance in the seemingly impenetrable walls surrounding the monastery. A small door on the west side seemed too small to be the entrance to this massive, fortress-like building. But when we discovered and then pulled a thick cord attached to the wall next to this door, a bell rang loud and clear. Soon a basket on a pulley was lowered over the wall, landing right next to us. It contained a note requesting our names. Once the night monk on duty, invisible to us, had read our names and established our identity, we were allowed in to the holy monastery of St. Catherine's.

The monks were asleep. Entering the courtyard, we passed a community kitchen with a large open fireplace for cooking. Too tired to think of food, we headed to the few rooms available for visitors. The rooms were simple but very clean. A washbasin in every room, filled with delicious, clear cold water was the most welcome amenity of all. The water, the night guard explained, came from the so-called Moses Well located in the middle of the monastery courtyard. In the darkness, wielding our small flashlights, we washed up as best we could. Electricity at the monastery was only a year old. But as a thank-you gift for the kind hospitality it received, the American film company shooting *The Ten Commandments* here at St. Catherine's in 1957, had left its generator for the monks. For the first time since the establishment of the monastery 1400 years ago, the monks could generate electricity for a limited number of hours every evening.

We heard highlights of St. Catherine's fascinating history. Christians had been coming to this harsh region since the second century. To be near biblical sites, early monks had settled in isolated communities in the southern Sinai. The lives of these hermits were neither easy nor safe. They lived in caves or stone huts, spending their days in prayer and silence. At the hermits' request the Byzantine Empress Helena, ordered the building of a small church, which provided shelter. These Christian hermits suffered not only persecution, but outright attacks by nomadic tribes and Barbarians.

According to legend, the ancient Israelites, led by Moses, wandered this region, when Moses encountered the Burning Bush. The Burning Bush is described in the book

Ulla Morris-Carter

of Exodus as having been on fire, but miraculously was not consumed by the flames. A voice, speaking out of the fire, commanded Moses to climb the mountain. Moses remained in the mountains for forty days and forty nights, after which he received two tablets inscribed with the Ten Commandments from God. Two hundred years after the church was built, the Eastern Roman Emperor Justinian I ordered the construction of the fortified Mount Sinai Monastery (548-565).

With the Burning Bush in its compound, it became a place of pilgrimage—holy to all three monotheistic religions. By the 7th century the monastery faced a new dangerous situation due to the Arab conquest. The monks requested the protection of Mohammed himself, who apparently granted that request and instructed his followers to protect the monastery. Even Napoleon, who conquered Egypt in 1798, placed the monastery under his protection.

Saint Catherine, after whom the monastery is named, was a martyr who died upholding her Christian faith. She was revered both in Byzantium and in the West. According to legend, her beheaded body was carried by angels to the top of the highest mountain in the Sinai, later named Mount Saint Catherine.

Early the morning after our arrival I was awakened by the sound of four bells in the bell tower. When I looked down at the courtyard from the balcony running alongside the second floor, the first thing I noticed was a Mosque from the 10th or 11th century right next to the Christian bell tower.

A prominent Egyptian newspaper, *Al Ahram*, ran a story in 2002 about St Catherine's under the headline, 'A Lily in the Wilderness':

> St. Catherine's geographical isolation "along with the consummate diplomacy practiced by its monks has ensured that the periods that followed, occupation by the British, independence, the Nasser era, the Israeli occupation and the Sadat and Mubarak years have largely washed over the monastery's walls, leaving it unaffected."

We spent most of our first day recovering from our journey, exploring the monastery, and learning more of its history. Saint Catherine's was built on the only available level land, a small plateau surrounded by, jagged, waterless mountains. Climbing the surrounding hills, we again experienced the solitude and stillness of this spiritual place. Not even mosquitos or flies or birds disturbed this silence. They didn't seem to exist here.

We were delighted to discover a lush garden behind the monastery. It contained cypress and olive trees, almond groves and vegetables. The dark green cypresses contrasted sharply with the sunlit mountains beyond.

Never before had I seen a bluer sky, so intense that it appeared unnatural. The weather on this first day of February was absolutely perfect. The light, dazzlingly bright, was almost hurtful to ones eyes.

Ulla Morris-Carter

Above: *St. Catherine's Monastery looking from above.* **Right:** *View from below.*

Our bottles of whiskey for Father Nikophorus evidently worked well. Not grumpy at all, he showed us some of the hidden treasures—ancient icons in vivid colors, some dating from the 5th century, supreme examples of Byzantine art. Lighting devices, candelabra and enclosed candle stands, were placed in such a way that the church was illuminated even on dark days or night vigils. Icons, we were told, were created especially for this kind of illumination. The gold on their surfaces sparkled in the flickering light of hundreds of candles. Lights were a most important part of the early Byzantine period. Candles and lamps had to be continually tended and replenished.

Yet another unbelievable piece of history appeared in front of us: the second-oldest bible in the world: the Codex Sinaitus. It is supposed to be one of four great codices—an ancient copy, handwritten on parchment, in Greek letters, dating back to the fourth century.

Another memorable discovery was the charnel house. Since there was no room for a cemetery, monks who died were buried just long enough for their bodies to decompose. Then their bones were unearthed, collected and placed into the charnel house: arm and leg bones in one chamber, skulls in another. Only the bones of the abbots were allowed to remain together and were placed in a small compartment in the wall. It was frightening to look at piles of human bones. The dry climate eliminated any odors.

The next day we climbed 7,200 foot Mount Moses (known as Jebel Musa in Arabic, meaning the Mountain of Moses). An icy wind blew when we reached the top. We were glad to have brought along our wool sweaters. Beauty surrounded us wherever we looked. The silence at this mountain top made for a spiritual experience, hard to imagine in the busy lives we had left behind.

Day three brought one more adventure. Richard, his mother and I climbed the higher and more difficult Mount St. Catherine, at 8,000 feet. We started at 6:00 in the

Ulla Morris-Carter

Top Left: *Father Nikophoros, the guardian of the most important collection of Byzantine icons.* **Top Right:** *The Charnal House of skulls.* **Bottom Right:** *Myself, Richard Weber and his mother at the top of Mount St. Catherine, 2680m (8793 ft).* **Bottom Left:** *The kitchen*

morning with the sun rising, walking into a translucent, glowing dawn. The cloudless sky changed from pink to amber to brilliant blue. By 10:45 a.m. we had already reached the highest point. Again we shivered from icy winds despite radiant sunshine. After an hour and a half of rest we descended, refreshed. We walked in complete silence. Discovering delicious rainwater in a three foot hole, we drank greedily and splashed ourselves with this cool liquid. Exhilerated and sunburned, we hurried on and entered the monastery at four in the afternoon.

Meanwhile our travel companions had managed to provisionally repair the Volkswagen's broken car battery by filling it with sulfuric acid and sealing it with wax. Our Ford 100 had lost three of its shock absorbers, and only six of the eight cylinders were still working. Richard worried that we might not have enough gas to make it back to the infamous gas station at Abu Zenima.

Ulla Morris-Carter

On the road.

Hoping for the best, we left at 6:30 am. It was another glorious day. Of course we got stuck in the sand again. But in the meantime we had become such experts in digging out that we no longer lost a lot of time.

Unfortunately, our Ford, without all the weight of the food and gasoline, was now very light. The three of us in the truck bed bounced up and down, and occasionally engaged in improvised gymnastics to put more weight at the tail end. Richard would drive full-speed through the sandy stretches, which meant that we in the back disappeared in a cloud of dust. The VW blew a tire. We had a spare and it was quickly repaired. Just when we arrived on the desert road to Abu Zenima, Richard realized our gas pump was broken.

And—we didn't have enough gas to reach Abu Zenima.

Never despair! We were lucky again. Out of nowhere appeared a truck, another Ford 100 just like ours, belonging to the Belgian Oil Company drilling for oil in this region. The driver, a friendly chap, took us to the company's workshop where all spare parts and gas were available. Only men lived out here in the desert. Consequently we women were quickly removed from the scene and ushered into a side room. The oil company had two private planes, a radio station, tennis and basketball courts and an open-air cinema. We were impressed. Without special permission no one was allowed out here. But the oil company employees and the chief engineer were welcoming and very helpful. Not only did they allow us to stay, they repaired our car completely, filled it up with gas and then invited us for a meal. Two hours later we were on our way again, grateful to have been so lucky.

The last part of our journey passed without incident. Only once more did we have to dig out of the sand before reaching the Suez Canal. The ferry took us across. It was

Ulla Morris-Carter

already dark when we embarked on the last 75 miles. By 10:30 p.m. we were back in Cairo, exhausted and exhilarated. It had been the trip of a lifetime.

Many years later I would write this little poem in a workshop, having been allowed less than 10 minutes to compose it.

Wind—Storm—Sandstorm

The soft desert wind grew and blew
Into a storm—a fierce storm
Tearing at the sands of the infinite desert.
It blew hard, hit my face full force,
Settled in my nose, mouth, eyebrows,
Scratched its sandy claws into my eyes,
Burnt fierce, my face.
Breath almost impossible,
I hid under the truck,
Hoping to escape the eye of the storm,
Hoping to escape before turning into a sand statue—
My face already a mask of brown and yellow.

St. Catharine's monastery from above.

Ulla Morris-Carter

Joe Alex and I on the tennis court at the Gezirah Sporting Club.

MEETING JOE ALEX MORRIS

CAIRO 1958

The Middle East, as far as I can ascertain, has never been, and probably never will be, calm, stable or without conflict for any length of time. 1958 was no exception.

Arab Nationalism, an ideology and a political force, was in the making. Growing numbers of educated Arabs were becoming enamored of Egyptian President Nasser's Pan Arabism movement. Nasser formed a union between Egypt and neighboring Syria that was later joined by Yemen. This union became known as the United Arab Republic, *UAR*.

A news flash suddenly announced the assassination of 23-year-old King Faisal II of Iraq during a military coup. He was killed together with his mother, his younger brother and wife and most of his household. Iraqi Prime Minister Nuri es-Said attempted to escape but was captured and executed in July, 1958. Faisal's regime marked the end of the Hashemite monarchy in Iraq, which thereafter became a republic. Only Jordan continued as the Hashemite Kingdom, ruled by the then 23-year-old King Hussein, a cousin of the assassinated King Faisal. King Hussein was frequently referred to as "the brave little King," following his ascendancy to the throne when only 16 years old. His grandfather, King Abdullah, had been assassinated in 1951 at the al-Aqsa mosque in Jerusalem in the presence of young Hussein.

After my return from Lebanon in early July, my life, just like the Arab world, was in turmoil and in need of a period of calm and reflection. My job kept me very busy with the government contract to supply all Egyptian villages with their first drinking water pumps, a huge undertaking. Our Cairo office consisted only of two German engineers

Ulla Morris-Carter

and me. We worked late during the hot Egyptian summer with little or no break. Even I learned to talk and write about pump outputs and technical details like a professional.

My 25th birthday was approaching in October, when George Ekonomakis, a Greek-Egyptian jewellery designer and good friend, invited me out for a birthday dinner. George, always immaculately dressed in three-piece suits regardless of Cairo temperatures, was an intelligent and gentle person. Quite unlike my other friends and acquaintances, he drove a Rolls Royce, which somehow suited his personality. On our way to the restaurant, we had to stop at a busy corner where a policeman was trying to direct traffic. Cairo's evening traffic, reckless, relentless and unbelievably chaotic, was not moving fast. Black-robed women on foot were competing with donkey carts, bicyclists and ancient European or American cars for a piece of the road.

A VW station wagon pulled up next to us.

"Hello Ulla," I heard someone shout over the horrendous din.

I recognized my German journalist friend Andy Elten.

"Hello Andy," I shouted back at him.

"Have you won the lottery, Ulla? Pretty fancy car you are riding in," Andy yelled through his open car window close to my side of the car.

He knew, of course, that I didn't own the car. I didn't even know how to drive.

A day or two later Andy and his wife Isis invited me to dinner. Also at the dinner table was the man Andy re-introduced as Joe Alex Morris, *New York Herald Tribune* Middle East correspondent. According to Andy, I had apparently met Joe in that dimly-lit elevator almost half a year ago. Joe had just moved his Middle East base from Beirut to Cairo. And, so the legend goes, Joe had remembered me from that elevator ride,and had also seen me in the by-now famous Rolls Royce with George Ekonomakis at the wheel, while he and Andy were riding together to a press conference. A lively evening at Andy and Isis's house with great conversation, interesting stories and, above all, a lot of laughter, made it an unforgettable dinner party.

Joe Alex Morris phoned me the next day, asking politely whether I might accompany him to a party at an Italian correspondent's house. I was rather flattered to be invited so quickly by this charming American journalist and gladly accepted. Joe was a handsome 31-year-old fellow, intelligent, artistic, and a writer with a quick mind and a wonderful sense of humor. He offered to pick me up at my residence.

I had recently moved from Heliopolis to central Cairo to be closer to my workplace. Mme. Bichara, my landlady, a widow, had rented me a lovely room with a large terrace at 32 Sharia Sabri Abou Alam, on the 7th floor of an old Cairo building overlooking part of the city. She hurried to the front door when Joe rang the bell, supposedly just to let in the visitor. Of course she wanted to know who I was going out with. She withdrew quickly after polite greetings and a bit of small-talk, but not without giving me a wink of approval.

During our taxi ride to the Italian correspondent's house, Joe told me about his father. Joe Alex Morris Sr., also a writer and journalist, was well known among the press corps as the foreign editor of *United Press (UP)* during World War II, and later as the foreign editor of the *New York Herald Tribune* and the *Saturday Evening Post.* He had covered the Blitz in London and reported from other warring European countries during the war, including a brief stint in Berlin. Working under him at *UP* had been such young, later famous, journalists as Walter Cronkite, Merriman Smith and Howard K. Smith. I marveled at how a German war child was now enjoying the company of a former enemy, and listening to his father's war stories.

"I love to play tennis," Joe told me while still driving.

Terrific, I thought. I was also an enthusiastic, though not terribly accomplished, tennis player.

"We must play together some day soon," I answered. "Do you ever go to the Gezirah Sporting Club? I like to swim there and play tennis. They have great clay tennis courts," I mentioned casually.

"As a matter of fact I just became a member of the Gezirah Sporting Club," Joe said.

We made a date to meet for tennis the next day.

Joe and I at the tennis courts.

For reasons I never learned, the Italian correspondent had decided on a costume party. Not dressed for the occasion, I said to our host:

"The least I can do is take off my shoes."

It was a lively party with drinks, food and dancing. Our enthusiastic Italian host asked me to dance, and in so doing he managed to step on my now shoeless right foot with such force that I thought I was going fall. I had to sit down. I was in serious pain.

Our host was inconsolable, but understood when I said I needed to go home to ice my foot. Hating to take Joe away from this joyous event and his many colleagues, I suggested I take a taxi home. Joe, of course, would not hear of my leaving alone.

The elevator in my house was, as often happened, not working. Walking up seven floors of high-ceilinged apartments with a painful foot, was an adventure. Joe, always the gentleman, tried to carry me, but I was really too heavy. With Joe supporting me as

Ulla Morris-Carter

best he could, we moved in slow motion, all the while distracting ourselves by talking about our lives and such. By the time we had reached the seventh floor, stopping frequently and resting every so often on the cool marble stairs, we knew a lot more about each other than we had earlier. Two days later, an X-ray confirmed that I had a cracked bone and serious bone bruises in my right foot.

So began an exciting relationship that moved ahead quickly. We spent as much time together as we could manage, both of us being quite busy. As happens occasionally in life, one meets a person with whom one is in harmony, in full understanding of the task at hand without questioning every move. That was true for us. We enjoyed each other's company immensely despite coming from very different backgrounds, and despite the fact that my English was by no means perfect. I had good technical English, but my conversational English still left something to be desired.

Scarcely two weeks into our relationship, Joe had to travel to Syria, Iran and Iraq. We missed each other terribly. He was away for more than three weeks. I was delighted to receive a cable from him at my office. He was in Baghdad:

"Life is hell, ohne Dich," it read.

That cable prompted the Baghdad censorship office to order Joe to appear immediately to explain the text. Iraqi censors read every word leaving the country.

"What do you mean by 'life is hell in Baghdad?'" a furious censor questioned Joe.

The man didn't speak German and consequently didn't understand that "ohne Dich" meant only "without you." The matter was amicably settled after a translator explained that the American correspondent had only sent a love cable to his lady friend and had not meant to reflect on life in Baghdad. The matter amicably settled, Joe was dismissed with best wishes for a long and happy life.

He returned to Cairo at the end of November, but short trips to Jordan and Syria were still on his agenda before Christmas. His many journeys covering Middle Eastern upheavals, were, unbeknownst to me at the time, a way of his life.

Christmas was approaching. Both of us, without families nearby, knew we wanted to spend Christmas together. Moslems and Christians alike celebrated Christmas in Cairo with firecrackers, colored lights and, what else? lots of parties. Joe presented me with a most beautiful book, *EGYPT: Paintings from Tombs and Temples*.

We spent time with friends, including my long-time friend Souraya, whom I had traveled with on the *S.S. Esperia* on my first journey to Cairo almost three years earlier. Souraya and her parents invited us to their vacation house near the Great Giza Pyramid. It felt good to be with people who were as close to family as we had.

Sadly, however, we also had to prepare for Joe's long absence right after Christmas and into the New Year. Syria, Iraq and Iran were on his schedule, as well as Pakistan

Ulla Morris-Carter

and Afghanistan. Returning to Cairo after the first three weeks of his trip, Joe could spend only three short days before continuing to Pakistan and Afghanistan.

While he was away, I worked on and decorated his still fairly new furnished apartment. It was located in a lovely old three-story building in Zamalek, on a quiet tree-shaded street, Sharia Willcocks. Zamalek, on the large Nile River island of Gezirah, occupies the Northern part of the island. It lies between downtown Cairo and Giza. Known as a beautiful garden area, it is the quietest part of Cairo and the choice location for embassies, schools and foreigners. Cooler than downtown Cairo and close to the famous Gezirah Sporting Club, established in 1883 by the British, Zamalik was Cairo's most desirable residential area.

Joe was obviously delighted when he walked into his apartment, seeing it now decorated and warmed up with flowers and personal items. Walking around, excited to be in his own place, he suggested that it might be even more wonderful if we could enjoy this place together, or better yet, spend our future together.

That proposal, casual as it was, left me momentarily speechless. Yes, we had indeed much enjoyed our time together, felt most comfortable with each other and missed each other when not together. But a future together had not quite entered into my thinking. After all, we had only known each other for ten weeks, six of which he had been away. On the other hand I knew that he was the person I wanted to be with. There was no doubt about that.

Joe thought it might be advisable to write to his parents and explain. His parents were planning a trip to the Middle East, to Cairo to visit their son, then to Morocco where Joe's father was researching a story for *National Geographic* magazine.

Dear Folks,

Welcome, in advance to the exotic Middle East. I think your idea of visiting me in Cairo is fine, but if I may be permitted to interfere just a bit, I'd like to give a hand in your planning, for personal reasons.

First of all, I think you should come to Egypt first. For one thing Europe will be too cold in the middle of March. Egypt will be just right. So why not come here and then go up to Europe?

. . . one of the reasons I think so is hanging over my shoulder right now. Her name is Ulla, and I think that by the time you arrive here we should be through all the complications involved in getting authorization to get married in Egypt. We would like you to be here, and will also try to get her mother to come down from Düsseldorf.

Ulla is 25, an in-between blonde, with eyes that look like peppermint Life-Savers, only a little bluer. She is 1.68 meters tall, 58 kilos, and also has very important other statistics which she won't tell me now. If I am very lucky she'll be in favor of

Ulla Morris-Carter

the idea by the time you get here, so I invite you now. She speaks a little English, in addition of course to German and Arabic, and, if necessary, can interpret for you when you talk to my prospective mother-in-law.

The greatest complication so far is the fact that I am not baptized. Ulla, like most Rhinelanders is Catholic, and, for her mother's sake more than anything else, would like to have a church wedding. Her mother, a widow since the war, runs a Klischee Anstalt (engraving company), founded by Ulla's father, which is sort of an industrial design and engraving firm. Like Dad, she needs a rest after building up the business again out of the ruins of the war. Ulla is writing to her to come down, and we hope she will.

You might think this is all a bit sudden. It is. I knew Ulla slightly before I moved to Cairo [from Beirut], and of course have improved on this since I've been here. Neither of us wants to wait any longer than we have to, but the formalities should take that long. We have been thinking about it for some time, but I didn't make any serious proposition until yesterday when I returned from Baghdad. My timing was great, but now I've got to go off to Karachi Saturday, so I won't see her for another two or three weeks. I suppose it's a good introduction for her to the kind of life she can expect, at least in the near future. I hope she can take the separation more easily than I expect I will . . .

For the next three weeks there won't be any progress at all. I am off to Karachi early Saturday . . . I'll be stopping off, enroute back, in Teheran (definite) and Afghanistan (possible). A helluva time to go away, but Ulla may as well get used to this life from the start. If things like this will have any effect on our future, which I doubt very much, it's best to know now.

Must sign off for now. Will write you from Karachi, Kabul, or Teheran if I get a chance.

Love Joe.

This letter must have been a shock to his parents. Until then they had never heard of the German girl who was about to be married to their son.

```
Beirut.  Beginning with entry on March 10, 1959, with me stopping over in
Cairo on way to Ethiopia: "Dinner tonight at Joe Alex Morris, Jr's flat, with
his bride, a German girl Ulla.  They'll be married April 4--day after my
birthday--and suggest I come back and we could have fine combination bachelor-
birthday party.  But maybe too far from Ethiopia.  She very pretty, vivacious,
competent and should make fine wife for Joe.  For honeymoon, they going to
use George Weller's cottage in Kyrenia, and sailboat...."
```

A later letter from Gordon Gaskill, correspondent for Readers Digest, *to Joe Sr., in which he recounts from his diary, meeting Joe and his bride to be.*

Ulla Morris-Carter

GETTING MARRIED
IN CAIRO

1959

Getting married in Cairo on a houseboat on the Nile? Does that sound romantic? Yes, indeed, and romantic it was, but there were a few bumps on the way to the altar.

Every couple preparing to marry envisions a special wedding to mark what is, arguably, the most important day of their lives. That was true for Joe and me as well. Having observed and experienced the nerve-racking preparations for some of our friends' weddings, often leaving bride and mother-of-the-bride at the edge of a nervous breakdown, we were determined to not let it happen to us. Ours would be a small wedding, intimate and joyous, with a minimum of fuss and preparation. Our families would arrive shortly before the actual wedding day, leaving our mothers with no time to worry about dress codes, bridesmaid's dresses, hair-dos, flower arrangements, etcetera. Joe and I would prepare our own wedding.

Joe's letter to his parents had only hinted at some looming problems. Little did we know what awaited us, an American journalist and a German secretary/office manager, trying to get married in Egypt. Foreigners frequently wed at their embassies, but because we were of different nationalities, that option was not available to us.

David Holden, a dear friend and chief Middle East correspondent for the *London Sunday Times*, was to be Joe's best man. He was happy to offer us his home for our reception. His was no ordinary house. David lived on a houseboat, a Nile *Dahabie*, an antiquated wooden paddlewheel steamboat dubbed *The Saphir*, that was moored permanently at the edge of the Nile in Giza. *The Saphir* had quite an illustrious history. At least three of our correspondent friends had lived there for varying periods.

Ulla Morris-Carter

One of these, *Associated Press* correspondent David Lancashire, who lived there briefly with his wife Dedee, later recalled their floating home:

> The Saphir hadn't sailed anywhere for years. Still, she remained unmistakably nautical: a tall funnel amidship, engines shrouded down below and a wheelhouse above, a huge shuttered stateroom, a galley and a saloon and deck cabins, and a poop big enough for dancing. Tattered canvas awnings hung between the decks to fend off the Egyptian sun. The main deck was only a foot above the water, so the Nile lapped past a few inches from the stateroom door. And from the upper deck we could watch the life of the river and hear the call to prayers from a mosque across the water, and the creak of the big felucas toiling past with their wing-like sails and cargoes of earthenware pots or bundles of wood.

Wedding invitation and reception card.

With Joe traveling and usually unreachable, I scrambled to deal with the Egyptian bureaucracy. I collected documents, had papers translated into Arabic, researched the specific legal requirements for an Egyptian civil marriage, obtained doctors' certificates and declared under oath that I had never been married before. One important issue was a sworn statement that the parties involved were of Moslem, Christian or Jewish faith. Evidently there was no exception for a person, such as Joe, without a religion. Everybody had to be something in Egypt. Eventually, with his parents help Joe procured a paper stating that he was a Christian, on grounds, not included in the paper, that his mother had once been baptized.

While traveling, Joe wrote from Kabul, from Karachi, from Teheran, from Beirut. None of his letters made my long wait for his return any easier. Of the five months we had known each other before getting married, he had spent three months traveling:

Ulla Morris-Carter

Karachi, January 19, 1959

This will be but a short note, I'm afraid. I have to go out with a big landowner in a few minutes, then have lunch with the minister of information. Very busy, nicht wahr? But it's good, because the bloody Baghdad Pact is over with and I can try to do some real work for a change. It was a very disappointing meeting, with little news and only the usual complaints. Now for a quick as possible investigation into the Pakistan situation, and then off to Afghanistan. Unfortunately I have been delayed a couple of days because there are only two flights a week into Kabul. So I'll go there Tuesday, and try to get to Teheran on Sunday, which means, my darling, I won't see you until the following weekend at the earliest . . .

I have many things to tell you, but they will have to wait until I have more time to write. My only complaint is that I am covered with mosquito bites. It's very warm here and they keep me awake all night. I get up once or twice every night and go on a hunt, but now I have changed rooms and hope that the nightly attacks will end. Karachi is very dull, especially without you being here . . .

Karachi, February 2, 1959

Today was a bad day. I hope writing you will make me feel better. The president is sick in bed, so the interview I was supposed to be having right now was cancelled. I made a mistake about the flight to Kabul, so now I have to wait until Thursday. This is very painful because I have finished my work here and want to get the rest of the trip over with so that I can return to you as soon as possible . . .

Joe wrote a loving letter in German language—charming, funny, with numerous amusing mistakes. He certainly deserved an "A" for effort:

Teheran, February 8, 1959

Meine Schatze,

Ich will nur ein kurz Brief schreiben weil es sehr schwierig ist fuer mich auf Deutsch zu sagen was ich will. Aber es ist auch noetig wenn ich in Zukunft nach nur Deutschspraechige Verwandte schreiben muss. Also, ueben, Morris.

Es ist auch sehr schwirig Dir zu sagen wie einsam ich bin. Hoffentlich wir werden wieder zusammen nach fier Tagen. Entweder Mittwoch oder Donnerstag ich werde bei dir sein. Aber je vier tage sind zuviel.

Es schneit hier und natuerlich ist es sehr kalt. Kairo macht mein Blut schwach (?) Aber die Atmosphaere ist sehr schoen. Teheran ist hoch, und wenn es nicht schneit, sehr trocken. Wir muessen hier zusammen kommen naechstmals. Bestimmet, mein Liebling? Ich denke wir sollten alle Dinge zusammen machen. Ohne Dich ist es genau wie ohne meine rechte Hand...

Ich bin eben von einem grossen Mittagessen zurueckgekommen. Bei einem alten Freund aus Beirut, ein Englaender. Er wohnt hoch im Unterberg, aussen der Stadt

Ulla Morris-Carter

(in der Naehe, ich meine). Ich habe meine Story nach dem Telegraf Amt gebracht, und bald muss wieder ausgehen fuer Abendessen mit AFP –Korrespondent, der einzige Auslaender Jounalist der im Teheran stationiert it. Er ist Alsatien, bei Name Faust, un ein sehr richtiger Kerl. Vielleicht kennst Du ihn. Er war vor der brutalischer Angriffe im Kairo.

Vergiss nicht, meine Schatze, mir zu schreiben beim St. Georges Hotel wenn Du etwas anderes von Beirut moechtest. Ich hoffe beim Air Liban nach Kairo zu fliegen, aber will Dir telegrafiern aus Beirut. Ich liebe Dich wie nie zuvor. Glaube mir. Nicht mehr versuchen diese Lage zu verstehen. Es ist, und davon bin ich zufriedig. Aber niemals zufriedig ohne Dich und weit von dir hier. Diese Lage endet sehr bald, inshallah.

Und bitteschoen, entschuldige du mein Deutsch. Du musst mir lernen, besser zu schreiben. Du musst mir vielen lernen, nicht wahr? Oder, ich sollte sagen, wir muessen viele zusammen lernen. Mit gern, bei mir. Dein, Joe

English translation:

My darling,

Just a short letter because it is too difficult for me to write in German a,nd to say exactly what I want to say. But if in the future I need to write to my German-speaking relatives, it's necessary [to learn writing in German]. Therefore, practice, Joe Morris!

It's also very difficult to tell you how lonely I feel. I hope we'll be together again after four days—either Wednesday or Thursday. But even four days are too long.

It's snowing, and of course very cold. Cairo has made my blood thin. But the surroundings are beautiful. Teheran lies high, and when it's not snowing, very dry. We must come here together the next time. For sure, my darling. I think we should do everything together. Without you it feels as if I am without my right hand.

I just returned from a big luncheon at the house of an old friend from Beirut, a British fellow. He lives in the foothills near the city. I just finished writing my story and carried it to the Telegraph Office. Soon I have to go out again, this time for dinner with the AFT (Agence France Press) correspondent. He is the only foreign correspondent based in Teheran. He is from Alsace-Lorraine, and his name is Faust—a really great guy. Maybe you know him? He lived in Cairo before the brutal upheavals.

Don't forget, my darling, to write to me at the St. Geroges Hotel in Beirut, if you would like me to bring you anything else from Beirut. I hope to fly to Cairo on Air Liban, but will cable you from Beirut. I love you, like never before—believe me!. I no longer try to understand this situation. It is what it is, and I am happy about it. But I am never happy without you and far away from you. But, inshallah, this situation will soon end.

Ulla Morris-Carter

And, please, excuse my German. You must teach me how to improve my writing. You have to teach me a lot, right? Or, I should say, we have to learn a lot together. That is fine with me. Your Joe

Our courtship continued via letters and cables. The mail in the Middle East was not known for speed or reliability. I struggled alone trying to learn whether we could have a church wedding, or for that matter, anything other than an Egyptian civil ceremony, a mere formality that would take place in the Civil Marriage Registration Office at the Ministry of Justice. A recent acquaintance, a German Franciscan father, Father Ludwig, came to the rescue:

"To marry you in the Church is out of the question as long as one of you is not baptized," Father Ludwig announced in no uncertain terms. "We could ask for special dispensation from the Vatican in Rome, but it will take a long time. Or, Mr. Morris could consent to be baptized, which will also take time. Or," he added after a long silence, "I could possibly marry you in the small chapel of the School of the German Sisters in Bab El-Louk, Cairo."

"Does that also need special dispensation from Rome?" I asked, fearing the worst.

He hesitated slightly before answering.

"Here in Cairo I am my own Bishop," he said, giving me a reassuring smile. Just tell Mr. Morris to see me so that I can instruct him in the Catechism and give him some advice about any children who might be born into this union."

Breathing a sigh of relief, I was dismissed.

After six long weeks, Joe finally returned. One morning on our way into downtown Cairo, we decided to stop at the Ministry of Justice to ask whether we finally had all our papers together and documents in order. We had never been inside the Ministry of Justice, a big imposing old building located on teeming Lazouglu Square. It had seen better days. I was on my way to work and to the market. Joe was on his way to the *United Press* office. Joe could read the signs inside the buildng, all of them in Arabic, directing us to the Registration Office on the fourth floor Annex. We climbed well-worn marble stairs and found ourselves in a huge high-ceilinged room reserved for registration purposes.

The noise was unbelievable. Utter chaos seemed to reign. The room was packed with people who stood in clusters around different desks or tables, Kohl-eyed village women in full black *niqaab*, full covering, or the slightly less modest covering of the *hijab*, and by men in *galabyas*, the long, shirt-like garment worn by men in Egypt. The galabyas were either striped or plain white. Was I the only Western woman in there? Men were staring at me despite my modest blue cotton skirt and white, long-sleeved blouse. I felt totally out of place.

Ulla Morris-Carter

We discovered that this registration office not only registered people who wanted to get married. It also served for the registration of people who had died, of babies that had been born and farm animals that had been traded. The wailing of the women who registered the death of their husbands or children, seemed to be out of key with the wailing of women on the other side of the room. Those who could neither read nor write used their inked thumbs to sign papers.

Finally, in the far corner, we found the registrar in charge of "Official Marriage Contracts", a Notary Public. If I had imagined a wood-paneled office, a dark-suited registrar sitting behind an imposing desk, flowers on either side, this certainly was not it. We waited in line only to discover that the registrar spoke no English or, any language other than Arabic. Most men in the room wore *galayias*, but he, as a civil servant, was dressed in western style, grey trousers and a well-pressed white shirt. He was not overly tall, but he made sure he looked important by straightening his upper body and lifting his head when we approached. In our rudimentary Arabic we asked at what date and time we could have an appointment to get married. Introducing himself as Abdel Aziz Wahdan, the registrar announced without hesitation:

"Stay right here, I'll marry you now. No need to come back. Where are your witnesses?"

Joe and I looked at each other, dumbfounded. We had difficulty understanding his rapid flow of Arabic and requested that he speak slowly or, better yet, find a translator.

"We do not provide translators. Where are your witnesses?" He repeated, this time in slow Arabic.

"Witnesses?" Joe questioned. "We have no witnesses. We had not planned to be married today," he managed to answer.

"No problem, we have witnesses here, I'll call them. They will be here momentarily. You will pay only a modest fee (bakshish, bribe) for their services."

He turned around and gestured toward two galabyah-clad men who seemed to be standing ready to be called for such services. They were introduced to us as "witnesses who are sane and know the contracting persons . . ."

The first one was Sayed Ahmed Mostafa, 24 Sharia Port-Said, ID card No. 19955/1958 el Khalife. We were shown his ID card, as if that made any difference to us. The second was Hafez Mostafa, 8 Zahr el Rabie, El Sayeda, ID card No. 30071/1956 el Sayeda. Sayeda evidently meant the district in which their ID cards were issued.

Hafez Mostafa was a handsome, tall man of Nubian extraction. Both witnesses wore white galabyas and small white crochet caps. They greeted us with respect and seemed familiar with the routine. The registrar checked our documents (luckily already translated into Arabic), nodded agreement, stamped and numbered them.

"Thirteen documents in all," he stated with satisfaction.

We had long since learned that the more documents one could produce, the better

Ulla Morris-Carter

the results. Without further delay he turned his attention to Joe, and I guessed, rightly or wrongly, that he might be asking him to "repeat after me," the marriage vows. The Arabic alphabet doesn't include vowels, which means that reading foreign names is a bit of a guessing game. I heard what presumably was my name when he referred to "Nursula Ann Mary" (instead of Ursula Annemarie Agnes, which are my proper first three names according to my birth certificate and passport).

No family name was ever mentioned, only Joe's passport number.

All Joe could answer was: "Yes, I accept."

Now the registrar turned towards me and I assumed that it was my turn.

He asked something incomprehensible, which prompted me to whisper to Joe: "What did he say?"

"It's my name, repeat it!"

All I had heard was "Joe Leeks" and again no family name.

Following Joe's example I mumbled, "I accept."

Nobody had warned us of any of this. The registrar then began writing rapidly on white, newspaper-sized, lined sheets of paper while we were still standing there, silent and puzzled. So this was our marriage ceremony, I thought. What a miserable way to get married.

The registrar had already filled two of the large sheets of paper with his calligraphy-like script, writing in Arabic from right to left, when he suddenly stopped, looked around, listened intently to an announcement that came over the loudspeaker, and said to us:

"The department is closed now. President Gamal Abdel Nasser has just announced a day of mourning for the dead of Mosul in Iraq. Come back tomorrow and we'll finish." [1]

With this announcement our registrar closed his books, put what would become our marriage contract into a folder, bowed respectfully and departed.

We couldn't believe what was happening to us. Walking out of the building into bright sunshine and the bustle of Cairo streets, we both burst out into unstoppable laughter. Who ever heard of a half-married couple?

"Let's celebrate our half marriage at Groppi's with a cup of coffee and a croissant," Joe suggested.

Groppi, on Midan Soliman Pasha, was Cairo's best-known teahouse and cafe, a crowded European style place that accommodated women as well as men. It had once been the most celebrated tearoom in the eastern Mediterranean, founded by a Swiss Chocolatier, Giacomo Groppi. Mr. Groppi was known for producing the best chocolates in Egypt. Even King Farouk had ordered boxes of them to send to his friends and relatives.

1. *A few days earlier a number of disgruntled Iraqi army officers from conservative Sunni Arab families who opposed the Iraqi leader, Brigadier Abdel Karim Qasim for his increasing links with the Communists, had attempted a pro-Egyptian coup, which failed. Many of the officers were massacred.*

Ulla Morris-Carter

On our way to Groppi we passed two little shoeless boys with dirty hands and flies around their eyes, sitting at the entrance to one of the nearby shops. They were selling necklaces of jasmine flowers on a cotton string. Their thin arms were loaded down with these necklaces, which they swung in the air and in front of every passer-by. The scent was strong and deliciously sweet. Joe bargained with the boys and bought two necklaces, which he put around my neck.

Wearing those lovely white flower necklaces I almost felt like a bride. We had a splendid late breakfast. Then we went our separate ways to do the routine chores we had set out to do in the first place.

Next morning, appropriately dressed and in the proper frame of mind for such a serious occasion, we returned to the Ministry of Justice. Abdel Aziz seemed to be expecting us. Without further ado he produced our unfinished Marriage Certificate and continued to write for the next half hour, in silence. Then he handed us the five-page hand-written document, signed and sealed, with a beautiful red ribbon attached. He congratulated us warmly. We paid our fees and departed happily, and legally, married. Before leaving we glanced briefly at our Marriage Contract, which we couldn't read except for the first sentence:

"On Wednesday, the ninth of Ramadan, 1378—the year of the Hegira—(March 18, 1959) at 11:10 a.m. at the registration office in Cairo . . ."

Outside, we discovered that some of our journalist friends had meanwhile found out about our civil marriage adventure. Carrying flowers, they were waiting for us to emerge from the Ministry of Justice. Congratulations, laughter and best wishes bubbled over us.

Among the wellwishers were two Egyptian journalists who scolded us for not having consulted them:

"You hire a lawyer and let him handle the civil marriage," said Ibrahim. "My wife would never have set foot into this registry. Our lawyer handled everything."

At that point I was still working with the German company. Mohamed, our messenger and helper, was greatly interested in my progress. He had only recently learned how to read and write, slowly at first, but he was improving by the day. He made delicious coffee, the sweet Arabic, *baladi*, coffee served in small cups, or mint tea in little glasses. And he ran errands. Phones were often not working and messages frequently arrived faster on foot than by waiting for the phones to come back on.

A couple of days after my so-called wedding ceremony, Mohamed had just finished reading his daily section of the morning newspaper when I entered the office.

He had barely greeted me with his friendly *sabakh el kher*, good morning, when he could no longer restrain himself:

"I just read in the paper that you were married two days ago. I can't believe that your new American husband paid only thirty Egyptian pounds for you. How is it possible?

Ulla Morris-Carter

I paid more for my wife when I married."

He was obviously extremely displeased and disappointed to read this news. After all, his salary was probably no more than five pounds per month. How could an American capitalist pay so little for a German lady! He looked disapprovingly at me and questioned whether he had read correctly.

Mr. Wieland who could speak and read Arabic, assured Mohamed that indeed he had read the text correctly. He showed me the article in the Egyptian newspaper *Al Akhbar* which reported on March 19, 1959:

> Alex Morris, correspondent of the Herald Tribune, Cairo, put an end to the story of his love. Yesterday at the registry office he paid thirty Egyptian pounds as a dowry to Miss Nursula, the German girl whom he met by chance in an elevator in October last year. The families of the bride and bridegroom arrived especially for the occasion to celebrate the wedding on April 14 [sic] in the church of the German Sisters in Boulak [sic]. The story of the marriage was the only story in the journalistic life of Joe, for which he received blame because he cabled the story to his mother only after he finished the marriage registration."

LE JOURNAL D'EGYPTE

Propriétaire-Rédacteur en chef Edgard GALLAD
Administratrice · Directrice : LITA GALLAD

الجورنال ديجبت بالّلغة الفرنسية

Journal égyptien de langue française

VENDREDI 20 MARS 1959   La plus forte vente et la plus grande diffusion des journaux de langue française d'Egypte et du Moyen-Orient   6 PAGES – 15 MILLIÈMES

Alex Morris, le correspondant du « Daily Herald Tribune » vient d'épouser Ursula Ann Mary.

Le journaliste anglais et sa fiancée allemande   («Al Akhbar»)

une ravissante jeune allemande qu'il a rencontrée dans l'ascenseur, au Caire, en octobre dernier et c'est au Caire qu'il convole en justes noces, après avoir payé trente livres de dot au Bureau de l'Enregistrement des actes civils. — Tous nos confraternels vœux de bonheur. — La bénédiction nuptiale leur sera donnée, le 14 avril, à l'Eglise de l'Ecole allemande de Boulac.

Wedding announcement in a Cairo newspaper, Le Journal D'Egypte, *March 20th 1959.*

I was bewildered. Money had never been mentioned in our very confusing marriage ceremony. Our Egyptian journalist friends later explained to us that Egypt's legal system was based on Islamic law and that the registrar had simply written a certain amount, in our case thirty pounds, into the required field of the official contract after realizing that we didn't speak Arabic fluently and probably wouldn't understand the Egyptian system anyway. The amount mentioned was what an Egyptian husband paid his wife if he divorced her. Divorce was an easy matter in those days.

"I divorce you, I divorce you, I divorce you!" was all it took.

Egyptian men could leave one wife and acquire another as long as he notified both the existing wife and the intended one and paid a kind of alimony, namely the amount stated in the marriage certificate. Mohamed, after the appropriate explanation, seemed consoled, but never quite understood why an American wouldn't pay more. All Americans were supposed to be rich.

Ulla Morris-Carter

Joe went to Father Ludwig to be instructed about rules and regulations of the Catholic Church. I waited almost three hours before he returned.

I wondered: "Did he have to learn the Catechism by heart or was he receiving an overload of Catholicism?"

I needn't have worried. When Joe returned he looked relaxed and was smiling broadly.

"Great meeting with Father Ludwig. His English is excellent and he couldn't have been more helpful. I now know all I need to know about the Catholic Church. Father Ludwig gave me a Catechism to study and lent me a book that describes and explains all the sexual positions allowed by the church."

I thought I wasn't hearing right, and for a moment questioned his sanity.

"And furthermore we discussed the Boston Red Sox in great detail. Father Ludwig is an avid baseball fan. He was delighted to find out that I came from New England and consequently rightly assumed that I would be familiar with the Boston Red Sox. He will marry us on April 4 in the German chapel."

On the top floor of the building on Sharia Willcocks, in which Joe occupied the ground floor apartment, lived Judge Jasper Yeates Brinton with his wife Geneva. Judge Brinton was no ordinary judge and lawyer. He was, rather, an international figure, "the grand old American," who had been a resident of Cairo since 1921.

Born in 1878, he came from a prominent Philadelphia family. After graduating from University of Pennsylvania Law School, serving as Lieutenant Colonel in the Judge General's Department and as a member of an investigative mission to troubled Turkish Armenia, he was nominated by U.S. President Harding as the first American Representative to the Mixed Courts of Egypt. The Mixed Courts of Egypt were an unusual institution, an experiment in international justice, "highly acclaimed for their solid achievement in the field of international cooperation." As such, Judge Brinton occupied a special position in Cairo society. In his days Egypt was still a British protectorate. Once a year, as the only American judge on the Mixed Courts, Judge Brinton had to pay his respects to the Sultan, the father of King Farouk, and later to King Farouk himself.

The Judge admitted, "I enjoyed that immensely. As an American it rather tickled me to be calling on a king. You don't go very often calling on a king like that, all by yourself, and sit there and talk to him. He was very pleasant."

Judge Brinton was a modest person, gentle but with the sharp mind of a lawyer, who never boasted of his many accomplishments. Every American Ambassador new to Egypt would call on Judge Brinton to pay his respects. Well-known writers, such as Graham Greene, were among the friends who came to visit him. At age 81, when we met him, the Judge still played tennis and frequently went rowing on the Nile. An

Ulla Morris-Carter

aristocratic-looking person, tall, slender and elegant, Judge Brinton volunteered to give me into marriage to Joe Alex Morris. What an honor!

Meanwhile, we prepared for the arrival of our respective families.

Joe's parents were the first to arrive in Cairo. They came from Morocco, where Joe's father, accompanied by his wife Maxine, had just finished an article for *National Geographic*. Not having met them before, I was extremely nervous. But Joe's father, a handsome, distinguished gentleman, whom no one could help but admire, made it extremely easy when he simply embraced me at the airport with a big hug and said,

"Hello, honey, welcome into our family."

Maxine was equally warm and welcoming, and I felt immediately as if I had known them all my life. A few days later my mother, traveling with her sister, my aunt Agnes, arrived by boat in Alexandria, where Joe and I picked them up at the busy harbor. What a joy to see them again!

We weren't quite sure how to deal with this influx of relatives who didn't know one another and who weren't conversant in each other's languages. Busy with preparations for the wedding, we decided it would be best for all of us if our families enjoyed some sightseeing before the event. We suggested a trip to Upper Egypt, every tourist's dream. Joe's parents were delighted that we had already made arrangements for them. They were to take the Nile boat to Luxor and Aswan and return by train to Cairo. My mother and Aunt Agnes were equally pleased. Having arrived later than the Morrises, they would be taking the train to Luxor and Aswan and would return by boat, the reverse of Joe's parents' trip. For two days all four would be in Luxor at the same time, staying at the Luxor Palace Hotel. We wondered whether they would meet, how they might find each other and how they would get along.

Aunt Agnes spoke a fair amount of English, definitely more than my mother. Returning from a long day of sightseeing in the Valley of the Kings in Luxor, Aunt Agnes asked the concierge whether Mr. and Mrs. Joe Morris, Sr. were staying at the hotel and if so where to find them. He accompanied Aunt Agnes and my mother to the dining room and pointed to a couple dining in the far corner.

"Oh my God," exclaimed Aunt Agnes, turning to my mother, "that is the same American lady we have run into a couple of times today while sightseeing. We have been laughing at her all day because of her outlandish outfit, so typically American."

Maxine apparently wore a tiger-patterned scarf over her head, topped by a straw hat with a large ribbon that fluttered in the ever-blowing desert wind. An extravagant belt over the matching trouser suit and wild Mexican jewelry completed her outfit. In contrast, my aunt and my mother, coming from still war-worn Germany, were modestly dressed in demure colors.

Aunt Agnes, 48, short and bubbly, courageously took the lead and approached the Morris family. The Morrises were evidently very pleased to meet the bride's family. Joe's

Ulla Morris-Carter

Above Left: *My mother Maria, Joe's mother Maxine and my Tante Agnes in Luxor.* **Above Right:** *Joe's mother Maxine on a camel.* **Bottom:** *Bellydancer entertaining the relatives before the wedding in Cafe Fishawi, one of Cairo's oldest cafe's in the Khan El Khalili Souk.* **Table:** L-R: *My mother Maria, Joe's father Joe Sr., Joe's mother Maxine.* **Behind the dancer:** *Tante Agnes and myself and various other friends.*

Ulla Morris-Carter

father, always the gentleman, charmed the German ladies immediately. Soon there was lots of laughter over linquistic gaffs on both sides. By all accounts they had a splendid time, communicating in broken English, gesticulating with their arms and hands, and occasionally consulting a small dictionary. As we had hoped, they became fast friends.

With all our relatives back in town, we were invited to a number of pre-wedding parties. My mother and aunt had the time of their lives. Dr. Wilson Ghobri Beshai, my dentist, a personal friend, took a great liking to my aunt and showed her the Coptic part of Cairo. Another Egyptian gentleman, whom my mother had met years ago in the hospital in Düsseldorf while undergoing one of her eye operations, escorted my mother. He spoke German and they had corresponded from time to time over the years. We had a hard time keeping track of these two middle-aged ladies, who were as excited as teenagers on a first trip abroad. Indeed, it was their first trip abroad.

Charly Arnault, *ABC* correspondent for the Middle East, a good friend, had known and worked for Joe's father at *UPI*. Charly insisted on inviting all of us to a splendid dinner party with dancing at the new Hilton Hotel, which President Nasser had recently inaugurated, a glamorous affair.

THE WEDDING

Finally the day of the wedding arrived. I had hardly slept the night before. Looking out of the window in the early morning of April 4, 1959, I couldn't believe my eyes.

It was raining. It never rains in April in Cairo. Occasionally there is a little rain in January or February, but hardly ever thereafter.

I was devastated. Nothing and nobody was prepared for rain. The reception on the houseboat, open on all sides, would be a disaster.

Pater Ludwig checked in with us by phone: "Don't worry about the rain. It's a lucky sign. Rain on the wedding day is a sign of fertility."

The phone rang again. The caterers called to announce that their waiters, almost all of them Moslems, could not serve alcohol because it was a Moslem holiday.

"Sorry about that, we forgot to tell you!"

What to do? We desperately called friends and colleagues hoping to find servants who were either Christians, Copts or Armenians to help serve drinks on the houseboat. Serving drinks was easier said than done. Champagne, not available in Cairo stores, was to have been shipped from abroad with the help of one of our diplomatic friends, but it had not arrived. Joe and I called all our diplomatic friends and begged them to each bring a bottle of champagne to the wedding reception. As diplomats they could buy it at their PX store.

"Forget wedding presents, just come with a bottle of champagne! We'll pay you back as soon as our champagne arrives."

Ulla Morris-Carter

It stopped raining at noon. The sun shone brightly in a cloudless blue sky. Everything looked fresh and clean. I relaxed a little. More and more however, this wedding was turning out to be a comedy of errors. Everything that could go wrong, did.

My mother was taken to the chapel by my 70-year-old good friend, Paul Lipshitz, a Polish Jew who had turned Moslem after emigrating from Poland to Egypt. I had met him on my boat trip to Upper Egypt. He insisted on driving my mother so that he could get acquainted with her. I was not very comfortable with his offer, because he seldom drove himself and was mostly driven by a chauffeur.

"My mother's English is not very good," I tried.

"No problem, I will speak Yiddish to her. I am sure she will understand. And I know a certain amount of German."

He picked her up at her hotel. On the way to the chapel he backed into a lamppost. No one was hurt, but both were shaken up.

I was getting dressed in Joe's apartment with the help of my aunt. Since I had neither a hairdresser nor any bridesmaids to help, we had to improvise. I wore a three quarter-length white dress with a full skirt and a lace jacket on top. A short veil held by a little crown, a truly Egyptian number made out of sequins, completed my outfit. The little crown caused all kinds of problems. It simply refused to stay on my head. I looked at my watch. I was late.

Finally, with the veil in place and the crown firmly attached, my aunt left for the chapel. I was left alone in the apartment for a moment of peace. I was still painting my fingernails when Judge Brinton came down the stairs to take me to the chapel. He gently tried to calm me down by suggesting we do a trial run in preparation for our walk into the church. The house on Sharia Willcocks had a long white marble corridor at the entrance of the building. The Judge offered me his left arm as we walked the corridor a couple of times in measured steps while I was still blowing on my fingernails to dry the polish. I asked the judge whether, indeed, I was walking on the proper side?

"Oh yes, my dear friend, I need to have my right hand free to protect you. If I were in uniform, I would be holding a sword in my right hand."

I had no doubt that he knew the protocol a lot better than I. He wore a well-tailored black suit with a white silk vest and sported a white carnation, a the picture of sophistication and elegance. In my opinion he was the best-dressed man in the wedding party.

His 1947 Dodge was waiting in front of the house. Driving with the Judge was an experience not to be forgotten. The Dodge started with a roaring noise, resembling a truck more than a passenger car. Judge Brinton drove with considerable speed, disregarding traffic lights as well as traffic police. The police sensing his approach,

Ulla Morris-Carter

Top left: *Joe with bridesmaids, Soraya (L) and Hugette (R) and Wieland flower children.* **Top right:** *Judge Jaspar Brinton walking me down the aisle.* **Middle left:** *Joe waiting for the bride.* **Bottom left:** *Father Ludwig conducting the marriage ceremony.* **Right:** *Newly weds and a flower child.*

Ulla Morris-Carter

promptly cleared the road for him. They jumped out of the way whenever they saw that dark red Dodge heading their way. All I could do was close my eyes, take a deep breath and pray for safe arrival.

When we reached the chapel, Father Ludwig was pacing up and down the courtyard in front of the chapel.

He had already announced to Joe, only half amused, "If she doesn't get here soon we'll have to start without her. I have to catch a plane for Jerusalem."

The daughter of a German business friend had volunteered to play the harmonium. The music sounded beautiful when I entered on the arm of Judge Brinton.

"But why wasn't she playing the Mendelssohn wedding march, as we had arranged?" I wondered.

Now was not the time to ask.

The chapel looked gorgeous, decorated with loads of white calla lilies and an assortment of other white flowers sent by friends. Joe was waiting to the right of the altar, accompanied by two maids of honor: Soraya Farid, my good friend with whom I had traveled to Egypt, and Huguette Atallah, the daughter of my former landlady in Heliopolis. Both looked elegant and exotic. The men, David Holden, correspondent for the *Sunday London Times* and Willy Lazarus, correspondent for the *Times of India*, stood to the left of the altar. The chapel seemed just the right size for our wedding party of 60.

Losing no time, Father Ludwig started the ceremony as soon as Joe and I were in place. What followed was a touching and heart-warming ceremony. Father Ludwig spoke in English. I have to admit that I do not remember exactly what he said, but I know he spoke from the heart. Our mothers shed a few tears. My hands were shaking when Joe put the simple golden wedding band on my finger.

Then the harmonium, sounding triumphant, played a final Beethoven piece. Mr. Wieland's children, ages four and five, recited a lovely little German poem for us as they threw rose petals on the red carpet.

We walked out to the applause of family and friends.

When I saw our harmonium-playing friend outside the church, she told me that, when she was practicing before the wedding ceremony, an angry Egyptian had come into the chapel and said:

"You are not allowed to play the Mendelssohn wedding march in Egypt. Don't you know that Mendelssohn was a Jew? It's forbidden to play his music in this country."

She was so taken aback that she did not dare to play it. But she had yet another problem. Unbeknownst to me, she had sprained her ankle the day before in a painful fall and could not press the bellows of the harmonium. Her foot was so swollen she could barely walk, let alone press the pedals. Unable to find a replacement, her father, a prominent German businessman, volunteered to assist his daughter. He sat close by

Ulla Morris-Carter

Top: The Family *L-R: My aunt Tante Agnes, Joe's father Joe Alex Sr., my mother Maria, Joe & I, and Joe's mother Maxine.*
Above left: *Opening the veil kiss the bride.* **Right:** *Joe Sr. welcoming me into the Morris family.*

Ulla Morris-Carter

his daughter's side, and at times was underneath the harmonium, doing the footwork, while she was playing up above. Luckily the harmonium was in the back of the chapel, unseen by most of the guests. However, those who could see had a hard time not breaking into laughter during the ceremony.

THE RECEPTION

Now it was time to proceed to the houseboat for the reception. The Nile flowed calmly, its smooth waters deep green in the late afternoon light. The river banks, still lush at this time of year, were shaded by the many jacaranda trees on the sidewalks, some of them already in a cloud of lavender-colored blossoms, others about to explode. Their fern-like leaves made the trees look like large umbrellas.

To reach the boat, one had to cross a wobbly and narrow gangway. A rope on either side was there to prevent visitors from falling into the water. Some of our elderly guests had to be convinced to at least try walking over the gangway. The Pakistani Ambassador, a charming gentleman of a certain age, with his beautifully gowned wife, almost went overboard, barely caught by our best man who was helping the guests. Madame Atallah, my former landlady, afraid of setting foot on the gangway, had to be convinced by David Holden that she woud be safe while holding onto his arm.

Finally, securely on board, she asked to use the restroom. When she emerged, her face had changed color. She looked greenish and faint.

"I am feeling seasick," she whispered.

We settled Madame Atallah in a quiet corner and hoped that we could finally toast our marriage with a glass of borrowed champagne.

Not so fast! Where was the bridegroom?

Joe had disappeared as had our best man, David. I went in search and finally found them standing on the gangway negotiating with a policeman.

"What is happening now?" I asked, prepared for anything.

The policeman, who had happened to pass by, had taken one look at the crowded boat and decided that *The Saphir* was overloaded. Indeed, the boat was listing dangerously to one side, the Nile side. Most guests understandably stood there, preferring the view of the Nile to the riverbank and the street.

"You have to stop the party or take some people off the boat. No more than 40 are allowed," droned the policeman.

We did have more than the anticipated 60 guests, at least 70, not counting helpers, and a few uninvited who had joined the festivities. David and Joe continued to negotiate with the policeman. They understood that a little bakshish would probably help to solve the problem. A few Egyptian pounds changed hands. Satisfied by promises the guests would be distributed evenly on both sides of *The Saphir,* the policeman departed. For

Ulla Morris-Carter

most of the evening I hardly saw either Joe or David. They were busy balancing the boat by moving guests from one side to the other.

Despite many obstacles, nobody complained and everybody seemed to have a splendid time. One of our Canadian journalist friends even wrote a story about the "Wedding in Cairo."

As it turned out we had enough borrowed champagne for everybody to toast our marriage. None of the generous providers wanted to be reimbursed. This meant we would have to give another party once our champagne shipment arrived. Joe, with his great sense of humor, moved easily through the evening as if everything was just normal. He had a way of handling crises that doubtlessly helped him with his often stressful work.

The sun was setting, one of those gorgeous Egyptian sunsets that paints everything orange and red. Time to cut the wedding cake. A light breeze made the sheets of canvas between the decks flap gently. The muezin called for sunset prayers from the mosque across the river:

Allah u Akhbar—God is most Great.
I testify that there is no god but God
I testify that Muhammad is the Prophet of God.
Come to prayer!
Come to salvation!
Prayer is better than sleep.
God is most great.
There is no god but God.

The muesin intoned the prayer loud and clear. It was a magic moment.

Once the sun had set, darkness fell quickly. I was exhausted, but happy. We had actually managed to be married. After final good-byes to our many wonderful friends from near and far, Joe and I made our way home to his apartment. We found it in a state of utter chaos, as we had left it.

Underneath a pile of clothing, hairbrushes and decorations, we extracted a couple of chairs—my feet were hurting—and sat down to a bowl of warmed-up lentil soup, a leftover from lunch when all our relatives and some friends had been there, ostensibly to help. We had hardly eaten anything all day, and the soup really hit the spot. We knew we would have only a few hours of sleep because Joe's parents were departing for Europe at the crack of dawn. We definitely wanted to take them to the airport and see them off.

A honeymoon would have to wait.

Ulla Morris-Carter

Above: *Official wedding photos and* **Below:** *Joe and I on our honeymooners in Cyprus.*

MEMORIES OF CAIRO

The news reached us via telegram from London: "Morris-Minor shipped yesterday, expected arrival in Alexandria, Egypt, May 14, 1959."

We had been married for a month but we had not so far owned a car in this city of terrifying traffic. As a matter of fact, I didn't know how to drive. Unless one wanted to explore the surroundings of Cairo or the countryside, a car was definitely not a necessity. Cairo's streets were packed with taxis, service taxis, buses, donkey carts, three-wheelers and everything else that had wheels, all at a reasonable price. Driving was a challenge, and God forbid you had an accident.

All excited about the news of our car's arrival, Joe and I shared a service taxi for the three-hour drive on the desert road to the port of Alexandria to welcome and retrieve our acquisition, the Morris-Minor convertible. Standing on the Alexandria dock, covered in dirt and dust, the small grey car looked, at first, a little miserable. Once washed, however, the newest edition to the Morris household sparkled, its dark-red leather seats cleaned and waxed to a high sheen. No BMW or Mercedes could have made us happier than this little jewel of a car. With the top down we drove back to Cairo.

The most important next step, after the lengthy but necessary customs registration had been completed, was for me to learn how to drive. Having spent my childhood and teenage years in Germany, my family did not own a car in the difficult post-war years. We didn't have money to buy one, and my mother had serious eye problems. Now in Cairo, at age 25, I was trying to catch up. Driving schools did not exist. Joe had to be my teacher. He was a patient and usually responded with humor when I didn't shift gears at the right time, or committed other beginner's mistakes.

Ulla Morris-Carter

First outing in the new Morris Minor.

Of course, even in Egypt, one had to pass a driver's test to get a license. No material was available with instructions on how to prepare for the test. The Al Jazeera Traffic Department, crowded mostly with men, suggested I come back accompanied by a lawyer. A few Egyptian pounds inserted in a document could be of great help in settling any problem. And so it was. The certificate from the opthalmologist stating that I had had a vision test was a perfect envelope for five Egyptian pounds. Even without a lawyer, I was given a date to return for my driving test.

I appeared on the appointed date at the Cairo Traffic Department. I had to answer a few questions in halting Engish about traffic signs, which hardly anybody in this city observed. Next came the actual driving test. I waited for the official to accompany me to my car and give me instructions for the test. He did not move from his office. He simply stood by the open window of the second floor room at the Traffic Department, overlooking the parking lot. A few minutes passed before he instructed me in Arabic, shouting out of the window, to get into my car and start driving.

"Where to?" I asked, totally puzzled.

"Six meters forwards and six meters backwards. Then park," he answered.

Too intimidated to ask any questions I complied with his instructions. Having completed this task I stood in the parking lot awaiting further direction. None came for a while. The instructor simply stood at the open window without saying or doing anything. After a few minutes more my driving instructor came back to life. He motioned me to drive around the partking lot in an S-formation while he was still standing at the second-floor window looking down. When I had driven in S's around the parking lot for a few minutes, my Egyptian instructor signaled me to stop.

Ulla Morris-Carter

"You have done well. Congratulations, you are now an Egyptian driver. Come to the office on the third floor to pick up your Egyptian driver's license."

I could hardly believe my ears. Was this all there was to it? I began to understand, or thought I understood why the Egyptian way of driving was so different from the European, or maybe just the German, way of driving.

One early morning, with me at the wheel of the Morris Minor, Joe and I were on our way to the Gezirah Sporting Club for an early morning swim. Joe, usually a tolerant teacher, crticised my somewhat unorthodox driving.

I was so irritated by his remarks that I stopped the car, jumped out, and shouted, "You better drive if you don't like my driving."

The traffic behind us stopped. As Joe moved quickly into the driver's seat, Egyptian men in near-by cars whistled, laughed and even clapped their hands. I looked around in disbelief and embarrassment while hurrying to the passenger side. I had totally forgotten that I was wearing a bathing suit with only a little wrap around my shoulders, not standard dress code for the center of a conservative Middle Eastern city. Cairo was a cosmopolitan city of almost 3.5 million inhabitants in 1959. Most of its female population did not wear head scarves or chadors. Women coming to town from the countryside or nearby villages did. Yet, Cairo was conservative enough to forbid young lovers to walk hand-in-hand along the corniche of the Nile, particularly when unchaperoned. Frequently such couples were reprimanded by police.

Eventually I learned to drive around town quite confidently in Cairo traffic. Summer was upon us and the temperatures rose above 100°F.

Once when I was driving on the inner lane of a roundabout in heavy traffic, a huge dark-brown object flew out of the tall trees growing in the center of the traffic circle. It chose to land in the décolleté of my summer dress. This dress was made of a particularly beautiful French material, not available in Cairo at the time. Our dear friend, Paul Lipchitz, had given it to me as a birthday present. The brown object turned out to be a flying cockroach, completely disregarding the special origin of the dress and the sensitivity of its wearer. It finally settled in my bra.

How can I describe what it feels like having a one-inch long flying cockroach wiggling and scratching, trying to escape the confines of a bra, *my* bra no less! Panicking, I tried to ease myself from the inner lane to the outside of the five-lane circle, while the cockroach continued its struggle. Reaching a safe spot to stop, I jumped out of the car, and bent over to shake this agonizied insect out of my underwear. Meanwhile, of course, while Cairo's traffic moved along slowly, the men again were whistling and shouting insults at this unaccompanied young foreign woman. There comes a time when foreign women tire of the attention to which they are subjected. The experience was traumatic enough that I remember it half a century later.

Ulla Morris-Carter

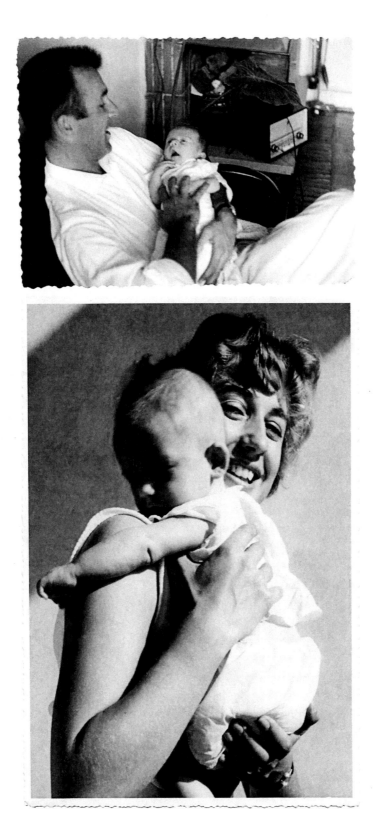

Above: *Joe with baby Maria.* **Below:** *Maria and I.*

BIRTH OF MARIA

1960

One evening in late June, 1960, Joe and I got into our gray Morris Minor convertible and drove into the desert. It had been a stifling hot and airless day, normal for that time of year in Cairo. But life at 110 degrees F, without air-conditioning, can be trying. It certainly was for me during those last few days of my pregnancy.

Expecting our first child, and comfortably seated now on the dark-red leather seats of our lovely little car, we hoped to catch some cool night breeze. At the outskirts of Cairo the desert sky glistened with thousands of stars. The Big Dipper seemed close enough to touch. In the shadow of the great Pyramids of Giza, we spread our blanket and stretched out over sand still warm from the intense heat of the day. For a few hours we were blessed with restful sleep.

Two photos stitched together from sleeping at the foot of these pyramids.

Ulla Morris-Carter

I had been uncomfortable all through the preceding days. Without a mother or knowledgeable female by my side to advise me, I did not know what to expect prior to the birth of a first baby. I disregarded the occasional labor pains, if that was what they were.

The day after our desert adventure, Joe and I went out to dinner with long-time friends including Arian and Arnaldo Lacagnina. It was a Monday evening. We splurged by going to the Semiramis Hotel roof garden restaurant, the coolest hot spot in town. The old Semiramis was Cairo's best hotel next to the new Shepheard's, which had been rebuilt after it burned down during the furious Cairo fire of 1952. But unlike the Shepheard's, the Semiramis had retained its old charm. History oozed from every room, every nook and cranny. It was the place to be almost anytime but particularly on a hot Egyptian night. Overlooking the Nile and a splendid Cairo skyline, the roof garden was washed in mellow light.

A band played the inevitable Italian rhythms, plus music by the Inkspots, "Only You" or "My Prayer at the End of the Day." Elegantly dressed Egyptians and a sprinkling of foreigners dined at beautifully appointed tables. Soft, balmy air enveloped us, interrupted now and then by a slight breeze. Cairo shimmered under a clear sky, the way only a desert city can sparkle once its eternal dust and dirt have settled. When I disappeared into the ladies room for longer than usual, Arian came in to check on me. I appeared "cool, calm and collected," she would remember. Actually I had had a couple of intense contractions that sent me to the floor of the ladies room to do some breathing exercises.

Returning home, as if nothing important were happening, we found an old friend sitting on our staircase, waiting for us. Keith Wheelock, a journalist friend of Joe's, was passing through Cairo. He wanted to see Joe and discuss a few things with him. The two men, seeing my discomfort and remembering some old wives tales they had heard somewhere, decided that the appropriate pain reliever, also a means of speeding up my labor process, would be a gin martini. I disliked gin but bravely tried a little. Then I went to bed while they continued to drink martinis.

Later the contractions intensified. When I thought the time had come to drive to the hospital, I had a hard time waking Joe. His heavy, first sleep had been deepened further by the martinis. Finally on our feet, we rushed to the garage where the car was parked.

It was blocked by another car. Panic set in. Joe was as nervous as I was.

It was three a.m. Our bawab—every house in Cairo had a bawab, a kind of caretaker and concierge—sitting in his little hut, was also fast asleep. Unable to rouse him, we tried to locate the owner of the car blocking ours.

Hopeless.

Finally we managed to find a taxi. The taxi driver sped to the hospital as if his life depended upon it.

Ulla Morris-Carter

At the hospital an Egyptian nurse went immediately into action. Speaking only Arabic, she declared, while preparing me for delivery, that I was indeed "very dirty." I thought I had misunderstood her. But no. In no uncertain terms, she repeated the statement. Finally it dawned on me what she meant. Almost all Egyptian women regularly remove all body hair, including pubic hair, once they reach puberty. Using a method similar to waxing, Egyptian women prepare a delicious smelling paste called *helawa*, meaning sweet, made of sugar, water and lemon and spread it over the area to be de-haired. I had not used helawa, and the nurse was not at all pleased.

But there was no time to spare. To my relief, Dr. Selim, my gynecologist, arrived. He was a caring, gentle Egyptian, short and slender, with a beautiful smile and a very comforting demeanor. Trying to cheer me up, he declared, after hearing the martini story, that in all likelihood the baby would be born with the hiccups. Joe had meanwhile been banished to the hallway. In those days fathers were not allowed into the delivery room, certainly not in Cairo.

Wisely, Joe had brought along the book he was presently interested in, a book on the Crusades. The aftereffects of the night before, plus very little sleep, combined with a nerve-racking taxi ride and the bloody stories of the Crusades, added to his suffering as a prospective father.

It took quite a while for the little darling to decide to enter this world. Maybe she felt she wasn't ready to leave the warm surroundings of the womb and face the harsh world outside. Finally, at 9:30 a.m., the nurse placed a lovely little girl with a fair amount of dark hair into my arms. The struggle and pain were immediately forgotten.

The Anglo-American hospital in Cairo was no cooler than the rest of the city. After four years of closure due to the Suez crisis in 1956, during which the foreign-owned hospital had been sequestered by the government, it had only recently been reopened under Egyptian management. Dr. Selim preferred this hospital to the local Egyptian ones because it had a better equipped operating and delivery room. As a matter of fact, most foreign women avoided Egyptian hospitals altogether, preferring to return to their home country or travel to Beirut to give birth.

The hospital had no nursery, so the baby was placed in a crib near my bed. The little darling did not behave angelically, suffering, no doubt, like her mother, from the intense heat. An Egyptian woman in the next room seemed to have gathered her whole tribe around her. They filled her room and spilled out into the hallway, where they set up a temporary kitchen, cooking on a primus cooker. Smells of spicy rice and the native foul (a type of kidney bean, the main staple of the Egyptian diet) and other intense odors drifted into my room.

After one day I knew that I had to find a way to leave the hospital as soon as possible, even though the normal stay after birth was at least four days. The Egyptian nurse appeared the morning after the birth in hair curlers, carrying a tin cup and a tin spoon with which she proceeded to feed this tiny baby some sugar water. I was horrified, but being totally inexperienced, did not know what to do. In her best Arabic she explained that this sugar water was to keep the baby going until my milk had come in and I could nurse. This was easier to accept than the cockroaches that occasionally ventured over my bed sheet or meandered under my bed. Joe took me home the next day.

One important decision had yet to be made, naming the baby. Tradition-bound as we still were in those days, we decided to name her after her grandmothers. Not wanting to offend either, we named the baby after both—after my mother "Maria" and after Joe's mother "Maxine." We only learned later that both grandmothers disliked their names.

So began the life story of one little Maria Maxine Morris. She weighed seven pounds, eight ounces and was 34 inches long. Her first residence was our tiny but lovely duplex penthouse apartment on the eighth floor at 8 Sharia Wilcox, Zamalek, near the Gezirah Sporting Club. Maria had come into the world during a period of relative calm in the city's turbulent recent history.

Such was the decade preceding the birth of our baby. The biggest news story in the Arab world in 1960 was the start of the building of the Aswan Dam.

An old journalist friend, Tom Little, wrote:

At precisely 13:50 hours on January 9, 1960, President Nasser dynamited 20,000 tons of granite to signal the start of work on the High Dam at Aswan.

None of which was of any interest to one Maria Maxine Morris.

Hand drawn dinner party invitation for our impending departure from Cairo.

Ulla Morris-Carter

CAIRO-NEW YORK

1963

In 1961, after six years as Middle East correspondent for the *New York Herald Tribune*, Joe was transferred to New York to get reacquainted with the United States. If I had thought that after leaving the turbulent Middle East we would have a quieter family life, I was mistaken.

When Maria and I landed in New York in 1961, Joe picked us up at the airport with the news that he had to leave for Florida immediately. He was to cover a developing political crisis, the invasion by CIA-trained Cuban exiles living in Florida, into Cuban territory at the Bay of Pigs. Recently elected President John F. Kennedy had become increasingly concerned about Cuba under its new leader, Fidel Castro, and Castro's close ties to the Soviet Union. The invasion in April of 1961 was quickly repulsed, but it prompted the Cuban government to build up its defenses, which eventually led to a U.S. confrontation with Russia and the Cuban Missile Crisis of 1962, a crisis that put the world at the brink of a Nuclear War.

Joe was away for six weeks, a long six weeks for me in a big new city by myself. Joe's cousin Molli and her husband, John Cloake, the British Consul General in New York, had graciously lent us their apartment in Greenwich Village temporarily while they were on home leave in England. But New York posed a challenge no matter how I looked at it. First was the search for an affordable apartment in the right part of town. Without Joe's presence, that posed a major problem for me, a newcomer who did not know one end of New York City from the other. An extensive search finally proved successful when

Ulla Morris-Carter

I found the small but attractive apartment on King Street, also in Greenwich Village. After paying a hefty amount of key money before I could sign the lease, we became the proud lessors of the King Street apartment for a monthly rent of $150.

I was terrified that I might have made the wrong decision, until Joe's parents, Maxine and Joe Sr., came down from Connecticut and set my mind at ease. They assured me that I had done the right thing. They liked the apartment and the location.

In this floor-through apartment we walked from our living room directly into the kitchen. The room next to the kitchen was the actual bedroom. It was small but airy and filled with light, so it became Maria's room. A five step staircase outside her bedroom took you up to what we considered a lovely miniature garden, a great luxury in New York. A seven-storey factory, spewing soot and occasionally dark clouds of smoke, was a close and undesirable neighbor. But one couldn't choose one's neighbors, and, as everyone knew, New York was not famous for its clean air.

Soot or no soot, a few flowers, including two rose bushes, thrived. The small lawn was nothing to write home about until I discovered, and planted, a tough kind of grass, poisonous green in color, that seemed especially designed to survive in New York's air. Our living room, its windows half-way below street level, afforded a view of an assortment of passing Greenwich Village feet and also served as Joe's and my bedroom equipped with a pullout Simmons couch-bed.

In the early morning, still lying in bed, I could watch all those feet walking by, and I considered doing a study of feet, some shoeless, some in fashionable high heels or sandals, others in sturdy workmen's boots, then guessing, or imagining, what the person who wore those shoes would actually look like. If I was curious enough about an interesting pair of feet, I squeezed myself into the small space between the armchair and the window, to actually examine the person walking by.

Looking upwards, my nose touching the window, I could get at least a partial view of the object of my curiosity.

Left: *Joe reading the newspaper.* **Right:** *Maria, Joe & I in our in our small garden.*

Ulla Morris-Carter

I felt trapped in New York, confined to my little neighborhood, which, in fact, was a very pleasant one. But I had not yet learned to adjust to a life without a job, without a built-in set of friends and without familiar surroundings. Finally, I discovered Washington Square, where young mothers with babies watched their offspring play in dirty sandboxes and discussed politics.

On occasion, during the summer, I walked barefoot like some of the other young mothers. Joe disapproved. He didn't care for me in the role of a hippy. On one of those excursions I met a young woman, Carol Gibson, pushing a stroller carrying her son Christopher. We discovered that both our husbands were journalists. Carol's husband Bob worked for *Business Week*, Joe for the *New York Herald Tribune*. We enjoyed each other's company and after a few meetings decided to try and bring our husbands together, a slightly daring project. We were lucky. They liked each other, had lots to talk about and we all became fast friends. The Gibsons lived just one block away from us, an added benefit.

After a few weeks in New York, when Maria was almost one year old, she was diagnosed with Celiac disease, a stomach disorder that had started in Cairo but was not diagnosed until we came to New York. She had to be hospitalized. The good sisters at the Catholic St. Vincent's Hospital told me that I was not allowed to see her for a few days while they administered a battery of tests, a ruling I considered cruel and inhumane punishment for both mother and child. I walked out of the hospital crying bitter tears.

When I was allowed to visit her after four days, Maria refused to look at me. Her blue eyes stood out in her pale face and seemed bigger than I remembered them. There were bruises on her cheeks, probably from forcing medicine or tubes down her throat. She turned her head away from me as if to say:

"I don't want to see you. You abandoned me."

I was heartbroken. After another day in the hospital we were allowed to take her home. From then on she would have to be on a strict diet until she outgrew the disease almost five years later.

While Maria was in the hospital, Bob and Carol Gibson invited us for dinner at their apartment. I was in a state, depressed and unsettled. I remember sitting at their dinner table with tears welling up in my eyes. Not normal for me.

Returning home that night I experienced severe cramps, abdominal pains and heavy bleeding. I realized at once that I was having an early miscarriage. I had no feelings of sadness or loss or desperation, just the realization that I wasn't ready yet for another child. Maria's illness required my full attention, emotionally and physically.

Unfortunately, Maria had to be hospitalized again that year for severe dehydration following an infection that brought her fever up to 106° F. I learned that the nuns in the hospital baptized Maria after seeing the inscription on her little hospital bracelet:

Ulla Morris-Carter

"Maria Maxine Morris—mother catholic, child not baptized."

Not much later Joe entered the same hospital for an emergency appendectomy. I had become a regular there.

In 1962 Joe was offered the job of associate foreign editor at *Newsweek*, a job he accepted, having noted the *New York Herald Tribune's* financial problems, which led to its collapse four years later. Joe now worked grueling weekend hours before *Newsweek* was "put to bed." He would leave the house Friday morning at nine a.m., not to return home until four or five a.m. next morning. He would sleep three or four hours, then return to *Newsweek* for another 12-14 hour day. He did then have a three-day weekend, Sunday, Monday, Tuesday, but he was often so exhausted that he needed more than a day to recover. So we didn't have a normal weekend to be with friends. New York, I quickly learned, could be a great city to live in, but great only if one had money, preferably no children and knew one's way around.

We did not have a lot of money, I knew nothing about New York, and we had a baby.

At age 35, Joe came down with a serious case of mononucleosis accompanied by high fever and liver pain that put him out of commission for more than four weeks. I was up day and night, sitting beside his bed with a bucket of ice water putting cold compresses on his forehead and legs trying to reduce the fever. He finally grew so frustrated and impatient that one afternoon, when his fever was again above 104° F, he screamed at his visiting physician, who still made house calls:

"You mean to say that there is nothing in 20th century medical science other than to prescribe Aspirin for me?"

So, life was not much fun that year in New York. Whenever possible we would drive to Guilford, Connecticut, to spend time with Joe Sr. and Maxine. I loved them, and their home was a safe haven for me, a house as warm and welcoming as any I had ever dreamt of.

In October we did manage a short excursion to Amagansett on Long Island for a few days of rest and recreation. It was late in the season for a beach outing, but Joe was convinced that a few days away from New York City would help him regain his usual positive outlook on life. He had had a particularly stressful period behind him and needed a few days off. It was not only the long weekend hours at *Newsweek*, it was also working in an atmosphere that was not conducive to creative thinking, and that put extra pressure on him. Frequently the editors, when taking a break for lunch or dinner, would go to the nearby pub for a couple of martinis, maybe double martinis. I do not know how one manages to work after a couple of martinis, but work they did.

Joe was driving our little Morris Minor convertible to the east end of Long Island on an overcast day. The streets were fairly empty in Amagansett. The summer season was long over. Suddenly, without any warning, Joe slumped over the steering wheel while the car kept moving, though slowly, barely missing a tree at the side of the road.

It seemed he had had enough foresight to step on the brake before collapsing. I was momentarily unable to move. I had no idea what was happening. Regaining my equilibrium, I managed to bring the car to a complete stop, run around to the other side and try desperately to move Joe's unconscious body from the driver's side to the passenger seat, not an easy matter in a small car with a heavy body.

Maria sat motionless in the back seat, her beautiful blue eyes as big as saucers, watching in silence. She must have realized that this was serious. Off to the nearest emergency room, well, a First Aide station was all I could find.

By the time we got there Joe had revived and opened his eyes. A friendly doctor emerged from the First Aid station and helped Joe inside. Color had returned to his face, and he could stand up by himself.

What a relief! After a thorough examination, the doctor assured us that Joe had neither had a heart attack, nor, as I had feared, a stroke. It was exhaustion from overwork and stress that had caused this collapse.

By the time all this was over and both Maria and Joe had recovered sufficiently, I had acquired a model's dress size 6—a first for me.

NOTICE

VILLAGE ORDINANCE IX

"Section 7. Public bathing in any of the waters within the corporate bounds of the Village, unless in a suitable bathing dress or covering, is hereby prohibited. NO PERSON SHALL WALK OR RIDE IN ANY VEHICLE UPON OR ALONG THE PUBLIC STREETS OF THE VILLAGE IN ANY BATHING SUIT, SHORTS, TRUNKS OR OTHER APPAREL WHICH DOES NOT COVER PROPERLY THE BODY AND LIMBS FROM MIDWAY BETWEEN THE KNEES AND THE HIPS TO AND INCLUDING THE SHOULDERS."

PENALTY $5 - $100

Another mishap: *Notice I received n Amagansett, Long Island, while shopping with Joe's sister Claire. The policeman threatened to arrest me on for wearing European 'too short' shorts, if I would not immediately get into a car and out of sight. Ironically, I felt well dressed with a button up shirt and not a strapless decolte which other women were wearing.*

Ulla Morris-Carter

View from our balcony on Rue Clemenceau

THE BEIRUT YEARS

Earth

How beautiful you are, Earth, and how sublime!
How perfect is your obedience to the light and
how noble is your submission to the sun!

How lovely you are, veiled in shadow, and how
Charming your face. Masked with obscurity!

How soothing is the song of your dawn, and how
Harsh are the praises of your eventide!
How perfect you are, Earth and how majestic.

I have walked over your plains, I have climbed your
stony mountains; I have descended into your valleys;
I have entered into your caves.

In the palins, I found your dream;
upon the mountainI found your pride;
in the valley I witnessed your tranquility;
In the rocks your resolution;
In the cave your secrecy.

– Khalil Gibran, Lebanese Poet.

TRAVELING TO BEIRUT

1963

One month to prepare for departure to a new assignment in a new country. We borrowed $2,000 from *Newsweek*, went shopping for items we thought necessary or that we might not find in Lebanon.

We cancelled the lease on our apartment and tolerated vaccinations, medical check-ups and visa applications. Nothing fazed me. On the contrary, the flurry of activity was a welcome change from the daily routine of a stay-at-home mother in New York. During my year and a half in this big city I had never felt at home. To me it seemed like an unfriendly foreign country. Now the excitement of going back to the Middle East overrode all the problems of leaving. Finally, we said our fond farewells to friends and family. Miraculously the three of us made it to the New York airport on time. It was a cold, grey morning in early March 1963.

Pan American took us to London. There we boarded Middle East Airlines to our final destination. My excitement was growing. Approaching Beirut I could see the Mediterranean Sea under a glorious spring sun. My heart jumped with joy at the first sight of tiny Lebanon, nicknamed "Switzerland of the Middle East." Approximately the size of Connecticut, Lebanon has both Mediterranean and Alpine climates, spectacular scenery and impressive ruins. I had visited Lebanon for a few days in 1958 while I was living in Cairo.

Landing at Beirut airport and stepping into the crowded airport hall, I knew I was back in the Middle East. Sweating porters, mostly of Kurdish origin, pushed their way toward us, fighting for our fare. There were Arab men wearing tarbushes, Arab women covered in black, men in white galabeyas, men and women elegantly dressed

Ulla Morris-Carter

in western style, The customs officials insisted on inspecting every piece of our vast load of luggage. They were a curious lot. They rummaged through everything. Finally through customs, we stepped outside into warm sunshine and hailed a taxi to take us to the Palm Beach Hotel. A ride in a Lebanese taxicab is an experience not quickly forgotten. Nothing is more frightening than one's first. Honking, speeding, zooming around blind corners, with the driver turning around now and then to talk. It was all part of the experience. Horrified, I clutched Maria in my arms and feared for our family's life. Joe, who knew Beirut, was unperturbed, seeming to enjoy the scenery.and being back in the Middle East.

Somehow we arrived in one piece at the Palm Beach Hotel, a modest, but comfortable hotel, just opposite the more famous and palatial St. Georges Hotel. We were only steps away from the Mediterranean. The Palm Beach was our home for more than four weeks while we searched for an apartment and waited for our furniture to arrive. From our room on the third floor I could see Lebanon's mountain range which seemed to grow out of the greenish-blue Mediterranean. It was said that one could drive to the ski resort of Farayah in the morning, ski for two or three hours, return to Beirut and swim in the sea in the afternoon. All this lay ahead of us.

In 1963 Beirut was a city of approximately half a million people. Crowded onto a narrow stretch of land at the foothills of the mountains, it was both a cosmopolitan and, historically speaking, a Phoenician and Arab city. While searching for an apartment I discovered Souk Tawila, meaning the long souk, in downtown Beirut. It became my favorite shopping area. The smells and the variety of shops reminded me of the larger souks in Cairo or the covered souks of Aleppo, Syria, that I had known and loved. Winding passages led from Souk Tawila into specialized markets. There was the Souk Franjieh, the flower, fruit and vegetable market, overflowing with produce of many kinds, mostly grown in the Bekaa Valley. The Bekaa, a fertile agricultural plain, is Lebanon's bread basket. Further along were the smelly fish and meat markets. Then came the gold souk, its store windows glittering with gold bracelets, necklaces and pendants.

In Souk Tawila tiny shops were as close together as sardines in a can. Every imaginable item could be found here, if one just spent enough time looking for it. What appeared to be no bigger than a hole in the wall might be a store filled with exquisite French lingerie, staffed by a Lebanese salesman, who, his eyes sweeping over your body, took "measurements" before recommending one or the other lacy item. Next door would be a store selling gorgeous fabrics for dresses, even including brocade. Most women in Beirut had their dresses made. Then there were record player stores, repair stores, toy stores, tobacco and newspaper stores. And money changers at every street corner. Beirut in 1963 was an important commercial and banking center, with a busy port. Lebanon, in general, had acquired a reputation as a free market and an "open" country

Ulla Morris-Carter

with fewer restrictions than in neighboring Arab states, such as Egypt, Syria or Saudi Arabia. Another attractive feature for the large foreign press corps was the fact that Lebanon, unlike other Arab countries, had no press censorship, except—as I would later learn—for articles specifically discussing Lebanese affairs.

Beirut was a city of contrasts. It had beautiful old villas and apartment buildings and houses with shady terraces, surrounded by lush gardens overflowing with jasmine and bougainvillea. In the process of rapid expansion, however, it had also acquired a number of architecturally uninspired buildings, some of them ugly modern structures. Nonetheless, the city was still called the Pearl, or the Paris, of the Orient.

Driving through Lebanon was like turning the pages of a history book, ruins of ancient Phoenician city-states, crusader castles, Greek inscriptions, ancient ports such as Biblos and Sidon and the famous temples of Baalbeck. Not far from Beirut one could find evidence of the earliest known civilizations— Phoenicians, Chaldeans, Assyrians, Babylonians, Hittites. It was all part of what made Lebanon a fascinating place to be.

In my search for housing I learned soon that one didn't just choose an apartment for affordability and convenience to job and schools. It was important to consider the noise level. Beirut was and would remain a very crowded city built on hills, with narrow, winding, criss-crossing roads and alleys. The many blind corners caused taxi drivers to lean on their horns. There were street vendors whose voices seemed to penetrate closed windows. There were the muezzins calling the faithful to prayer, there was the coffee man selling bitter Arabic coffee in small cups, clinking two cups together to announce his arrival, and many many more sounds, some pleasant and some unbearable.

The view from our apartment.

Ulla Morris-Carter

227

Our extensive search for a place to live finally proved successful. We rented a seventh-floor penthouse apartment in a relatively modern building on Rue Clemenceaux. It was affordable and seemed just right for us. From its many terraces we had a perfect view of snow-capped Mount Sannin towering over Beirut and the Mediterranean. Below us lay the hotel district with the celebrated St. Georges hotel right on the water. By the time our furniture arrived, Joe had already departed for Egypt for an interview with Egyptian President Gamal Abdel Nasser.

These were busy and at times lonely days for me. I had not had enough time yet to make new friends and get settled. Where to find babysitters? Where to apply for residence permits? Where to find a car that was affordable? How to obtain a Lebanese Driver's License?

Left: *Joe meeting with President Nassar.* Bottom: *A ski trip to Fariah in the mountains of Lebanon, with my visiting mother, Omi, and our car, a Rambler convertible, that we called 'The Golden Rocket'.* Below: *Joe and Omi.*

Ulla Morris-Carter

228

GUNS AND GHAT

JOE TRAVELS TO YEMEN

We had not yet moved into our new apartment in Beirut before a civil war in tiny Yemen threatened to destabilize the entire Middle East. The situation prompted Joe and his British Daily Telegraph colleague, Dick Beeston, to depart for Yemen via Saudi Arabia in early June of 1963.

Traveling to Saudi Arabia and Yemen in the 1960s was not a routine journey. It required physical stamina, patience, quick thinking and, if possible, a good sense of humor to overcome the inevitable frustrations one was likely to encounter. At the time, the civil war in Yemen, long since forgotten, or ignored, threatened the peace of the Middle East. The issue went beyond the political division of Yemen into Royalists in the north and Republicans in the south. It was all about oil.

The Saudis took the part of the north, while Egypt, under Nasser, who wanted a foothold on the oil-rich Arabian Peninsula, aided the south with arms and Russian Ilyushin bombers flown by Egyptian Air Force pilots. The Saudi government, keen to publicize Egypt's role in the bombings, was willing to supply the journalists with the necessary visas, an open truck for the first part of their journey, and two guides.

Isolated and extremely tribal, Yemen had been ruled by a dictatorial tyrant, Imam Ahmed, until his sudden death in 1962. His son, Mohamed al Badr, took over as the new ruler. Only a few days after his installation, a seemingly successful revolution, led by Brigardier Abdullah al Salal, drove the weak and inexperienced al Badr out of his palace in Yemen's capital Sanaa into the mountainous region of North Yemen. There al

Ulla Morris-Carter

Badr established headquarters in an elaborate four-foot high cave, surrounded by loyal tribesmen who rallied around him. Suddenly Yemen was involved in a little war—a war that quickly developed into something much more dangerous.

Arriving in Jeddah, Saudi Arabia, Joe and Dick Beeston immediately proceeded to their next stop, the Saudi Red Sea Port of Jizan on the Yemeni border. Waiting for their Yemeni guides to arrive, Joe and Dick were stuck in a guest-house/customs shed in Jizan, where the Saudi government had suggested they should overnight. Joe's report indicated that it was one of the hottest (125° F), most humid and most squalid places he had ever stayed.

Years later Dick wrote a vivid description of the guest house, in his memoir *Looking for Trouble:*

> The days were unbelievably hot and humid and all we could do was to lie, stripped, on camp beds waiting for evening when the temperature would drop to about 100° F. Our room faced the harbour where glassless windows overlooked the rotting bags of cement. Before midday each day a hot, on-shore breeze would pick up, gradually covering our sweat-soaked bodies with powdered cement. When we were coated grey and the cement began to harden, we would leap up, throw buckets of tepid water over ourselves then return to our camp beds where the torment would start again. In the evening, the governor of the province would send over a huge brass tray full of stewed sheep, camel and rice, tinned cheese, bread and jam and Coca-Cola. It all seemed a long way from the terrace of the St. Georges.

From Joe's photos. **Above:** *Dick Beeston in Yemen and the armed rebels.*

Ulla Morris-Carter

After two days the guides arrived in full regalia, with bandoliers of cartridges across their chests and wicked-looking Yemini daggers in their belts. The journalists' expedition started out in an open truck, across desert and flat land but when they reached the higher elevations of the Yemeni mountains, Joe and Dick had to proceed on foot, walking mostly at night for fear of being strafed by Egyptian bombers. They tried to rest during the day, if they could find a safe, shady spot.

After eight days Joe cabled *Newsweek:*

> Unable to beat the Yemeni tribesmen on their own ground, the Egyptian jets strafe everything that moves in the mountains and deserts of northern and eastern Yemen. They are even using Napalm, blister gas, and, say the royalists, poison gas.

> 'They dropped a can on us in Aula village on the eastern front. We were sick for three days, vomiting and bleeding from the mouth and nose,' said Ibrahim el Hejwa.

Joe's article continued:

> To visit the Imam's headquarters, I traveled for two nights up precipitous slopes. When I arrived outside his split-level cave at the crest of a 7,000-foot peak, some 3,000 tribesmen were on hand, chanting war whoops, brandishing daggers, shooting rifles into the air... Dozens of camel trains loaded down with ammunition and rifles and other supplies under straw camouflage worked their way up into the mountains...

> Inside [the cave], across a floor covered with Oriental carpets, sat the Imam. He wore a black turban and a dark ankle-length robe. We talked about guerilla warfare and Arab politics.

> The Imam told me indignantly: 'The UN will not decide this war. The Yemenis will decide it.' As he bade me farewell, he smiled brightly: 'I'll see you in Sanaa.'

Below: *Joe at the cave .*

Ulla Morris-Carter

Above: *The Iman and his soldiers outside the cave.* **Below:** *Yemeni mountain range from Joe's photos.*

Ulla Morris-Carter

During adventures of this kind I had no news of Joe's whereabouts or of his well being. I was in Beirut with Maria, worried about him, but trying to be brave and moved into our new apartment by myself. Three weeks into the Yemen journey, Joe called from Saudi Arabia, seemingly happy and healthy. Another week passed before he returned to Beirut.

"Yemen was an extraordinarily beautiful country with scenery and views unlike any other I have seen before," he said.

And he had traveled widely.

"We must visit Yemen together one of these days, when Yemen is peaceful again." But neither peace nor our return visit ever came to pass.

Though accustomed to Joe's frequent absences, I had to get used to the unpredictable pattern of Middle Eastern life and its never-ending crises. Joe's frequent trips on a moment's notice became routine. He and I would pack his suitcase in five minutes, then race to the airport to catch the next plane. Yet he never forgot his tennis racket. Joe loved playing tennis. It kept him sane when work pressures and deadlines weighed heavily.

Beirut attracted a colorful contingent of foreign nationals and expatriates, businessmen, bankers, journalists, artists, architects and builders. There were a multitude of embassies with large numbers of diplomats from all over the world. Visitors and tourists arrived from Europe year round. The summer visitors from Egypt, Saudi Arabia, the United Arab Emirates, Bahrain, Kuwait and Iraq came to escape the unbelievably hot climate in their home countries and spend time in the refreshing air of the Lebanese beaches and mountains. Others came from Asia, the Far East and Australia to enjoy what Lebanon had to offer, spectacular scenery, entertainment and pleasures not unlike those of the Riviera, casinos and nightclubs and excellent restaurants.

In addition to the good life, Beirut offered another important advantage: sophisticated banking connections. The American Embassy in Beirut was considered one of the best in the Middle East with numerous Arabists and Middle East experts among its diplomatic corps. Because the Middle East has never wanted for crises, coup d'etats and other upheavals, those experts were much in demand.

Through a stone gate in the Yemeni mountains.

Ulla Morris-Carter

Joe and I dancing at Le Bal des Petits Lits Blanc, *a prestigous charity ball, in Bait Eddine Palace in 1964.*

BEIRUT

1963-64

To live in Beirut in the early 1960's was the envy of many. "Lebanon had its happiest period then", a Lebanese politician said.

The city was filled with a strange mixture of warring political factions and continuous social life. The sheer exuberance of the Lebanese, rich and poor, great and small, was contagious. We foreigners loved it and shared in it. One was always welcome at a Beirut dinner party, with or without a husband or escort.

Unlike Germany, where dinner parties were formal and the guest lists demanded equal numbers of males and females, Beirutis were more flexible and extraordinarily hospitable. Out-of-town visitors appeared unexpectedly and joined in, no questions asked. If there was a curfew, which happened occasionally during tense political times, one had a "pajama party." Friends simply stayed overnight until the curfew was lifted at 5 a.m. If there was tension in the air, and the Middle East was never tension-free, what better way to spend the evening than to have a get-together, argue politics late into the night, and never settle anything.

Not all was politics however. I remember an absolutely beautiful July evening in 1964, attending a charity ball, *Le Bal des Petits Lits Blancs*, 'the Ball of the Little White Beds', held at the Beit Eddine Palace in the mountains of Lebanon. Beit Eddine, house of faith, was built by the Emir Bechir Chehab around 1812. A good example of early 19th century Lebanese architecture, Beit Eddine, approximately 50 kilometers southeast of Beirut, provided a romantic setting for a summer ball. Dancing under a full moon on one of the many terraces of the palace, was unforgettable.

Ulla Morris-Carter

Of course, there was another side to Beirut. Ever since gaining independence from France in 1943, Lebanon had had a problem trying to find a balance between Christians and Moslems, between rich and poor, between the many religious factions that all wanted a share in its government, Maronite Christians, Sunni Moslems, Shiites, Druze, Armenians, Greek Orthodox, Assyrians, Chaldeans, as many as 17 religious groups were represented in Lebanon. The Maronite Christians, though a minority today, have dominated the government since independence. Up to this day strict rules govern the political appointment of Lebanon's president, prime minister and speaker of the House. The President must be a Maronite Christian; the Prime Minister a Sunni Moslem and the Speaker of the House a Shiite Moslem. The last census, taken in 1932 and by now completely outdated, still forms the basis for the formation of government.[1]

Life in Beirut in 1963 seemed relatively quiet. October 26 was a perfect day, sea-scented, bright and sunny. It was my 30th birthday. I was four months pregnant with our second child, and I could not have felt better or happier. Joe had recruited friends to prepare a surprise birthday party for me. Many showed up at our apartment, journalist friends, ex-patriots who now called Beirut their home, and local Lebanese. They were a happy crowd, warm-hearted friends of many nationalities. Joe had just returned from a trip to the Persian Gulf. He surprised me with a beautiful pearl necklace. Shiny, iridescent and perfectly beautiful, the pearls made me feel like a queen.

Among our acquaintances was a Soviet journalist working for Izvestia. Constantin Vichniyewski, a lively and fun-loving fellow with a passion for gambling, seemed rather un-Russian. He spoke fluent English and Arabic, even wrote poems in English. We often wondered whether he might be with the KGB. Unlike his Soviet journalist colleagues and the Soviet Embassy diplomats, who were usually not allowed to associate with westerners during the Cold War era, Constantin happily consorted with his western colleagues. He loved parties, and he gambled in the Casino du Liban.

"May I bring a friend?" he asked on this occasion.

We were astonished by such an unusual request from a Soviet journalist.

"Of course, we would love to meet your friend," we answered.

We expected another Soviet journalist. To our surprise, Constantin appeared with a gorgeous Russian blonde. He introduced her as Natasha. I wondered why she had come to our house. Soviet visitors to Western households were definitely not the norm. I sat down with her, away from the noise of the party to get to know her a bit.

"My husband is a diplomat with the Soviet Embassy," Natasha explained.

Her English was not fluent, but easily understandable.

1. *In 2007-2008 Lebanon remained completely deadlocked for many months over the election of a new President, a problem that has since been repeated in 2014-16. Clan warfare between religious factions however is not new. It goes back centuries.*

Ulla Morris-Carter

"Life is sometimes boring around our house, somewhat monotonous. We don't go out a lot. I am delighted to be here tonight."

"And where is your husband?" I asked.

"He is babysitting our four-year-old daughter."

"Oh, I see," was about all I managed in response.

I was astonished by her frankness. We were not exactly close friends, and this was a most unusual situation. but Natasha and Constantin seemed to have a good time. They mixed with our friends and left at around 10:30 p.m. Very early the next morning the phone rang. Barely awake, I ran to the phone and tried to understand the heavily accented voice.

"Who is calling? I can't understand you. Could you please repeat your name?" I shouted, hoping for better communication.

"I am Natasha's husband," the unknown voice said. Pause. ". . . I want to thank you for inviting Natasha to your house."

"We were delighted to meet her," I replied in my sleepy state.

"You must have had a good party," Natasha's husband continued.

His English was excellent, but with his heavy accent he was hard to understand. "I am very sorry that she stayed so late, and I apologize for her," the unknown voice continued.

Suddenly I realized where this conversation was heading. Totally awake now, I remembered that Constantin and Natasha did not stay late. 10:30 p.m. in Beirut was early. People always arrived late and stayed late.

"We are used to staying up late when we have a party," I tried to reassure him.

"I apologize again for the inconvenience." He hung up the phone.

We never saw either Constantin or Natasha again. Over the next few months we tried to contact Constantin at the only telephone number we had. No luck. Had he gone one step too far? Neither gambling nor contact with Westerners was allowed by the Soviets. And Constantin had told us he had a wife in Moscow. Maybe an affair would be tolerated within the closed Soviet community but probably not when it played out in Western circles. Not knowing Natasha's family name, we had no way to find out what happened to her. To call the Soviet Embassy was out of the question. We never did learn what had happened.

JUDY

Judy came to visit us at our apartment on Rue Clemenceaux, "us" being three-year-old Maria and me. Joe was traveling, from Syria to Jordan, to Saudi Arabia and Iraq. The Middle East was never without tension, or an imminent coup d'état, or a re-structuring of government, or other serious upheavals. Joe covered it all for *Newsweek*.

Ulla Morris-Carter

I met Judy in my twice-weekly French class, where we struggled to master vocabulary, read French authors such as Racine and tried to write intelligent essays in French. Judy, who was of British origin, sat next to me. I had not known her before we attended this class. She usually came to class unprepared and rarely had her homework done. She just wanted to learn to speak French, she said. In her mid-twenties, long-legged and tall, she had a strong, statuesque body. She was attractive without being outstandingly beautiful. With her hair tied carelessly into a ponytail, and without any make-up, she looked wholesome. One day, very casually, she mentioned that she really envied people like me with a "normal family life."

"I work in the entertainment industry", she said. I have no relatives here, and I miss my family and the comforts and closeness of home." She sounded somewhat lonely.

"I particularly miss my grandmother. My grandfather was a British Civil Servant in India, and Grandmother had a huge repertoire of Indian adventure stories that I loved to listen to."

"Well, maybe you would like to visit us, a relatively normal, somewhat boring family," I said.

She took me up on the offer. The next Tuesday afternoon she appeared unannounced at our apartment on Rue Clemenceau. She seemed delighted to play with Maria, and also gladly participated in a few household chores.

Helping me make tea, she told me: "To be here is a great treat for me. I feel right at home."

"Come back and visit us again. I'm so pleased you came."

Indeed I was delighted to have such good company and felt that I had acquired a new friend.

"But tell me, what do you actually do? And what is it that prevents you from doing any homework for our French class?" I questioned.

"Well, I work 364 days a year, except Good Friday. A pretty tight schedule."

"I can certainly understand that. But I still don't know where you fit into the mix? Don't you have any weekends?"

"Well," she hesitated for a moment, obviously doubtful whether she really wanted to tell me the rest.

"I am the principal dancer at the Casino du Liban."

Speechless for a moment, I gathered myself together and managed to answer: "Principal dancer? In the Casino du Liban, you said?"

"Yes, that's who I am. And that's what I do."

I had once been invited to the Casino du Liban, a high-class nightclub and cabaret with an elegant gambling casino. The Casino du Liban presented a spectacular show, which, some people claimed, was better than the famous Folies Bergère in Paris. Indeed, Judy told me that she had been one of the famous "Blue Bell Girls," dancing at the

Ulla Morris-Carter

Folies Bergère before coming to Lebanon. The Blue Bell Girls were a well-trained group, beautiful to look at and strictly supervised by the founder of the troupe, an Irish lady by the name of Margaret Kelly. Margaret Kelly had striking blue eyes, hence her nickname, Miss Bluebell.

In an interview with the *Los Angeles Times* Miss Bluebell once said:

They [the girls] must have long legs, be at least 5-foot-10, with high, well-formed derrières, firm breasts, but not too large because, since the demise of the brassiere, dangling, voluminous breasts appear unpleasant, anti-esthetic.

On my first visit to the Casino du Liban I had admired the glamorous dance ensemble, decked out in fantastic feathered headdresses, sequined G-strings, high heels, and not much else. At the end of the show a huge glittering cage in the shape of a ball descended slowly from the ceiling, containining, I just learned, Judy, in an enormous feathered headdress, high heels, a silver G-string, and topless.

In Lebanon these dancers put on a spectacular show. They could do the catwalk, dance the Charleston, shimmy, shake and kick up their legs higher than I thought anatomically possible. At the end of the show a small train would cruise slowly through the audience, its rails running on the second step of the two-tiered table arrangements. Most of the participants sat on the train, waving to the audience. And who sat at the front, right on top of the little locomotive? The principal dancer. Judy, of course.

Having revealed her secret, Judy seemed relieved and could now talk easily about her past and her life in Beirut. Interestingly, she came from a family of civil servants, not a theater family.

"My grandmother would be horrified if she knew I was dancing topless in the Casino du Liban. She knows I am a dancer, but she believes I am a dancer in classical ballet. Indeed, that is how I started. But being as tall as I am, I sadly had to leave my ballet group. That is when Miss Bluebell showed up, recruited me, she was looking for tall girls only, and off to Paris I went."

Of course rich Arabs, sheikhs from the Persian Gulf or princes from Saudi Arabia were always close at hand to invite the dancers to their royal suites, in luxury hotels. Foreign women were considered available and free game, whereas their own wives were not allowed out without a chaperone. Judy explained that this situation had become a continuous battle. Luckily she had acquired a Lebanese boyfriend, Lucien, who helped her escape after the shows. He came from a prominent farming family. But society in general simply did not allow him to appear with Judy at any social function. As a dancer, no matter how sophisticated, she was simply not accepted in Lebanese society.

When we invited the two of them to one of our dinner parties, he confided that this was the first time they, together, could attend a social function in a family setting. The morning after the party, our doorbell rang. In front of me stood a chauffeur in

Ulla Morris-Carter

uniform and matching cap, carrying two large crates of fruit.

"You must have the wrong address, I did not order any fruit." I said, about to close the door.

"But this is a gift from Monsieur Lucien," the chauffeur insisted. And there it was, a thank you from Lucien for the dinner invitation, one box of delicious looking apples and one box of rosy-cheeked peaches. Judy and Lucien became our friends who visited whenever Judy could manage an evening off.

Birth of Karin

As winter approached, I needed a new maternity dress. I located a little store in the Souk Tawila, the only place that carried pregnancy clothes. Most women had their dresses made, particularly when pregnant. But I thought it would be easier to just buy a dress, no trying on, no waiting. I was astonished to see that the the sales people, even in this store, were men. I picked a black dress, simple, with a little collar of fake fur, very soft and becoming, I thought. I paid for it and was ready to leave when the salesman insisted that I try it on.

"I am sure it fits just fine," I said, not wanting to be assisted by this young salesman.

Besides, who had ever heard of a maternity dress needing to be fitted? His attitude was annoying, particularly as he stood blocking the narrow door, insisting on helping me try it on. In the tiny fitting cabin I became more annoyed. He whistled approval through his teeth, put a few pins around the bottom seam, while never missing a chance of touching me or running his hands over my body. Too embarrassed to make a scene, I just slapped his hands, quietly.

"A little tighter under the arms, madam?" he suggested.

Then, in the mirror, I noticed that he had unbuttoned his trousers. Revolted, disgusted, and humiliated, I stormed out of the fitting room, demanding to see the owner. He appeared, impeccably dressed in a dark suit, smiling condescendingly at me while I furiously stated my complaint in French and broken Arabic. His demeanor smooth, he pretended to be listening.

Then, adding insult to injury, he gave me a most pitying look as if to say: "Madam, who do you think would be interested in a woman as pregnant as you?"

With contempt in his voice he said coldly: "You must be mistaken, madam!"

I ran out of the store, almost in tears. I was wearing the pregnancy dress, some pins still in the seam, carrying my clothes under my arm. I realized that I, as a foreign woman, could never win such an argument. I should have known better, having had an equally distressing experience in a shared taxi.

Later Joe gently scolded me: "Don't ever put yourself on the level of a Lebanese taxi driver or a salesman and argue with them."

Ulla Morris-Carter

Joe was right. I had a lot to learn. Pregnant Lebanese women rarely ventured outside their homes. If going out, they made sure they were accompanied by their husband or a chaperone.

My gynecologist was a wonderful Lebanese woman by the name of Adma Abu Shdeed. Against tremendous odds, Abu Shdeed had become the first woman with an M.D. from the widely respected American University of Beirut , AUB, in 1931. Now in her fifties, distinguished looking, her shiny black hair pulled back into a chignon, Dr. Abu Shdeed commanded respect all over the campus. Her warm, dark eyes exuded understanding. She was a champion of women's reproductive rights. Her reputation as a female doctor who could possibly help infertile couples had spread throughout the Middle East. It was a subject that could never be discussed openly in the Arab world. I noticed with interest that I was one of very few women who entered her clinic alone. Normally Arab women were accompanied by their husbands. Dr. Abdu Shdeed was famous enough in this part of the Arab world to have been called to Jordan to deliver the children of King Hussein's wives.

On the morning of March 19, 1964 I set out to buy a few items for Easter, just 10 days away. Anticipating the birth of my second child, I wanted to make sure I would be ready for the Easter egg hunt and a few Easter presents for Maria, now 3 ½. The basket on my arm contained only a few items. I began to feel uncomfortable, maybe a little more than uncomfortable. Labor had started. And strongly! One contraction followed the next in rapid succession. I was still walking around a crowded souk.

"Take a taxi and get to the hospital as fast a possible." I told myself.

Thank God, Joe had just returned from Syria and could help. Racing home, I grabbed my suitcase, which I had prepared ahead of time, and hurried to the AUB Hospital, known around the Middle East for its excellent doctors and nurses. Dr. Abdu Shdeed arrived promptly to check on me and guide me along during labor. After seven hours of a fast, hard and complicated labor, Dr. Abdu Shdeed decided to give me an epidural, a pain relief injection into the spine. Until that moment, I had never heard of an epidural.

One hour later she gave the thumbs-up sign. A beautiful little girl was born. The new baby looked absolutely perfect to me when the nurse put her into my arms. Dr. Abdu Shdeed, however, seemed distressed. She left the delivery room to talk to Joe, who was not allowed to attend the birth:

"I really wanted to present you with a boy," she told Joe, almost in tears. "All along I knew it would be another girl, but I hoped desperately that I would be wrong and it would be a boy."

Joe was delighted to have another girl, particularly one that looked so beautiful.

While I was resting he left for home to tell Maria about her new little sister. Returning to the hospital around nine or ten p.m. he found me in a temporary recovery room.

Ulla Morris-Carter

All the other regular rooms were occupied. The nurses must have assumed that I was sleeping, or perhaps they simply forgot where I was. Nobody had looked in on me. I had had a terrible reaction to the epidural. I was hemorrhaging and momentarily paralyzed. Unable to speak, move or ring the bell, I was alone and terrified. Joe raced through the hospital, shouting for a doctor. I had lost a lot of blood and felt extremely weak. I recovered quickly and needed to stay in the hospital only an extra day.

Among all the mostly Arab babies born at the AUB hospital during my stay, here was this little blond number. In the nursery, where all the babies were lined up in little bassinets when not in their mother's room, I could easily find my daughter.

We decided to name her Karin after my dear and equally fairhaired friend and kayaking companion from Düsseldorf.

Left top: *With Karin looking mischievous.* Left bottom: *With Karin on our balacony.* Above: *Joe with Karin and Maria, a little later on.*

Ulla Morris-Carter

NINE EVENTFUL MONTHS

1965

The phone rang early in the morning. I rushed along the corridor to reach it, hoping it might be Joe calling. He had been traveling in Saudi Arabia for the past two weeks, and we had had only minimal cable contact.

But it was not Joe calling, rather, it was his father, Joe Sr., my beloved father-in-law. He and his wife Maxine, Joe's mother, had been on my mind all during the night because I longed to tell them our exciting news. I had just found out that I was pregnant with our third child.

It was March, 1965. But Joe Sr. had a more urgent message.

"Maxine is in the hospital. She has been diagnosed with pancreatic cancer. Her oncologist gives her only a few days to live."

His voice was shaking. I could feel his distress.

"Please, find Joe. I hope he can be here soon."

The news hit me right in the stomach, as if I'd been punched. How could it be? Maxine was still so young, only 58 years old. Her last visit to Beirut was less than seven months ago, when she came to see her grandchildren, particularly our new baby, Karin.

Maxine had appeared healthy, so politically aware, so smart and witty. But suddenly I recalled an incident that I had somehow put out of my mind. By mistake I had picked up her glass of orange juice one early morning. Drinking it quickly, I just about keeled over. The orange juice was spiked with gin.

Still nursing Karin, I was not drinking any alcohol. What was the matter with Maxine? I didn't understand, nor did I dare raise the question for fear I might be wrong, or for fear of embarrassing her if I was right. Both Joe Sr. and Maxine enjoyed a drink,

Ulla Morris-Carter

sometimes before lunch, and definitely before dinner. But early in the morning? Never. I decided to forget about the incident. Now, seven months later, I wondered whether she might have felt unwell without mentioning it to us. At the time she told us proudly about her check-up before traveling, when she had been given a clean bill of health.

Most important right now was how and where to find Joe. He was still traveling somewhere in Saudi Arabia. I spent hours on the phone, dialing desperately. Finally I located him in Jeddah. Could he make it in time to Guilford to see his dying mother? For a long moment Joe did not say anything.

"I will try to find a way to get there as soon as possible, but I won't be able to stop in Beirut to see you and the children."

No further conversation. I knew Joe would get to work immediately. He and his mother were very close. They operated on the same wavelength, both with quick minds, great senses of humor and no end of curiosity.

Finding a way to fly directly from Saudi Arabia to Connecticut without stopping in Beirut, Joe did manage to see his mother for a few days. She lived slightly longer than her doctors had anticipated.

It was hard to take it in, that this so unique person would no longer be part of our lives. I loved and admired her. She was the one who accompanied her journalist husband on important interviews and took shorthand when he interviewed not only President Eisenhower, but also, later, Richard Nixon.

There was no more interesting mother-in-law than Maxine. The two of us had often sat up deep into the night, talking, smoking, and trying to solve the problems of the world.

What a spring that was! Death and a new life so close together.

While Joe was in America, another event required my attention. Joe had received a cable that Mrs. Kay Graham, the new publisher of the *Washington Post* and *Newsweek*, would be arriving in Beirut for a short visit. Accompanied by *Newsweek's* editor-in-chief, Oz Elliot and his then wife Deirdre, Kay Graham was making her initial foray into the media world following the suicide of her husband, *Washington Post* publisher Phil Graham.

Mrs. Graham's tour was to introduce herself to her troops as their publisher and their new boss, a courageous venture. She and the Elliots had been in the Far East visiting foreign bureaus, particularly war-ravaged Vietnam. At 3 a.m. I drove to Beirut airport to greet them and to accompany them to the St. Georges Hotel.

A sleepy concierge showed them to their respective rooms. Meeting them the next morning, I noticed that they were not a happy team. They had had an uncomfortable night, they admitted, and not because of jet-lag. Mrs. Graham had requested a room with a king-sized bed, and the Elliots, a room with two beds. In the middle of the night,

Ulla Morris-Carter

Left: *Joe's mother Maxine Morris in Guilford, shortly before her death.*
Above: *Joe with Kay Graham, publisher of Newsweek, in Egypt.*

the sleepy concierge had mixed up the instructions. The Elliots ended up in the room with the king-sized bed, and Mrs. Graham in the room with two beds. I didn't know that the Elliots were in the middle of a divorce. Sharing a king-sized bed was not part of the deal. And Mrs. Graham had been too tired to switch.

Before his departure for Saudi Arabia, Joe had sent out invitations to the Beirut press corps, a number of Lebanese ministers and political dignitaries, to attend a large cocktail party at the St. Georges Hotel in honor of the *Newsweek/Washington Post* visitors.

I was frantic. How was I to deal with this without Joe?

Over the phone Joe suggested I call Mark Riachi, a well-known Lebanese journalist and good bachelor friend of ours. Mark came to the rescue. He volunteered his services to stand by my side, make introductions and, in particular, look after Mrs. Graham. This arrangement was a huge success. After the cocktail party, Mark Riachi took Mrs. Graham and the Elliots to one of Beirut's most famous nightclubs, the Cave du Roi. Mark had requested a special belly dancer to perform for the visiting dignitaries. They all loved it and danced the night away. Mark and Mrs. Graham got along so well that Mrs. Graham insisted Mark accompany her to the interview with the Lebanese President.

The next day Mark personally drove Mrs. Graham to the airport while the chauffeured limousine took the Elliots.

Ulla Morris-Carter

A little later I received an invitation to an all-ladies dinner at the home of Adnan Khashoggi, a well-known and immensely wealthy Saudi business man and shady arms dealer. The extensive Khashoggi family always summered in Beirut, when the temperatures in Saudi Arabia frequently reached an uncomfortable 120° F. This year was no exception. When in Beirut, the Khashoggi family occupied a large apartment building with a spectacular view over the Mediterranean. Their fairytale existence was enhanced by a lush garden and a swimming pool illuminated at night with floating candles. As soon as the Saudi women set foot on Lebanese soil, they threw off their black abayas and head coverings and slipped into stylish Western clothing, which this year featured mini-skirts. A few Saudi princesses, in Beirut for the summer or possibly en route to Europe, rounded out guest list.

When I entered the Khashoogi apartment, I could hardly believe what I saw. The 18 or so ladies were decked out in their most elegant evening gowns of silk and satin and wore an astounding display of jewels, from diamonds to emeralds to rubies. With their black shiny hair elegantly arranged, they were stunning. I, by contrast, in my beige dress with matching jacket, felt like an abandoned orphan or Cinderella after midnight.

The Khashoogi women spoke excellent English, but most of the Saudi princesses did not. In my limited Arabic I tried my best to chat with them about the weather, about children and kitchen matters.

Finally the door to the dining room opened. The light came from crystal chandeliers. Most of the floor space was taken up by an enormous table covered with enough food to feed an army. In the center of the elaborately decorated table sat a whole roasted lamb on a silver platter, its skin gleaming under the light of the chandeliers. The lamb had an apple in its mouth. Arabic rice with raisins and nuts, and dozens of delicacies in small dishes filled every available space on the table. Dining was to be buffet-style, and I was starving and wanted to try everything.

Just as I was handed a plate to help myself the hostess appeared carrying a small crystal bowl, which she handed to me:

"You are the guest of honor. This is for you, our special foreign guest," she exclaimed.

Startled, I paused for a moment, then looked at the dish, first in disbelief and then horror. Two eyeballs rolled happily around the bowl. Occasionally they stood still and stared at me. I thought I was going to be sick. The sheep eyeballs, I said to myself. Joe had mentioned this tradition and told me how he had eaten them in Saudi Arabia. It is an insult to the host family if one refuses this special treat.

"One must swallow them whole, not chew them," Joe had explained. "Just swallow them whole like a marble or a large pill."

Impossible, I thought to myself. I must find an excuse, and fast. I closed my eyes for a split second, then turned to my hostess.

Ulla Morris-Carter

"Thank you for the honor, but I really can't accept it. I hate to be impolite, but," and here I hesitated and took a deep breath, "I haven't told anybody yet, but I am pregnant. You know yourself, I am sure, how miserable one can occasionally feel during the early part of pregnancy. I simply cannot swallow a bite."

"Oh, I understand completely, and congratulations!" she said. I'll get you a cup of tea and I am sure you will feel better."

I thanked her profusely for her help and understanding. Though I was truly hungry, I had to stick to my story. Sadly, my first and only ladies dinner party ended early, and I hurried home for something to eat.

FROM NEWSWEEK TO THE L.A. TIMES

The year 1965 turned out to be a tumultuous year, not only in family affairs, but also in world affairs. Lyndon Baines Johnson was inaugurated as the 36th U.S. President. Martin Luther King led thousands of nonviolent demonstrators from Montgomery to Selma, Alabama, in the 54-mile freedom march. 770 marchers were arrested. The first U.S. two-man space flight, the Gemini space program, was launched. The Vietnam War made daily headlines, and the first haunting photographs of the U.S. bombing there appeared in our newspapers.

Early that summer, Joe left *Newsweek* as their Middle East correspondent and joined the *Los Angeles Times,* opening their first Middle East Bureau in Beirut in the Press Cooperative Building on Rue Hamra.

Mrs. Graham was not pleased. She called the *Los Angeles Times* publisher, Otis Chandler, to complain about the theft of one of her top foreign correspondents. Because of the move from *Newsweek* to the *Los Angeles Times*, we lost the U.S. home leave that had been due us with *Newsweek*. Instead, we would have to wait another two years before being eligible for leave under the *Los Angeles Times*. That meant no home leave for four-and-a-half years.

But this wasn't the only problem. The question of health insurance to cover the birth of the baby due in November became an issue. Who would cover the cost? Was this a pre-existing condition? The baby, conceived with *Newsweek*, would be born to the *Los Angeles Times*. I was embarrassed by the back-and-forth letter exchange on this subject. In the end the *Los Angeles Times* volunteered to pay.

Summers in Beirut were hot and sticky. The summer of 1965 was no exception. Beirut emptied out. Many locals moved to the mountains. Most foreigners, and Beirut was full of foreigners who had established their business bases there, traveled to their home countries. We couldn't afford to fly to the U.S. or Germany. We barely managed a short family trip to Cyprus

Ulla Morris-Carter

Cyprus

Few things in life turn out exactly as planned. Most of the time, minor adjustments will rectify a situation. But occasionally one finally just has to declare defeat.

We needed this much-delayed vacation, R&R from the turbulence, the heat and humidity of Beirut, and most importantly a quiet time and a coming together of our family. Joe had been constantly on the road covering wars, revolutions and upheavals, which in the Middle East were and are never far away. Our children were now five and 1½ years of age, and I was seven months pregnant with our third child.

A correspondent friend had offered us the use of his house in Kyrenia on the Island of Cyprus. We accepted his generous offer. Cyprus, the third largest Island in the Mediterranean Sea, seemed ideal for us, just a short plane ride from Lebanon. Even if the temperatures in the summer were often as high as those in Lebanon, the air in Cyprus, unlike Beirut's, was dry and the evenings balmy. And beyond that we had a beautiful beach right below our house, just minutes down a small path.

Joe and I had spent our honeymoon on Cyprus in 1959 in that same little village of Kyrenia, one of the most picturesque places imaginable. Its tiny crescent harbor seemed like the ideal place to slow down, sit back, relax and forget the problems of the world. Its small streets and walled gardens, rosy with pomegranates, and the green fields surrounding the village, looked to me like the most romantic and beautiful places I had ever seen. The neighboring village of Belpaese was home to the writer Lawrence Durell, famous for his novels, the Alexandria Quartet, and, in 1965, his new book on the Cyprus conflict, titled Bitter Lemons.

To make this vacation easier for all of us, but particularly for me, we brought along our Armenian babysitter and household helper, Marie. She wasn't feeling too well when we started our journey. I thought that it was because she had never flown. The Kyrenia vacation house of our friend was lovely, not luxurious, but perfect in its simplicity and it was surrounded by an untended but lush garden. Clearly the house needed some major attention. It hadn't been lived in for a while. Mice and other critters obviously found it a pleasant nesting ground. No problem, I thought. Between Marie and me we would be able to whip this place into shape in no time at all.

Marie, however, feeling worse, took to her bed the minute we arrived. I wasn't sure exactly what troubled her, but she looked pale and frightened. We communicated in broken Arabic. None of us spoke any Armenian, and Marie spoke no English. That turned out to be an obstacle.

After some difficult probing, I discovered that Marie was hemorrhaging. She needed a doctor, this was an emergency. Because we couldn't read the telephone book, it was in Greek only, we didn't know where to start to find a doctor. Luckily, Joe remembered the names of some local journalists from the days when he had covered the

Ulla Morris-Carter

independence of Cyprus in 1960, and the following civil war between the Greek and Turkish communities. These journalists came to our rescue. A pleasant Greek-Cypriot doctor appeared fairly quickly. He spoke excellent English, but obviously no Arabic or Armenian, which meant that I had to translate the untranslatable.

To our dismay he soon discovered that Marie had attempted an abortion. It had gone wrong, and she was hemorrhaging. He tended to her as best he could but recommended that she return to Beirut as soon as possible as she needed further care and possible hospitalization. Add to that the tremendous language problems. I had not counted on playing nurse to Marie, rather the opposite.

After two days of full-time nursing duty on my part, helped greatly by our friendly doctor, Marie seemed stable enough to fly back to Beirut. The airline managed to organize a first class ticket. Joe carried Marie, a pillow under her head, on board the Middle East Airlines plane, which whisked her back to Beirut and to her family.

Meanwhile, five-year-old Maria developed a high fever. Our Cypriot doctor, by now almost a family friend, diagnosed it as pneumonia. She would have to go to the only hospital on the island in Nicosia, the capital, for treatment and X-rays. It was about an hour's drive from us. In Cyprus, which had been a British colony since 1925, driving was on the left, a problem for me. I had never attempted to drive on the left-hand side of the road. My American husband, on the other hand, did not find this a problem at all as he had lived and worked in England and had covered Cyprus for his newspaper. It meant that he was the one to make daily trips to the Nicosia hospital with Maria.

I was still waiting for the relaxing part of this vacation. Seven months pregnant, I had pictured going to the beach, sitting in a small harbor taverna sipping Uzo and gazing at the sunset. The house was now habitable, if not perfect. Maria's health was improving.

Were we now ready to start our real vacation?

Suddenly the weather turned extremely hot, oppressive and overcast. The sky, until now clear and bright blue, turned a dirty beige-brown, part of it almost purple and frightening to look at. No doubt, a sandstorm was approaching. We knew sandstorms from living in Cairo and Beirut, the Khamseen that blows from the Sahara desert and stifles the air.

Joe didn't want to let on that also he too wasn't feeling too great. He continued to help until I noticed his flushed complexion. When Joe's fever reached 103° F, our Dr. Papadopoulos diagnosed a virus that appeared to be going around Cyprus.

Not to worry, he declared. "In three or four days you will be as good as new, just rest and drink lots of liquids."

Little 1½ year-old Karin, my cute blond girl with bright blue eyes and a big smile on her face, had been a bit neglected while the surrounding commotion took up most

Ulla Morris-Carter

of my time and energy. The Cypriots, mostly dark-haired and olive-skinned, adored Karin, wanting to pat her on the head and stroke her silky blond hair. To make up for my recent neglect and despite the approaching storm, I took Karin out to do some shopping and to look at the wild ocean. Waves as high as 30 feet crashed against the stone sea wall. Our delightful harbor was fairly well protected. We settled into a quiet cafe for a cool, delicious lemonade and a rest. The wind rose, and suddenly the storm blew in at full force. Walking home, we had a hard time pushing against tremendous gusts that almost blew us off the unpaved road.

Karin was an adventurous little girl, almost always good-humored and happy. She didn't even complain when the sand blew into her tender face. She just soldiered on, holding tightly to my hand. It required all our strength to make any headway. A good trooper, she actually seemed to enjoy this adventure. We soon reached the front garden of our home away from home. The wind had blown the latticed garden gate closed. Usually it stood open. I tried to open it. Without warning it unhinged itself and landed right on top of Karin.

I was too stunned to scream.

Joe was upstairs in bed with a high fever. I remember lifting the heavy gate off my child. She was lying totally still, face up on the dirt road. The pattern of the lattice work was imprinted on her face and body. No crying, no screaming, no complaining! Nothing but the howling sounds of the storm. And no sign of life from Karin. I picked up the limp body, and charged against the wind to the house.

Convinced she was dead, I gently lay her into her crib and rushed to the phone. By now I had memorized Dr. Papadopoulos's telephone number. We were, no doubt, his best clients. Panic stricken, I raced back to the crib. Karin was moving slightly, and yes, she was opening her eyes. Her bruised body and bloody face did not matter, she was breathing, she was not dead. Arriving promptly as usual, Dr. Papadopoulos told me that she might have a concussion. She had obviously lost consciousness for a while, but no, he assured me, she was not going to die.

Joe began to feel better, his temperature dropping to near normal. Karin's accident, however, was the straw that broke the camel's back. We decided to return to hot and humid Beirut, where we hoped for a few peaceful, quiet days, in spite of the heat. And, indeed, to be safely back home never felt better.

Our vacation? Not as expected. Such is life, a never-ending series of surprises.

No sooner had we returned to Beirut from Cyprus, than the Indo-Pakistani conflict, fought over Kashmir, broke out. It had simmered since early August, but by the end of that month it had escalated from a Pakistani guerilla war into a full-scale Indian offensive toward West Pakistan. Both countries, Pakistan and India, laid claim to the entire state of Kashmir. The *Los Angeles Times* instantly called Joe into action to cover

Ulla Morris-Carter

the story, even though it was not actually a Middle Eastern conflict. He took off for Rawalpindi and Lahore, Pakistan. Communication was sketchy, of course, as he traveled with the Pakistani troops. I was growing increasingly worried, sitting at home with two small children and a third one to come.

How long would this war last? After three weeks of sometimes heavy fighting, both countries agreed to a UN-sponsored ceasefire at the end of September. That stopped the fighting but changed little politically. Both countries, under pressure, withdrew to their pre-war positions.

Meanwhile the news out of Los Angeles was equally grim. In August race riots broke out in Watts, a section of Los Angeles. Over a period of six days more than 35 people died and more than 1,000 were injured. Among those killed was a *Los Angeles Times* reporter, Ruben Salazar. The National Guard had to be called in to stop the riots.

Joe returned to us briefly in October before taking off again, this time for Iraq and other hotspots. Interestingly, one of his articles out of Baghdad ran under the headline:

Iraqi Chief Offers Kurds Anything but Secession if they'll End War.

As I write this, half a century later, I can hardly believe how little has essentially changed. The Middle East has never stood still.

By November 18, 1965, our baby was due any day and Joe was still on the road somewhere in the Middle East. Never before did I feel happier and more relieved to see him come home than when he appeared just days before the baby's birth. A huge weight was lifted from my shoulders. I felt almost light-footed despite the load I was carrying.

What a relief to have him home.

On November 23, John Fistere, a former journalist, and his wife Isobel invited us to a special dinner party in honor of Henry Luce III, son of the founder of *Time* magazine. As *Time's* vice-president and a journalist Luce was touring the Middle East. Joe was hesitant about taking me to a dinner party, but I insisted that I was feeling just fine.

After all, who would enjoy sitting at home waiting for labor to start?

I decided to wear that black dress I had bought in Souk Tawila in downtown Beirut for just such occasions. The Fisteres had an elegant sit-down dinner. I was placed next to the guest of honor. Henry Luce was a man of the world, an interesting person with knowledge of the Middle East. I enjoyed him as a dinner partner, but halfway through the main course I suddenly began to feel the well-known signs of early labor. I took a deep breath and carried on, trying to hide my discomfort from the dinner guests. More pains followed in rapid succession. I really couldn't eat anything, but having defied Joe earlier that evening, I didn't want to admit I was wrong. I managed to hang on until dessert and coffee were served in an adjoining room. At that point it was past time for me to move to the AUB.

Ulla Morris-Carter

Joe was frantic: "I'll take you to the hospital immediately. No, we can't go home first and pick up your suitcase."

He was right. There was no time to lose. Arriving at the hospital, I knew where to go. Karin was born there, too.

"I can find my way," I told Joe reassuringly, "Just call Dr. Abu Shdeed and tell her that I am in the hospital."

Dr. Abu Shdeed, my gynecologist, had already delivered Karin. I was very fond of her and grateful to be her patient. Over the last two years, she had become a friend of the family. While Joe was calling Dr. Shdeed, I stood at the entrance of the maternity station. A nurse passed by, looked at her watch.

"It's almost ten o'clock. You cannot visit at this time."

"But I am not visiting. I am having a baby, please hurry."

She looked surprised at this woman in a black dress with a black evening coat over her shoulders, carrying nothing but a little handbag. I am not sure she took me seriously, because I did not look terribly pregnant and was standing there all by myself.

When she disappeared, I called after her, begging her to believe me, to let me lie down. The pains were increasing and coming more rapidly. I could not stand up much longer. After what seemed like an eternity, she returned and pointed to an empty room where I could lie down. By this time ten minutes or more had passed.

Apparently, Dr. Abu Shdeed had called the hospital to tell the nurses that she was on her way and to prepare me for birth. Finally, there was some action, and I received the attention I desperately needed. Labor this time was fast and furious, different from the births of Maria and Karin, when labor dragged on for many hours.

Dr. Shdeed's face suddenly appeared, like an angel looking down on me as I was struggling to catch my breath. When I saw her familiar gentle and comforting face, I immediately relaxed. Joe had returned to the hospital and was allowed to see me briefly. In those days a father's presence during delivery was not appreciated, usually even forbidden. Doctors feared that they might have to take care not only of mothers but also of faint-hearted fathers.

I had been in the hospital less than two hours when I was rolled into the delivery room. By my recollection it was just a few minutes before midnight when I heard the new baby's first cry. From where I was lying I could see the clock with the large Roman numerals. At that moment I was not concerned about the exact time of birth. I was just overjoyed, unbelievably happy and relieved when Dr. Abu Shdeed announced that our baby was a perfectly beautiful and healthy little girl, all fingers and toes intact. Only later did I realize that the nurse registered our baby as having been born on the next day, November 24 at 12:05 a.m. What I also didn't know then, was that Dr. Abu

Ulla Morris-Carter

Shdeed left the delivery room to talk to Joe, who was waiting nervously outside, to tell him, again with tears in her eyes:

"It's another girl. I so much wanted for you to have a boy. I was pretty sure it would be a girl, but I hoped that this time I would be wrong."

Joe, seeing Dr. Abu Shdeed in tears, immediately assumed that something was terribly wrong with either mother or child. He could hardly believe she thought a third girl would be a disappointment. But in the Arab world, and she knew the Arab world well, it was important to have a boy in the family. Girls frequently were not even counted when children were mentioned.

On Dr. Abu Shdeed's special request, Joe was handed a white robe and allowed into the delivery room. Seeing and holding his beautiful new baby daughter, he was as happy as I was. There is no way to describe the tender feelings and delight that holding a tiny new creature brings out in whoever is involved at birth.

After a day of rest in the hospital, I was released to face a tumultuous reunion with Karin and Maria, both delighted to have a new little sister at home. A congratulatory telegram from my mother called our family the "Dreimäderlhaus," the house of three girls , after a Viennese operetta with music by Franz Schubert.

The new baby remained nameless for almost three weeks until we finally settled on Julia. Actually, we wanted to call her "Julia Augusta," after the old Roman name for Beirut. But the fear that she might be called Gussy, made us eliminate "Augusta."

Below left: *My mother, Omi, came to visit with the new grand-daughter.* **Below middle and far right**: *On a short summer vaction in Laqulouk, a cool mountain resort, as a substitute for our missed homeleave and escaping the heat and humidity of the Beirut summer. Joe with baby Julia at the pool and myself with Julia.*

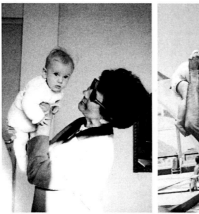

Ulla Morris-Carter

253

Los Angeles Times

**INTER-OFFICE
CORRESPONDENCE**

DATE: December 15, 1965

FROM: Ed Gilbert

SUBJECT: Fatherhood (Overseas Division)

TO: Joe Alex Morris Jr.

Although Among Ourselves does not make much of a
fuss over new babies of Times employes, you have
forced us to make an exception. For, as you
probably have been informed, your recent contribution
to the population explosion made history when your
youngster became the first foreign-born xhihd Times
child.

This epochal event should be heralded in the proper
manner. So would you please forward me all of the
pertinent data, or better yet, an "I was there" piece
by you. Also--and this is where we really break
precedent--please send along a picture. We have na
turned down all baby pictures in the past for pretty
doggone obvious reasons, but then we have never had
one born in Beirut before.

Must have this by Jan. 4 to make the January issue.

Thanks much, and of course, Congratulations

Editor, Among Ourselves

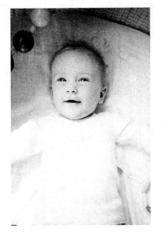

Above: *Letter from the* L.A. Times 'Among Ourselves' *internal
magazine. 'First Times baby born abroad' prompted them to run a
story about it.* **Left:** *Passport photo of baby Julia for the piece.*

Ulla Morris-Carter

Winter beach in Beirut: Joe with the three girls.

Ulla Morris-Carter

Joe Sr.'s painting from our beautiful Patriachie balcony.

PATRIACHIE

On December 1, 1965, just a week after our third daughter's birth, we had to change apartments. The rental contract for the Rue Clemenceau flat had run out at the end of November, we had no choice but to move at a most inconvenient time.

By sheer chance, a place we had always admired became available following the departure of a British Embassy couple who had occupied it.

"What a view! Unbelievable!" Joe and I exclaimed in unison when we first stood on one of the many balconies of the old Arab house in Patriarchie.

Overwhelmed by what we saw, all of Beirut streched out in front of us as well as the narrow but fertile seaboard, wedged between the sea and the 10,000-foot mountains we decided then and there that we would sign the lease. It was a most romantic, though slightly impractical, place for a family with three young children.

Patriarchie, a section of Beirut originally the seat of the Greek Orthodox Patriarch, became our new home. Our top floor duplex apartment also overlooked the edge of the Basta, the old Moslem quarter. We had almost as many balconies as rooms.

Because of its age, our apartment had a few design problems. The kitchen was definitely not state-of-the-art. The square granite sink had an old-world look, hand-hewn and charming, but only admired by those who did not have to do the daily dishwashing. Certainly nobody before our arrival had ever considered anything like a dishwasher. The kitchen cabinets had screens instead of glass. The apartment had no central heating system. Beirut, like other seaside cities, turned cold and damp in the winter months. On any given winter morning I would fire up the kerosene stove, then

Ulla Morris-Carter

light the fire in the fireplace before proceeding to the next room to light a gas heater.

Earlier, Joe, returning from Afghanistan, had presented me with a sheepskin-lined Afghani shepherd's coat. He suggested that it could be worn as a "bathrobe" in the early chilly morning hours or when nursing the baby. No sooner did I feel warm in my new Afghan fur coat, than the untreated sheepskin began to smell rather nasty, a rancid odor I found impossible to tolerate for more than a few minutes. Ah, the price of living in a romantic place!

Frequently the creaky elevator would not work. No problem as long as I didn't have to carry babies, strollers and groceries up to the third floor. From the street to the entrance of our building, we ascended an imposing flight of stairs, 50 old stone steps, to a courtyard and the main entrance of our house. Across the courtyard from us stood a splendid old Arab building, occupied by Assem Salam, a nephew of then Prime Minister Saab Salam, and his Palestinian wife Josephine. They became friendly neighbors.

Because this was a "local" move, the *Los Angeles Times* did not provide any financial assistance and, therefore, many of our spirited friends and journalists pitched in. This meant that the changeover turned out to be chaotic. Every room was filled with boxes, but not necessarily the boxes that should have been there. Joe was traveling again before we were properly settled. I had little help. A newly arrived German au-pair, uncomfortable and unhappy in Beirut, turned out to be more trouble than help and departed after a few days.

After the birth of Julia and the sudden move that followed, I was incredibly tired. I do not recall any other point in my life when I felt so completely and continually exhausted. The old apartment on Rue Clemenceau had had to be packed up while the baby had to be nursed. Two young children had to be looked after and furniture moved, then re-installed, into the new apartment. At times, after the children had been tucked into bed, I fell asleep in front of the fireplace, waking up with my front roasting and my back freezing.

As well as being one of the more picturesque places we had ever lived, the new apartment had quite a history. Our immediate predecessor was a British Embassy diplomat. We learned that Mr. Rowley had been with MI6, the British equivalent of the CIA. I thought he was a rather mysterious man.

Before our move into this place, we had been invited to one of the Rowleys spectacular cocktail parties. At the entrance to the apartment, beyond a narrow foyer, Mr. Rowley had installed two small mirrors, on either side of the wide doorframe. These were placed to allow him a view of the spacious high-ceilinged living room whenever he and his wife entertained. He always stood at that same spot, greeting his guests,while consulting his mirrors so as never to miss anything that might be occurring at the other end of the long living room. Elsewhere, we found strange holes in two walls, holes that

Ulla Morris-Carter

contained neither electrical plugs nor any other fittings. Our imaginations ran rampant, conjuring mysterious plots and spy stories.

When spring approached, life became more pleasant and a lot easier. Sunshine and flowers filled our house and terraces. Julia and her two sisters adjusted happily to their new surroundings. Madame Arslanian, a mature and very kind Armenian lady, came to help out. She absolutely adored Julia and filled in for mother whenever necessary. Other than "mama," Julia's first words were in Armenian, none of which I could understand.

Madame Arslanian, we all called her simply Madame, was multi-talented. A great seamstress, she sewed identical dresses for all three girls of pink and white-gingham material, with a dark blue trim. This drew strong protests from Maria and Karin, who disliked being dressed in identical outfits. At almost three and six, they were already individualists.

Joe returned home one evening with unusual news.

"The Greek Orthodox Patriarch of Jerusalem is visiting Beirut and will join us for breakfast tomorrow morning at eight a'clock. He has agreed to an interview and conversation here at our house rather than in the Patriarchat."

I was used to have sudden dinner guests or visiting journalists, but a Greek Orthodox Patriarch? Never.

Karin, Maria, Julia and I. Girls in their identical dresses made by Madame Arslan.

Ulla Morris-Carter

Joe interviewing the Greek Orthodox prelate Bishop Saleeby, archimadrate of Beirut and Mount Lebanon, of Patriachie.

"A Patriarch for breakfast?" I exclaimed in horror. "What do I have to do? What does he eat? Do I have to kiss his ring?"

I was deeply concerned. As every mother knows, eight in the morning is a busy time. Children have to be ready for the school bus to take them to kindergarten or nursery school, the baby has to be fed, and the breakfast dishes cleared away. Joe, with his usual equinimity, calmed me down.

"The Patriarch will just have a cup of coffee while we discuss some of the problems of Jerusalem. And don't worry about kissing his ring. That's for Catholic Archbishops."

The Patriarch, a tall man with dark brown eyes that couldn't hide a little twinkel, arrived promptly at eight. He turned out to be a friendly and gentle person. With his white beard and long black robes he made an impressive figure. Comfortably seated in our living room, he appeared at ease when the children came in to greet him and even insisted on kissing baby Julia when I carried her into the living room. Soon , he and Joe were deep in conversation, giving me a chance to quietly disappear.

Later that first year in Beirut, Antoinette entered our lives. A 29-year-old no-nonsense lady, blonde and strong, she came to help with the children. Madame Arslanian had decided that looking after three children daily was more than she could handle at her age. With Joe gone over half of the time, moving from one crisis to the next, I needed more help. Antoinette spent six hours a day with us, Monday through Friday, plus occasional babysitting at night. Her parents, her two brothers and her sister resided to the north in Tripoli, Lebanon's second largest city. We settled into a pleasant working routine with Antoinette, and our household was running as smoothly as one could expect with three young children under foot.

Seven months after Antoinette joined us, we received a strange phone call from someone named Joseph. A Lebanese-American from Texas, he told us he had returned to Lebanon for the sole purpose of finding a bride. Not just any bride. She had to be from the northern region, where he originated. She had to be Christian, preferably good looking, and willing to move with him to Texas.

He asked to have a "conference" with us. Puzzled by this unusual request, Joe and I invited him to come over. Joseph showed up dressed in suit and tie. He looked around 30 and spoke excellent English.

Ulla Morris-Carter

"What shall I do?" Joseph asked, wasting no time on lengthy introductions. "After a few days of looking around, my eye fell upon Theresa, Antoinette's younger sister. I want to marry her, and I need your help. I have enough money to take care of her and her family. Antoinette, as the oldest daughter, is the one that, by tradition, I should marry. But it's Theresa I love and want. Her parents will insist on having one daughter at their house to help out and look after them. They will not be happy with my request. If they allow me to take away Theresa, they will want Antoinette at their house instead. Would you, please, try to convince Antoinette to return to Tripoli to look after her parents? I will pay her a decent salary. I have plenty of money to make up for the loss of her job with you. Please, convey to her that I am most sincere and will be waiting anxiously for her answer."

This was one of the strangest requests either of us had been presented with.

"Is he asking us to be a marriage broker?" we asked each other. "What can we do? We haven't even met the parents."

One thing we saw immediately was that Joseph and Antoinette had a language problem. Antoinette spoke French and no English and Joseph spoke only English and no French. And his Arabic was rusty, he admitted.

How did he communicate with Theresa? we wondered. And the last thing we needed was to be involved in a Lebanese-American family feud. We knew how difficult, even dangerous, these feuds in traditional Arab families could be. Before we could become more involved in this transcontinental love story, events conspired to solve the problem.

It was May 1967. Suddenly, Joe had to leave for Cairo and Jordan. Tensions were running high in the Middle East. Anxiety over the possibility of yet another Arab-Israeli war was everywhere. What would become known as the Six-Day War was spreading its shadow over the region. Antoinette's mother called, hysterical, wanting her daughter to come home immediately.

When the first dramatic news stories of hostilities came over the radio, half of Beirut fled the city for the mountains, many to their ancestral villages. Foreigners were evacuated in droves. I decided to stay in Beirut with my children. I did not know exactly where Joe was at that moment. More important, I knew he would have to cover this developing crisis for the *Los Angeles Times* and could not be expected home any time soon.

Better, I thought, to stay in place.

Ulla Morris-Carter

To get the news in a land where almost no one will talk for the record...

...it takes a Joe Alex Morris in Beirut

Covering the Middle East calls for a very special set of reporting skills and talents. Joe Alex Morris Jr., head of the Los Angeles Times bureau in Beirut, has what it takes to do the job – the rare ability to cut through the difficulties of distance, language barriers, intrigue and official secrecy in covering his complex news beat.

During his years as a foreign correspondent, Morris has reported revolutions and uprisings in many Arab, African and Asian countries. He spent weeks covering both sides of the Yemen civil war. His special report on India in 1964 won international recognition and acclaim.

He has ranged from the Himalayas to Equatorial Africa on news stories of worldwide significance.

Joe Alex Morris is typical of the 22 bureau heads who represent the Los Angeles Times in key news areas around the world. The excellence of his work reflects the emphasis on quality which characterizes his newspaper. By seeking, attracting and challenging men of outstanding editorial ability, The Times continues to strengthen its position of leadership among news media, reaching Western America's largest and most influential audience every morning of the year.

The Los Angeles Times
A DIVISION OF THE TIMES MIRROR COMPANY

L.A. Times ad featuring Joe Alex Morris in the Wall Street Journal.

THE SIX-DAY WAR

JUNE 1967

If I were to live a thousand years,

Never would I forget Jerusalem

Which still seems to breathe with the grandeur of Jehovah

And the terrors of death.

~ Chateaubriand, 1811

"**N**othing fits together. Nothing is in place," I mumbled to myself on Monday morning June 5, 1967, the day the Six-Day War began. Tension was running high not only in Beirut, but all over the Middle East.

Joe was somewhere in Jordan, but we had no contact. All means of communications had been cut. I was alone in Beirut with three small children in an old Arab house that towered over the neighboring dwelling. The building had emptied out within hours of the first news of the outbreak of war. Most of our neighbors fled to their ancestral villages in the mountains.

Where was I to go? What was I to do?

I didn't have enough cash in the house. I hadn't stocked up on food. Our residence permits had expired. Joe had not been in Beirut long enough lately to renew them. Residence permits were not only necessary to reside in Lebanon, but would be also required when leaving the country.

Ulla Morris-Carter

We had been looking forward to home leave in the US and Germany. Having missed our scheduled home leave two years earlier, in the summer of 1965, due to Joe's change of jobs, we looked forward to introducing our children to their grandparents and to taking them out of the hot and humid Beirut summer. But as had happened before, the perplexities and the politics of the Middle East interfered with our plans.

I had been by myself in our house in Patriarchia for the past three weeks. I had seen Joe only for half an hour at Beirut airport on June 2, 1967, a Friday. He had been reporting from Cairo and was transiting Beirut on his way to Amman, Jordan, fearing that yet another Middle East crisis was in the making. Most of his colleagues preferred to remain in Cairo. He always had a good nose for being in the right place at the right time. After arriving in Amman, he rented a car, and, unbeknownst to me or anybody else at the time, he was immediately on his way to Jerusalem, where he correctly suspected confrontations would start. Communications had been erratic during the past few days, but they worsened daily with the mounting tension. As Israeli troops were massing at the Egypt–Sinai border, the radio news was confusing, unsettling and mixed with unreliable rumors.

By 1967, the modern state of Israel had been in existence for 19 years. It had been created out of another war—the 1948 War of Independence. Frustrated by the losses of this first Arab-Israeli war, the war the Palestinians would continue to call "The Catastrophe", *Al Nakba*, Arab countries had lately increased their fierce and almost hysterical anti-Israeli rhetoric. Following the 1948 war, some Palestinians had fled their homes in Palestine out of fear, others had been expelled from their land in what had been Palestine and was now Israel. Quite a few Palestinians went to Kuwait, others to Syria, Jordan and Lebanon.

By 1967, Lebanon had absorbed large numbers of Palestinian refugees, some of whom had been successfully integrated into Lebanese society and business life. But thousands of others still lingered in the Palestinian refugee camps such as Sabra and Shatila on the outskirts of Beirut. Emotions ran high in the camps. The refugees, stateless, without jobs and without much hope for their future, were fiercely anti-Israel.

Arab hostility toward the State of Israel was the direct cause of the present tension, anxiety and unrest. Israel grew more and more alarmed by warlike threats from Egypt that President Nasser might close the Gulf of Aqaba, the three-mile-wide Strait of Tiran through which Israeli ships had to pass to reach Eilat, Israel's only Red Sea port. Indeed, on May 23, 1967 President Nasser ordered the closing of the Gulf of Aqaba to Israeli shipping. In addition, Egypt, Syria and Jordan had joined in a defense pact, which prompted Israel to start massing troops at the border.

In Beirut, the rumbling of guns could be heard in the distance, gripping us all in fear of another Middle East war. Nervously, we watched and waited, while the United

Ulla Morris-Carter

Nations and the United States scrambled to find a peaceful solution. At 6 a.m. Monday, June 5, 1967, Israel launched a pre-emptive attack on Egypt. Its suddenness surprised everybody. Heavy fighting erupted. Each side claimed the other had invaded. Israel issued an appeal to Jordan to stay out of the war. Jordan refused. Jordanian forces joined the war with a massive bombardment of the Israeli sector of Jerusalem. Shells began to fall on Jerusalem at 11 a.m. In short, it proved a brutal war, an accidental war, provoked by misperceptions. It was a war that nobody really wanted. In the end it brought a humiliating defeat to Egypt, which was followed by the resignation of President Nasser.

As it turned out, Joe had made the right move by traveling to Jerusalem. Immediately after the hostilities started, all foreign journalists in Cairo were placed under house arrest in their hotels by the Egyptian military. The journalists in Amman, Jordan, experienced a similar fate. Confined to their hotels, they were denied access to the front lines. Since Jordan, at that point, had already cut all communications, Joe could not inform me of his exact whereabouts. I had heard that he was not in Amman. I was frantic when the *BBC* announced that three journalists had been killed in Jerusalem. No names were given at first, and nobody had any direct information. The *BBC* later carried the news that an American *NBC* correspondent and a *Life* photographer had been killed while filming from the roof of the National Hotel in Jerusalem. The Israeli army had mistaken the photographer's tripod for an anti-aircraft gun.

The *Los Angeles Times*, via *United Press* telex, asked whether I—a housewife and mother—would give a short description of how I fared by myself during this crisis. I had never written anything other than letters during my then 33 years of life, and I did not have either time or leisure to sit down and write during those commotion-filled days. Later, though, when Beirut was for long days under curfew, I made an attempt. My one and only article ever eventually appeared in the *Los Angeles Times*, shortened and with an editor's introduction:

> Among those caught up in the chaos and tragedy of the Middle East war were thousands of foreign residents. Many had to cope with blackouts, angry crowds, and eventually, hasty evacuations. One who did not go was Ulla Morris, wife of Los Angeles Times correspondent Joe Alex Morris, Jr., resident in Beirut. She was alone with her three children throughout the one-week war, while her husband was covering the fighting. Her story follows.
>
> BEIRUT--Monday, the day the war broke out, started like any other day. I packed the children off to school at 7 a.m., and was rushing out of the house for my French lesson.
>
> There was just enough time to listen to the 8 a.m. BBC news from London, the fourth news bulletin I heard that morning. And there it was: Fierce fighting has broken out between Egypt and Israel in the Sinai Peninsula."

Ulla Morris-Carter

One little handful of words,not completely unexpected, but finding all of us unprepared for what was to come. This short announcement was enough to transform immediately the scene in Beirut. People huddled around transistor radios on every street corner. Those not listening seemed to be walking faster than usual. Most of them appeared to be rushing downtown, towards the banking district.

I joined the rush. Having only slightly recovered from the first shock and knowing that with my husband in Jordan I couldn't count on his presence for some time, I turned to immediate problems like finances. The local branch of the First National City Bank, a busy place in normal times, had turned into a solid mass of people desperately anxious to draw money. I couldn't even see the counter, let alone get near it to cash money. Travelers checks had already been scarce the week before, and today there were none.

After this unsuccessful mission I went up to the UPI office to read the incoming ticker. The news was even grimmer than I had imagined. The war had really started, not only in the Sinai but a fierce battle was raging in Jerusalem. All Beirut was gripped by the news. Tension was mounting everywhere. My next project—trying to stock up on food—was only slightly more successful than the trip to the bank. People were buying for weeks to come. The supermarket resembled more and more a football field after a rough game. Empty shelves, slightly dusty, stared back at me where I was accustomed to see sugar, rice, flour, and even matches.

I stocked up with whatever I could find and tried to make my way home through traffic jams, people lugging heavy food packages, frightened people rushing off to their mountain villages—the only place they would feel safe, even if the village was located only nine miles from the Israeli border.

At home, equal confusion awaited me. Our babysitter and house helper, Antoinette, was in a panic because her hysterical mother had ordered her to come home to their mountain village immediately. Also there was our next-door neighbor, the wife of an American University professor, in an extremely nervous state. She was just about to have her first baby. As I walked in, the telephone rang. It was the American Embassy saying they were to start evacuating Americans in about five hours, on a voluntary basis first for non-official families. In the fast-moving events of the morning, the idea of leaving the country had not even entered my mind. I politely declined the offer but asked them to keep me informed.

Exhausted and hot from running through downtown Beirut in the summer heat, lugging packages of whatever groceries I was able to find, I collapsed at home into a chair in our living room. A sudden excruciating pain running through my back made it almost impossible to get up again. All I wanted to do was lie down on the cool stone floor and rest. But there was no rest for the weary: Antoinette, our babysitter, following her mother's orders, departed instantly for the mountains, but children needed to be fed and decisions to be made.

An American Embassy official came around that evening and presented me with

Ulla Morris-Carter

an"evacuation kit" or—as I called it—the"how-to-make-sure-to-be-molested" kit. The first thing I pulled out of the large brown envelope was a big American flag, with instructions to paste it on our car's windshield before leaving. As events later in the week were to show, this would have had the effect of making absolutely certain our car would be burnt or smashed up. Various little flags were also included, along with signs in Arabic to mark our flat as being occupied by Americans—a virtual invitation to sacking.

Tuesday morning began with more calls from the Embassy, this time with the more urgent advice to leave town, particularly since I was there by myself with three small children. Meanwhile the Embassy itself was attacked by a mob, which did some damage before police brought it under control.

By lunchtime I had another call from the Embassy, this time trying to evacuate me from our apartment to another in a supposedly safer area. We lived right on the edge of the Moslem quarter, Basta, the source of the fervently anti-American demonstrators now roaming the streets. I declined once again, but started thinking that at least I should pack some bags for an emergency evacuation.

This posed a new problem: How to leave? My traveling husband had not been in Beirut long enough recently to have our residence permits renewed. Theoretically at least we could not travel. Even more important was how could I travel with only a very limited amount of cash? I had no news from Joe and had no idea where he was. It was all too much, and once again I abandoned any thought of leaving.

The phone rang at 5:30 the next morning, Wednesday. It was the Embassy man again. Lebanon was about to break relations with the U. S., he said, and the security of American citizens could not be guaranteed.

At this point I started packing in earnest. All Americans, I learned, had been strongly advised to leave on the evacuation charter aircraft. Then a new problem arose. The embassy called back to advise me that, since I still carried a German passport, I was not eligible for evacuation. My three American children could go, but I did not fall into the category of 'strictly American citizens.'

Then the Germans called with their evacuation offer, somewhat more attractive since the Bonn government was picking up the whole bill, whereas the Americans were charging prices considerably higher than normal airfares. I was considering this when the hitch came up again:

"What did you say? Three American children as well? The flight is strictly reserved for German citizens only. We might be able to take you all on a later flight—if there is one. But you will have to pay for the children."

An hour later the American Embassy informed me that I would be allowed to travel with my children on a flight for "businessmen and others." But by then I had decided to stay on, for better or worse. Things just seemed too difficult to be sorted out in a hurry.

Later, I realized how glad I was with my decision. Friends confirmed that the

Ulla Morris-Carter

American University's School of Agriculture, where the processing of evacuees was going on, was total chaos. Two thousand Americans were gathered there, mostly women and children. Many spent the night trying to sleep on the floor, dined on dry sandwiches and sipped black coffee while they waited for buses that would take them in convoy to the airport. The airport was, of course, closed to civilian traffic by then. Most of our foreign friends had evacuated to either Turkey, Greece or Frankfurt, Germany. The pilot's wife, one floor below us, had also fled to the mountains to be with her family.

Beirut was quiet that Wednesday night. A strict curfew had been imposed and the blackout was complete. The stars in the heaven never seemed brighter and more beautiful, contrary to the mood and anxiety of all of us. The reality of the situation was grim indeed.

A first glimmer of hope was reported on Thursday, when Jordan accepted the U.N. ceasefire proposal. By Friday morning all parties had accepted the ceasefire. I was hoping the tension would ease up. But there was more trouble to come. The news of the Arab defeat was slowly sinking in, and the voices blaming American and British intervention were rising. Thousands of angry demonstrators gathered and marched toward the American and British Embassies. They were stopped within 200 feet of the Embassies by security forces.

The demonstrators were not discouraged. Friday they marched along Beirut's Corniche, the beautiful promenade running along the Mediterranean Sea, to the heavily Western residential district. There they managed to do considerable damage.

If we thought this would be all for that Friday, we were wrong. That night President Nasser resigned, acknowledging his responsibility for the "grave setback" on the battlefield. Before the last word had been spoken, new demonstrations were forming next to our house, shouting:

"Nasser, Nasser, we want Nasser."

In spite of curfew restrictions, the crowd grew. From our balcony I could see the marching shadows in the blacked-out streets. I heard occasional explosions and more shouting for Nasser, now combined with cries of "Johnson Assassin."

Then I smelled something burning. I walked all around the house, but found nothing. Aside from my children and myself our building was empty. The elderly landlord and his wife had also fled to the mountains. Not too comforting a thought in case of an emergency. Finally I traced the smell it was just another burning car.

The only people still around were our friendly neighbors, Josephine and Assem Salam.

"Dont worry, you can stay with us. We will protect you and your children. Behind our walls you will be safe," Assem assured me.

I never had to take them up on their kind offer, but considering the fierce anti-

American feeling that many local people loudly expressed, the Salam's offer provided great comfort.

The next day, Saturday, major demonstrations formed near our apartment house to protest Nasser's resignation. Our building, located at the edge of the Moslem quarter, Basta, stuck out like a sore thumb, standing as it did, 50 steps above street level. Under curfew, we couldn't leave the house at all. Stores were closed, our food supply was running short, the children were like caged animals, and I was in constant back pain.

I suddenly realized I didn't know where the children were. I searched the house. All was quiet. Worrying that they might have run out into the street, I opened the shuttered doors to one of our many balconies to look down. And there they were, all three of them, Maria, 6, Karin, 3, and Julia 1½, on the balcony. Knowing they were not allowed outside, they had closed the shutters behind them. Shouting in Arabic with the masses in the street below, they were throwing their little fists up in the air.

"Nasser, Nasser, Nasser, we want Nasser!"

Maria, the oldest, was draped in a wool blanket despite the 100 degree heat, no doubt to increase the dramatic effect of her action. Even little Julia participated. I broke out laughing despite the seriousness of the situation. Maybe their three little voices helped to support the cause, because President Nasser withdrew his resignation that day. But more demonstrations and more curfews followed. And more endless, lonely days in a shuttered house.

Five days later—we were still under curfew—the doorbell rang. Nobody had rung our doorbell in days. The sound of the bell frightened me. No one was supposed to be outdoors, nobody dared to walk the streets without fear of being arrested. Our whole building was devoid of people. The bell rang a second time, this time more urgently. I moved quietly to the door and tried to listen to any sound that might give me a hint of what was happening on the other side of the front door. Nothing. The small opaque glass windows in the door didn't allow me to see out. I was scared, fearing I might be confronted with an anti-American hothead.

When the bell ran a third time, I decided to be brave and open the door. And there, miracles beyond miracles, stood Joe, like a ghost, in the silence of the round-the-clock curfew. No suitcase, no jacket, no briefcase, no typewriter, just Joe in shirtsleeves, carrying nothing but a passport in his shirt pocket.

My back suddenly gave out completely and I collapsed into his arms.

"Where are you coming from?" I finally managed to whisper.

Before he could answer, three little girls appeared from the back of the apartment racing into his arms:

"Daddy, Daddy. Daddy. Where have you been?"

For a number of minutes I was still in a state of shock. My knees were wobbly and

Ulla Morris-Carter

I had to lie down because my back was no longer holding me up. But the joy of seeing Joe alive and well overtook all the worry and anxious days of waiting.

There is a postscript to my above mentioned article. Every story had to be taken to the censorship office to be censored before it was allowed to be telexed or cabled to the home office.

As I was flat on my back at home, Joe took the article to the censor.

"Housewife's story, non-political," he told the censor, who, late in the evening was very busy and didn't bother to read the whole article.

The next morning we received an urgent call from a journalist friend, inquiring worriedly about Joe. Had we not heard that Joe had been ordered to leave the country within 24 hours, our friend asked.

"Why?" Joe asked incredulously. "I haven't heard anything,"

"Because of yesterday's article."

"I didn't write anything yesterday."

Apparently the censor was re-reading yesterday's copy and found a couple of objectionable sentences pertaining to Lebanese behavior in my article, something not tolerated by the Lebanese censor's office. One was allowed to write anything, good or bad, about any Middle Eastern country, but not about Lebanon. Apparently there was quite an uproar in the censorship office, but Joe, rushing down to the censor, could blame it all on his ill-informed wife and managed to settle the problem. The pitfalls of journalistic endeavors by non-journalists! I had written only one story and already the damage was done.

Joe told us his story. After his arrival in Jerusalem by rental car from Amman, Joe had booked himself into the National Hotel, a hotel where he had often stayed and knew well. Its location close to the Mandelbaum Gate, named after Mr. Madelbaum whose house stood where the gate had been built, the sole access to Israel from Jordan, was very convenient for many reasons.

When Joe found out that all communications in Jordan had been cut but that communication lines in Israel were still open, he went into action. He marched the short distance from the National Hotel to the Mandelbaum Gate, and, forever the optimist, he nonchalantly and brazenly crossed through the Gate without any problem. The guards were obviously not expecting visitors to Israel at that moment. He quickly found a small Israeli post and telegram office, filed his story and, as fast as his feet would carry him, returned to Arab Jerusalem.

After this successful mission, he tried to cross the Mandelbaum gate a second time in this brazen fashion. This time he wasn't so lucky. The Israeli border guards immediately stopped and arrested him.

Ulla Morris-Carter

Not knowing what else to do with this strange American fellow who entered Israel from enemy territory at a time of high tension and full military alert, they locked him up in a small wooden hut near the gate, a place where the guards, under normal circumstances, could take shelter when needed. After three hours of being locked up, Joe saw the familiar figure of the cigar-chomping mayor of Israeli Jerusalem, Teddy Kollek, passing by the hut. Joe knew Teddy Kollek from an earlier interview and started banging on the dusty window as hard as the windowpane would allow. Nobody paid any attention at first, but Joe continued his noisy attempt to make himself known.

Irritated by the ongoing noise, Mayor Kollek finally looked around and noticed the man in the hut. Questioning the guards, he unlocked the door, and recognizing Joe, Teddy Kollek yelled at him: "

What on earth are YOU doing here? You are on the wrong side of the fence."

Joe explained and apologized.

Teddy Kollek was quick to answer: "I'll let you go this time. But don't EVER try that again."

With this Joe was dismissed and deported to the Arab side of the Mandelbaum Gate. Despite his deportation, Joe was pleased with himself for managing to cable two articles to the *Los Angeles Times* when nobody else could file from the Jordanian side of Jerusalem.

The *Los Angeles Times* headlines:

MIDEAST WAR: Heavy Fighting erupts.

Heavy fighting broke out in the holy city of Jerusalem Monday. Concentrated small arms and heavy mortar fire began less than an hour after Egypt and Israel locked horns.

Israeli infantry and tanks entered the Arab-held sector of Jerusalem Tuesday and captured portions of the city against little or no resistance.

Three Newsmen Killed, Three Others Wounded

U.S. Proclaims 'Neutrality' — Asks for Cease-Fire

The journalists staying at the National Hotel were badly shaken upon learning that their *NBC* colleague and a *Life* photographer had been killed while filming from the roof of the hotel (the third newsman killed turned out to be an Israeli journalist). The National Hotel had been under fire for hours. Only Joe and two British journalists were still staying there, spending most of their time on the floor, when the light bulb above their heads was shot out. There was no electricity, a great shortage of food, but plenty of whiskey in the bar.

"The only problem," Joe remarked, dryly, "we had no ice."

The capture of the Jordanian part of Jerusalem on Day Three of the war by Israeli troops, meant that Joe and his two colleagues from *Reuters* suddenly found themselves in

Ulla Morris-Carter

enemy Israeli territory, rather than in Jordan. The Israeli military quickly informed them that they were "persona non grata" and instructed them to leave Israel without delay.

"Go back to where you came from. You are not welcome in Israel."

If one lived in the Arab world, one was not allowed to travel to Israel. To leave Israel was easier said than done. Joe's Jordanian rental car had been confiscated, and airports and seaports were closed. When the cease-fire was announced on June 10, Joe managed to walk to Lydda Airport, Jerusalem's domestic airport close to town. By luck he found a flight leaving for Nicosia, Cyprus. At Nicosia airport, a sympathetic Lebanese Middle East Airlines pilot, who had flown evacuees out of Beirut to Nicosia, offered Joe a ride to Beirut on his now empty evacuation plane. This was a risky maneuver, because Beirut airport was closed. Neither passport control officers nor security personnel were on duty, and the city was under a complete curfew. The pilot and Joe managed to arrive safely in Beirut and maneuvered through the airport and back into town via a military convoy that took pity on them. They still had to walk part of the way to their respective homes.

Before leaving Jerusalem, Joe and three of his colleagues traveled in a borrowed car to Bethlehem. Among the stories Joe had written for the *Los Angeles Times* was this one, describing the aftermath of the war and its devastation and misery:

Bethlehem Road Littered by War

Bethlehem, June 11, 1967

The long, twisting drive from Jerusalem to Bethlehem is strewn with the debris of war.

Burned out Jordanian tanks and jeeps mounted with recoilless rifles littered the roadside, along with taxis, trucks and other vehicles caught up in the tides of war . . .

The Bethlehem-Jerusalem road was also sprinkled with growing groups of Israeli tourists and civilians—denied access to some of their holiest shrines for 20 years by the Jordanians—who took advantage of this first day of the cease-fire to visit the land they formerly saw only through Jordanian barbed wire.

They gave an unreal air to the scene, generating almost a holiday atmosphere, as they arrived in Volkswagen minibuses, the women in slacks and with bandanas around their heads.

Their evident happiness and joy were in stark contrast to the Arab civilians, who plodded down the same roads carrying most of their precious belongings in huge bundles atop their heads. These new refugees were everywhere and apparently moved aimlessly. On the Bethlehem road and on the road to Jericho, they were traveling in both directions under the broiling sun. Some were lame. Others carried babies. A young girl and a boy were lugging an old foot-operated sewing machine.

Many were obviously hungry. They tried to wave our car down and pointed desperately at their mouths.

Ulla Morris-Carter

So far, no effort has been made to clear away the Arab bodies, which lie in Jerusalem's streets and along the surrounding roads. The electric power is still off, and the food problem is getting worse. The situation of the several hundred thousand Palestinian refugees, living in camps was described by one U.N. official as serious.

The Church of the Nativity, one of Christendom's most sacred shrines, was only superficially damaged . . .

Inside, the funeral of a youth killed in the shelling Wednesday, went on. Outside, a guide approached four western journalists and asked, "Excuse me, do you want a guide to the church?"

The town of Bethlehem, which has unashamedly commercialized Christianity to the profit of its citizenry, was ready to do business again . . . .

To fully understand the tragedies of war, here is another short story that Joe wrote from Amman, a couple of weeks later, July 4, 1967:

"In 'Valley of the Lost,' Even Fear is a Mirage"

The little girl stood patiently in line. She was barefoot, and her once brightly colored smock was grimy brown after weeks of continuous wear. In her right hand she held a bright tin water pail.

The line of women moved slowly forward, toward the back end of the water-tank truck. The driver, a big rough Bedouin with his kaffiyah wrapped around his head against the desert breeze, manipulated the rubber hose skillfully from one water pail to the next.

Their pails filled, the women balanced them gracefully on their heads and moved off to their tents.

At last it was the little girl's turn. As she held forth her pail, the last drops of water splashed into the bottom. She just looked and continued to hold up the pail.

"Ma feesh mai," (no more water) the driver told her, a cigarette dangling from his lower lip. She stood there, as if she didn't understand, with the pail still proffered. The driver repeated it several times, his voice rising in volume each time. Still the barefoot little girl stood there. Finally he shrugged and turned away, got into the cab and drove off.

The little girl watched, not a trace of emotion on her face, as the big truck lurched across the desert towards the highway. She was a refugee from the recent Arab-Israeli war, and perhaps there was no emotion left in her, not even fear.

Dickensian scenes like this one are everyday occurrences in the Middle East today in the wake of the war. This one took place at a spot appropriately named Wadi Daleil, or "Valley of the Lost."

Ulla Morris-Carter

When the brief war of 1967 ended, Israel was in control of a vast area outside its own borders. In fact, in less than a week, Israel had more than tripled the size of its territory. It had crushed the Egyptian and Jordanian armies and beaten the Syrians. It was in control of the Golan Heights, and, most important, it had access to the port of Eilat, whose closure had triggered the war. The Middle East had seen wars before, many of them, and this one, as we know now, was not to be the last. But it proved to be a transformative war in that it defined boundaries for half a century to come and longer.

LOS ANGELES WORLD AFFAIRS COUNCIL

612 SOUTH FLOWER STREET, LOS ANGELES 17, MADISON 9-3194

LUNCHEON MEETING

Thursday, September 7, 1967

12:00 Noon, Biltmore Hotel

$4.50 per person

AFTERMATH OF THE MIDDLE EAST WAR

to be discussed by

JOE ALEX MORRIS, JR.
Los Angeles Times Bureau Chief
for the Middle East

Joe Alex Morris, Jr. joined The Times in May, 1965, as Chief of the new Middle East News bureau in Beirut, Lebanon.

When the Middle East war broke out Morris was in Jordan covering the Israeli-Jordanian front. He was in the old city of Jerusalem when it was captured by the Israeli troops and witnessed the fighting first-hand. Since cessation of active hostilities he has gone back to Jordan from his Beirut base to cover developments there, and has also visited Yemen.

A 1949 graduate of Harvard, Morris served with the U.S. Army in Belgium and Germany during and after World War II. He has been a foreign correspondent in Germany, England and the Middle East for United Press and later for the New York Herald Tribune. He then served as Middle East correspondent for Newsweek before joining the Times.

This World Affairs Council meeting provides an opportunity to hear an experienced reporter and regional expert describe the current outlook for the Middle East.

- -

Los Angeles World Affairs Council
612 S. Flower Street, Los Angeles, California 90017

An invitation by the World Affairs Council in Los Angeles where Joe gave a presentation on the Six-Day War.

Ulla Morris-Carter

SPIES I MET

Cairo was and would remain a fascinating city, mysterious, chaotic, dusty and hot, a place where past and present co-exist, where ancient palaces sit next to ugly modern buildings, and where bare-legged fellaheen, peasants, walk next to elegantly dressed businessmen and attractive women. It is also a place that has always been rumored to be full of spies of many nationalities and backgrounds.

Half a century ago, even messenger boys or household help were sometimes observed removing discarded carbon copies of letters or newspaper articles from garbage cans. We saw it often. What did they do with them? Where did they take them? To the Secret Police? We never knew.

In 1956, shortly after I started my new job with the Cairo office of a German pump manufacturing company, KSB, *Klein, Schanzlin & Becker*, I met a 35-year-old bachelor, Franz Kiesow, who represented a major German industrial firm headquartered in Düsseldorf, my hometown. He invited me to a cocktail party given by a friend of his at the friend's home. New to Cairo and only 22, I was flattered to have been invited by this mature, well-established businessman. Having recently escaped the hardships of post-war Germany, I was overwhelmed by the elegance of the guests, the luxury of the apartment, and the free-flowing champagne.

Everything in those early days in Cairo impressed me.

At the party Franz Kiesow introduced me to his friend, Wolfgang Lotz, one of many German businessmen who lived in or visited Egypt at that time. I had not thought of either of them for many years.

Ulla Morris-Carter

Nine years later, in 1965, I was living in Beirut. One morning, as I was reading an article in the *Daily Star,* Lebanon's only English language newspaper, I came across the name, Franz Kiesow. He was described as a close friend of Wolfgang Lotz, the wealthy and well-known breeder of horses and longtime resident of Cairo, whom I had met in my early Cairo days. Mr. Lotz and his attractive German wife, Waltraud, as well as Franz Kiesow, were on trial, the paper said, accused of spying for Israel.

Herr Lotz was found guilty of "repeated acts of espionage and sabotage on behalf of Israel and directed against the United Arab Republic."

His sentence was life with hard labor and a fine of 330,000 Deutschmark.

Waltraud was sentenced to three years with hard labor. Kiesow was found not guilty of all charges. The trial was a sensational show that lasted for a month and drew in many leading names from Egyptian society and the military.

In the end, the Lotz's served two years in Egyptian prisons but were saved by the Six-Day Arab-Israeli War of 1967. The Israelis made the repatriation of their prisoners, some 5,000 Egyptians including nine generals, conditional on the release of the Lotz couple.

Lotz was an interesting person. He was born in Mannheim, Germany in 1922, but in 1933 emigrated with his mother to Palestine. In 1948, when Israel was established, he added Israeli nationality to his German roots. Lotz had blue eyes and was described in a biography as "… blond, stocky and a hard drinker . . . the very epitome of an ex-German officer."

In 1956 the Israeli Intelligence Service, *Mossad,* approached him to work for them. Hardly looking like an Israeli, and not having been circumcised, he had great advantages for *Mossad.* His active social life in Cairo allowed him to penetrate the tight circle of former Nazi scientists, who, at the end of WWII, had fled to Egypt to avoid prosecution and de-Nazification in Germany. The Egyptian government asked these former Nazi scientists for help in developing missiles for use against Israel. One of those German scientists recruited by the Egyptian government was Dr. Wolfgang Pilz.

He had begun his work at the German rocket station in Peenemuende, Germany, where he assisted Wernher von Braun in the development of Hitler's V-1 and V-2 rockets.

In 2013 Mohamed Hassanein Heikel, former editor of *Al Ahram,* Cairo's highly regarded newspaper, wrote of Pilz and his colleagues:

> The production of chemical and biological weapons was easy… it was all based on German scientists who had fled Germany. Some of them had knowledge of nuclear energy, like Dr. Wolfgang Pilz, who came to us for a while and then started working on missiles and moved to China.

I had known nothing of Dr. Pilz before arriving in Cairo, and met him there only briefly. But being one of very few young and single German women, I was frequently and wrongly associated with Dr. Pilz's work in the German science community—an assumption I did not much appreciate.

The mysterious Middle East grew even more mysterious and obscure for me after living there for over three years. I believed that I was beginning to understand its traditions, its religions, its way of life and some of its people.

The next episode taught me otherwise.

A few months after our wedding in Cairo in 1959, Joe invited me to accompany him on a trip to Beirut, a rare treat for me. For one thing, I had a full-time job. And as I was not a journalist, I could rarely obtain a visa to countries such as Saudi Arabia or Yemen. And, there was the high cost of air travel.

When we arrived in Beirut one of Joe's many journalist friends, Kim Philby, invited us to a "late wedding celebration." Our host was a highly intelligent man, a member of the British establishment who spoke fluent Arabic and French, some Spanish and some Russian. He was born in the Punjab, India, and was named Kim after Rudyard Kipling's fictional character. Kim was the son of St. John Philby, a brilliant and eccentric linguist, well-known scholar and political advisor to King Ibn Saud of Saudi Arabia.

From 1951 to 1953, Joe, as a young journalist and public relations man for ARAMCO, the Arabian American Oil Company, had lived and worked in Dahran, Saudi Arabia. While there, he had met the senior Philby and on rare occasions saw Kim when Kim visited his father in Dahran. Joe and Kim became better acquainted later when both were accredited journalists, Joe as Middle East correspondent for the *New York Herald Tribune* and Kim as correspondent for the British publications, the *Observer* and the *Economist*.

On our way to Philby's apartment Joe warned me that Kim enjoyed alcohol more than food and was rarely without a glass in hand, and that Eleanor, his third wife, frequently joined him. She was the Seattle-born, recently divorced wife of the *The New York Times* correspondent, Sam Pope Brewer. Kim and Eleanor were married in London and now lived on Rue Kantari, one of Beirut's best neighborhoods.

I cannot remember details of the luncheon because vodka was served in quantity. I had never even tasted vodka let alone drunk it during the day. There were toasts by Kim and toasts by Eleanor and then more toasts when dessert was served. Lively conversation made for a lengthy luncheon. Kim had piercing blue eyes and a slight stutter, and he was a charming conversationalist. Because of his unassuming personality and relaxed, courteous manner, women were drawn to him, I noticed. He had traveled the world. He had covered the Spanish Civil War for *The (London) Times,* and parts of WWII while he was living in France. He had lots of stories to tell.

I don't remember what we ate, but I do remember, vividly, that after a four-hour meal with lots of vodka I walked down the five flights of stairs from the Philby's apartment feeling as though I were floating on a cloud. My head was in a delicate state. I was afraid it might splinter, like a light bulb dropped onto a concrete floor, if anyone so much as touched it.

I had first met the newly-wed Philby couple while they were on a visit to Cairo. At a party in the apartment of an Indian journalist friend, Kim and Eleanor, both drinking heavily, got into a noisy and unpleasant argument. It ended with Kim picking up the nearest *objet d'art* and throwing it across the room at his wife. Luckily, it missed Eleanor and the bystanders before it crashed and shattered.

In the early days of 1959 we knew nothing of the darker side of Kim Philby and of his secret life as a member of what became known as the Cambridge spy ring. Two of his colleagues, Guy Burgess and David MacLean, were exposed in 1951 and fled to Moscow. They had been spies for the Soviets for years, and though it was rumored that Philby might be the so-called "third man" of that ring, it was not until 1963 that he was exposed as a high-ranking member of British intelligence, who worked as a double agent for the Soviets. At that point Philby, too, managed to defect from Beirut and fled to Moscow.

In 1968, Philby wrote his autobiography *My Silent War,* with an introduction by British author Graham Greene, Philby's fellow spy in London for a few years while both worked for the British Military Intelligence Service MI5. They had been good friends.

My Silent War became a best seller:

"More gripping than any novel of espionage I can remember," wrote Graham Greene. "Philby lived out his days in a drab Moscow apartment awash in alcohol," Malcolm Gladwell reported in the *New Yorker* magazine.

Philby died in Moscow in 1988. His former employer, *The Observer,* said that he was:

> . . . perhaps the most lethal double agent in the annals of British espionage. As a member of the Cambridge Five (formerly the Cambridge Three) spy ring and a secret servant of the Soviet intelligence services, Philby was responsible for the betrayal of countless national secrets as well as the brutal elimination of many British agents.

Some 30 years later, when I was living in California, a journalist who was writing a book, one of many about Philby, called me to ask about my stay in Lebanon in the 1960s. I acknowledged that Joe and I had originally met Philby when we lived in Cairo and had visited him in Beirut, but that by the time we moved to Beirut in 1963 Philby had just defected on a Russian freighter bound for Moscow.

The journalist who called me had heard from a mutual friend that behind our first Beirut apartment on Rue Clemenceau there was an alley. I remembered the alley well. We often used it as a shortcut to reach the next street over. It was a small alley, not

Ulla Morris-Carter

drivable, and not visible from Rue Clemenceau. The journalist asked the name of the alley. But I did not remember. It probably didn't even have a name.

"Do you remember a large white wall, maybe the back of a house?" she asked.

"Yes, indeed," I said. "I remember that wall exactly, not a very attractive wall, neither clean nor interesting, full of graffiti."

"Exactly!" she exclaimed. "That was the wall where Philby left little xx's in a specifi ccorner when he needed to be in touch with his Soviet handlers."

Of course I had never noticed the xx's.

Ulla Morris-Carter

The Rhine near Oberwinter

back to GERMANY

return to LEBANON

evacuate to GREECE

Above: *Arriving at one of many press cocktail parties in Germany.* **Below:** *Joe looking a little peakish post treatment.*

GERMANY

1969—1975

Departing for Germany from Beirut in December 1968 was truly a traumatic event. It meant leaving behind my beloved Middle East, where I had spent 12 eventful years of my life, where I had been married and where our children were born.

Our years in Cairo and Beirut had not always been easy, but they had never been dull. In comparison, the German horizon loomed cold and grey, with winter coming on.

Joe had been assigned by the *Los Angeles Times* to cover East and West Germany and some of the Iron Curtain countries, in addition to the Benelux states, which included Brussels, the seat of the European Community *(EC)*, plus the Nordic countries. We were to reside in Bonn, the city the German Parliament had voted, in 1949, to become West Germany's capital.

The choice of Bonn had been preceded by a major public debate. Many argued that Frankfurt would be a much more appropriate place, a city in which German kings had been crowned for 1,000 years, in which the revered author Goethe was born in 1749, and where the first German parliament of 1848-9 had been formed. More important, Frankfurt was the business capital of Germany. But Chancellor Adenauer favored Bonn, a relatively small city on the western side of the Rhine, because Bonn was to be only a temporary capital. He hoped that Berlin would, in the near future, become the capital of Germany again.

Because of its size, Bonn did not have enough buildings to house the government, its ministries and the many diplomats and civil servants that are connected with any government. Even 20 years later, when we arrived in Bonn, there was a severe shortage

Ulla Morris-Carter

of housing. Consequently, with a family of five we had a particularly hard time finding accommodations. We ended up renting a house in the small town of Oberwinter, a 30-minute drive to the American School in Bonn-Bad Godesberg, where Maria, now 8, was enrolled. It also meant a longer commute for Joe to his office in the Pressehaus in Bonn.

Our two younger daughters, Karin, four, and Julia, three, entered the Kindergarten in Oberwinter. They had to adjust to children who spoke only German. Karin, always determined, rose to the new challenge quickly. Julia, on the other hand, dealt with the language problem by simply not speaking at all. She went on strike and stopped communicating. I understood her protest. In Beirut she had an Armenian babysitter, Madame Arslan, who adored her, but spoke only Armenian. Arabic, French and English contributed to the potpourri of languages Julia had to deal with. The addition of German was just too much for her. Increasingly worried about Julia's silence, I wondered whether Joe and I were exposing our children to too many challenges. It was quite a while before Julia started to speak again.

In the meantime we enrolled Karin, who was bored at the German Kindergarten, in the small *British Embassy Preparatory School*, BEPS, in Bad Godesberg. The British school system started children at age five. In typical British fashion, pupils had to wear uniforms. Dark-blue tights or knee socks, white long-sleeved shirts and striped blue-grey ties, grey skirts, dark-blue blazers and berets. Joe would stand, with Karin in front of him, before a large mirror, to teach her how to knot a tie. A year later Julia joined Karin at the British school.

Julia, Karin and the Fiat in front of the house in Oberwinter. It was Julia's first day of school, 1970.

When Joe was not traveling, he liked to drive the children to school, because he enjoyed ogling the young, good-looking British teachers and their fashionable mini skirts.

"Miss Sinfield looks particularly attractive today," Joe would tease Karin, who was most embarrassed.

Finally she burst out, "Don't drive me into the school parking lot again. I can find my way alone."

Small as BEPS was, it provided excellent academic preparation for future school changes.

Despite my original complaints about Bonn as a dull place, I had to change my mind when, in September 1969, Willy Brandt, a Social Democrat, was elected chancellor of the Federal Republic of Germany, *FRG*. The election of Brandt and the coalition he formed with the

Ulla Morris-Carter

Free Democratic Party, *FDP*, under the leadership of Walter Scheel, marked the most momentous change in German politics since Chancellor Adenauer.

The noted German writer Heinrich Böll wrote of Willy Brandt:

> Willy Brandt's life provides material for a legend, almost a fairy tale come true. The man who became chancellor in 1969 was . . . the illegitimate Herbert Frahm from Lübeck, who even managed to aggravate this blemish, the idiotic original sin, in the eyes of bourgeois society, by becoming a socialist and an emigré.1
>
> *- Bracher, Republik im Wandel.*

This political change made Bonn a more exciting place to be, certainly for a journalist like Joe. He spoke German well and soon became deeply involved in covering Willy Brandt's new government and his important *Ostpolitik*, Eastern policy.

NEW YEAR'S EVE IN BAVARIA

A highlight of our first winter in Bonn was an expedition to the Bavarian Forest with Dan Morgan, *Washington Post* bureau chief in Bonn, and his family and my brother Hans and his family. None of us had a lot of money to spend on a winter vacations, but we found rooms for rent in an interesting place, a Bavarian pig farm in a small village.

With fresh snow on the ground, we tried to teach our seven children, ages three to nine, the basics of skiing. Without the availability of a lift to tow everybody uphill, Joe devised a system that allowed the children to be pulled uphill, by hanging onto a rope attached to the back of our VW station wagon.

I am still horrified to think of the exhaust our children must have breathed in. Of course, they all loved it.

We ate breakfast and dinner in the only pub in the village, where Bavarians enjoyed vast quantities of a foul-tasting schnaps, called Beerwurz, which means made from the roots of berries. The locals insisted we try this specialty. They spoke with such heavy Bavarian accents that we at first thought they were speaking a foreign language. Not wanting to offend them, we all agreed to try it.

It was New Years' Eve, 1969. I almost keeled over after taking my first gulp. But the men, when informed that this particular schnaps was a great aphrodisiac, consumed more than the women did. It wasn't long before we heard noisy laughter coming from outside the pub.

Curious, we ventured outside to check. There we found three bare-chested males, happily drunk, engaged in an outrageous snowball fight. It was a freezing night. The thermometer showed 20 degrees below zero. The church bells of the nearby small church were already ringing in the New Year, 1970.

---

1. Willy Brandt had taken this name in 1933 to avoid possible discovery and assassination by the Gestapo.

Ulla Morris-Carter

Oberwinter 1973-1974

Joe had just returned from six weeks in Egypt, traveling with the Egyptian troops fighting the Israeli army during the Yom Kippur War of October 1973—so named because it began on the Day of Atonement, the holiest day of prayer and fasting in the Jewish calendar. Golda Meir was Israel's leader, and Anwar Sadat was president of Egypt. Egypt was hoping to win back territory lost to Israel during the 1967 Arab-Israeli War.

Supported by a major U.S. airlift of arms to Israel, the Israeli Defense Forces beat back the Arab forces. It was a hard-fought war on several fronts. Egyptian troops swept deep into the Sinai Peninsula, while Syria, aligned with Egypt, sent its troops to the Golan Heights. After almost three weeks of fighting, a UN-secured cease-fire went into effect on October 25, 1973, with the help of then American Secretary of State, Dr. Henry Kissinger, who acted as peace broker.

Back from Egypt in November, Joe did not look well. He had lost almost 15 pounds, which I first attributed to the hardships of traveling with the Egyptian army with little food and not enough water, while marching in the hot Egyptian desert. Our doctor insisted on a few tests. But before they could be concluded, Joe had to leave again. This time he rushed off to Greece, where students of the Polytechnic University of Athens had been staging a massive protest.

For more than six years, Greece had suffered under the harsh dictatorship of the military junta, which had abolished civil rights, imprisoned and tortured politicians and citizens, and interfered heavy-handedly in university life and affairs.

On November 14, 1973, the Greek students went on strike, and thousands of Athenians joined the protest. Three days later, a military tank crashed the gates of the barricaded university, killing and injuring many students. Though tragic, these events helped to dislodge the military junta and eventually ended the regime of the dictatorial Greek Colonels in the spring of 1974. Joe, based in Bonn, covered the Greek crisis because he was well-acquainted with the politics of that country.

While Joe was still in Greece, the test results came in. They were not good. Our doctor insisted that Joe return immediately, Greek crisis or not. Twelve hours later I picked him up at the airport and took him straight to the Johanniter Hospital in Bonn-Bad Godesberg, where a biopsy was to be performed.

"You can pick him up in the late afternoon," the hospital doctor had assured me.

At 6 p.m. on that Friday afternoon, the hospital was eerily quiet. I could not find anybody to give me information. There was no Joe, no doctor, no nurse in sight. Finally a friendly male attendant told me, "Friday afternoon the staff leaves on time. I will help you."

"But where is my husband?" I inquired. "I brought him here this morning for just a biopsy."

Ulla Morris-Carter

The male attendant smiled reassuringly, while opening a few doors to hospital rooms.

"But my husband is not hospitalized. He is an out-patient," I protested. "I was told I could take him home this afternoon."

After another five minutes of search the male attendant turned to me: "Here he is," pointing to a sign on the door, "Joe Alex Morris. Didn't you tell me that this is his name?"

"Yes, indeed, that is his name."

The attendant opened the door to the hospital room and politely gestured for me to enter first. I stopped cold at the entrance: Joe was lying in bed, motionless, his eyes closed, completely still, his face white as the sheet that covered him. Was he dead?

I screamed for help, not once, probably twice, or three times, loud enough to bring immediate action. A young resident doctor appeared running, with two nurses in tow. They took one look at Joe and immediately went to work.

He had had a complete circulatory collapse with nobody in attendance. He had been left alone in the room after an operation of an unknown nature.

"I am not the operating doctor and don't know what was done," the resident said. "The surgeon is not on duty now. You have to call his personal physician who admitted your husband for a biopsy. I am sorry, but I cannot tell you anything."

I was speechless. Was I not hearing well or was I losing my mind? How was it possible to perform surgery without notifying the next of kin? Calling me, the wife? And what was the unknown operation all about?

Nobody could give me any information until Monday, three days from now, I was told, when the surgeon would be back at the hospital.

I was in a state of shock. My legs were shaking and I had to sit down. Never before had I experienced such a totally unreal situation. It reminded me of the German expression about doctors, "Gods in white coats," unreachable, unapproachable, God-like.

"May I please have the telephone number of the surgeon?" I asked.

"Oh no, we never give out private telephone numbers of our doctors."

I kept looking at Joe, wanting to hug him and tell him that everything would be ok. But I had no idea whether he would be ok. I still knew nothing.

To this day, forty years later, I have not fogotten or fogiven those doctors for their incomprehensible inhumanity.

I was angry, but mostly I was worried about Joe. I called our family doctor, a gentle soul, but he was equally uninformed. I raced around the hospital trying find someone to give me some news.

There seemed to be nobody.

The nurses assured me that Joe would be fine once he came out of the anesthesia.

"Anesthesia for what?"

No answer.

Ulla Morris-Carter

"The doctor will tell you on Monday."

How could I go home without some kind of reassurance? I had left our three children at home with a babysitter, for what I thought would be an hour. The children had been excited that their beloved Daddy was coming home after two long absences. By now several hours had passed, and I still knew nothing.

Finally the nurses eased me out of the hospital room, saying that I could not spend the night there. Of course I had to go home and see my children.

I needed to talk to somebody to help me calm down. Near the hospital lived friends of ours, the *Financial Times* correspondent, Malcolm Rutherford and his wife Elisabeth. They were at home. Visiting them for a short time helped me to regain my equilibrium before driving the rest of the way home

Saturday and Sunday passed with hospital visits. Seeing Joe alive and responsive helped, but he looked pale and grey, uncomfortable, but not in serious pain. Monday was a dull November day, typical for Bonn. I met Joe at the hospital. He was now allowed to walk around.

We entered Dr. Sommers' office on the second floor, a well-appointed room with impressive old furniture. After a few minutes of polite conversation, Dr. Sommers was ready to discuss the real reason for our visit. He explained that, while doing the biopsy, he had discovered a tumor in Joe'a abdomen, which he decided to remove while Joe was under anesthesia.

"Please, don't worry," he assured us, "the tumor was encapsulated, therefore, no reason to be concerned. We are conducting more tests to make sure all is in good order. Let's meet again in a week."

This God-in-white dismissed us with a handshake and good wishes.

A week later we were back in Dr. Sommers' office.

This time he offered:

"A small whiskey, Mr. Morris? I know Americans love whiskey."

He opened his impressive, carved wall cabinet to take out a bottle of whiskey and a glass. It was three in the afternoon. Joe was not ready for a drink.

"The tumor was not quite as good as we had originally thought, in fact it was malignant. But because it was encapsuled, it had not spread. Please, don't worry. You can rest assured that you don't have to be concerned about it any more than you would about a cold."

With a friendly slap on Joe's shoulder, Dr. Sommers bade us good bye.

We were certainly not reassured, nor did we feel any better than we did after the first visit. In the Germany of 1973 the word "cancer" was only quietly whispered, not openly discussed. Returning home, we started a telephone marathon with friends

Ulla Morris-Carter

in the medical field. My friend Karin and her husband Wolfgang, both experienced gynecologists, were astonished that Joe had not had tests of the lymphatic system.

"Frequently cancer will spread from a tumor into the lymph system. The surgeon did not suggest any further tests?"

Wolfgang could hardly believe it.

Joe did not recover as quickly as we had hoped. The *Los Angeles Times*, worried about their usually reliable foreign correspondent, suggested Joe fly to Los Angeles to be checked out and get a second opinion. In the 1970's, the United States had by far the most advanced cancer research centers in the world.

Joe flew alone to Los Angeles, where, indeed, after extensive tests, doctors at the Good Samaritan Hospital found that his lymph system was filled with cancer cells. He was given a 50% chance of survival. Chemotherapy did not yet exist in those days. The highest feasible dose of radiation was prescribed. That could be done in Germany as well as in the United States as long as it was started immediately.

Two days before Christmas, Joe flew back from California to Germany to be with us. Despite the difficult medical news, it was a most happy reunion. We sat around the fireplace, grateful to be together again after almost three months of separations. The only serious problem arose when the German doctors decided they would not start radiation treatment because of the Christmas holidays. January 3, 1974, would be the earliest day of treatment despite the U.S. doctors advice to begin treatment immediately.

Having absorbed the latest bad news, we sat down for a serious discussion of life and death and the future. We were still young. Joe was 46, I had just turned 40, and the children were 13, 9, and almost 8.

Where to go if Joe was unable to continue at the pace required for covering wars, revolutions and upheavals? Major tensions in Germany between East and West brought enough headaches, even without the necessity of long-distance travel to the Middle East. Would Joe have to give up his work as a foreign correspondent? Where would we live? How would we survive? More important, how would HE survive?

Friends and colleagues visited and gave support and advice. During the week after Christmas, a new idea began to take root. Our friends Bob Ball, Bonn bureau chief of *Time Magazine*, and his German wife Inge, had recently bought an old farmhouse in the small village of Ameno near Lake Orta in Northern Italy.

Would that also be a possibility for us? We called Bob and Inge Ball's friend Maleen, who lived in Ameno.

 Could she help us find an old farmhouse? we asked her over the phone.

A few days later Maleen called back.

"There is an old farmhouse for sale, *una casa rustica*, not exactly a house ready to

Ulla Morris-Carter

move into," said Maleen. "But it's beautifully located with two acres of land around it. One part of the house is probably 300 years old. If you are interested you must come quickly. Another person also has an eye on this property."

I eagerly agreed to visit soon. Maleen invited me to stay with her and her partner Günther while in Ameno. Joe insisted that he felt well enough to look after the children despite the radiation treatments, which often left him nauseated and with second-degree burns on his body wherever radiation had been directed.

I left shortly after Christmas.

Spring 1974
Tuesday

Dear Joe,
        Sorry to be so uninformative lately. It wasn't really
on purpose, but I was until today in the midst of a series of
tests so I couldn't really say much definitely.

What happened (I think) was that when they took an X-ray
recently, they saw something suspicious outside of the
lymphatic system, this led to a kidney test and then, today,
a prostate test. All ke negative. There is an unpsecific
swelling or k enlargement of my prostate, but the doct says
it has no connectionwith what ails me.

So far so good. The X-ray showed a good response to radiation
treatment. I should be finaished by mid-month or so, then a
final check-up, and we send all the information to LA. After
that, it's a question of periodic checkups. Curiously, the
clinic here has close ties with the lady doctor who runs the
Moscow clinic. All I need to do is take their introduction
and I'll get VIP x treatment there, they say.   This should be
good enough for the quarterly treatments, or rather inspections.
Then, since we come out from Moscow twice a year anyway, I'll
come back to Bonn for the thorough checkups.

So... unless you hear otherwise, don't worry. If something
goes awry, naturally I'll tell you, but am assuming from here on
out it will be smoother sailing. We are now actively planning our
Easter vacation in the French alps. I'm feeling much better as
the radiation tails off--- I'm now in the final phase and getting
only one-third of what I was getting at the peak. The doctors still
think I'm some sort of a freak, what with playing tennis and all
that (not to mention the carousing that went on during Carnival).
But it seems to amuse them to have a freak on their hands. One
of them is a Syrian, so I keep up my Arabic with him. This of
course makes me even more freakish to the others, but what the
hell, if you can't be a public personality, be a spectacle.

Otherwise not much new here. Bonn is pretty dull and I can't travel.
We did have Henry K the other day, but he wasn't all that much
news either. The kids are brattier than ever --- I take that back,
they're actually getting better, but everyone's come through a
warm, damp winter pretty well. Will try to be a somewhat better
correspondet in the future.

                    Love,
                    Joey.

Ulla Morris-Carter

A JOURNEY TO ITALY

During the 12-hour overnight train journey to Arona on Lago Maggiore in Northern Italy's Lake district I had time to reflect.

"50% chance of survival."

What did that really mean? Was it a glass half-empty, or a glass half-full?

Momentarily overwhelmed by these cold numbers, I was glad to be lying on the top bunk of the couchette where nobody could see my tears. Soon though my dark mood lifted, and I began to dream about Italy.

Just the name Italy evoked delicious images of sun-drenched hills, celebrated frescoes, glorious sunsets, cathedrals and convents, fountains and cloisters, bell towers from which the bells tolled hourly, and of traces of an Etruscan past. Visions of vineyards and olive groves floated in my mind. Lago di Orta, the smallest, most western and loveliest of the North Italian lakes, is located close to Lago Maggiore. We had passed through this area in the summer of 1973 when we were traveling by car from Germany to Yugoslavia. Ever since we had been intrigued by the idea of finding an old farmhouse for our family. We did not own property anywhere. We always traveled to wherever Joe Alex was transferred, renting apartments or a house. Somehow we never settled anywhere, for lack of time or lack of money.

At Lago di Orta, Maleen and Günther, both stage designers, lived in the village of Ameno and worked for theaters in Germany. They had just done the sets for *Schwarzwaldmädel,* Black Forest Girl, a revival of a 1917 operetta playing in Stuttgart.

When I entered their house, I couldn't help smiling. It resembled a stage, black and white marble floors, columns, a spiral staircase leading to the guest bedroom, a

Ulla Morris-Carter

dining room appointed with silver candelabra and dark-red velvet curtains. A most unusual house with a great view of Lake Orta. Maleen, who was of Romanian origin, was probably in her early fifties, with flaming red hair cut short and a dramatic demeanor. She spoke fluent Romanian, German, Italian, and some English. She truly suited this house and the house, her. Günther, a few years younger, good-looking and, as I found out that evening, a most wonderful cook, had obviously adjusted his life to Maleen's. She was the driving force in this household.

Soon we were off to visit *La Casa Rustica*. Günther and Maleen invited Signora and Signor Baroni to join the visiting team. Nothing could be done in Ameno without consulting Signora Tina Baroni. An impressive lady about my age, Tina acted as real estate agent, tax advisor and assistant to her contractor husband, Carlo. She proved knowledgeable on such things as building permits, dealings with the *Municipio*, City Hall, and signing contracts at a lawyer's office.

Her first and foremost task was to locate the owners of *La Casa Rustica*, who turned out to be five different individuals, sons and daughters of the original farmer. They had long since abandoned the family farmhouse in search of better lives.

"But where are they now?" I asked.

"I don't know," said Tina, undaunted.

"We shall find them, no problem. I know their uncle, who lives in the next village."

While traveling I could not stop worrying about Joe and our three children. How was he surviving the radiation treatment? Was he nauseous or was he well enough to deal with the daily adventures and problems of three children 13, 9 and 8? And most importantly, would he recover sufficiently to continue his job as a foreign correspondent?

Maleen and Günther, were most understanding, but also full of good cheer and positive thoughts. They helped me to stay calm and collected.

"After all," they said, "you will be away from home for only two more days: one day to inspect the farm house, and the next day to board the overnight train back to Germany."

Snow was on the ground the next morning, when Carlo Baroni, the contractor, picked us up in his four-wheeled vehicle, to chauffeur us to *La Casa Rustica*. Bumping over an unpaved forest road, unsuitable for ordinary cars, Carlo drove us safely to what we hoped would become our future home.

Emerging from the forest road, all I could see at first was a thicket of brambles, overgrown hedges, tangles of weeds run rampant and a bit of a tiled roof in need of repair. The house looked like a dilapidated "Sleeping Beauty Castle," surrounded by wild, overgrown rosebushes, their branches long and thin, bare of leaves in winter. There seemed to be hardly any doors, window frames or even floorboards, just the shell of a house built of heavy stones with walls more than a foot thick.

Ulla Morris-Carter

"The Sleeping Beauty Castle". Our future house and myself standing in front of it during my first visit.

I entered hesitantly through an open doorway, wondering what on earth had possessed me. In the middle of the room on my right, which Tina described as the kitchen, stood a large iron bed frame. A shepherd had apparently made his headquarters here. The whole ground floor, as far as I could tell, was wall-to-wall sheep dung. Left of the entrance was a small, dark room, which I baptized The Cave. Fifteen hand-hewn stone steps led up to the second floor, but ended in a big hole instead of a room because all the floorboards were missing. No place to go but back down. A shaky-looking wooden staircase on the outside of the house reached up to the third floor, where, according to Tina, the hay had been stored when the house was a working farm. Tina encouraged me to go upstairs and take a look.

"You will have a beautiful view of the Monte Rosa, the highest massif of the Alps, and the church tower of Lortallo," she said, encouragingly.

It was a relief to reach the third floor without the staircase collapsing!

Once up there, I could hardly believe what I saw. The view truly was spectacular. Snow-covered Monte Rosa was clearly visible on this cold winter day. If, on a clear and sunny day, one woke up early, Monte Rosa, located on the Swiss-Italian border, would be a splendid pink, its 15,203-foot high peak glistening in the morning sun. It was a stunning view, unlike any I had ever seen. The huge open room, the former barn, was filled with light. No windows, no doors, only parts of an earlier thick wall. I imagined two splendid bedrooms with views of the Alps and the surrounding villages.

The ground-floor stable, once attached to the house, had all but disappeared. We managed to find only traces of rugged stones where it had stood. Tina assured me we

Ulla Morris-Carter

would be able to build a living room, where once the stable had stood. This area was nature-protected, therefore, new construction was forbidden. One was allowed to re-build only where a structure had originally been, but no changes to the outside of a house or additions were allowed.

Despite the fact that this ruin wasn't exactly what I had expected, my imagination ran wild with how we could transform it into a wonderful family retreat. I was forgetting for the moment that we might need a place to live in the near future, not three or five years from now. When we returned to Maleen's and Günther's house, I called Joe and gave him a detailed report.

"If the price is right and you like it, buy it!" he said simply and without hesitation "I trust your judgment. I loved the region and the village right away when we traveled through last summer," he announced, sounding completely confident and convinced that this was the right thing to do.

Well, the price was right for our limited budget, but we had no idea how much it would cost to repair, rebuild and refinish an old abandoned farmhouse. There was no water, no electricity, no gas line, no proper road. And we still hadn't found the owners.

"Grappa time," announced Maleen after our return to her house.

She produced a crystal decanter containing a clear liquid and three glasses. Günther brought in a bowl of glistening herb-covered green olives. We sat on low chairs around the fireplace in one of the small, cozy downstairs rooms. I had no idea what Grappa was, but soon found out that it was a potent liquid, to be consumed in small doses. It certainly warmed ones stomach on a cold winter's day. After two or three glasses of Grappa my doubts about buying *Casa Rustica* had practically disappeared. Günther was preparing dinner and refused help from us ladies. Maleen, the stage designer, was already designing our future living room where the old stable had been. I was imagining vines on trellises, wisteria in delicate purple colors, marigold so brilliant they seemed to be on fire, and clusters of purple and white irises. And not to be forgotten, a fig tree on the hill.

By eight o'clock Günther rang a bell. He announced that dinner was being served. A beautiful table set with flowers and silverware awaited us. I was overwhelmed by the hospitality and also the formality of dinner in a village of no more than 350 people. But Günther and Maleen were theater people, and their house was a stage. Günther had the air of a maitre d' in a first-class French restaurant. With a napkin over his arm, he first poured Prosecco into Champagne glasses, then announced Champagne risotto with fresh porcini mushrooms, while, with a grand gesture lifting a heavy silver cover off the risotto dish.

Even now, many years later, I can still taste and remember that exquisitely delicious risotto. I don't quite recall the other courses, but in typical Italian fashion, a meat

Ulla Morris-Carter

and vegetable dish followed the risotto. Salad and cheese, plus dessert completed this incredible dinner. I had no problem falling asleep after a long day, and the previous night on the train. The Grappa and *vino rosso* with dinner also helped to put me into a deep, dreamless slumber.

Finding the heirs of the abandoned farmhouse in northern Italy was not as easy a task as Tina Baroni had promised. After a few months of searching, questioning and writing letters to far-away places, the heirs turned out to live in five locations in three different countries. Because of the snails' pace of mail in and out of Italy—letters could take as long as four or five weeks to arrive, if at all—this process turned out to be a lengthy ordeal.

At one point, a mailman in our region of Italy, after a long postal strike, took one look at the mountain of mail that had accumulated at the post office, made a little fire and burned the whole lot.

Three heirs lived in France, one each in Versailles, Montreux, and Nice. Another resided in Geneva, Switzerland, and one sister lived in Monza, Italy. Every document that arrived from France and Switzerland had to be translated into Italian by a certified official translator or the Italian Consulate or Embassy.

At that point we were confronted with another unresolved matter of major importance: money. Not that we had never thought about payment, but we had not clearly approached the problem of money transfer—how to pay for a property that we almost owned? Maybe a check from our German bank would do? We could carry it personally to Italy, we thought. We knew that the Italians preferred hard currency, such as Deutschmark or Swiss Francs, instead of the weak Italian Lira. But the officially stated price of the house had to be paid in Italian Lira.

What to do? Tina Baroni to the rescue.

"You have to open a bank account, of course," Tina's matter-of-fact voice on the phone to Germany made it sound as if we could just go to the corner store and pick one up.

"However, you first have to acquire a residence permit before you can open a bank account," she continued.

I began to experience that unpleasant feeling in my stomach that I knew preceded problems—I felt that I needed to sit down.

'Please, not another bureaucratic obstacle,' I remember thinking. My experiences with the Italian bureaucracy had already taught me that Tina's simple announcements meant trouble.

"How can I obtain a residence permit?"

I was almost too afraid to ask the question, immediately suspecting that another overnight train trip to Italy was unavoidable.

Ulla Morris-Carter

"First we need to fill out forms that require your signature—it won't take long. You can get the permit in a day or two."

Tina tried to sound reassuring and confident. My heart sank.

"A day or two" in Italian time did not mean just two days. I realized that this was the price to be paid for venturing into a foreign country whose language I did not speak well and whose laws I did not know. But we had no choice if we really wanted to buy *La Casa Rustica*. And we did. So off I went to Italy on another overnight train trip.

Filling out forms for the whole family to obtain a *codice fiscale,* a type of Italian Social Security number, one for every member of my family, was my first job. It included such questions as maiden name and birth date of mother, name of father and grandfather, residences during the previous ten years and much more. But without *codice fiscale* no residence permit, without residence permit no bank account. A *codice fiscale* is an absolute must for all transactions, such as paying electricity, gas and water bills, property taxes, telephone bills and more.

Bureaucratic wheels in Italy turned slowly, however.

Completed forms in hand, I stood in line at the *Municipio*, the City Hall, in Novara, Piemonte's capital about an hour's drive from Ameno. I was elated when I reached the head of the line. Victory was in sight.

But not so fast! A smiling Italian lady closed her window just as I was approaching and announced a two and a half hour lunch break.

It was pasta time. No self-respecting Italian would dream of eating a dry panini at his or her desk. Off she went, together with her colleagues, to *la mama, la sposa,* the wife, or *la nonna,* grandmother, for ministrone or pasta. Hundreds of Italians stream out of their offices or leave construction sites at exactly 12 noon, run to their cars, their Vespas or—less frequently—their bicycles and race home.

Understandably, I learned quickly, they are starving. Most Italians don't eat breakfast—a quick espresso, bitter and dark, and often no larger than 26 drops in a small espresso cup at a coffee bar—is all they consume before starting their daily jobs. I learned to avoid being on the road at 12 noon, fearing to be run down by one of those hungry Italians. They tend to drive in the middle of the road. Maleen Pacha explained to me that, because the Italians are dizzy from hunger, they avoid driving the curves and simply ride in the middle. I am not sure I quite believe this theory, but driving at noon can be scary.

At least this time the Italian bureaucracy cooperated. I received five *codice fiscale* and a temporary residence permit within three days with Tina's help and connections. She always knew a signora with connections.

"She is a good friend of mine," Tina would say.

Ulla Morris-Carter

La Casa Rustica in the snow, under construction.

Luckily, Tina seemed to have a good friend in every department. With all the required, precious documents in hand, I was allowed to open a bank account at *Banca Populare di Novara* in Orta. The bank employee who helped me, Signorita Maria, was a young, gorgeous looking Italian lady. She wore heavy gold jewellery and complemented her outfit with one of those splendid, luxurious Italian silk scarves.

Somehow she did not fit into this small old bank building, which actually was one of the ancient, attached houses in the historic part of Orta. She certainly could not understand why anybody coming from a big city in Germany would choose to live in Orta—or worse—in Ameno, a small village, where nothing ever happened. She herself was ready for big city life, where she hoped to find a husband, she told me.

Money transfers and writing checks in Italian language meant learning to write numbers that went way beyond my comprehension and knowledge of the language. The numbers ran into the millions ($1 was worth I.L. 650). It's a frightening experience to suddenly have to transfer thousands if not millions of lire.

Finally, on April 29, 1975, the big moment had arrived—the signing of the sales contract. All the heirs, or their representatives, equipped with powers of attorney, gathered at the *Notaio's*, Notary Public's, office in Omegna, a small town on the north end of Lago di Orta. The *atto notarile,* the sales contract, was to be signed. In Italy

Ulla Morris-Carter

a notary public is an important person, of much higher standing than in the United States. He usually has a law degree and resides in splendid surroundings. So it was with Dottore Giancarlo Bertoli, our *Notaio*. We had met him during a previous visit. Dressed in an Armani suit, his beautifully polished Italian designer shoes peeking out from underneath an antique desk of enormous proportions, he was the perfect image of a proud Italian. His high-ceilinged office was decorated with beautiful frescos. We always wondered whether the cost of this elegantly appointed office and its occupant would be factored into our bill.

All interested parties assembled at 11 a.m. Signora Tina Baroni was representing us in our absence. The group waited patiently until 2 p.m. for one missing person. After three hours had elapsed, it was established that the missing person was a lady who lived in Paris. She owned, said the *Notaio*, one quarter of ONE room, which turned out to be the no-longer-existent stable, *la stalla*.

But, the *Notaio* continued:

"*La povra,* the poor dear, is very ill; she is too ill to sign any paper. She lives in a mental institution in Paris."

Tina Baroni politely translated:

"She has *malatia di testa*." "She is sick in the head."

The *Notaio* proceeded:

"*Ma non che problema* , but there is no problem, signing the contract without her. She will never recover and has no heirs. After she dies we'll write an additional contract."

This detail would turn into a major problem when we wanted to sell *la Casa Rustica* thirty years later. In the Italy of 1975 however, nobody paid much attention to it. Laws existed to be broken—not every Italian paid taxes, one-way streets could easily turn into two-way streets, and one missing signature by an heir *un poco pazzo*, a little crazy, who had no family or heirs and would never leave the mental institution, did not seem the least bit worrying.But Signora Baroni, as our representative, refused to sign the contract without our specific agreement.

Another month went by before our consent reached the *Notaio*.

All in all it took almost a year and a half after my initial visit before we had all the paperwork in place. The final sales document did not reach us until the summer of 1975, by which time the *Los Angeles Times* had transferred Joe to Beirut, Lebanon. We had moved out of Europe.

Ulla Morris-Carter

The finished house a few years later.

Ulla Morris-Carter

SUN SEP 28 1975

Confusion Grips Beirut These Days

BY JOE ALEX MORRIS JR.
Times Staff Writer

BEIRUT—This must be the most confused city in the world these days.

It is only halfway, if that, out of a vicious civil war.

There is a curfew every night.

Those shops which are not bombed are shuttered tight. Those Lebanese who can afford it have long since removed their families to the safety of the mountains, so houses and apartments are unlit.

Armored half-tracks move on metal streets, scaring the cats and rats as heaps everywhere. There has been no lection for more than a week.

The movie houses are dead. So are

Beirut scene, say they are simply gunmen who haven been paid off yet to stop fighting.

The gasoline situation is a good example of the chao Officially, there is plenty of gasoline on hand.

Ghassan Tueiny, the minister of petroleum, said so, an everyone knows that Tueiny is an honorable gentlema Yet the gasoline stations remain closed.

The man at the station around the corner is no excep tion. But drive up at a quiet moment, and he'll back yo car into the lubricating shed, and fill it up.

But things are slowly getting better. The Renaissa

8 Part I—Thur., Oct. 9, 1975 Los Angeles Times ★

PLO Threatens to Intervene as Outbreaks
of Fighting Dash Lebanon Peace Hopes

BY JOE ALEX MORRIS JR.
Times Staff Writer

BEIRUT—Hopes that civil war torn Lebanon was retu mal were shattered earl by sharp outbreaks of fi nit and the northern cit

The renewed shooting broke an uneasy five-d fourth round of civil v the country this year, time, security forces involved.

Also for the first ound, which began a here was a threat from n establishment to inf now, the Palestine Libe -ation had been active with the government l top the bloodshed.

Huge fires were ragi rol in downtown Beir shelling early Wednes nen were not able to g ause of snipers.

In the worst single i ar shell landed close t le outside a bakery in Moslem district. At le

The renewed fighting came on the last day of a Moslem feast, Id el Fitr, marking the end of Ramadan, the

WAFA accused the Christian Falan gists of breaking the cease-fire and warned that "the Falangist gangs

Beirut Almost
Without Hope

TUE OCT 21 1975

1,600 Reported Killed
in 6 Weeks of Fighting

BY JOE ALEX MORRIS JR.
Times Staff Writer

BEIRUT—This Lebanese capital Monday was a city almost without hope. There appeared to be no end in sight to the factional warfare between Christian Falangists and Moslem left-wingers. In the last six weeks, the fighting has raged virtually unchecked except for a dozen o so fragile, short-lived cease-fire per ods.

On Sunday, the prospects seeme brighter. There was practically n shooting, and tens of thousands o war-weary Lebanese took their fam lies to the beaches and mountain

14 Part I—Tues., Oct. 21, 1975 Los Angeles Times

Fighting Intensifies
in the Heart of Beiru

Lebanese, Foreigners Alike Are Target
in Once-Safe Hotel, Shopping Districts

WED OCT 29 1975 BY JOE ALEX MORRIS JR.
Times Staff Writer

BEIRUT—Rockets and mortar shells rained down on helpless Lebanese foreigners in the main hotel district and elsewhere in the capital Tues ... huge palls of smoke and starting fires. Previously safe shop rted as the batt d.

ns), hastily evac n bullets begun v tayed closed Tue tween Christian reached a new p ps guard detachn matic rifles and from its dress combat fatigues el shutters were indows.

d other foreign ebanese who c flood of evacua ng of most emb 0 American of lependents left

Fierce Fighting in Beirut
Ebbs With New Cease-Fire

MON OCT 27 1975

BY JOE ALEX MORRIS JR.
Times Staff Writer

BEIRUT—The fierce fighting day morning. Their American guests in armored cars.
an residents and oth ho were determined e first flight of eva oing—some of them y, but others have ecided to move out as spread into areas

War-Torn Beirut Abandoning Hope

OCT 21 1975

Continued from First Page

The renewal of violence also halted political efforts to resolve the crisis, efforts which a Moslem deputy has described as a merry-go-round leading nowhere. A meeting of the political subcommittee of the National Reconciliation Committee set up by Premier Rashid Karami wa called off—the streets were too dangerous for some members to get to the meeting place.

For the first time, the local American school shut dow U.S. Ambassador G. MacMurtrie Godley has been tryin to keep the school open, realizing that, should it clos hundreds more Americans living here would pack up ai join those who have already left for safer climes.

The Lebanese schools have remained closed, and Pres

These schools and others are in severe financial difficulties and fear drastic drops in their enrollments. The city's reputation as the educational center for the Arab world is threatened.

Although the shooting stopped later Monday, the wave

BEIRUT BRIDE GETS DEADLY GIFT

It Was Just Another Wedding, Alm

BY JOE ALEX MORRIS JR.
Times Staff Writer

APR 18 1976

BEIRUT—"Dearly beloved, we are gathered together

army, big or small—brought in a present wrappe orful paper. He gave it to the bride.

She unwrapped a shiny new Kalashnikov sub

ANY INDIVIDUAL TRAGEDIES IN MIDST OF CHAOS

War Takes Heavy Personal, Economic Toll in Lebanon

BY JOE ALEX MORRIS JR.
Times Staff Writer

BEIRUT—Theophilus Irani sat
idly stirring a cup of masoboutm,
bittersweet Turkish coffee.

he warm winter sunshine speckl-
the bright red tablecloth on the
her table of his restaurant, a place

orful past which included six years
service in Hilter's army.

Doris Irani was long associated
with Wernher von Braun, the German rocket chief, at the installation
at Peenemunde. In those days, sh
was nicknamed "V-2" after the German missile.

the manager of the Phoenicia Hotel,
died of asphyxiation after refusing to
be evacuated from the hotel when it

tradespeople and office workers
Since the fourth round of fighting
began in September, most of thei

Law of the Gun in Beirut: Bank Robberies
THU APR 8 1976
MON DEC 2 2 1! ## Killings and Macho Bandits in Jeeps

ebanon Civil War
Regaining Past Fury

BY JOE ALEX MORRIS JR.
SUN JAN 11 1976

BEIRUT—Armed bands battled in t
s of downtown Beirut Saturday, brir
war situation rapidly back to its pr
nce and senseless bloodshed.

Fighting raged between Christian an
h mortars, rockets and machine gu
alties varied, but police sources repor
s killed and 200 wounded in the last
The U.S. Embassy, located on the co
district, was reported under sniper fi
Christian Falangists moved into th
ins of the 26-story Holiday Inn, wh
e fire-gutted Phoenicia Hotel 50 yard
Kidnapings and counter
pped during a recent lull in the
cc.
The latest round in the conflict beg
en Falangists blockaded the Pale
Tal Zaater and Jisr al Pasha on Beir
The Falangists blocked attempts

some miracle, staggers along. Electricity, telephone service and water
supply break down continually, but
somehow are restore.

Garbage collection is a sometime
thing, and huge piles of rotting re-

one would dream of challenging
new gladiators who have taken o
the city.

Breaking into banks has becom
popular advocation. The Banco
Roma was the latest but proba
not the biggest prize.

ANARCHY IN BEIRUT

Continued from 10th Page

The crisis has brought about a
change in Lebanese life-styles. Beirut
is a dead city at night, inhabited only
by gunmen.

In the old days, Lebanese gay

ing like Elvis Presley's, as
takes the corners.

Meanwhile, the sanitation
out every morning to pick
latest crop of dead, maimed l
They miss a few, of coo

U.S. Orders Embassy
in Beirut Evacuated

Spreading Fighting Envelops Building;
Americans Urged to Leave Lebanon

BY JOE ALEX MORRIS JR.
Times Staff

BEIRUT—The American Embassy was ordered evacuated Monday after-
when it

THE RETURN
TO BEIRUT

ITTER POLITICAL RIVALRY

Civil War Threatens to
Tear Arab World Apart

MON JUN 7 1976   BY JOE ALEX Times Staff

BEIRUT—Never has the Arab
world seemed so close to falling apart.
The bitter falling out of the two
main Arab protagonists over the past
w months—Egypt and Syria —has
en capped by a rupture in their re-
tions.

War Leaves Lebanon
SUN JUL 11 1976
Ruined, Still Divided

BY JOE ALEX MORRIS JR.

BEIRUT—In the past 15 months,
Lebanon degenerated from the most

Many Lebanese Christians will

Your reason and your passion are the rudder
and the sails of your seafaring soul.

If either your sails or your rudder be broken,
you can but toss and drift, or else be held at a
standstill in mid-seas.

For reason, ruling alone, is a force confining;
and passion, unattended, is a flame that
burns to its own destruction.

Therefore let your soul exalt your reason to the
height of passion, that it may sing;

And let it direct your passion with reason,
that your passion may live through its own
daily resurrection, and like the phoenix rise
above its own ashes.

–Khalil Gibran

MY LOST YEAR

BEIRUT 1975-76

Beirut Battered by Heavy Artillery Fire, Making Chances for Peace Seem Remote

Strife-Torn Lebanon Faces Turning Point

Beirut Violence Hits New Peak

Beirut at Point of Total Confrontation

Such were the headlines in April and May of 1975 in the *Los Angeles Times.* I was packing up our house in Bonn-Bad Godesberg, West Germany, where we had lived for the past four years, to move back to Beirut, Lebanon.

Originally, in January of that year, the *Los Angeles Times* had assigned Joe to become the Moscow bureau chief. But the aftereffects of his illness did not seem appropriate for living in the Soviet Union with uncertain follow-up medical attention. By the early spring of 1975 Joe had completely recovered from a year and a half of treatments and was ready for his new assignment back in the Middle East. Our children were in the middle of their school year, prompting our decision to have them finish school in Germany. I remained in Bonn-Bad Godesberg with the children until June. Joe returned briefly from Beirut to help me pack up the house.

In the early summer of 1975 we spent three weeks in the U.S. visiting Joe's father in Guilford Connecticut. It was always a great treat and pleasure to see and stay at our beloved Joe Sr.'s house.

Ulla Morris-Carter

Joe Sr. and Joe Jr., in Guilford in the summer.

Meanwhile, the news out of Beirut sounded ominous and sometimes threatening. But Joe's usual optimism was contagious, and all of us quickly set aside our worries. We looked forward to returning to a place we knew well and loved. In the 1960s, life in Beirut had been full of adventure and exciting, and we had much enjoyed living there. Luckily, we didn't know what lay ahead of us.

Still, why would any rational, sane person move to a country in such turmoil?

I asked myself a few times. Easy answer: we wanted to stay together as a family. Surely, the situation would improve. We had always known the Lebanese people to be irrepressibly hopeful and resourceful, as well as full of contradictions. A country made up of so many different factions and religions cannot exist without friction. And as long as Joe worked as a foreign correspondent, we would, of necessity, confront obstacles now and then.

On April 13, 1975, a spark ignited what would later become the catalyst for a devastating 15-year-long Civil War in Lebanon. Gunmen killed four Christian militiamen. Believing the assassins were Palestinians, Christian militias, known as Phalangists, retaliated by attacking a Palestinian bus transiting the east Beirut suburb of ain al-Rummaneh. Twenty-six passengers were killed.

From this incident, inter-communal fighting between Christian and Moslem sects spread quickly throughout the city and beyond. The Lebanese Christian parties believed that the Palestinian military presence in Lebanon was the main problem. Beirut's normally frenetic nightlife ground to a halt. As restaurants and nightclubs closed, a short truce brought deceptive quiet and relief. But the security soon deteriorated again. The various factions began shooting indiscriminately. Beirut turned into a "dead" city after one weekend of violence left 175 killed and many more wounded.

Ulla Morris-Carter

While reporting on all this, Joe had been trying to find an apartment or a house to rent for his family in what he considered a safe area. He opted for a place in a mixed religious neighborhood, neither the mostly Christian East Beirut, nor the predominantly Moslem West Beirut. He found a spacious apartment in the Manara Building, which overlooked the ocean and the Bain Militaire, the military beach.

Nearby stood a magnificent landmark, the black-and-white striped lighthouse of Manara. The people who lived in the impressive Manara building were a mixture of Lebanese and foreigners, including an American Morman Bishop, a Lebanese general, and the Military Attaché of the American Embassy. Sunni and Shia Moslems, Christians, Maronites, Druze and other religious sects lived harmoniously in the Manara area, a peaceable microcosm in the crazy quilt that was Lebanon.

Beirut airport was in its usual state of chaos when we arrived in early August, 1975, people shouting, running, smoking, sweating. After orderly Germany, it felt good to be back in the Middle East. It was like a homecoming when we moved for the second time into the Palm Beach Hotel, where we had stayed twelve years earlier. For two weeks we awaited the arrival of the moving van that carried our furniture from Germany via Yugoslavia, Greece, Turkey and Syria to Lebanon. On arrival, one of the two German truck drivers, knowing little of the political upheavals in Lebanon, phoned from Tripoli, Lebanon's northern city near the Syrian border.

"There is unrest and sectarian fighting here. We are not driving any further," he announced.

After confirming that the road to Beirut was open, we assured, bribed, and promised the drivers that it was safe to drive. They could unload at our new apartment, then depart immediately. After a peaceful night in Tripoli, the drivers decided to risk it. They drove the last 85 miles to Beirut without incident. But when the truck tried to turn the corner into Manara, we saw with chagrin that our street was too narrow for their huge vehicle. Everything had to be unloaded, then reloaded onto a smaller truck.

That was only the first obstacle.

Permission from the customs authority, whose offices at the port area were closed because of "les évènements," was necessary for the import of furniture. A customs official had to be bribed to come to our house, unseal the truck, then list the import of furniture in Joe's passport. Otherwise it would be impossible to take our belongings out of the country at a future date.

The inspector barked at our washing machine.

"A Whirlpool!" he shouted. "Not allowed in Lebanon! This brand has been boycotted in the Arab world for some time."

More bakshish. More disallowed items.

Then came the piano, an old, light-brown upright we had acquired in Germany.

Ulla Morris-Carter

The local Kurdish porters were accustomed to transporting everything on their backs. They would strap a heavy leather band around their heads, then attach the piece to be transported, including the washing machine, and carry it up the stairs. That would not work with our piano. Finally, our two hefty German truck drivers stepped in. With two heavy straps, they hoisted the piano almost effortlessly over their shoulders, and up it went to our third floor apartment.

The next day we moved into our beautiful home on the third floor of the six-story building. We had a large, airy living room overlooking the ocean, an attached dining area, three balconies plus a glassed-in terrace that served as breakfast or sun room, three bedrooms, a small maid's room that we used as an extra bedroom, and a large, old-fashioned kitchen. While hanging up curtains, I noticed that our upstairs neighbors who occupied the penthouse, were packing up, leaving Beirut for Athens, Greece, they said. I had hardly met them. We were unpacking, they were evacuating.

Post offices had closed. Mail delivery had stopped. Telephones worked only erratically. And yet, ten days after we moved in, I found a way to send a letter to my mother in Germany via an acquaintance leaving for England:

> Joe really chose a good place for us. Our area is relatively safe and calm. Our neighbors call it "the Switzerland of Beirut." We hear the shooting and explosions, but they are not in our street. John and Inge's apartment, on the other hand, is located in a terrible part of town, unreachable at the moment. Their quarter is completely closed off following an explosion, which caused major damage. Reuter's news agency nearby doesn't have a single window left intact. The city is completely dead. No stores are open with the exception of a few small stores in safe areas. In the morning there are long lines in front of the bread stores, reminding me of wartime Germany. Our second problem is money. We are running out of cash. Six days ago the banks closed. Some stores are happy to sell on credit, particularly when they know the customer, which cannot be said for us.
>
> Other than that we are fine. The children are bored; we are under curfew. Karin has already baked her third cake this week, but now we are running out of sugar. We miss fresh vegetables, fruit and dairy products. There is no bottled gas for sale at the moment, something we need for cooking and hot water. Fortunately we bought enough when we moved in. The washing machine has not been installed, and heaven only knows when we shall find a plumber who is not busy shooting or fighting. The cease-fire is obviously not holding. Joe went downtown today, where fighting continues. He even took a wounded fighter to the hospital. The old, beautiful souks are all burnt down. Only Joe, who of course has a press pass, can move around. We enjoy the people in our building, and we get together with them while we are under curfew.
>
> School is supposed to start next week. Needless to say, the situation needs to

Ulla Morris-Carter

become a lot calmer before that happens. Luckily, we live close to the school, so that the children can walk there once the situation normalizes.

Our apartment is in pretty good shape right now. Julia has just been polishing furniture. I, unfortunately, am fighting a losing battle against cockroaches, despite the fact that our whole apartment was fumigated before we moved in. A mouse just appeared in our corridor, which Karin proclaimed to be very cute. Strangely enough, our children seem to adjust to this situation without any problem.

Must close now and cook dinner. Journalist friends are joining us tonight . . . .

In early October our daughters, Maria, 15, Karin, 11, and Julia, 9, started school. All three enrolled in the American Community School, ACS, which had an excellent reputation and was walking distance from our house. But despite our optimism that *la situation* would improve soon, we could no longer ignore the shooting. Exploding shells kept us awake at night. Beirut was now plunged deeply into sectarian warfare. Every morning we called the school switchboard, which was manned from 6 a.m., to ask if there would be classes. If told "It is a quiet day," we would send our children to school.

Three weeks later, a friend was flying to Germany. She carried a second letter to my mother in Düsseldorf:

Since yesterday the mood in Beirut is lifting. A new cease-fire seems to be holding. We are eagerly waiting for tomorrow, Monday, to find out whether Beirut will indeed return to life. Banks, with the exception of one day, have been closed for three weeks now. Only grocery stores open occasionally in the morning to give us a chance to shop at least for the most important items. We have had enough to eat so far, but no milk and no dairy products, and very little bread. The queues at the bakeries, often between 20 and 50 people long, are remarkably disciplined. We lead a rather unreal life. Every morning is devoted to organizing food, every afternoon and evening Beirut is a dead city. Daily curfew from 5 p.m. until 5 a.m. is strictly observed. Nobody dares to go out in any case for fear of snipers. The problem is that one never knows where those "crazies" sit and why they are shooting. But our apartment is indeed in the safest part of town. The American School, so far the only one, opened two weeks ago and is operating despite the crisis. However we have been instructed to take children to school only if and when we can get there without problems. Some days only 60 percent of the students are in attendance. Nobody knows when any of the other schools--the German School, the Lebanese schools and the French School—will re-open. Many teachers and students have fled to the mountains or never returned from summer vacation. Quite a few bankers, their employees and businessmen, are presently living in London, Athens or Amman, waiting for an end of the crisis. Some plan to move away permanently because of the communication problems: no mail, erratic telephone service, at

Ulla Morris-Carter

times problems of getting to the airport, etc. The American University, which is to open next week, has only 1,200 registered students compared to the normal 5,000. Economically speaking, Beirut is a great fiasco. Damages and losses are estimated to be $2.5 billion—and that sum does not include the losses of the last few days. All the souks and the bazaars have been destroyed. We are not allowed to enter downtown, but Joe told us of the unbelievably horrific destruction. Beirut is completely covered in garbage. Stinking garbage fires are burning on many street corners. We are desperately fighting cockroaches and other pests. The children seem to find all this rather exciting. Luckily, they have found friends who live nearby, so they can visit. We all hope things will normalize next week.

Today we went to the beach. Fantastic weather, and very few people. We no longer have hot water, because we are out of butane gas. We just have enough for cooking. The gas factory is in a part of Beirut that has had a lot of problems. Since two weeks ago there is no gas anywhere. The large luxury buildings have not had hot water for three weeks, because of lack of heating oil. It's remarkable how quickly one can adjust to these situations. Now that we finally have our washing machine running, we simply wash with cold water. That doesn't work with our dishwasher, however. Well, we are back to washing dishes by hand.

We are happy with our apartment. Many small things are still missing, such as curtain hooks. You can't hang curtains without hooks. But we feel lucky that we were able move in. Quite a few people—journalists and business people—have been living in hotels for more than three months, waiting for their furniture to be released from the port, which of course has been closed since May. As far as mail is concerned, in emergencies please consider calling the Los Angeles Times Bureau in Bonn and ask them to relay messages via telex. You may of course try to phone us—unlikely that it will work. Our telephone number is 354083.

Just now Hannelore, the secretary to the Press Attache of the German Embassy, called to tell us that, in emergencies, you are allowed to send mail via the diplomatic pouch to Beirut. Use a normal envelope addressed to us and put it into a second envelope, addressed to Hannelore Rusch, Deutsche Botschaft Beirut, 53 Bonn, Postfach 1500. Hannelore is a friend and lives around the corner. Also the German Ambassador is a friend from Bonn days. Please use this opportunity. We are longing for news from you. . . .

And don't worry about us. As long as one keeps ones head down, all is well.

But the city's despair was deepening. For the first time, rockets appeared to be landing in or near our previously spared western sector. The stores on once elegant Rue Hamra remained closed, prompting thousands of street peddlers to set up shop on the sidewalks or even on the main road. They sold everything from cigarettes to men's suits. The suspicion was that these goods came from downtown shops that had

Ulla Morris-Carter

been looted. Banks had been closed for weeks. Many stores, which at first had gladly accepted checks, now took only cash. But people were running out of cash, even though some of the old streetside money-changers were still around, happy to change foreign currency if one had any. Life staggered on. Ones days centered on how to obtain bottles of butane gas for cooking and hot water, and where to buy bread or gasoline. Driving or walking to school became too dangerous.

In late October the American school shut down. American Ambassador MacMurtrie Godley had been trying to keep it open, realizing that, should it close, hundreds more

Los Angeles Times
BEIRUT BUREAU

JOE ALEX MORRIS, JR.
PRESS COOPERATIVE BUILDING, BEIRUT, LEBANON
TELEPHONE XXXX 354083

Oct. 21, 1975

Dear Joe,
         We have a pigeon departing tomorrow, so thought would
try to get something in the mail. She's the NYTimes wife, going
to Athens to sweat it out --- I wish I could say await the final
denouement, but in this situation, the end may come by frittering
away, not with a bang. Anyhow, her husband was in Vietnam, and
he's nervous.

We old Middle East hands are not, of course. Even though xxx our
sanctuary here in West Beirut has of late come into the noise
zone from the nightly go-arounds. We haven't had any hits in the
region, unlike our old digs in Patriarkiya, which has been a
madhouse, complete with explosions plus the whizz of the RPGs
as they zoom by on their way to destinations which even those who
fired them know not.

We were up there today, visiting the Moffetts and the Davies, who
live across the street from our old place. Our successor by
three in the old flat, Buchalla of the Sueddeutsche Zeitung,
moved into a hotel today, having packed his family off to Germany
a couple of weeks ago. He, like many, had a good reason: the
German school here has shown no signs of reopening, and what do
you do with the kids?

We have --- cross fingers --- been lucky in this respect. The
American school is the only one here to have reopened on a normal
basis (the Brits are trying to make do by holding classes in
the embassy and in people's houses). We missed school Monday, after
a particularly bad night, but they were back in business today.

The kids seem to be adjusting well enough. Julia with groans of
protest, Karin with alacrity but somewhat confused by terminology
and new Math, with which I cannot help her much. Ulla too is
slowly reacquiring her Beiruti orientation, much taken up with
infernal battles, not with Palestinians but with the cockroaches.
With no garbage collections for six weeks now, they are having
a field day. I've been trying to help --- plastering up cracks
between walls and window frames, etc., but the outcome is still
in doubt and Ulla suspects the roaches are winning. We are more
or less settled in, with mainly nagging details still to be
settled like getting the car re-registered, picking up our
resident permits which were supposedly ready a month ago but
the office has been closed ever since "lay zevenements", as the
Lebanese call it, got under way again in full force.

Ulla Morris-Carter

Fighting Intensifies in the Heart of Beirut

Lebanese, Foreigners Alike Are Targets in Once-Safe Hotel, Shopping Districts

Beirut Almost Without Hope

U.S. Orders Embassy in Beirut Evacuated

Spreading Fighting Envelops Building; Americans Urged to Leave Lebanon

BY JOE ALEX MORRIS JR.

Headlines of some of Joe's articles in October 21, 28 and 29, 1975.

Americans would pack up and leave. The American Embassy and others ordered evacuation.

Joe had to stay. We were desperately trying to keep the family together, rather than joining the exodus to Turkey, Cyprus or Greece. Evacuation would mean sitting alone with my children in a foreign country, probably in a small, furnished apartment, hoping Joe could visit occasionally. We had had too many separations already, too many schools, too many changes. We had no home to return to in either the U.S. or Germany.

Beirut airport turned into a scene of chaos as most foreigners tried to leave. Our oldest daughter, Maria, became one of the refugees. At age 15, with no school in Lebanon to go to, she needed a special solution. After a few unsuccessful attempts we managed, via *UPI* telex and the help of a journalist friend in Geneva, to enroll Maria in a boarding school in Switzerland.

TASIS, The American School in Switzerland, was located in Lugano. Because of the bank closures, we could not equip Maria with money for her trip or to pay her school fees. *United Press Telex* to the rescue: journalist friends in Switzerland phoned my mother in Germany asking her to send money to Maria once she had arrived.

Amid hundreds of other foreigners leaving Lebanon, Maria was understandably apprehensive about her future alone in Switzerland. She would have to walk into an already existing class in the middle of the semester in a school she had never visited before.

"Will I find friends? Will I be accepted?" she asked.

My heart was heavy just looking at her. Knowing how she felt, I was truly depressed for the first time since our return to Beirut.

Maria put a brave face to a sad situation.

To add to her uneasiness, the *Time Magazine* correspondent in Beirut, one of Joe's colleagues, asked Maria to carry film for the cover story of that week's issue. Communications in Beirut were mostly down.

He instructed her:

"No matter what may happen, never let go of the film. It's the most important thing

Ulla Morris-Carter

you carry. You will be met at the Geneva airport by a *Time* correspondent, who will wear a red carnation in the button hole of his blazer."

I watched Maria board the plane clutching the film tightly under her arm. She hardly had time to cry, unlike her mother.

Meanwhile we had managed to register Julia and Karin at Broummana High School, *BHS*, an excellent British Quaker boarding school, located in the mountains. One of the few schools in Lebanon still functioning, it was far enough from Beirut to be safe, or so we believed. BHS had been founded in 1873 by a Swiss missionary, a converted Quaker. Karin and Julia had attended British schools in Germany, so they would have no problem academically.

But many of the boarders had already evacuated, or were leaving, just as Joe and I arrived with Julia and Karin in our white Fiat convertible on a balmy October day. It was heartbreaking to leave the children in the mountains. From being a mother of three, used to a lively and noisy household, I had become a childless mother in an empty apartment. I cried all the way home.

Julia and Karin called us occasionally from a faltering public telephone, when it was functioning. Occasionally we received hand-carried letters via someone who had managed to travel to the mountains. Julia had to live in the section for the younger students, where she turned out to be the only girl among a noisy group of boys. She was very unhappy.

In Karin's age group, more boarders were still staying at the school, most of them from Saudi Arabia, Yemen, Jordan, Dubai, Syria and other Arab countries. Karin, being Karin, always self-directed, adjusted well and made friends easily. As the civil war intensified and more students left, Julia was allowed to join the big girls, a major improvement. She was much happier being with her sister and other girls.

As winter approached, it was getting pretty cold up in those mountains. Frequently the school had no heat, which was also true for us in Beirut. Urgent requests for hot water bottles and heavy sweaters arrived over the intermittent phone line. Karin and Julia also wanted judo outfits. Judo had been added to the school curriculum to help the students to keep warm. Food was available some days more than others and was pretty meager. If the school baker had flour, he could bake bread.

For Joe and me, visiting the girls became more difficult by the day. We had to cross the so-called Green Line, the division between the two warring parts of Beirut near the Museum. Sniper fire was the norm. One never knew where the shots were coming from. There was no clear border or division between one side and the other.

One day, Joe and I were surprised to receive a hand-delivered letter from our children asking us not to try to come to school:

Ulla Morris-Carter

"We are just fine, don't worry about us," it read. "No need for you to drive up."

We were puzzled at first. But when we heard that the father of a British student at BHS, on his way up the mountains to see his daughter, had been shot dead, we understood. Our children were terrified something might also happen to us, but they never said so outright.

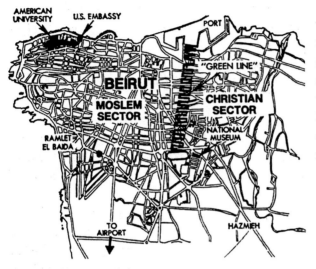

In Beirut the situation worsened. Rockets and mortar shells rained down, sending up huge palls of smoke and starting fires in the main hotel district. The heavy fighting focused first on the Holiday Inn near the waterfront. This luxury hotel took rocket shells and had many windows shattered. Fifty foreign guests plus about 200 personnel were now trapped there. Some

Above: *Map of a divided Beirut.*
Below: *Julia, Karin and I on a previous visit to Broumana, 'putting on a brave face'.*
Right: *The letter written by Karin and Julia from Brou-mana, February 1976, expressing concern about our visit. The father of a school classmate had recently been shot and killed driving past a check point to visit his daughter.*

Dear Mum & Dad,

I'm very sorry you couldn't come up on Saturday but next week we'll have the holidays and we can see you for 2 whole weeks. Right now, we are not allowed off school grounds because 2 men were kidnapped in Broumana We are all alright and I hope I have to go now because MR. Johannites must go.

Love Julia
& Karin

P.S. School is going alright and this weekend, we pretended we were camping and we slept on the floor!

Ulla Morris-Carter

tried to leave, but were driven back by gunfire. Next door, the Phoenicia Intercontinental Hotel sent its guests into a downstairs basement room for protection.

Previously safe shopping areas echoed with small arms fire and were quickly deserted as *The Battle of the Hotels* intensified. Violence and chaos had become a way of life. Nights were differentiated between those that were calm, allowing sleep, and others in which the sound of mortar shells kept everyone awake. But many residents were reluctant to leave for fear of having their apartments occupied by squatters and their belongings stolen. First National City Bank pulled out some 200 employees and their families.

"How many will return?" we asked ourselves. "Can the government get a grip on the situation?"

But the Lebanese Army did not intervene. There were mounting demands from both Christian and Moslem leaders that President Franjieh, a Christian, resign. For weeks he had not been heard from, not even to publicly appeal for peace. Throughout the city the atmosphere was one of increasing desperation and depression. Centuries-old social, religious and political rivalries were exacerbated by the presence of the large number of Palestinian refugees, siding with the Moslems and operating as a state-within-a-state.

The Lebanese Civil War had wider dimensions. It became a national war between Right and Left, between Moslems and Christians, between Haves and Have-nots. Outside forces helped their favorite factions. Both Syria and Israel became involved in this proxy war. Through the officially closed Port of Beirut, weapons and ammunition poured into an intricate political jungle that had once been a small serene nation.

Chaos alternated with quiet days. One beautiful morning, to relieve the tension, Joe and I decided to get out of the house to try and play a game of tennis. The radio assured us that it was a quiet day. At 8:30 a.m., tennis rackets under our arms, we walked down to the nearby Renaissance Tennis Club. Although the Club was officially closed, we knew the gate was unlocked. As we passed the building next to ours, our Lebanese neighbor came out and got into his red Peugeot sedan. He was dressed in a dark suit and tie. Under his arm he carried a Russian-made Kalashnikov submachine gun.

We exchanged friendly good mornings. It wasn't until later that we realized the absurdity of the situation: we with our tennis rackets, the neighbor with a machine gun under his arm. That was Lebanon. At the Tennis Club, we first had to clear the hard-surface courts of shrapnel and dirt. But then the game was a big treat.

Individual Tragedies

Amid the re-opening and re-closing of banks and shops, surrounded by accumulating mountains of garbage and lack of public services, Beirut was full of individual tragedies. Many acquaintances, having made Beirut their home for years, were stymied. They didn't want to leave everything behind, and frequently they had nowhere to go.

Ulla Morris-Carter

Our friends, Louise Severino and her daughter, for example, permanent residents of Beirut for more than a decade, were cooped up in their apartment for fifteen days in one of the most contested areas, while shots and shells whisked about them. They survived, but ran out of food and lived without running water and no telephone line to call for help. We could not reach their house without risking our own lives. Roadblocks manned by different factions appeared and disappeared with the speed of light. These "flying roadblocks" could only be maneuvered with the right kind of permit, a pink-colored permit for a Palestinian roadblock, another color to pass a roadblock manned by Phalangists, yet another to pass a Sunni or Shia roadblock. The trick was to whip out the right kind of permit at the right time. A Lebanese citizen who passed one of those roadblocks had his fate marked on his identity card, which stated his religion. If he were a Moslem and the roadblock was Moslem, he was lucky. But if he were Christian he would likely be taken away, perhaps released hours later in exchange for Moslems taken by Christians elsewhere. Or he could become one of those many unidentified corpses carried away by the sanitation forces every morning.

Our dear friends, John and Inge Markarian, lived near Louise, in the same dangerous area of Beirut, called Kantari. Dr. John Markarian, President of the American-Armenian Haigazian College, was married to my good German friend Inge. John and Inge had already taken to sleeping in the hallway on a couple of mattresses for fear of being hit by glass or shrapnel in their many-windowed upstairs apartment. They had decided to stay in Beirut, not only to protect their apartment, but, more important, to protect the nearby college of which John had been President since 1955, for 20 years.

The main building, the beautiful Mugar, dating back to the 1920s, held John's office. It, too, was eventually hit and partially burned. The adjacent college buildings, however, escaped major damage, mostly because of John's presence and wise interference. As a Doctor of Theology from Princeton University, John knew how to deal with the gunmen. When they threatened him at the door, he would invite them in for coffee. He disarmed them with charm and a good sense of humor.

His Biblical motto, "When your enemy is thirsty, give him a drink," often stopped the gunmen in their tracks.

BUT BEIRUT PAIR ARE STAYING PUT

War Moves Into American's Apartment

SAT NOV 1 1975
BY JOE ALEX MORRIS JR.
Times Staff Writer

BEIRUT—Dr. John Markariah and his German wife, Inge, were busy packing up their valuables Friday.

per fire in the area, they want to get their most precious possessions to safety. Also their cat, a Siamese named Balthazar.

But they have no intention of mov-

was taken over by left-wing Moslem gunmen of the Nasserite Movement, one of many factions on that side.

"I was terrified when they shot their way through the front door."

Joe's article in the L.A. Times about the Markarians.

Ulla Morris-Carter

Occasionally, when fighting was so fierce that John and Inge could not leave their house, Joe would take them bread or other food, using his press pass to move past the many roadblocks.

Another case was that of Theophilius "Theo" Irani, a Lebanese Christian, and his German wife Doris. They owned a small restaurant called Rhenania, named after the Rhine River, in Beirut's hotel district. Doris, the driving force behind the Rhenania, had a colorful past, which included being a hurdler on the German track team in the 1936 Berlin Olympics, plus six years in Hitler's army.

During WWII she had worked closely with Wernher von Braun, the German rocket scientist who developed the first ballistic missile. In those days Doris was called "V-2" after the missile, *Vergeltungswaffe 2*. If you knew her well and asked her, she might bring out her photo albums and show you the photos of herself with the famous scientist, who after WWII had been recruited by the Americans to work closely with NASA.

Rhenania was known more for giving homesick German engineers and businessmen a touch of the home country than for gourmet food. A mural of the legendary *Lorelei Maiden*, sitting on a cliff above the Rhine, combing her long blonde hair, covered one wall. A painting of Germany's Black Forest covered the other.

During Beirut's *Battle of the Hotels,* Rhenania was forced to close. Theo and Doris were trapped, unable to get out. Theo, desperate and a little drunk, decided to walk to the nearby Phoenicia Hotel, which was momentarily occupied by the Christian Phalangists. His somewhat crazy idea was to ask his Christian brothers to please stop shooting. He thought he could save his restaurant and his home.

Approaching the Phoenicia Hotel, he was shot in the leg by a sniper. He was left lying in the street, bleeding profusely. When help finally reached him, his leg had to be amputated. The Rhenania burned down completely. Doris and Theo, no longer young, had lost everything; Theo died shortly thereafter.

And then there was the sad story of Jon Randal's displacement. Jon, the *Washington Post* correspondent, our close friend and colleague, lived near the Markarians in the beleaguered Kantari district. In late October he found himself trapped in his penthouse apartment during a two-day battle. When he was ordered out of his apartment at gunpoint by a group of Moslem fighters belonging to the Communist Party, he was not allowed to take anything with him. Dressed only in boxer shorts and a T-shirt, Jon finally convinced the militiamen to let him put on blue jeans, a shirt, socks and shoes. They admitted that it would be difficult to walk barefoot over shrapnel and glass. But he had to leave behind his passport, his travelers checks and everything else.

When he told his captors that the Algerian Ambassador, a Moslem, was a good friend who could vouch for him, Jon was taken to the Algerian Ambassador's residence

Ula is desolé because suddenly she has no children around. She lost three daughters and, as I told her, she gained a son--- namely Jon Randal who moved in for three or four days. Poor Jon lost practically everything including his passport when goons kicked him out of his apartment. The experience has not lowered his level of nervous tension.

Otherwise all is well here. The airport's still open, MEA flies on time most of the time even if other airlines chicken out. We still have a curfew which is almost unnecessary because so many of our friends have scooted --- both foreign and Lebanese --- that I don't know where we'd go if we could. Let's hope for the best, keep our fingers crossed, etc. KMPC called me the other night and one of the questions was: when are YOU evacuating? The guy was astonished when I said I had not intent of doing so.

Bests,

Joe's letter to L.A. Times *foreign editor Bob Gibson about recent events and conditions. November 5, 1975.*

in the wee hours of the morning. The pajama-clad Ambassador managed to have Jon released. The militiamen apologized profusely and assured Jon that absolutely nothing would be touched in his apartment. Worried because we hadn't been able to reach Jon by phone for at least two days, we were overjoyed when he suddenly stood in front of our apartment.

For the next three days he walked around in Joe's clothes, hoping to be able to return to his apartment once the shooting had died down. When he finally did reach his building, he watched armed looters carrying out Persian carpets, clothes and furniture. Slowly climbing the stairs to his sixth-floor penthouse apartment, he knew there was trouble. The penthouse had been ransacked and completely burnt out.

Just before Christmas 1975 another cease-fire went into effect. During this quiet period we managed to pick up our two children from their school in the mountains. All of us then traveled to Germany to spend a normal Christmas with friends in Bonn and with my mother and brother in Düsseldorf. The best part was Maria's arrival from Switzerland, completing our joyous reunion.

In early January 1976 Joe, Karin, Julia and I returned to Beirut. Maria went back to her school in Switzerland. Nothing much had changed in Beirut. Cease-fires were arranged only to be broken within a few days. The American University of Beirut, AUB, was trying to start its delayed fall semester, but security conditions had hardly improved. Nonetheless BHS was still functioning, so we took our two children back to that mountain school in Broummana.

We were delighted when 18-year-old Jay Bruder, the son of the American Military Attaché, came to live with us and to occupy one of the empty bedrooms. His parents had had to evacuate together with other Embassy diplomats and employees at the end of October. Already enrolled at AUB, Jay was waiting eagerly for classes to start. AUB reopened in early January without incident. Our apartment was walking distance

Ulla Morris-Carter

from the college, and Jay was grateful to be able to stay with us. He told us that 2,200 students were attending.

Less than two weeks later, Lebanon's civil war sank to its previous low level of violence and senseless bloodshed. At this point the 'Battle of the Hotels' was in full swing. The luxury hotels, Holiday Inn, Phoenicia Intercontinental and the famous St. Georges Hotel, all located close to the ocean and within a city block of each other, became, once again, part of the bloody skirmishes that engulfed Beirut. Fighting raged between gunmen armed with mortars, rockets and machine guns. Christian Phalangists moved into the bombed-out remains of the 26-story Holiday Inn, while Moslems seized the fire-gutted Phoenicia Hotel 50 yards away.

The city shook under the worst fighting yet in the eleven-month struggle among various factions. Kidnappings, the grisliest events of all, continued in force. A dear friend of ours, Edouard Saab, editor-in-chief of the French-language paper in Beirut and correspondent for the Paris paper, *Le Monde,* was killed by a sniper while driving with the *New York Times* correspondent, Henry Tanner. Edouard left behind a wife and three young children. His death sent chills down our backs.

In February 1976, I was left alone in our now nearly empty building for a few days while Joe was traveling. After a particularly bad night of shelling, no electricity, and an invasion of cockroaches in the kitchen, I was so frustrated that I swore I would never again stay by myself. To battle the cockroach invasion I had closed all windows and doors of the kitchen, stood on a chair and sprayed the originally white ceiling, now black with cockroaches, with three cans of poison. As they were dropping right and left of me, I felt not only disgusted, but suddenly very sick. I just managed to climb off the chair and ran to the bedroom where I collapsed on the bed.

After this ordeal, the *Los Angeles Times* allowed me to accompany Joe on his next trip to Kuwait and Bahrain. But, away from Beirut, I could not relax. I was worried about the children. What if the airport suddenly closed? From Kuwait we were unable either to phone or telex Beirut. Was there now no electricity, I wondered?

While in Bahrain, Joe and I were interviewed by the *Gulf Mirror,* a Bahrain newspaper.

"Survive with a Smile" read the headline. "People who work for newspapers sometimes have to run strange risks, as do their wives," opened the article.

By the time we returned to Beirut, the Christian militia had mounted a huge 85mm gun in front of Broummana High School. Occasionally, it was shooting down on our district in mostly Moslem West Beirut. Ironically, we too had acquired a very noisy 85mm gun, placed by the Moslems right below our living room window. Our gun tended to shoot in the direction of Broummana. When the gun went off, our windows rattled. The noise was awful. It could literally rock you out of your seat. Our windows were now taped up to prevent flying glass hitting us when the gun went off.

Joe would call out, "Outgoing, darling, don't worry!"

Easier said than done. Men apparently have a higher tolerance and a different emotional response to the sounds of guns going off than women. In my case, memories of World War II loomed with frightening images. Later, our children told us that, after the installation of the big guns, they and their classmates in Broummana frequently had to go down to the basement of the school, carrying their sleeping bags to spend the night.

During the spring semester Julia and Karin came home only once. That was in March, 1976. And what a weekend it turned out to be! Traveling conditions were worse than ever, and Joe and I were relieved that we had managed to have the children with us. The city rocked to the explosion of artillery shells. The continued thunder of rockets and mortars, which we had formerly heard only during the day, came closer and closer during the night.

Page 16, GULF MIRROR, Feb. 16 — Feb. 21

SURVIVE WITH A SMILE...

VISITORS to the Gulf this week are Ulla and Joe Alex Morris, who have found that in wartime Beirut facial expression could be the subtle little difference that makes all the difference — between life and death.

Joe has covered the civil war in Lebanon as a correspondent for the *Los Angeles Times* and Ulla — the only Western journalist's wife to remain in Beirut throughout the war — has been serving as a mother-surrogate to the foreign press corps. During this time the Morrises found it imperative to seem friendly and calm when guns were waved in their faces.

"A friendly 'Marhaba!!' ('Greetings!') in the right place can keep you alive." says Joe, a 48-year-old American Middle East hand who has covered four

(compliments of his newspaper) "as a reward for braving the war in Beirut instead of sitting in an Athens or London hotel at the rate of $100 per day!" She admits, however, to being a bit chagrined when, eight months into the civil war, the newspaper casually cabled one day to Joe: "By the way, how are Ulla and the kids?"

The "kids" — the Morrises' three daughters aged 10, 11½ and 15 years — were with their parents in Beirut until late October when the American Community School they attended closed after a big shootout in nearby Ain Mreisse and Kantari districts. At that point the eldest was sent off to school in Switzerland and the two younger girls were taken to a boarding school in Broummana, in the mountains outside Beirut.

Their parents remained

PEOPLE who work for newspapers sometimes have to run strange risks — as do their wives.

BETH ANN WILSON this week interviewed in Bahrain one of the leading American correspondents in the Middle East, about how he and his wife managed to survive in Beirut during the worst of the civil strife. Joe Alex Morris and his wife Ulla were the only married couple among foreign correspondents to stay through all the troubles...

d'oeuvres no dessert. It was usually pea soup or lasagna. I had plenty of German wine in stock and we always drank too much, but even then it wasn't very jolly.

"Often the people who came to us would have a gun poked in their ribs

"When I worry about my two younger daughters freezing in the mountains outside Beirut from lack of heating oil, my husband tells me not to be silly 'You have suffered more than that' he says."

However she does worry then discovers her shiv

Article written in the Gulf Mirror, Bahrain, February 1976, *as Joe was on assignment in Bahrain and due to the unstable situation in Beirut, I was allowed to accompany him.*

Ulla Morris-Carter

Joe, who rarely wrote about himself or his family, did write a short article about this particular night:

War Finally Shatters Beirut Quiet Area

By Joe Alex Morris Jr. (March 23, 1976)

About 1 a. m. Monday, the Lebanese civil war came to the residents of the Manara quarter of Beirut.

The sounds of battle, previously remote and muffled in Manara, suddenly became very loud. The Christian Phalange militia, smarting under the loss of the Holiday Inn Hotel, unlimbered its big guns in Ashrafiyah, a few miles to the east, and began to pour artillery and tank fire into west Beirut.

Manara, which means "lighthouse," is the section of town most remote from the battlegrounds of the past 11 months. Lebanese call it "The Switzerland of Beirut," envying its relative tranquility. But Manara lost its neutrality a few weeks ago, thanks to Lt. Ahmed Khatib and his rebel Lebanese Arab Army. Khatib's men set up a headquarters down on the coast, at the military beach, just a few hundred yards from the lighthouse.

Of course, the Phalange knew about it. And so we, who live in the district, began getting calling cards from the Phalange early Monday morning as part of their artillery offensive.

No district of Beirut has completely escaped the civil strife. Manara had the occasional bombing and, more frequently, bold car thefts and holdups, often in broad daylight, by gangs of youth armed with Kalashnikov submachine guns.

But by and large, life had been nearly normal. Street vendors had peddled fruits and vegetable as usual, and even the shoeshine man had continued his regular rounds.

But early Monday morning, this honeymoon ended. It was a source of perverse satisfaction for some. My wife, for example.

For weeks I had slept peacefully through the remote thunder of rockets and mortars, while she had lain wide awake in bed, waiting for the next round. This time we shared a sleepless night.

In contrast, the children down from their mountain school for the weekend, slept until early morning when Khatib's men directly below returned fire for the first time in retaliation against the Christian barrage. A few hours later, Ashrafiyah began hitting back, raggedly bracketing the military beach and rattling our windows with each concussion.

The Khatib forces took several good hits, one just a few feet from an armored car which miraculously continued to function.

Building superintendents hurriedly rounded up those still living in this sector and took them to air raid shelters in the more modern buildings. The shelters were built against Israeli air raids. Now they were being used because Arab was fighting Arab.

As for our family, the best that could be said was that we did not panic.

Ulla Morris-Carter

Others were less lucky. One correspondent, also a Manara resident, decided early in the day to get out and headed for the Commodore Hotel as a temporary residence. On the way, he ran into a funeral, complete with mourners shooting weapons into the air, a traditional way of showing grief. He dived under his vehicle and waited until the funeral had passed.

My children—ages 10 and 12—were terribly sophisticated about it all. They kept asking when they could get back to school. When asked whether they had been frightened during the night, they said simply: "We have had it louder in Broummana" where the school is.

We took the children back to school Sunday evening wondering and worrying how much longer we would be able to travel up and down the mountain roads. But we were still hoping to continue living in Lebanon, though most of our friends had left. I was one of very few wives still around. I cooked many a dinner for those wife-less journalists who lived on our side of Beirut.

We didn't have to wait long for the other shoe to drop. Suddenly, because of heavy fighting, all roads to the mountains and to Broummana were cut off. Gun law was the rule of the day. The government had ceased to function altogether. Private armies and militias were all that remained of public order. There was no way to cross "sniper alley", the Green Line, to reach the mountain roads without being killed in the process. Just at that moment the school sent a message telling us that they had to close down immediately, and what to do with the children?

Most of the remaining students were lucky enough to travel from Broummana via Damascus, Syria, to meet up with their parents who were living in Saudi Arabia or Cairo or Amman. We did not have that choice. Our children could only leave by crossing the extremely dangerous Green Line to travel into the part of Beirut where we lived. And we were unable to leave Beirut to retrieve our children.

What to do?

Our friend Ghassan Tueni came to the rescue. A member of Parliament and, at that point, Minister of Information, he was also publisher of *An-Nahar,* a Lebanese daily newspaper. His family had evacuated from Beirut to their family estate in Beit Mary, a small town near Broummana. Ghassan himself had to remain in the city and could not leave.

He told us, "You cannot, under any circumstances, drive to Broummana. I myself am unable to travel to see my family. I will never never speak to you again if you even attempt to cross Green Line. Do you want to get yourselves killed? "

Telephone communications had stopped altogether. As Minister of Information, Ghassan had radio contact with his wife, Nadia, in Beit Mary. Beautiful Nadia was one of Beirut's best known poets. Ghassan radioed Nadia that she was to send her driver to rescue two Morris girls from BHS, and, in addition a third child, a British girl, Susan,

Ulla Morris-Carter

whose parents lived near us in Beirut. Nadia Tueni, Ghassan reassured us, would look after the children until the roads were safe to travel.

"What have we done to our children?" I asked myself.

I was worried beyond belief. I couldn't sleep. But I had nobody but myself to blame that I had not left Lebanon earlier. We had no way to alert the children that Nadia Tueni or Nadia's driver would pick them up from school. Nor could we explain why. They knew, of course, that the school was closing, but nothing else. I spent anguished nights thinking of Karin and Julia alone in a strange house with people they had never met. Karin had turned 12 a few days ago, and Julia was just 10. All children, including ours, had been taught never to go with any stranger when approached. How would they know who Nadia's driver was? Would they pack clothes to wear? Where were their passports? And school books? I was frantic, but there was nothing we could do short of risking our lives. We trusted Ghassan and Nadia, who soon assured us via their radio contact that our children were safely installed in their house. We had no way of communicating with them.

It took at least five days before a telephone call came through from Beit Mary. Relief on all sides. Karin was on the phone. She sounded less distressed than I had expected. Both she and Julia were fine but understandably worried and homesick. They needed reassurance from us. Nadia had tried to be extra nice to them. She had managed to find a jar of black market peanut butter, which she assumed all American children loved.

How could she know that this was not the case in our family? We all hated peanut butter. Julia and Karin, realizing the trouble Nadia had gone to, pretended to eat the peanut butter sandwiches with pleasure, and, when Nadia left the room, stuffed them into their pockets. But what to do then? Deposit them in the toilet, was their decision. Horror on horror! The sandwiches would not go down. They floated! I hope Nadia never learned of the sandwich disaster.

After waiting a week for a break in the fighting, Joe and I decided to try again to reach Broummana and Beit Mary. Joe instructed me to wear a bright-colored shirt—I chose hot pink—and to leave my long blond hair uncovered so that we would be easily identifiable as non-militia. We drove our only car, the Fiat, with the top down.

Crossing the wide-open, eerily empty street that divided the city, the Green Line, we traveled in complete silence.

Suddenly, out of clear-blue sky, a shot hit the right fender of our treasured little car. An invisible sniper must have been hiding in one of the nearby ruined houses. The noise of the bullet hitting the metal fender echoed in the silence surrounding a closed-up gas station. Joe made a dramatic, hair-raising turnaround while yelling at me to keep my head down. I will never forget the drama of that moment in a deserted gas station—every pump covered with bullet holes.

Ulla Morris-Carter

No time to stop. No time to discuss the situation. The only thought we had was to get out of this terrifying place as fast as possible. Despite Joe's desperate maneuver and the bullet hole in the fender, the Fiat was still driveable. The tire seemed to hold. We were pretty shaken up. Worse, we had to return home without having been able to retrieve our children.

A second attempt, two days later, was more successful. When we were stopped by masked gunmen at the foot of the mountain road, one of them, it turned out, wanted a ride to Broummana: *Achlen wa sachlen*, please, be our guest.

We were thrilled to have his company. The militia fellow, his face covered by a menacing mask, sat proudly high up on top of our folded roof. The Fiat didn't have much of a proper backseat. He was holding his Kalashnikov up into the air. With our guest-companion sitting visibly high in the back of our car, we encountered no further problems on the mountainous road to Beit Mary.

After depositing our still-masked militia guest at his family home, we arrived at Nadia Tueni's house. Karin, Julia and Susan, waiting outside the house, jumped into our arms. We held them for a long embrace, and I silently promised myself never to part from our children again. They looked worried but otherwise well and much relieved to see us. I had been concerned that this ordeal might leave our children in a state of anxiety. But they seemed self-assured, unruffled, more mature and quite composed.

After fond farewells and many thanks that could never be expressed in words, we squeezed the three little girls, Karin, Julia and Susan, into the narrow back seat of the Fiat. I prayed that our trip down the mountain road would not bring another unexpected confrontation.

Much to our dismay, Susan's parents had refused to drive up to Beit Mary to pick up their daughter. We could not possibly take responsibility for a child that wasn't ours, should something happen on the way. On the other hand, leaving Susan at Nadia's house was out of the question. Susan's parents had never met either Nadia or Ghassan. We decided to take Susan along. Luckily, the trip home was uneventful. With a communal sign of relief, we saw our landmark lighthouse come into view. Our first stop was at Susan's parents' home. Delivering her to her anxious parents and having our own children back were the greatest gifts we could have asked for. We had had to leave behind most of the children's clothing for lack of space, in addition to lack of access to the school. But the tension that had been with us stayed in my bones for a long time.

THE LAST STRAW

Two days after our return to Manara, Julia, Karin and I ventured out for a bit of shopping on Rue Bliss near the American University of Beirut, only a few minutes from home.

Ulla Morris-Carter

"It is a quiet day," the radio had announced.

It was not only a quiet, it was also a gorgeous spring day with brilliant sunshine. The world looked a lot better than it had two days ago. Though many establishments were closed, a few minor food stores were open. The streets were full of pushcarts, selling everything from fruits and vegetables to probably stolen French silk scarves. French perfumes, any brand one desired, were offered at half the normal price.

Suddenly, without any warning, we heard the whizzing sound of a rocket. All hell broke loose. A car exploded next to us and burned. The balcony above our heads took a hit and came crashing down inches from us. Pandemonium. People were screaming and crying. The man next to me was badly wounded.

Someone pulled Karin into a little butcher shop, where sheep were being slaughtered. Julia was pulled into another small store. Karin ran out of the butcher shop revolted by the smell and the sight of the freshly slaughtered lamb which she considered worse than being hit by shrapnel. She lost her hearing for a while from the horrendous impact of the explosion. I had lost one of my shoes in the commotion, and a piece of shrapnel grazed my finger. Karin insisted on picking up a few pieces of shrapnel as souvenirs.

We gathered ourselves together and ran home. I collapsed into a chair, shaking all over. This episode was the last straw. No way could we afford to remain in a city where life was so cheap and chaos reigned.

We must leave the country.

Returning home from one of his forays into the even more dangerous parts of town, Joe tried to book a flight to Cyprus. Not possible. There were no longer any flights to Cyprus. There were, in fact, no longer any flights to anywhere. Except one: Middle East Airlines to Athens. All other major airlines had stopped flying in and out of Beirut. Not easy to find space for the three of us on that one flight to Athens.

The next morning, each of us carrying only a small suitcase—we were not allowed more than carry-on—we made our way to the airport through numerous roadblocks and other obstacles. Joe managed to accompany us to Athens, but had to turn around and go back immediately. The Beirut airport was about to close, and he had to be in Beirut to cover the worsening crisis.

What I had always feared, now had indeed come true. We were the latest refugees in Athens, where thousands of Lebanese had already taken shelter. Schools were overcrowded. Housing was impossible to find. Desperation overtook me at the prospect of another long separation from Joe.

In a handwritten letter to Joe's father and friends in the US shortly after our arrival in Athens, I described our situation:

> Now we are in Athens, and God only knows what next. We arrived nine days ago.
> Actually we had hoped to go to Nicosia, Cyprus, but there were no flights. No

Ulla Morris-Carter

space in Nicosia schools anyway. After two days in Athens Hilton Hotel (which was much too expensive) followed by three days in a small furnished hotel apartment, we found a minute furnished flat, clean, and not too far from the British Campion School, where Karin and Julia are now registered. It's their fourth school within one year. No doubt, we'll all turn into neurotics shortly. But the kids have adjusted remarkably well after a rather nasty and hectic three weeks in Lebanon. They find this school easier than the Lebanese mountain school, which is good for a start. Karin immediately qualified for the finals in the 100-meter-dash and hurdles of the 12-14 year olds. No doubt that helps to get into the swing of things. Also Julia did very well on all levels; so they are reasonably happy.

The days before our departure were filled with anxieties, doubts and questions. We had to get the children down from the mountains, when suddenly their school was in the firing line. They had a few bad days a la World War II. . . .

Well, since then things have deteriorated unbelievably. Here I sit now, with few clothes, no school supplies, no toys, no car, no typewriter, and I really feel like a refugee, maybe a luxury refugee, since I am not sitting in a tent. If I ever write my memoirs (hahaha!!!) I will call 75/76 my lost year.

Meanwhile we had Maria's Easter vacation coming up coinciding with a four-day airport strike in Athens—just to add to our problems. She could not get into Athens—stuck in Zurich—no friends and not enough money for four days of hotel (her school did nothing to help). Instead she flew to Beirut to where she was originally booked (too long to get into all details). The main problem, no communications—nobody was in place. We didn't have a phone as yet—we had only been in our new apartment for a day—Maria didn't even have our new address. Desperate telexes between UPI Zurich and UPI Beirut to find Joe and inform him of Maria's imminent arrival at the beleaguered Beirut airport, which also threatened to close down. Joe managed to pick up Maria, kept her in Beirut for three days, which she mostly spent with our friends John and Inge. When riding in the Fiat convertible, always with its top down, Joe made her wear a bright pink hat with a black ribbon that said in Arabic Sahafi (meaning Journalist). He himself wore a yellow cap with the same identification, wanting to make sure they were not mistaken for militias or fighters. While Joe had to work, he didn't want to leave her alone in our now completely emptied out building, nor could he take her along, which meant Maria spent most of her time with our friends John and Inge Markarian. Maria was terrified, when, standing in a breadline with our friend Inge, one of the gunmen shot his way to the front of the line. Thereafter she did not feel very welcome in Beirut. Luckily the Beirut airport remained open long enough until Joe could send her on to Athens. By this time I was a nervous wreck and ready to give up . . .

Well, now I am here with my three daughters in a tiny apartment (two small

Ulla Morris-Carter

324

bedrooms), and a husband in Beirut with whom I cannot communicate other than urgent messages via friendly UPI people. I am afraid I am boring you to tears, but life hasn't been easy. I don't know what next. Joe has written to the L.A. Times saying that Beirut is and will be uninhabitable for families for a long time to come. There is complete anarchy—all our neighbors have left--their empty apartments broken into and robbed. Joe is afraid that ours will be next in line, because he is out so much, and there is nobody left in the building. Most journalists have moved into the Commodore Hotel--convenient for filing stories, and meals (if available). All families are in Cyprus and Athens or back home, wherever home is. Athens is overflowing with Lebanese and others, terribly expensive and difficult on housing. As far as Joe's job is concerned, Athens is outside the Middle East, though he also covers Cyprus and Greece, which helps. Cyprus has an uncertain future as well.

Language problems are tremendous. My German, English, French and Arabic help very little. The first thing I have to do after Easter is to take a crash course in Greek, though I don't know what our future holds. In any case there is no way of getting our furniture out of Beirut--the port is closed. Only air-freight is available, which is what banks and other wealthy organizations such as Coca Cola--also Time Magazine--are using. The L.A. Times is not that generous, I am afraid, and I have almost given up caring . . . .

Our apartment looked so comfortable when we left—and now we are gone. I must sound terrible, please forgive me. I am in the process of recovering. I have shed my three tears. I know that Beirut is passé, and I am trying to live with it.

Poor Joe has so much to do and to think about. I don't know how he is managing alone in our house. I know he was happy to get Maria out as fast as possible. They together cooked dinner for some friends and packed a suitcase for us. It contained mostly clothes we can't use--outgrown or too big--it really was funny. They forgot the only two important things I really wanted: the typewriter and my jewelry.

All our children have grown up quite a bit through this ordeal. They are very understanding and matured, if you can believe it. So maybe it will all work out in the end.

If Beirut is quiet, I'll take Karin and Julia (after Maria's departure for Lugano) for a few days back to Beirut to try and retrieve some of the most necessary things. All Karin's and Julia's clothes plus their passports are still in the mountains. They are now traveling on emergency passports made out in Beirut.

Please give me your news. We are longing to hear from you. Write to us via UPI Athens--Nobody knows us in our new neighborhood.

Despite wanting to stay under the covers and never get up, I faced every day and life continued. I had lost my foothold. I was homeless. The rented apartment contained not one personal item, nothing but ugly furniture and a small, ill-equipped kitchen. Endless

Ulla Morris-Carter

numbers of bureaucratic demands kept me running from one department to another. Greek bureaucracy, too, can be archaic. New bank accounts needed to be opened, a telephone line had to be applied for, a matter of great importance but hard to get.

We might have managed, if Joe, as a journalist, had been in Athens, but without his press credentials, it was probably a hopeless undertaking. Then there was the question of a car. Discussions with my brother in Germany followed. Would he be able to buy a car for us, then ship it to Greece, or have an acquaintance drive it to Athens? Would Joe's press credentials enable us to import it without the hefty customs duties? Cars cost three times as much in Greece as in Germany.

Many questions, no answers. If only I could talk to Joe.

BEIRUT BUREAU

JOE ALEX MORRIS, JR.
PRESS COOPERATIVE BUILDING BEIRUT, LEBANON
TELEPHONE 290352

March 26, 1976

Dear Joe,
        Sorry we missed your call the other day. I was out changing our elusive president around the countryside, and Ulla had just taken the kids down to the street for a little shopping where she promptly managed to get herself pinned down when three shells landed in the xixi vicinity/

By the time you get this they should be out of the country. We haven't rushed it, but there seems no end to the crisis here and now Beirut is a dangerous city, with artillery likely to hit anywhere. We don't feel particularly exposed, although a few days ago the Christians opened up on the military beach just down below us where the Moslem army deserters have a Hqs.

But the school up in Brumanna is stopped, and is not safe either. Our Christian friends have put some heavy artillery up near the school, and naturally they draw retaliatory fire. Everyone up there is living in the Dorm basement and I guess they're all miserable. We're just happy we got the kids down last weekend before the shit really hit the fan.

Anyway, the tentative plan is to get Ulla and the kids over to Cyprus on Sunday. If we go, you'll probably hear from us before you get this. If the letter arrives with no call beforehand, it probably means we didn't go after all, or they didn't. But right now, we thought we'd look into the school situation there, the housing on a temporary basis, then I'd come back here --- if I go at all.

Say hello to Ruth and Larry for Ulla, tell Ruth we got her letter. Must rush to get this to someone leaving for Amman --- and the U.S. That's the other sad part of it: all the hard liners who refused to join the first wave of emigration are now disappearing slowly. We are probably the last in our building soon, although a couple of other suddenly single men are still in principle around.

More later. Love
                Joey

Joe wrote a letter to his father, Joe Sr., chronicling our ordeals. March 26, 1976.

Ulla Morris-Carter

A note from Nick Williams, the acting foreign editor of the *Los Angeles Times,* arrived in Athens in the mail. It made me smile.

```
Dear Ulla,

        Welcome out!  I would send you your campaign ribbon, but not sure
which color fits your Athens wardrobe.
        I know you had mixed feelings about leaving Beirut--though, God knows
from here I don't know why.  If nothing else, those midnight calls from
the desk must have driven you mad.
        At any rate, though The Times does not give awards for spouses coping
under deadline pressure, I'll give you my own.  And thanks for the many
times you jumped in to help us out in reaching Joe, who damn well better
win one of the awards that are given.
        Gerri, who never asks "How're things at the office," hask been asking
after you and the girls since things came apart over there. We both
are delighted that you're getting a breather.

                                Best to you all, and to Joe.
                                        Nick Williams
```

Journalist friends offered help. Athens-based Cokie Roberts and her husband Steven, the *New York Times* correspondent, lived nearby. They appeared with a stack of towels and other needed household items. Monti Stearns, the Chargé d'Affairs at the U.S. Embassy, invited me to lunch to discuss the question of a residence permit and other important matters. He and his wife Toni had been much involved in the establishment of the British-curriculum Campion School, which Karin and Julia now attended.

The children, thoughtful and loving, kept me on track. Doubtless, they felt as uneasy as I did. And they missed their father. They kept asking why he wasn't with us. Other Beirut-based correspondents had already joined their families in Athens.

Five weeks after our arrival in Athens, Joe telexed. Beirut was quiet. A new cease-fire had been brokered.

"Do you think you could come to Beirut?" he asked. "I really need some help packing up a few of your and the children's most necessary things."

The *Los Angeles Times* had given us permission to airfreight a few boxes to Athens. I spent a sleepless night. Did I dare to fly to Beirut, leaving the children in Athens? What if something happened? What if Beirut airport closed down? Yes, the children could stay with friends, yet I was reluctant to leave them in Athens. On the other hand, I could not possibly take them with me to Beirut. It was important for me to clear up a number of important items left unfinished during our rapid departure. Finally, I decided to risk flying into Beirut while the going was temporarily good.

Shortly after my arrival in Beirut Joe wrote to his father, trying to explain what was happening. I mailed the letter after my return to Athens:

Dear Dad,

Having been through what may have been the worst, we are now half-way pulling out of Beirut. The packers are here to do a small airfreight shipment to Athens. Ulla

Ulla Morris-Carter

is here, having arrived amid the sound of artillery bombardment at the airport. I think we are more or less moving to Athens, although so far no firm agreement from L.A. If we do, we will live gypsy style in a smallish apartment until summer. Then probably the family will spend a month on an island, maybe me too.

It is sort of simmering down here, and we hope to go up to Broumana in the mountains tomorrow to pick up the kids' things from their school. It is all very sad. But even if peace would break out, Beirut will be no place for a family for a long time. With the past twelve months sordid experience, we don't have much desire to stay, even though the weather is beautiful, and the apartment is so comfortable. I had my car lifted off me as I drove down a main street the other night. Then got it back a couple of days later thanks to the Palestinian connection. It is thoroughly wrecked however and will probably never again be in good shape.

Ulla took all the kids to Crete for a few days before Maria went back to school. Maria is getting to be a pretty fair traveler, although she misses family life more than I ever would have suspected of her. . .

Love, Joe

What Joe didn't tell his father was the horrendous ordeal he went through, after his car was taken by masked gunmen. On his way home from filing a story at the Reuters bureau, he was kidnapped by two Arab thugs.

Joe wrote a story about the carjacking of his beloved little Fiat:

Two gunmen waving their Kalashnikovs flagged the car down. Beirut was at that point crawling with control points set up by virtually all of the many factions engaged in the conflict, and the cautious driver kept his eyes wide open on the dark and deserted streets. These two were different, however. They didn't want to check identities. They wanted, they said, a ride. Looking down the barrels of the Kalashnikovs, the owner decided that wisdom dictated he give them a ride. It turned out, of course, that it was he who was taken for a ride. And a hairy ride it was, ending with the owner being rudely deposited on the outskirts of town. His passengers considerately permitted him to detach his apartment key from the key ring before driving into the night. Because it was an unusual car for Beirut, the Fiat was spotted a few days later by a friend of the owner, a Palestinian with good ties to Fatah, the biggest guerilla group. It was sitting outside the office of a Lebanese left-wing resistance organization. A low-level Palestinian confrontation duly took place with the eventual result that the car was returned to its owner. With many apologies and assurances that its abductors were not members of the Lebanese organization.

The car papers were missing, however. And the car was hardly maneuverable, and appeared to have been driven over nothing but twisted metal and broken glass in

Ulla Morris-Carter

the interval. The abductors had also done their best to destroy its pristine beauty by applying a thick coat of black creosote paint. Among other things, they had painted a large "F" on one door—a complete mystery since no "F" appears in the name of the organization involved."

When Joe was dumped in a Moslem district, he had no choice but to try to walk home through dark, deserted areas. Thereupon he was stopped by other masked men, who thought he was a *Phalangist*, Christian, spy, because he was walking in a Moslem area at night, something nobody did any more. And Joe no longer had any identification, no press pass, no passport, no driver's license. They took him into the basement of a house he did not recognize, where he spent several hours.

In the early morning he was allowed one telephone call, which he made to the Algerian Ambassador, Mohamed Yazid. We had all memorized the Algerian Ambassador's telephone number. He was known to be a friend of the foreign press, and he had the right kind of connections to the Palestinians, when needed. With the ambassador's help, Joe was released shortly thereafter.

In his usual laconic writing style, Joe messaged the *Los Angeles Times:*

"All this followed a day in which I was first shot at crossing into the Christian quarter, then mortared on the way back."

Law of the Gun in Beirut: Bank Robberies, Killings and Macho Bandits in Jeeps

THU APR 8 1976

BY JOE ALEX MORRIS JR.
Times Staff Writer

BEIRUT—Volkhard Windfuhr, a German and one of that increasingly rare species—a foreigner living in Beirut—was returning from a business trip.

Emerging from the airport, he got into a taxi for the drive home.

On the way, the driver pulled a pistol and demanded his money. Windfuhr gave him what was in his pockets—about 150 Lebanese pounds ($60)—and was left stranded on the airport road.

But Windfuhr got another taxi.

What the first driver didn't know was that, as his plane descended toward Beirut, Windfuhr had stuck several thousand dollars in his shoe.

This is standard practice now in Beirut, a city where the only law on the streets is the law of the gun. You carry enough money in your pockets to be credible, but no more.

It is a city in anarchy which, by

some miracle, staggers along. Electricity, telephone service and water supply break down continually, but somehow are restore.

Garbage collection is a sometime thing, and huge piles of rotting refuse have for months been a standard, stinking sight.

Officially, things are looking up. There has been an armed truce in effect since last Friday. First steps are being taken to resolve the political crisis.

But at the same time, people are being killed, abducted, and mutilated at a rate not far off the average of recent violent months. "More than 55 Dead Tuesday in Beirut," said the headline of a Wednesday paper.

Lawlessness has become a matter of routine. Brigands who hijacked an American Embassy car are driving it around town without even bothering to disguise the theft. There is the occasional traffic cop on the job, but no

one would dream of challenging the new gladiators who have taken over the city.

Breaking into banks has become a popular advocation. The Banco Di Roma was the latest but probably not the biggest prize.

That award must go to the British Bank of the Middle East. Its strong room was broken into, allegedly by foreign experts brought in specially for the job, and the safe deposit boxes were emptied.

The bank itself lost several million dollars in cash, but this is thought to be chicken feed compared to what was in the safe deposit vaults. One of Beirut's biggest jewelers, for example, kept all of his precious stones there, sending messengers from his shop just around the corner to bring the required pieces whenever a rich Saudi prince dropped in looking for baubles.

The total loss will probably never be known.

Please Turn to Page 11, Col. 4

Joe' reports on Beirut's descent into lawlessness in the L.A.Times, *April 8 1976.*

Ulla Morris-Carter

April 6, 1976

Mr. R. W. Gibson
Los Angeles.

Dear Bob,

First of all I want to express my appreciation for the understanding shown by home office by our moment of crisis. The whole thing has been an unnerving, trying experience for Ulla in particular, but the path was eased by the lack of static, indeed, the seemingly full comprehension of our plight which was the echo I got from Los Angeles.

It's been rough on Ulla, she thought she was going to Athens for a brief respite. I guess I knew from the start she wouldn't be returning, but I had to win her over slowly. First, find the right school for the kids, then a place to live. By a series of happy miracles, we did both. Finding a flat was the luckiest of all, since furnished places on short-term leases are virtually impossible to get in Athens (particularly since the Beirut refugees began streaming into Athens last Sept.-Oct). But we did, and it's quite close to the school.

The kids have had it bad too. They really toughed it out in Lebanon, and it only began to hit them when they were reasonably secure in Athens. Karin faced it with her usual poise, but in the end, her stomach betrayed her anxiety. She began having tummy aches for no apparent reason. With Julia it came out in fretfulness and unreasonable whining and crying. Of all things, she objected violently to the flat, which is furnished sort of Egyptian kitsch style (the owner is Egyptian). She declared she wouldn't move in there under any circumstances. Quite a show.

I hope by now they are settling in at school, their fourth inside 10 months. If all goes well on that side, I would be tempted to keep them there.

In any case I can't at this point see bringing them back to Beirut (nor Maria, who is unhappy with her school in Switzerland). The American School here may or may not try to reopen next September, depending of course on the political conditions. But it is not hiring any teachers from abroad, which means if it does open it will be with a motley coalition of locals --- American women married to Lebanese, etc. ---- some perhaps good but certainly they won't have an adequate program.

Joe wrote a letter to Bob Gibson, after our evacuation to Athens, describing our situation.

Ulla Morris-Carter

**INTER-OFFICE
CORRESPONDENCE**

DATE: April 23, 1976

FROM: Bob Gibson

SUBJECT:

TO: Foreign Correspondents

Joe Morris had four bad hours in Beirut Monday night. On his way home from filing at Reuters, Joe was kidnapped by two Arab thugs who stopped his car at gunpoint.

The kidnappers took Joe on a hairy chase through uncomfortably deserted parts of Beirut, then stole his car and all his papers, and dumped him in a Moslem district.

Thereupon Joe was stopped "by other goons who thought I was a Falange spy because I was walking in their area at night--something nobody does any more.

"All this followed a day," Joe messaged, "in which I was first shot at crossing into the Christian quarter, then mortared on the way back."

On Thursday, Joe got back his car, a four-year-old Fiat Spyder, thanks to an alert friend who works with Al-Fateh and spotted it on a back street.

"It's in bad shape and was partly repainted when we got it back from the Qawmeeyeen, or Syrian Popular Party, who claimed, of course, they hadn't stolen it," Joe cabled. "It just happened to be parked outside their office and they had the keys plus my Lebanese press pass. One problem is that the car papers are still missing. The apologetic Qawmeeyeen promised to try and get them back. If not, I may have trouble, although I can get temporary Fateh papers of ownership."

###

For the one week Joe was resettling Ulla and his children in Athens, Jack Foisie covered Lebanon for Joe. Upon Jack's return to Cairo, he wrote in a letter of Joe's resumption of duties in Lebanon and Jack's response to Lebanon:

"Morris came back with the zest that is always a Joe Alex trademark--along with his beret. Joe was ready to resume a story that, in one week, had left me exhausted. What had been exciting, droll or ghastly for me when I first arrived in Beirut was now routine. I had become quickly jaded. I was written out on features.

"I will add those ten days in Beirut (I had been in Beirut often, of course, but never to work the civil war) to my memory book. I sure learned to say 'sahafi' quick enough, for it means correspondent. Just like I learned to shout 'Bao Chi' in Vietnam. Otherwise, my linguistic capacity, as you know, is limited."

###

Foreign Editor Bob Gibson's weekly internal newsletter to L.A. Times *correspondents, April 23, 1976.*

Ulla Morris-Carter

Joe's handdrawn map describing our Beirut neighborhood at the time of our departure

THE MORRISES' BEIRUT, 1976 (SUBJECT TO IMMEDIATE CHANGE)
L.A. TIMES SYNDICATE

AMBULANCE MISSED CURVE AT HIGH SPEED HERE

HOTEL RIVIERA (2 HITS + KAMLEUCK'S WEDDING)

A.C.'S TENNIS COUR (CLEAR SHRAPNE BEFORE PLAYING)

6 BURSTS NARROWLY MISS SUNDAY FISHERMEN

SOFT DRINKS - ICE - ANY TIME!

FOOTBALL FIELD CUM HELICOPTER PAD (EVENTUAL U.S. EVACUATION)

EXTREMELY NOISY SOVIET 85 MM GUN

P.S.O.L.I.R.A. TRAINING FIELD

RENAISSANCE CLUB

BALCONY

3RD FL. HIT

PAUL (WHEN NOT AT H'S)

NEW MALAS. BLDG.

9TH FL. WIPED OUT BY 155mm SHELL

HANNELORE! GERMAN TV MAN HELD UP

KIENZLE & CO. GERMAN TV ROBBED: 0230 BY 12 GUNMEN

KHALIL THE BARBER

UNCLE SAMI'S BOOKSHOP — PAPERS — SOMETIMES

NEW APT. BLOCK — UNINHABITED, THANK GOODNESS

UNICEF CHIEF'S MERCEDES STOLEN

CONCORDE

RUE BLISS

153 mm SHELL 9TH FL.

INT. (CHANGED?)

ULLA + 2 KIDS UNDERNEATH THIS ONE

NEW GARBAGE DUMP

WHERE IS PACHELBEL ANYHOW? + WHO?

NEW GERMAN EMBASSY (WELL MOVED BY THE MOURABITOUN!)

ST. PAUL HOTEL (EGYPTIAN WHORES LONG SINCE GONE)

SAMI KHAZEN INTERIOR DEC. (BOMBED)

NEW VEG. MARKET

SMITH'S WAGON K.O.'D

RY'S. NEW STORES BUILT W.O. PERMITS

SPORT

U.N. BLDG. HIT 6TH FL.

GET "SAHAFI" (JOURNALIST) T-SHIRTS HERE

DEUTSCHE EV. GEMEINDE KIRCHE — JOHN MAKARIAN PREACHES HERE — WHEN NOT PLAYING TENNIS (OR GOLF).

MRS. SMITH'S GROCERY (1 BOMB, 2 MORTARS)

RUE SADAT

RDATI

ALSO NOT IN PIX: JON RANDALL TEARING HIS HAIR

NOT IN PIX: MORRIS BEING RELIEVED OF FIAT

RNITURE STORE BED OUT

2 Kms →
RUE ABDEL AZIZ.

In front of the Diamantidou St. house..

FROM BEIRUT
TO ATHENS

1976

By the time Karin, Julia and I had departed Beirut for Athens in April 1976, the tragic confrontation which had begun as a feud between arrogant Lebanese Christians and presumptuous Palestinians in 1975, was one year old.

It had broadened into an ideological struggle between Left and Right and into a sectarian struggle between Moslems and Christians. The Palestinians had formed their own state within the state of Lebanon and were running their own roadblocks.

In early June, with the Beirut airport still open, Joe flew to Athens for a two-day visit, hoping to retrieve our newly acquired German car from customs. Customs officials insisted it be registered in Joe's passport, he being the accredited journalist. Starting at 6 a.m. the morning after he arrived, we raced from one office to the next, from port to mid-town departments, in order to complete the formalities and registration of the new white VW station wagon.

The minute Joe set foot in Greece, the situation in Beirut went from bad to worse, requiring him to return to Beirut immediately. He worried that Beirut airport would close again following shelling of the airport tower and the partial destruction of one of the runways a few hours earlier. Exhausted though we were after a whole day of running around and working on car documents, we managed to complete the necessary paperwork. Joe made it to Athens airport to catch that day's only flight back to Beirut.

He had been in Athens for less than 24 hours.

There seemed no end to the tragedy that had befallen the small, beautiful country of Lebanon. Syrian diplomatic intervention during the first half of 1976 met with

Ulla Morris-Carter

little success in restoring order. Therefore, shortly after Joe's return to Beirut, Syria decided to send 6,000 troops into Lebanon to help the Lebanese Christians fight the Palestinians. Syria tightened its grip around the beleaguered capital. The main power station had been hit, and Beirut came to a complete standstill. There was no bread or gasoline, and electricity only infrequently. Beirut airport closed.

The "siege of Beirut" had started. The question was, how long could Beirut sustain this isolation?

Joe wrote a diary during this siege of Beirut, starting Monday, June 7, 1976. It detailed the daily struggle to file stories, find food, bread and gasoline plus survive the summer heat without a refrigerator and without butane gas for hot water and cooking.

Joe's remarkable daily account, frequently hourly, included the kidnapping of U.S. Ambassador Francis E. Meloy Jr. together with his senior aide, Robert O. Waring, and the embassy bodyguard-driver in June. All three were found shot to death. The slaying of the two diplomats and their driver capped an ugly new turn in the Lebanese civil war, in which tens of thousands had died over the past fifteen months. Three Lebanese nationals, allegedly belonging to a Trotskyite cell, were arrested in connection with the slaying.

Driver Also Seized, Killed in Leftist Area
THU JUN 1 7 1976
BY JOE ALEX MORRIS JR.
Times Staff Writer

BEIRUT—U.S. Ambassador Francis E. Meloy Jr., a senior aide and the embassy bodyguard-driver were kidnaped here Wednesday and shot to death.

Their bodies, wrapped in blankets and with the blood still flowing, were found on a garbage dump on the southern outskirts of this war-torn city.

Slain with the 59-year-old ambassador, who arrived here only last month, were the economic counselor, Robert O. Waring, 56, and the Lebanese driver, Zoheir Bomoghrabil.

In Washington, President Ford denounced the killings as "an act of senseless, ontrageous brutality," but declared that the "United States will not be deterred from its search for peace (in Lebanon) by these murders."

A State Department spokesman said that contingency plans for the evacuation of the remaining 1,400 Americans in Lebanon would be un-

War Leaves Lebanon Ruined, Still Divided
SUN JUL 1 1 1976
BY JOE ALEX MORRIS JR.

BEIRUT—In the past 15 months, Lebanon degenerated from the most prosperous and highly advanced nation in the Arab world into a battered, bloody arena, riven by religious and political hatreds.

For months there has been no effective government. The army split

Joe Alex Morris Jr. is the Times correspondent in Beirut.

up into rival factions—largely, but not entirely, determined by how the soldiers and officers worshiped God.

The economy has come to a near-standstill. Factories were turned into smoking ruins, the workers either returning to their mountain villages or fighting for one side or the other. Some of them are making more money as looting warriors than they did at the work bench.

Many Lebanese Christians will honestly and indignantly deny this. But little else can explain the Christian assault on the Palestinian refugee camp at Tal Zaatar, the last remaining hotbed of Palestinian-Moslem resistance in the area the Christians would expect to control under a federal system.

Everything about the 15 months of struggle here seems irrelevant to the outside world, except for a few unforgettable factors.

The United States was largely unconcerned un.'t the Syrians began to play an active role in Lebanon and Israel began making threatening noises about the tolerable limits of Syrian intervention. Washington then served as a channel to head off a Syrian-Israeli confrontation.

Lebanon's Arab brethren were even more callous than the Ameri-

Right: One of Joe's reports on the assassination of U.S. Ambassador Meloy and his aide Warying, June 1976. Above: Joe reporting on the situation in Lebanon deteriorating even further after we've left.

Ulla Morris-Carter

Paros

When Joe finally managed to take a break at the end of June, he was exhausted and definitely ready for a vacation. Reunited, we were able to take a holiday on the Greek Island of Paros, one of the Cyclades islands we had visited once before in 1972. We all wanted desperately to escape the claustrophobic unairconditioned apartment in the Athens suburb of Halandrie. Athens was sweltering in the summer heat with temperatures as high as 104°F.

A Greek ferryboat took us on an overnight journey from the Athens port of Piraeus to the island of Paros. In the small village of Naussa, ten kilometers north of Parikia, the capital city of Paros, we rented a modest stone house with two bedrooms, a bathroom, a primitive kitchen and cold outdoor showers.

Naussa, in 1976, had neither hotels nor apartments for rent. Quiet time on the island was exactly what we all needed. No war, no newspapers. Only the shortwave radio with its BBC broadcast connected us to the world. No journalist would ever miss that. Mornings started slowly with Greek coffee, fresh bread and Greek yoghurt, sitting by the absolutely charming harbor of Naussa. The morning sun was still mild. The waves of the Aegean Sea lapped quietly at the coastline. At least for these short moments we could forget the less peaceful world not far away. Our days were spent swimming or lounging under one of our homemade shades, reading and resting.

For years Naussa had been the almost secret meeting place for those in the know, old-timers, mostly writers and poets, who spent their summers in this quiet, not yet touristy village. They all were characters. The often drunk but talented and charming Irish poet, Desmond, had acquired an entourage of mistresses, all of whom returned to Naussa every year. Then there was the British playwright, Richard, and his wife, the mayoress of a small town in England. A couple of German journalists and their attachments, plus a small contingent of the Berlin Ballet Company, all delightful homosexuals, rounded out the foreign contingent that summer. Someone remarked that we, the Morris family, apart from the local Naussa residents, were the only "normal" family in Naussa.

One of our friends, Boris Kidell, a French journalist of Russian descent, writing for the French newspaper *Liberation*, lived part of the year on the north coast of Naussa, where he had built a dramatic-looking stone house with a separate guesthouse. Like most Greek houses, both were painted brilliant white, with bougainvillea in startlingly deep reddish-purple adding a special effect. A large, half-moon-shaped terrace, overlooking the turquoise waters of the Aegean Sea was everybody's favorite place to relax, visitors and owner alike.

Not only did Boris have a great house, he also had what we called a "private" sand beach of spectacular beauty. Actually, nobody can own stretches of beach in Greece, but

Boris Kiddell's house on Paros.

Boris's beach was located in a hidden alcove only a few steps away from his house and not easily visible. Boris would sit there every afternoon before taking his daily swim, looking like a Buddha, short and round and seemingly content.

No proper roads led to Boris' house. When we visited him, we borrowed a donkey to carry food and supplies for us, plus extras for Boris. We walked along the coastline or over wide-open acres of land, covered with wild thyme and sage. In the summer heat the air was filled with the intense aroma of dried herbs. Boris's house, four to five kilometers north of Naussa, seemed cut off from the world. Without electricity, his refrigerator and kitchen stove ran on gas. His record player ran on batteries, as did his large radio receiver. At night kerosene lanterns illuminated the house and terraces.

He lived by himself. His wife, a French concert pianist, had returned to France. Although Boris had managed to have one of her grand pianos shipped to Naussa, she found it impossible to live in a place where the closest tiny grocery store was an hour's walk away, and where the only piano tuner had to travel two days from Athens. Not her style, she told Boris.

In the back of my head, however, there was always the dreaded thought of Joe's inevitable departure back to Beirut and to other Middle Eastern hot spots. Three weeks on Paros went by all too quickly. When we left to return to Athens, our now 16-year-old daughter Maria remained on Paros, staying with our Egyptian friend, Isis, and her teen-aged daughter Bettina.

Back in Athens, I continued my search for a house or an apartment.

Ulla Morris-Carter

LOOTERS SCOUR REFUGEE CAMP

Tal Zaatar's Dead Lie Where They Fell

SAT. AUG 14 1976

BY JOE ALEX MORRIS Jr.
Times Staff Writer

BEIRUT—The dead of Tal Zaatar refugee camp lie neglected under the burning Mediterranean sun.

Many families died together as they attempted to flee. Dead mothers hold dead children in their arms.

Many are disfigured beyond recognition.

Those who dropped on the roads remain there, their bodies flattened by the vehicles of the Christian conquerors as they rolled over them.

Tal Zaatar once was a bustling Palestinian refugee camp of about 30,000 people. It is now a dead town, with hardly a building intact and many still burning.

Beirut Refugee Camp Overrun by Christians

Escaping Civilians Trapped by Shelling From Both Sides; Many Reported Killed

BY JOE ALEX MORRIS JR.
Times Staff Writer

FRI. AUG 13 1976

BEIRUT—The Palestinian refugee camp of Tal Zaatar fell to right-wing Christian forces early Thursday, pro-

Christian sources put the number at around 5,000.

Although, the camp was largely

A few headlines from Joe's articles on the massacre at Tal Zaatar, August 1976.

Joe returned to Beirut. The struggle between the Palestinians and the newly formed Lebanese Front, a Christian right-wing coalition of most Christian parties, continued unabated. It reached its climax when the Lebanese Front began the siege of Tal Zaatar, a densely populated Palestinian refugee camp in East Beirut.

By the time the siege ended after 52 days of fighting, the casualties numbered in the thousands. It was August 1976. Joe, of course, had to cover the siege and eventually the fall of Tal Zaatar refugee camp. He later revealed that he had to walk over massacred babies, children and women, a scene so grisly, so horrendous, so shocking that it made him feel sick. Joe had covered many wars, but, he admitted, he had never seen anything as gruesome and as unbelievably devastating as the deliberate slaughter of so many Palestinians by the Lebanese Christians. At least 1,500 Palestinians died in Tal Zaatar, and many more were wounded.[1]

While such events preoccupied Joe's life and time, he also learned of a so-called black market freighter that would try to make the journey from Beirut to Greece. An ingenious and inventive shipper, tired of waiting for the port to reopen, chartered a ship and decided to take the risk of navigating these dangerous waters to ferry out the belongings of some Beirut refugees who had left the country. The ship was to depart from the southern Lebanese port of Sidon, which meant everything had to be trucked through dangerous Shia territory, then transferred into a small boat before being loaded onto the large chartered freighter. Desperate times call for desperate solutions.

Of course, such risk-taking did not come cheap. The price was extremely high. But many Lebanese evacuees, about 50 to 75 families, were desperate enough to try this risky maneuver to get at least some of their belongings out of the country before they

1. *Note: Six years later that disaster would be overshadowed by the similar, but even larger, atrocity at the Sabra and Shatila Palestinian refugee camps. These 1982 killings, carried out by Lebanese Christian militiamen assisted by Israeli soldiers, claimed some 3,000 lives, mostly women, children and old people.*

Ulla Morris-Carter

were either looted or destroyed. No insurance coverage was available, and there was certainly no guarantee that the shipment would safely arrive at its destination.

Joe consulted the *L.A. Times*. Hesitantly, they agreed to pay for a shipment of some of our belongings. The paper admitted they had no provision for war losses and could not reimburse us in case of theft or destruction of our belongings. Strangely, the bean counters were willing to pay the hefty price for shipping but not for replacement. Joe queried me by telex. I said yes, I was in favor of the risk. However, there was no way I could travel to Beirut to help sort and pack what should be shipped.

Joe reported that amid total chaos in Beirut, two local Kurds appeared at our apartment to help pack up our belongings. No wrapping paper, no proper cardboard boxes, no string or tape. Therefore, every piece of clothing came in handy. Cups and glasses disappeared in soft wool socks, plates and bowls into underwear and T-shirts. Paintings were draped with dresses and sheets.

The final result was a most unusual pile of stuff that indeed resembled a refugee's belongings. Joe decided to leave behind a number of chests of drawers, balcony furniture, washing machine and dryer. And, of course, there were the inevitable small pieces missing that the packers decided they could take while nobody was looking.

Meanwhile an Arab League peacekeeping force, consisting of Syrian, Libyan, Saudi Arabian and Sudanese soldiers, had been assembled. Predictably, this force was not welcomed by all factions involved. A fragile cease-fire, like earlier ones, failed to hold. The U.S. Embassy now urged "in the strongest" terms that the 1,400 Americans remaining in Lebanon leave the country. The U.S. Sixth Fleet tied up near the Hotel district to ferry those willing to leave to the mother ship. In all, 263 foreigners, including 120 Americans, took up the offer.

Lebanon had become a nation partitioned along Christian-Moslem lines, not formally agreed upon, but workable in practice. When the Arab League peacekeeping force had moved in at the Green Line that separated the city, the fighting died down. The Christians in East Beirut, supported by Syria, were putting their house in order and organizing their part of Beirut. Shops were re-opening, gas stations had gas, and traffic jams returned. Mostly Moslem West Beirut, in contrast, was struggling with electricity cuts, water and gasoline shortages, and bread lines.

The town of Jounieh, in the Christian sector north of Beirut, had become the capital of Christian Lebanon. With the Beirut airport still closed, Jounieh was the principal outlet to the rest of the world. A small flotilla of boats made regular trips from Jounieh to Cyprus. Not only Lebanese Christians, but also foreigners and others could depart from there to Cyprus. A converted German torpedo boat named "Marder" guaranteed the fastest trip from Jounieh to Cyprus. An assortment of other yachts and refurbished motorboats rounded out the fleet. For Moslems and Palestinians the larger port of Sidon, in the South, served the same purpose.

Joe, on his way to visit us, found himself on a motor vessel named Tanya, a shabby converted private yacht flying the Cyprus flag. It ferried him from Jounieh to Larnaca, Cyprus. From there he flew to Athens. Not having seen him in a while, we were shocked. He seemed like a different person. Instead of his usually upbeat self, he was quiet and appeared depressed. For two days, he sat, mostly silent, on the couch of our small living room in the rented apartment. We had never seen him like this before. Not even the rambunctious children could lift him out of his depression.

Later he told us that he needed time, peace and gentle acceptance to overcome the nightmare of the Tal Zaatar massacre. But the world did not stand still waiting for Joe to recover. After a week he returned to Beirut.

While waiting to hear whether our belongings had left Beirut, I had found a Greek house for rent in an area called Paleo Psychico, Old Psychico. It was a delightful place with enough bedrooms and space for an office for Joe. After 6,000-plus Lebanese refugees had streamed into Athens, rents had skyrocketed. I had decided to rent the house before Joe saw it. It was extremely rare to find houses for rent, and this one seemed a perfect place for us. Even if the furniture failed to arrive, we could camp out in the house, buy a few beds and kitchen equipment, but have the luxury of lots of space around us. Space and room to maneuver had become a major issue in our lives after six months in very cramped surroundings.

Joe telexed that the first group of Palestinian refugees had appeared in our Beirut district trying to move into empty apartments. Our apartment would have been occupied by refugees as well, had Joe not been there to fight them off. All the more reason to ship out whatever possible, risk or no risk.

Finally, three weeks later, the anxiously awaited news arrived. The Lebanese black market freighter had docked at the Athens port of Piraeus.

More customs problems. Again Joe's passport was needed to register our belongings before they would be released from customs. This time Joe made it out of Beirut in the record time of 16 hours, as he excitedly reported:

> Crossed the Green Line into Christian territory out of our Moslem quarters; boarded a converted German torpedo boat; arrived eight hours later in Larnaca, Cyprus; rushed to airport and boarded an Olympic Airways plane that happened to be taking off for Athens. Fantastic, fastest time ever.

He was relieved, obviously, to be briefly out of Beirut. I kept my fingers crossed that he could at least stay long enough to help us move into our new house on 72 Diamantidou Street. But we already knew that he had to be back in Beirut in September, three weeks hence. Later, in a letter to friends, Joe wrote that we were near bankruptcy

Ulla Morris-Carter

Back of the Diamantidou house.

due to the many moves and the loss of so many things that were either stolen or never made it onto the freighter. Within less than a year and a half we had transferred from a house in Germany to an apartment in Beirut, evacuated to a small, furnished flat in Athens for almost six months, and then moved into a rented house. Julia and Karin had attended four different schools within one year. Maria was in boarding school in Switzerland.

The house on Diamantidou Street turned out to be a wonderful place. We were overjoyed to live again in a place that made us feel at home. It had a spacious back yard with a lawn and blooming hedges and plants. Underneath the house we discovered an old ping-pong table that we managed to restore to its former beauty.

With its gazebo-like front overhang, full of gorgeous white wisteria and fragrant jasmine, the house was inviting and welcoming.

An American movie company thought the house interesting enough to request the filming of one episode of the then famous series called "Lassie" at the house. Lassie, the beloved dog, was supposed to jump from the bedroom window on to the gazebo. Luckily this project never materialized, because the company wanted to take over the whole house, bedrooms and all. They offered a fair amount of money, but not enough to really tempt me. The children of course thought this was just the most fascinating prospect they had ever heard of. But I had visions of paper plates with pizza leftovers and Coca Cola bottles scattered through the house, cameramen sitting in trees and actors roaming around our bedrooms. I decided no, and I had the deciding vote.

Our lives in Athens seemed to normalize. The 18-month old Lebanese Civil War, however, continued unabated. Joe commuted between Athens and Beirut. In addition, his assignment covered the whole, vast territory of the Middle East, which included Turkey, Saudi Arabia, Syria, Jordan, Egypt, Iran and Iraq.

He was rarely home.

On December 21, 1976, he wrote to a friend: "I hope to be home at least through Christmas, having arrived yesterday. My wife and children look more like total strangers on each 'visit' home."

The Lebanese Civil War did not end until 1990, after a total of 15 years. One of Lebanon's leaders summed up our own feelings in an interview he gave in 1976, only two years into the conflict:

"This is the most horrible civil war since the Spanish civil war."

Ulla Morris-Carter

THE IRANIAN REVOLUTION 1978-79

In September 1978, while still living in Athens, Joe surprised me with great news: "Can you find a babysitter for a few days and travel with me to Scotland? Peter Jennings (*ABC* correspondent) and I have been invited to speak about the Middle East, and about Oil in particular, at a conference of American company presidents in Gleneagles in Scotland. I would love for you to accompany me."

What a question!

Of course I loved the idea of traveling with Joe to Scotland, where I had never been. Friends helped out, inviting our children to stay with them while we were away for a few days.

Meanwhile the world did not stand still—especially in Iran, where Joe had been covering the growing anti-government demonstrations. A major crisis was developing in the once prosperous oil-driven economy of the Shah's regime.

Unpopular fiscal reforms, including the stop of funds to pay the clergy, coincided with a rise in dissident activities from Islamic fundamentalists. Riots broke out in Qom and Tabriz, followed by major uprisings against Shah Reza Pahlavi's authoritarian rule over more than the past quarter century. Street demonstrations reached an unprecedented level.

Many cities were placed under martial law. Soldiers were ordered to shoot. More than 600 people died in Teheran's Zahleh Square alone. That day, September 8, 1978, became known as *Black Friday*.

As the news reached Gleneagles, both Peter and Joe raced to the phone to find the first available flight out of Scotland to London, for Peter, and to Teheran, for Joe. They knew that they would have to cover these developments.

The Foreign Minister of Kuwait, who was also attending the conference, offered the two journalists and me a ride to London on his private plane.

From there I flew back to Athens alone, while Joe boarded a plane to Teheran. He would spend the next six months covering the Khomeini revolution, allowing only a few precious family days in Athens.

Beyond Any Hope of Repai

BY JOE ALEX MORRIS, JR. SUN DEC 1 7 1978

TEHRAN, Iran—After months of upheaval, Shah Mohammed Reza Pahlavi is virtually isolated from his people, dependent on the army for his very survival.

He has turned the government over to a military man with no political experience, Gen. Gholam Reza Azhari, and as a consequence, Iran's political and economic life are paralyzed. The army, using force when necessary, has maintained order but has accomplished little more.

The prime minister, Gen. Azhari, has little contact with the palace, even less with moderate political leaders who would like to salvage the situation by restoring the 1906 constitution. This provides for a constitutional monarchy, complete with a European-style parliamentary system and a shah who reigns but does not rule, and gives religious leaders a veto over any legislation they view as contrary to the principles of Islam.

Joe's article in the L.A. Times, *December 17, 1978 (continued next page).*

Ulla Morris-Carter

Decisions are taken without even consulting the shah—as when Azhari ordered his troops off the streets of Tehran

Joe Alex Morris Jr., The Times' correspondent in Athens, has been reporting on events in Iran.

last week to permit the largest anti-shah demonstrations to date.

Thus, the question being asked here—and, presumably, in Washington—is no longer simply "Will the shah survive?" Instead, many are pondering a far more complex uncertainty: Even if the shah manages to retain his seat on the Peacock Throne, has the current unrest so crippled him that he never will be able to govern effectively again?

The shah's supporters are ever fewer. Some, like former Premier Amir Abbas Hoveida, have been thrown into jail on questionable charges to feed the public's ravenous appetite for victims. Others, among them Hushang Ansari, a top financial adviser, have taken the hint and fled. So has most of the royal family.

The voice of the people was heard last weekend, when millions turned out in huge processions in several cities to demand the shah's ouster. But the unrest also reaches high into the establishment and into the middle classes that have benefited the most under the shah.

One Iranian, a multimillionaire with an international business, said last week that the shah "is finished."

"He has had it," the man went on. "They looted this country and the shah cannot put it back together again."

This was a man who still had hope earlier this year, when the shah installed an intelligent, hard-working technocrat, Jamshid Amouzegar, as prime minister.

"But he couldn't do it," he said. "He couldn't buck the system."

The army is an increasingly uncertain factor. Recent reports of dissention in the ranks reach into the Imperial Guard itself, supposedly the best and most loyal of the troops supporting the Peacock Throne. The commander of another crack unit, the air cavalry, is reported to have been the target of an assassination attempt organized by his own men.

Morale has plummeted as the troops have faced off daily against demonstrators from their own class. At times, they have been torn between their orders and an appeal by top religious leaders not to fire on fellow Moslems. Desertions are reportedly running high, 150 per day according to some sources. Americans in Isfahan say the troops there are becoming antagonistic toward them and other foreigners.

The shah "is remote and chasing shadows," a Western

These political leaders are mostly old men, survivors of Iran's experiment 25 years ago with representative government, an experiment that ended when a CIA-inspired coup restored the shah to power. They have no organization and no real support among the people.

The support now goes largely to an exiled religious leader, the Ayatollah Ruhollah Khomaini, who wants to scrap the constitution and set up an Islamic republic. Opposition political leaders generally disagree, as do other religious leaders, who say that Khomaini, after 15 years in exile, is out of touch with reality.

Surprisingly, the impasse seems to bother very few Iranians. There is a strong element of nihilism in Iranian politics, and even those who stand to lose most view with some equanimity the prospect of chaos engulfing the country should the army split up and the shah be ousted.

"If 90% of the people want the Communists to take over, let it be," the millionaire businessman said.

A factory owner, who employs 1,200 people, said, "The price of freedom is bloodshed. There is no other way. One generation should be sacrificed for the nation."

Both these men, and others who share their views, can afford to talk this way. They have investments abroad, and the prospect of another life elsewhere if Iran should go up in smoke.

Obviously, many members of the Iranian establishment do not think this way. But they are keeping quiet. The only recent expressions of support for the shah have been of the rent-a-crowd variety, involving farmers brought in from the countryside to terrorize cities lying sullen under army rule.

The masses, plagued by inflation, poor housing and years of political suppression, voted with their feet last Sunday and Monday in the huge anti-shah demonstrations.

"When you're at the bottom, the only way to go is up," an oil engineer said.

Economically, the country has to a great extent ceased to function. The bazaars, the lifeblood of the economy, are closed, and oil production, which provides 80% of the foreign exchange needed for imported food and guns, plus the shah's huge development projects, is getting close to the minumum needed to meet domestic needs.

The schools are closed, and the government works only fitfully, plagued by politically inspired strikes. There are mounting demands to get the country going again, but they are blocked by Khomaini's appeal to keep the economy paralyzed until the shah steps down.

Many people, including some of the shah's most outspoken opponents, think that all is not yet lost, and they are waiting for the shah to act.

But the shah, sitting high on the hill in the Niavaran Pa-

On January 14, 1979—six months into the revolution—Joe wrote the story *The Face of Iran's Unrest Casts a Darkening Shadow*—a precursor to the return of Ayatollah Khomeini to Iran, and the departure of the Shah on February 6, 1979.

Graphic illustration of the Ayatollah Khomeini with oil pipes as head-dress which accompanied the article, The Face of Iran's Unrest.

Ulla Morris-Carter

The Face of Iran's Unrest Casts a Darkening Shadow

BY JOE ALEX MORRIS JR.

TEHRAN, Iran—The aftershocks of the prolonged Iranian crisis on the world's most important oil-exporting region have only begun. Destabilization has set in, and comfortable relations between conservative Middle Eastern governments and the United States are crumbling.

The United States, it appears, is still searching for the answers, both here in Iran where Shah Mohammed Reza Pahlavi's authority is being challenged in the streets, and elsewhere in countries not yet infected.

The Washington response to the challenge in Iran has been belatedly to support efforts to build a civilian govern-

---

Joe Alex Morris Jr., The Times' correspondent in Athens, is currently in Iran.

---

ment and to diminish the shah's supremacy without removing him from power totally. It is clearly a policy of too little and too late.

Iran is, or was, the world's second-largest oil exporter and a greedy absorber of U.S. and European military, industrial and agricultural technology and production. Just across the gulf lies Saudi Arabia, the biggest exporter of them all, a vast desert land with an archaic and repressive system of government which, in its fundamentals, dates back to the time of the prophet Mohammed, 13 centuries ago.

As with the shah, the United States has no policy there either, except to support the establishment—the princes of the realm and their supporters. About the only difference is that the Carter Administration has never pretended to be concerned about human rights in Saudi Arabia as it has in Iran.

The Saudis are clearly worried that the revolt in Iran could spread across the shallow waters of the gulf. The United States has responded with what amounts to an updated version of 19th-century gunboat diplomacy.

At the Saudis' request, the United States is sending a 12-plane squadron of its most advanced fighter aircraft, the F-15, to Saudi Arabia on a week's visit to demonstrate U.S. concern and support for the monarchy there. The U.S. Navy has doubled its presence in the Indian Ocean-Arabian Sea area, although Washington apparently has decided against sending the huge carrier Constellation.

All this is seen as a blunt warning to the Soviet Union not to mix in the turmoil brewing in the region, even though there have been no signs of Moscow becoming involved in the troubles in Iran.

Moscow has reacted predictably, by denouncing American gunboat imperialism.

The outcome in Iran is still in doubt, but Saudi nervousness is fully apparent. Gunboat diplomacy aside, the Saudis are showing signs of growing discomfort with their close ties to the United States.

The most striking example of this was the recent meeting of the oil-producers' cartel, the Organization of Petroleum Exporting Countries (OPEC). For two years, the Saudis had effectively vetoed any increases in the price of crude oil.

At their December meeting in Abu Dhabi, the 13 OPEC member countries decided to raise prices by 14.5% in stages during 1979. The outcome was a shock to the United States, which had been assured by the Saudis that a price increase was inevitable but would be modest.

Further, since the price rise the Saudis have shown signs of emerging from their self-imposed cocoon onto the international stage. Prince Salman Ibn Abdul Aziz, the governor of Riyadh and a key member of the royal family, indicated that the desert kingdom was considering the establishment of diplomatic ties with Communist nations, including the Soviet Union.

The Saudis had always rejected this, on the grounds that Communism was an atheistic philosophy and that their state was based on the holy Koran and was the guardian of Islam's holiest shrines. Salman, in a recent interview, said "It is impossible to ignore a superpower like the Soviet Union."

There is little doubt that Salman speaks for the royal family, which acts in concert to manage the kingdom. The close Saudi-American relationship had already been strained by the Camp David peace accords between Egypt and Israel, fully supported by Washington but unacceptable to most Arabs, including the Saudis.

The conservative Arab states have not abandoned the shah, but, like the Americans, they see little they can do to help him.

King Hussein of Jordan tried to mediate between the Persian monarch and the exiled religious leader, the Ayatollah Ruhollah Khomaini, but was rebuffed by Khomaini.

"The feeling among the Arabs is that the United States has let down one of its staunchest allies in the region," a conservative Arab diplomat said here. "If the United States cannot help Iran, what can it do for us?"

The issue is complicated further because any new government in Iran is going to cut back decisively on the shah's illusions of becoming a regional superpower. The whole multibillion-dollar military program is being thoroughly reexamined, and much of it—like the plans for a deep-water navy based on the Indian Ocean at Chahbahar —already have been scrapped.

Iran is abandoning all ambition of being the policeman of the gulf, a factor that could encourage the Arabs on the other side to drop their reluctance to cooperate with Iran in regional security. But, for the time being, there will be a vacuum in the strategic setup of the world's busiest oil-tanker route.

The concern is not limited to pro-Western Arab states. There is equal nervousness in neighboring Iraq, if for different reasons.

Most Arabs in Iraq are Shia Moslems, the same branch of Islam that has spearheaded the revolt in Iran. The leadership of Iraq comes from the Sunni Moslems, however. The Sunnis are the orthodox sect that is dominant in such countries as Saudi Arabia, Egypt and Jordan, but which is a minority in Iraq.

Although they are no friends of the shah, the Iraqi leaders responded with alacrity four months ago when the Iranians asked them to expel the Ayatollah Khomaini, who had been living in the Shia shrine city of Karbala.

Khomaini went to Paris and has been conducting his campaign against the shah from there ever since. His easy access to the media there has increased his power, and the shah's maneuvers to get him out of Iraq appear to have been a mistake.

Despite a significant switch in policy last week, Washington still appears to have no real policy on Iran except to salvage what can be saved. The United States is now urging the shah to leave the country—in the hope this will

Ulla Morris-Carter

345

Everybody Wants to Tell His Story

Jan. 29, 1979

Dear Bob,

Now that I'm (briefly) away from the turmoil and panic of Tehran, I thought you might like to know what it's like covering the Iranian crisis.

Summing it up, and for different and all valid reasons, the coverage is a remarkable example of journalistic cooperation. The major reason for it is the communications problem, but it has spread beyond that to a situation where news (not strictly exclusive stuff, but developing stories) are widely shared by journalists many of whom in the past had kept everything close to their chest, relevant or x irrelevant, important or no.

As I said, it all began with the communications chaos. As you know, there is no telex operating, the agencies have their own direct communications but they have enought to do on their own, and the frequent power cuts plus the curfew make them extremely weak crutches.

All that's left is the 'phone, and that means incoming calls, not outgoing. Nick Williams and the operators at the Times can tell you the troubles they have been having getting through to Tehran, so this too is a slender reed.

As a result, the "piggyback" is in full swing. It operates with a fairly small Mafia --- the Times, the New York Times, the Washington Post, the Chicago Tribune, the Baltimore Sun. But the practise is that when one of these gets a call from the States, he immediately informs the others. Anyone with copy ready then gets in line and transmits it when his turn comes.

It has not been without problems. The N.Y. Times once dictated to the Washington Post, which only recently installed a recording machine. The Post sent the tape over txx to the Times' Washington Bureau, where they discovered it played at a different speed than their own machine.

Some people do better than others by using their European bureaus to take copy. The Chicago Tribune girl in Bonn calls regularly --- aided by the fact that she can direct dial Tehran, something you can't do from the U.S., despite all our pretensions to advanced technology. Don Cook once called me from Paris, and I dictated to him slowly, and he repeated into his own tape recorder. Ixx We were saved by a call from Los Angeles that time, and I hope word got to Cook not to take the tape home and transcribe it.

Once I actually managed to call Los Angeles. It was 6:30 a.m., and I had just heard that the airport had been closed to prevent Khomini from returning. It was 7 p.m. in Los Angeles, plenty of time to make the paper, and I simply went down to the hotel telephone exchange, sat down next to the one operator on duty at that obscene hour, and asked him how to work the switchboard. After about 30 tries, I got through. Then L.A. got through to me twice more that morning to add to the story, and I think I filed my last add about 11 a.m. my time.

Ulla Morris-Carter

The communications problems make for little sleep, however. Calls come through late, often at 3 a.m. our time, and the choice is to stay up drinking in the press bar (thoughtfully provided by the Intercontinental management) or try to get some sleep, wake up, and try get to get back to sleep, often unsuccessfully after shouting over a bad line for half an hour. Understandably, there are a lot of bad tempered journalists who pile groggily into the breakfast room, moved up to the rooftop cafe after mobs wrecked the ground floor installation, along about mid-morning.

The cooperation is not limited to the Americans, but it joined by some of the British and French journalists on hand as well. Some people have special connections: Martin Woollacott of the Guardian, whose wife is Persian, Keneize Mourad, a French girl working for La Nouvelle Observateur, who is close to the local Tehran Ayatollah. Everybody lends a hand, and the practise is to hand over notes on a special subject to someone trying to do a story you've already done.

The zenith of all this is due when Khoemini actually returns, something which at the time of this writing had not yet occurred. John Apple of the NYTimes organized the whole battalion to cover the event, assigning spots for everyone to cover. Jon Randal of the Washington Post, who got the Behest Zahra cemetery detail, where Khomeini was due to make a pilgrimage immediately upon arrival was at last reports planning to take a sleeping bag out there, far to the south of Tehran, and spend the night in a mosque, figuring he would never get through the traffic on the big day. For this, he gets top marks for devotion to duty.

Apple's plan was for everyone to 'phone in his report to one of three correspondents on duty in the hotel, who would then type it all up as a pool report. Available to all who participated, of course, provided they could get back to the hotel in time to file and before curfew.

Aside from these problems, life hasn't been too bad in Tehran, unless something unfortunate happens such as Don Schanche falling into a pothole (?) and breaking a bone in his foot. The hotel comes up with passable meals despite supply problems, and manages to get enough fuel to keep the heating going and the auxiliary power when the city power goes off (practically every night). The crisis has led to something of a breakdown in the worst of all Iranian burocratic practises, and you can get ministers, even the prime minister, on the 'phone when it's important. I've even taken to calling up the No. 2 general in the military ranks with late night questions, and if he minds, he doesn't say so. In the old days, appointments with ministers took weeks, with formal letters being written by the Information Ministry, dates set, etc.

Language is something of a problem, of course. But confrontations with hostile crowds can usually be ended with the magic words "Man Khabarnegar Hastem" (I am a journalist). Then it's difficult to shut them off. Everybody wants to tell his story. The problems still abound here, but the people feel suddenly liberated, after years of looking over their shoulders to see if a Secret Police (Savak) agent is nearby before telling you the time of day. For the foreign press, at least, the Iranian revolution has already begun to pay off.

                    Bests,

                  Joe Alex

During a brief visit back to Athens in late January 1979, Joe wrote a letter to L.A. Times *foreign editor, Bob Gibson, describing conditions of reporting in Tehran, ironically declaring that "(f)or the foreign press, at least, the Iranian revoloution has already begun to pay off."*

Ulla Morris-Carter

From an earlier ski trip in my purple ski suit with Joe in France.

Under the Oracle at Delphi

February 10, 1979 in Athens
February 9, 1979 in Los Angeles

The snow was perfect for skiing that Saturday. Mount Parnassos near Delphi in Greece showed its best face. Its slopes were bathed in brilliant sunlight. I was full of joy, grateful to be alive on this most beautiful day.

The skiers passing me appeared to be in the same mood, smiling and waving. Forgotten were the fearful thoughts that had disturbed me yesterday evening, when a strange, incomprehensible foreboding had gripped me. It had come unannounced, out of nowhere. I reminded myself that I had spent twenty years as the wife of a foreign correspondent who roved through dangerous countries, particularly in the volatile Middle East, that many weeks alone with the children were never easy, but they were a part of the life that I had chosen in marrying a journalist. In yesterday's late Friday-night telephone conversation from Teheran, Joe urged me on to go skiing. He wanted me to take the chance of a brief respite from the worried waiting that he knew most correspondents' wives endure when their husbands are on dangerous assignments. I promised I would.

Leaving the house at 6 am with George and Jean Angelopoulos, newly arrived acquaintances from Los Angeles, I was glad I had followed Joe's advice. Under the warm February sun and a cloudless blue sky, the skiing near the archeological site of Delphi and its Oracle, was simply fantastic[1]. I noticed a ski patrol roaming up and down the slope with a message on a pink slip that seemed to interest no one.

1. Delphi is known as a center of worship for the God Apollo. Dating back to 1400 BC, the Oracle offered a spiritual experience when one consulted Apollo for advice on personal or public matters.

Ulla Morris-Carter

"Mr. Morris from the American Embassy," he called out, as he whizzed by.

Nobody answered. I perked up my ears on hearing our name, but I had nothing to do with the Embassy and I was not Mister Morris anyway. The same ski patrol came by a little later, same message, no response. Wrong name, wrong place. Who cared on a day like this?

"Hello, Ute and Bill, I didn't know you were here today. Great to see you!" I shouted across the ski slope.

I recognized dear, long-time friends, former neighbors from Beirut, now fellow-refugees in Athens. Ute was a beautiful German lady married to Bill Bonnillas, an American businessman and fellow Arab-world veteran.

"Unfortunately we have to leave right now, going to a big event tonight, black tie and all," Ute shouted back.

About four in the afternoon we decided it was time to drive back to Athens. The trip would take us three hours. Daughters Karin and Julia would soon be home from a school basketball tournament they were playing in at the British School in Athens. We planned to have dinner together. On my way out I ran into the ski patrol again.

"Did you ever find Mr. Morris?" I asked him out of curiosity.

"No. Seems there's nobody here by that name."

When I said that my name was Morris, he assured me that he was looking for a Mister Morris from the American Embassy. Obviously, I was not a Mister. Still curious, I decided to check with the ski office. Who was this Mister Morris and what might the message be all about? The office was crowded with people wanting information on weather, transportation and ski passes. It took time to find anybody I could ask. Finally a secretary appeared, pink slip in hand.

"This is the message for Mister Morris from the Embassy. Are you related?"

"No, I am not related nor am I from the Embassy. But my name is also Morris. I just thought I'd ask in case the message concerns me."

Then, staring at the pink slip in the woman's hand, I saw it had two telephone numbers, OUR telephone numbers, our home telephone number and Joe's office number. The manager appeared and directed me to a telephone.

I still remember that black rotary phone. My hands trembled as I dialed. Both numbers were busy, busy, busy for almost half an hour. Quietly I cursed my teenaged children who had just recently started doing phone marathons with their friends. Finally someone answered. It was Clair George, counselor at the U.S. Embassy in Athens and a friend and neighbor, but not normally a frequent visitor.

"Clair, what are you doing at our house?"

My stomach felt tight.

"Are you coming home now?" he queried.

Ulla Morris-Carter

A cold chill ran down my back. I was terrified and at the same time irritated by his non-answer.

"Of course I am coming home, what a silly question, you didn't try to find me on the ski slopes to ask me whether I am coming home? What is it, something wrong with the children?"

My first thought was that they might have had an accident, or worse, been run down by a truck. Athens traffic was dangerous under the best of circumstances.

"I'll tell you when you come home."

Clair's voice was drifting off. The telephone line seemed to falter.

"Do you in all seriousness expect me to drive home for three hours not knowing what happened after you tried to find me on the ski slopes? " I shouted. "This is ridiculous."

Silence.

"Are you still there, Clair?"

Bathed in cold sweat now, I could barely hold the telephone receiver in my jittery hands.

"Yes, yes, I am still here."

Clair's voice, normally strong, precise and clear, seemed to have lost its vigor. Was the line fading I wondered?

"Please, please, dear God," I prayed, "Don't let the connection break up."

Clair's answer was hesitant, barely audible:

"No, it's not the children. It's Joe, Ulla. He's been shot. He's dead."

I listened in stunned silence. I heard what he said. I did not react. I couldn't speak.

More silence.

"Jon Randal is here. He wants to talk to you."

"No. I don't want to talk now. I'll be on my way."

"Don't hang up, Ulla, please! We need to find Joe's father. He is not at home. Do you know where he could be?"

"Try Jane Condliffe in New York. She is Joe Sr.'s longtime lady friend. The number is in my black telephone directory."

I hung up.

Jon Randal, *Washington Post* correspondent for the Middle East, was one of Joe's best friends despite the fact that they were journalistic competitors. But Jon should be in Beirut right now, I thought. I just saw him yesterday before he departed Athens for Beirut. How could he be back in Athens? Nothing made sense.

I turned to George and Jean. They were standing in the doorway of the ski office, patiently waiting for me, looking puzzled. I told them calmly what I heard on the phone. No emotion. Nothing. I was simply giving them a message as if it had nothing to do with me. Immediately the busy office turned into a high-tension, turbulent and emotion-laden place.

Ulla Morris-Carter

"We need a doctor," yelled George, "We need tranquilizers."

"I don't need a doctor, I don't need tranquilizers. I just need to get home."

The parking lot was located downhill from the ski office, a short distance on skis. George Angelopoulos decided that I would not be in any condition to ski down to the car. Instead, he arranged to put our skis on the lift. We would walk down the short distance. At the bottom of the slope, where the lift arrived with our skis, the attendant did not pay much attention. The bindings of my skis were caught in the ropes.

George, unnerved by the whole dilemma, exploded.

"Can't you be more careful. You damaged the ski binding!"

He was speaking in Greek now, but with an unmistakable American accent. The lift attendant shrugged his shoulders in the "who cares" manner. George, now obviously angry, hurled a Greek insult at the lift attendant, who quickly prompted with, "If you don't like it why don't you go back to where you came from!"

The next moment, George and the lift attendant had come to blows. I was aghast.

"Do we have nothing better to do than to start an ugly fistfight?"

I had, so far, patiently followed orders.

Now I had to interfere: "We need to drive home. And I mean now, not an hour from now."

George looked sheepish, obviously embarrassed over having lost his temper at an inappropriate moment.

I climbed into the back seat of George's Mercedes. George and Jean sat in the front. I was numb. The news over the phone had simply not reached me. It's impossible, I told myself. Mistakes, I had learned, were often made during revolutions, during coup d'etats, during civil wars. Mistaken identity was certainly possible. It had happened just four weeks ago to the wife of the *Voice of America* correspondent, when a body near the Syrian-Jordanian border was misidentified as that of her husband. Distressed, I had arrived at her house to commiserate and help but was fortunate enough to be there when the news was corrected. The body, identified as a blue-eyed male, turned out to be that of a Syrian, not an American.

In twenty years as a foreign correspondent's wife, mostly living abroad, I had my share of commotion, upheavals and evacuations. But I had arrived at a point where I believed that Joe was invulnerable. He had survived so many outrageously dangerous situations, I was convinced that luck was always on his side. Accidents only happened to other people!

We traveled silently through the picturesque Greek countryside, along narrow, winding roads. Jean and George Angelopoulos had never met Joe. In fact, they knew nothing about me or my family. Two days ago, mutual friends had invited us to a

Ulla Morris-Carter

dinner party, during which George and Jean, newcomers to Greece, had asked me to accompany them to Delphi on the ski trip.

My first answer had been, "Thank you, but no."

However, I had changed the "no" to "yes" after last night's telephone call to Joe, who was in Teheran. The Iranian revolution was his assignment.

Now, in the car, I told Jean and George about my anxiety last night, how I ended up driving around our neighborhood for a while, trying to calm myself. Here I was now, sitting quietly in the backseat of the car of people who were strangers to me. I tried to recreate the events of last night. I told Jean and George how desperately I had tried to reach Joe by phone in Teheran, even though it wasn't our pre-arranged telephone night. Our arrangement was to try calling Wednesday and Saturday nights. But yesterday was Friday. Joe could not call out, but, if I were lucky, maybe I would get through. We had agreed that both of us would try to remain in place on the arranged days, I at home, Joe at the Intercontinental Hotel, where all the foreign correspondents were staying. Communications had become increasingly difficult over the last few weeks. The Iranian sea and air borders were closed. Telephone lines were rarely open, particularly via Greece. Telephoning out of Athens required patience and endurance. Last night I had dialed and dialed to reach the Greek operator. Then I waited for the operator to catch an open line to Teheran. But luck had not been on my side.

"If only I could talk to him, I would feel so much better," I had told myself. "Maybe after midnight I will have a chance."

Jean and George listened patiently as I recounted last night's desperate telephone marathon.

"Please keep trying," I had begged the telephone operator. "It's important."

Knowing that Teheran had imposed a midnight curfew, I was determined to reach Joe. And indeed, the call went through at 2:30 am.

Jean and George let me talk when I felt like talking and gave me space and time to be silent as well. Then they gently asked me about Joe and his life as a journalist. Newcomers to the Middle East, they had not followed the Iran crisis in detail.

Joe had been in Iran for the last six months with only short breaks of a few days to see us in Athens. He had come home for four days over Christmas and was gone before New Years Eve. And now it was February.

Ever since Black Friday in early September, 1978, Iran had been in uproar. Social uprisings and street demonstrations against Shah Mohammed Reza Pahlavi's authoritarian rule had sealed off all outlets for political expression except for the mosques and their highly politicized clergy. This had prompted the Shah to place the major cities under martial law and to send the army to confront the people. Soldiers with weapons had shot at demonstrators.

Ulla Morris-Carter

On September 8, 1978, more than 600 people had been killed in Zhaleh Square in Teheran alone. Ayatollah Khomeini, the spiritual leader of the Islamic Shiites, had been exiled by the Shah, first to Iraq and then to Paris. Now he issued calls from abroad for an Islamic Republic. The Shah tried to deflate the opposition, but it was too little too late.

By the end of January, 1979, the Shah was forced to leave the country. On February 1, Ayatollah Khomeini, after more than 14 years in exile, returned home to Iran. Joe covered his triumphant and turbulent entry into Teheran. A tall, impressive man in black robes, black turban and white beard, Khomeini remained determined to return his country to religious purity after what he considered years of Western corruption and decadence.

During the telephone conversation, Joe had understood my anxiety and frustration. He knew he had been away much too long. He loved his family and did not like these long separations any more than we did. He told me to be patient and explained that he was trying to ask for a break from his assignment in Iran.

Joe's *Los Angeles Times* colleague, Don Schanke had arrived to replace Joe in Teheran two weeks ago while Joe took a few days off to visit us. Covering one of the violent demonstrations with thousands of people crowding the streets, Don had slipped and fallen into one of the many shallow, uncovered canals that run alongside Teheran's streets. His broken leg, set in a cast in a Teheran hospital, developed gangrene, so he had to be flown out to a military hospital in Germany for treatment.

Joe, always looking on the positive side, made me promise to take the chance to go skiing.

"You don't usually sound so upset," he said. "You'll feel much better doing something for yourself. Please, promise you'll join the Angelopouloses for a day of skiing."

I had promised.

I had gone skiing.

Now I was on my way back to Athens.

Ulla Morris-Carter

THE HOUSE AT 58 GIZI STREET

IN ATHENS

At 7:30 pm on that Saturday, February 10, 1979, darkness had already fallen when I arrived home from Delphi. Cars were parked alongside narrow Gizi street, as far as one could see. The American ambassador's black limousine, flag flying, was in front of our entrance door.

Close by I noticed Ute and Bill's white convertible. Why were they here when they were supposed to be at a black-tie gala event they had mentioned to me on the ski slopes? Clad in the purple ski suit Joe had bought for me (though I had thought it was too expensive) and carrying my ski boots under my arm, I entered the house. More than 30 people crowded the front hall. They all fell silent as I approached.

Who are they all? I wondered.

The scene was unreal.

"What a nightmare!" I whispered more to myself than to anybody in particular.

Suddenly I remembered the title of our landlady Margaret Papandreou's book, *Nightmare in Athens*. She had described the brutal arrest, twelve years ago, of her husband, Andreas Papandreou, by the soldiers of the Greek Junta in this house that I just entered.

Yes, what a nightmare! The first person I encountered was the wife of an embassy official, carrying, she said "a lasagna for dinner." I looked around desperately for someone to rescue me. Jon Randal, *Washington Post* correspondent and good friend, emerged from the crowd. He hugged me, held me close for a while and answered my unspoken question, quietly. "Yes, Lovie, it's true. Go upstairs now and see the children."

Ulla Morris-Carter

I fled this chaos and rushed upstairs. Karin and Julia had spent the whole day in their rooms, not wanting to come out to talk or to meet anybody. Hearing me coming up the stairs they ran out and flew into my arms. For a long time, I don't know how long, the three of us huddled at the top of the staircase, out of view of the crowd. They were not crying, but they were shaky and frightened. Fear made their beautiful blue eyes look darker and bigger than I remembered.

What had they gone through in the last 12 hours, being told that their father had been killed? And without me or anyone else in the house they felt close to?

The first to hear had been U.S. Embassy counselor, Clair George, a neighbor and friend, who had been informed by *United Press International* that the BBC carried the news item of the shooting death of a *Los Angeles Times* correspondent, Joe Alex Morris. Apparently the family had not been notified by then. Clair had raced over to our house, arriving breathlessly at 8 am, hoping to prevent me from hearing the news on the morning BBC. But he did not find me at home, only my two youngest daughters, Karin and Julia. They were just getting ready to leave the house for a school basketball tournament. Now joined by his wife Mary, Clair suddenly realized that he and Mary would now have the unenviable task of having to deliver the sad news to two girls, age 13 and 14. Mary and Clair had asked the children to stay at home, fearing they would run into hard questions about their father's death. Mary and Clair stayed at the house. Karin and Julia fled upstairs to their rooms and remained there, waiting for me to come home. Overwhelmed with worry, sadness and concern for them, I was otherwise too numb to dwell on anything.

"Later, later," I told myself. "We'll discuss everything."

Trying to be brave and wanting to comfort me, the first thing Karin said, "Don't worry Mommy, we can help. We don't need to take lunch money to school every day. We can make sandwiches at home."

Silence. Then the question I had feared.

"Where are we going to live?"

Without their father and breadwinner in the house they thought we would immediately be impoverished. They already understood, correctly, that we could not stay on in Greece. We had to find a new home somewhere.

Home? Where was home?

This temporary house was all we had.

Noise and voices from downstairs.

"I must get out of this ridiculous purple ski suit, take a shower and go downstairs."

Standing under the warm shower with the water soothing my tired body, I cried for the first time. What better place to cry than under the shower? Tears are washed off and nobody notices. I tried to delay going downstairs by dressing slowly, but I knew they were waiting for me.

Ulla Morris-Carter

I put on a flannel skirt and a turtleneck sweater. It was cold in Athens at this time of year. Our rented house at 58 Gizi Street, a white stucco structure in the Paleo Psychico district, was built to keep the heat out during the hot Greek summer, but it hardly ever warmed up in winter.

Stepping slowly and hesitantly down the stairs, I saw Hawthorne "Hawk" Mills, deputy Chief of Mission of the U.S. Embassy waiting for me at the bottom. Ambassador McCloskey had come to the house earlier but had left after waiting an hour for me. Now Hawk Mills took over the official duties. Many decisions had to be made, "immediately," Hawk said, obviously uncomfortable at having to overwhelm me with the unpleasant details that accompany any death.

"Where is Joe to be buried? We need to get a message through to Teheran."

"Buried?" I almost shouted. "I don't even know whether he is dead."

Hawk was trying to be gentle, but there was no gentle way to ask hard questions at a time like this.

"Well, Joe told me some time ago that he would want to be buried in Ameno, the cemetery near our old farm house in Piemonte. It's a beautiful old cemetery."

"Ameno?" Hawk asked, incredulous, perhaps questioning my state of mind. "You mean in Italy?"

"Yes, Italy," I answered firmly. "Why not?"

Still struggling to be gentle, Hawk tried to tell me to be realistic.

"Joe was shot in Teheran. He is a U.S. citizen who worked for an American newspaper. You are German and you live in Greece. How can we possibly get Italy into this mix? Please, call Joe's father, He is waiting for your call."

My heart was heavy. Joe Sr. was 72. He would be devastated by the news of his only son's death. TV networks and BBC radio had carried the news before the family could be notified. Bob Gibson, foreign editor of the *Los Angeles Times*, had been informed by *L.A. Times* Paris bureau chief Don Cook, who heard the news on the BBC. Gibson, worried that Joe's father might also hear the news on the radio, had tried to call Joe Sr. in Connecticut at midnight, immediately after being informed by Don Cook.

But Joe Sr. had not been at home. After consulting with Clair George about Joe Sr.'s possible whereabouts, Gibson called Joe's longtime lady friend, Jane Condliffe, in New York. Indeed, Gibson found Joe at Jane's house, fast asleep at four a.m. Gibson had no choice but to relay the terrible news.

When I reached him that Saturday evening, Joe Sr. was, as always, full of love and concern for us. I needn't have worried what to say. Joe Sr. was, next to my husband, my favorite man in the whole world. He was a truly compassionate man, a great journalist and writer, who attracted people of all walks of life. Politicians, artists, actresses, actors and many others felt comfortable with him. They all wanted to tell him their life stories,

Ulla Morris-Carter

their worries, concerns and problems. Occasionally, to his dismay, the interviewee would use him as a psychiatrist and tell stories "off the record," thereby preventing him from publishing them. Now he was reaching out to me and his grandchildren with all the love and tenderness he could muster at what must have been for him a moment of unbearable sadness.

"If only we could be together to hold each other and not be separated by an ocean," I thought.

"Bring Joe's body to Connecticut, We'll deal with the details later," was his advice.

More important at this moment,was the question of the whereabouts of my oldest daughter, Maria. Nobody seemed to have any idea how to reach her.

Why isn't anybody in place? I thought to myself.

Trinity College in Hartford, Connecticut, where Maria was a freshman, knew only that she had gone skiing for the weekend with her roommate Liz Engelke. Joe Sr. finally located Maria at Liz's home, where the young skiers were spending the night before heading early for the slopes. Liz's parents, Dr. and Mrs. Engelke, were a loving and caring couple. Suddenly, they too had the unenviable task of telling Maria that her father was dead.

A religious family, the Engelkes called their priest and asked for his help. Could he possibly come to the house at the crack of dawn before Maria and Liz planned to leave, they begged him?

"I just received this ever-so-funny letter Daddy wrote from Baghdad when he forgot to pack his underwear. He went shopping in the Baghdad souk for pure Iraqi cotton underpants," Maria cried over the phone, when I reached her.

She sobbed uncontrollably, incapable of continuing to speak. If only I could hold her, be with her.

"These damn distances," I said aloud.

Joe's letter must have taken forever to arrive at Trinity College. His Baghdad trip was more than six weeks ago. Maria was soon on her way to her grandfather's hourse, in Guilford, Connecticut.

Many decisions had to be made quickly. Hawk Mills suggested we go upstairs, away from the noise. We settled in my bedroom because it had a phone line. Sitting on the unmade bed, I had left in a hurry at 6 am, I noticed that one of the drawers of our dresser just opposite us was half open, an item of underwear, a black slip,was hanging over the rim.

I can see it clearly even today. Strange, how one can remember unimportant details precisely, but not have any clear recollection of the big things, such as one's emtional state. I must have put my emotions on hold. I was functioning normally, or so I thought.

Ulla Morris-Carter

I still knew little beyond the few facts I had been given after arriving home. Nobody had a clear picture of what was happening.

Iran was in the middle of a revolution. All borders were closed. Telephone lines worked sporadically, if at all. Most of our news came from the still operating *United Press* telex or from an occasional call from the *Los Angeles Times*, if and when they could get a call through to Teheran. The U.S. Embassy in Teheran, surrounded by violent demonstrators, was little help. Embassy personnel had no direct knowledge of the shooting and could not get to the airbase on the outskirts of Teheran, where the battle in which Joe had died, still raged.

All we knew so far was that Joe had been at the Doshan Tapeh Air Base, supposedly checking out reports of a clash between the Imperial Guard, the elite fighting force loyal to the Shah, and Iranian Air Force cadets, supporting opposition leader, Ayatollah Ruholla Khomeini. Khomeini had arrived from exile in Paris a few days before. Ironically, the two opposing military forces were battling each other with American weapons.

When the shooting started, Joe, along with Arthur Higbee of *United Press International*, and later joined by Ray Mosley of the *Chicago Tribune* and Bill Brainigan of *The Washington Post*, had fled to a second floor photo studio near the Air Base. The photo studio had a telephone and a window overlooking the street. Ken Freed, Joe's *L.A. Times* colleague, who had only just arrived in Teheran on his first foreign assignment, was new to the Middle East. He had remained at the Intercontinental Hotel, where most of the press corps was installed. Apparently, Joe had phoned Freed from the photo studio minutes before he was shot to inform him of the intense firing with automatic rifles and heavy machine guns, much of it "swirling around the building where we had sought refuge," according to Bill Brainigan.

Hawk Mills and I spent two hours upstairs away from the crowd, telephoning and trying to make sense out of the chaos around us. When I came downstairs, Jon Randal handed me a glass of whisky and motioned me towards a comfortable chair in the corner of the living room. It was late now, maybe midnight or one a.m. People had left. The house was quiet. We were talking about Joe. I couldn't think. I just wanted to sit quietly and reminisce.

Jon was staying at the house for the second time. He had lived with us once before, after being kidnapped in Beirut in October 1975 during the early part of the Civil War. Now, when I arrived home from Delphi, Jon had already installed himself, typewriter at the ready, in the little room near the kitchen, which had once been the maid's room.

Ginny Papadopoulo, an American friend married to a Greek-Cypriot, stayed overnight with us as well. She knew the children and was helping however possible. She brought dinner, but I could not eat a bite. By 3 am, we finally all went to bed. I

Ulla Morris-Carter

was exhausted but I could not sleep. Finally I dozed off. At 5 am the phone rang. I sat up straight in bed. David Lancashire, *Toronto Globe and Mail* reporter and his Dutch wife Dedee, were calling from Canada. They knew it was the middle of the night.

"We are sure you can't sleep anyway. We just had to call you as soon as we heard the news." David and Dedee were close to tears: "We are devastated. What can we do?"

"I don't know. I really don't know. I can't think straight right now." My mind was blank and I was unbelievably tired.

Suddenly I became aware that I was alone in our double bed. This was by no means the first time. Joe was away more than he was home. But it hit me then and there, at five a.m., that this was going to be permanent. Joe was not coming home, ever. I pulled the covers over my head. I wished never to come out from under. Hardly sleeping, but needing to be alone, I stayed in bed until nine o'clock.

The Embassy left me with a whole list of questions, my task for this morning, Sunday, February 11.

Still in my bathrobe I went upstairs to Joe's study to search for some of the required documents. The third floor study was the most beautiful, if somewhat dilapidated, room in the house. Surrounded by balconies on all four sides and windows and glass doors on three, it allowed glorious views over the city and surroundings. Greece has the most brilliant light of all European countries. That never ceased to amaze me.

The floor of the study was covered with documents and papers to be filed and sorted. On Joe's last visit home we had started this project. But no sooner had he arrived in Athens, than the *L.A. Times* called him back to Teheran to replace his injured colleague Don Schanche.

Standing in this sea of papers, the harsh truth, the finality of death, hit me again. I was surrounded by all that represented Joe, his typewriter, his files, his pipes, which he had stopped smoking but were still sitting in the hand-carved wooden stand, unfinished stories, press passes, even a certain smell of shaving soap that usually surrounded him.

```
TELEX 215572

ATHENS

JOHN RIGOS

PLS ONPASS TO MORRIS' WIFE

BOTH OF US SEND OUR DEEPEST SYMPATHY. JOE WAS A FINE MAN AND A

PROFESSIONAL WITH FEW EQUALS. PLEASE KNOW THAT THE TIMES STANDS

READY TO HELP YOU IN ANY WAY YOU NEED US.

    OTIS CHANDLER AND BILL THOMAS

SENT FEB 10 1110 AST
```

One of the first telexes to arrive , from L.A. Times *Publisher Otis Chandler and editor-in-chief Bill Thomas.*

Ulla Morris-Carter

What was I to do? Yesterday I was numb, today I had to face realities I did not want to face, did not know how to face. It was heartbreaking, harder than anything I had ever known. Nothing prepared me for this kind of loss.

The phone rang, my mother calling from Germany. I had only been able to leave her a short message yesterday, when I didn't find her at home. It turned out that she had heard a news item on the radio announcing that a *Los Angeles Times* correspondent had been killed in Teheran, no name. Worried, she called my brother, who in turn called the *Deutsche Presse Agentur, DPA,* who confirmed the news, and the name, Joe Alex Morris, Jr. My mother was devastated. I simply couldn't understand why the news of Joe's death had been on radio and television before the family had been informed. How many others would have to hear the news via radio? Joe's aunt in Washington dropped the milk carton she was carrying when she heard the news item.

My mother loved Joe. Besides, she had lost her husband, my father, killed during WWII in France when she was only 34 years old. She knew all about loss and pain. She did not want me to have to go through that experience. It was harder and more painful to talk to my mother than it was to Joe's father.

When I went downstairs, the house was already filling up with people. As the flow of visitors continued, I had to extract myself occasionally to see my children and tend to other matters of immediate importance. There was, of course, some comfort, in seeing so many friends, acquaintances and journalists paying tribute to a wonderful man, husband, father and journalist that many admired. The customs and rituals of the Middle East and Greece required that friends and acquaintances come to the house to pay their respects and offer condolences. Family privacy and quiet mourning were not part of the ritual.

After treatment in Germany, Don Schanche and his wife Marybelle arrived in Athens to help. His right foot in a cast, Don hobbled into our house, doubtless in pain, but he never complained. He and Jon Randal manned the phones.

Next to arrive was Bill Tuohy, *L.A. Times* London Bureau chief. Given the mission of retrieving Joe's body from Teheran, he had tried in vain to fly to Teheran from either London or Paris.

What we did not know until later that day was that nobody knew where the body actually was. Nobody had been able to contact anyone who might have given us detailed information.

That evening, *L.A. Times* foreign editor, Bob Gibson, arrived at the house, worn out after a long flight and many hours of organization and preparation before departing Los Angeles.

Ulla Morris-Carter

The downstairs phone was now used solely for continuously dialing of the Greek operator to try to reach Teheran. Our second line fielded calls to and from Washington, London, Paris, Bahrain, Beirut and Amman, all in hope of finding help to bring Joe's body out of Iran.

With dismay the *L.A. Times* team learned from Ken Freed in Teheran that "the body probably, but not certainly, was inaccessible in an Iranian air force hospital on the east side of Teheran."

The hospital was under heavy fire for several days. All air and seaports remained closed. Freed courageously tried to reach the military hospital near the air base where Joe had been taken after he was shot. But the taxi he was riding in had its tires shot out. Continuing on foot, he was forced to abandon his task when pitched battles erupted all around him.

Adding to the pandemonium in the streets of Teheran was the forced resignation of the Shah-appointed Prime Minister Shapur Bakhtiar and his whole government. Ayatollah Ruholla Khomeini had taken over military and government installations, wiping out the last vestiges of the Iranian monarchy under the Shah. Mehdi Bazargan was appointed premier of a provisional republican government.

Jon Randal, who had spent as much time in Iran as Joe had, finally managed to contact Prime Minister Bazargan's office on the *UPI* telex, asking for assistance in finding Joe's body and for permission to get it out of the country.

DAY THREE

While all this was happening in Teheran, we continued our wake in the house on 58 Gizi Street in Athens. We no longer counted hours. Now it was days.

By Monday, Day Three, we seemed to have a continuous wake that resembled a cocktail party. Some people came to help, some came to comfort, to commiserate or give advice. Others, whom I hardly knew, seemed to be there for the entertainment. With four foreign correspondents floating in and out of the house, there was an endless supply of entertaining stories.

Partly from lack of sleep, and partly from not being able to eat, I was exhausted. I functioned like a robot. Sad moments alternated with light-hearted remembrances about Joe and his adventurous life. Monday afternoon the sun came out. We sat on the terrace as if having a lovely spring picnic, drinking coffee and wine and eating assorted sweets and pastries that people had brought.

So far Karin and Julia had not been back to school. They were uncertain about how to handle themselves with teachers and school friends who wanted to express sympathy. But they missed their friends who had not visited our house, probably on advice from their parents not to disturb us. By Monday night, after a long talk about

Ulla Morris-Carter

the pros and cons of going back to school, Karin and Julia decided to return to school the next morning, Tuesday.

There was still no sign of Joe's body.

The revolution in Iran turned more explosive by the day. We had to resign ourselves to waiting. We could not leave for the United States. Athens was headquarters, and the waiting game continued. Our house no longer seemed ours. It resembled a newspaper office, dealing with deadlines, non-stop telephone calls and an endless stream of people. Only a telex machine was missing.

DAY FOUR—TUESDAY

Tuesday morning started like any other normal school day, or so it seemed. I had breakfast with Karin and Julia, prepared their lunch boxes, and off they went to school. They could walk to their British school, but today their steps seemed slower and more hesitant than usual. Last week they had raced out of the house to be on time. Julia, just 13 and Karin, almost 15, did not want to be accompanied. What brave little soldiers they were! Watching them walk down Gizi Street, my heart was heavy with sorrow. They would have to grow up without the father they had so loved. Joe had always been so full of good cheer. Unlike me, he could make them laugh and pull them out of their occasional teenage bad moods. I felt guilty for not having spent enough time with them over the last three days.

Early that Tuesday morning, before anybody was up, I had walked downstairs. For the first time in three days, I felt the need to look at what used to be the daily tasks of ordinary housekeeping. Until now I had not even thought about daily chores. My life seemed to be run by others.

Looking around the house I noticed an embarrassing number of empty whiskey bottles, wine bottles, beer bottles and juice bottles, the kind of uninspiring morning-after debris one finds after a late-night party. I quietly collected all those leftovers, put them into a large garbage bag and carried them out to the garbage cans, which were placed at the right-hand side of the house, visible from the street. I was particularly careful not to be seen by my conservative Greek neighbors, who were friendly without ever being chatty. Why, they would have wondered, would a new widow be carrying out all those empty bottles?

I concentrated on the task at hand and placed every bottle slowly and gently into the garbage can, trying to avoid the clattering noise of glass bottles hitting the metal bottom. How could we have consumed so much liquor? After all, it wasn't a party, though some people may have thought it was.

I was surprised to notice that I was beginning to lose my cool. I was no longer functioning like a robot. I could feel anger and frustration welling up in me. The

Ulla Morris-Carter

telephone marathon was ongoing. Still nobody had had any contact with anyone who knew what was going on. Jon Randal and Bill Tuohy received provisional permission to fly in to Teheran with the first U.S. military evacuation flight to take U.S. citizens out of Iran, should such a flight be allowed. The *British Royal Air Force* granted the same type of permission. Sir Anthony Parsons, permanent second undersecretary of the British Foreign Ministry, and a good friend from earlier days, when we had known him as Ambassador to Saudi Arabia, facilitated our request. He was happy to be able to help.

I managed a few household chores. Upstairs, I straightened out the children's rooms where they had lived for most of the last three days.

On Julia's desk I discovered a beautiful blue card, larger than a postcard. Writing with a silver pen while she was waiting for me to come home, she had composed a poem on the day of her father's death. She had never shown it to anyone:

The card that Julia had made, in silver ink on blue paper.

Everyone is free,
Free to live and
Free to die,
But,
In his freedom to kill,
He is killing someone else's
Freedom to live.

I took it downstairs and read it to those assembled in the entrance hall, gathered as always around the phone. More than anything else so far, the poem written by his youngest daughter brought home the cruel fact of Joe's death. In the right-hand bottom corner she had drawn a little heart that said J.A.M. + J.A.M., Joe A. Morris and Julia A. Morris. She did not actually have an "A" in her name. Her name was simply Julia Morris. Later Julia reminded me that Joe and I had originally wanted to call her Julia Augusta, the old Roman name for Beirut, which would have given her the initial "A."

Ulla Morris-Carter

Day Four dragged on.

My impatience was growing. By afternoon I knew I had to do something, anything. I suspected that my informants at the house weren't telling me everything they knew. Later I learned that they were trying to spare me some of the sordid details of the search for the body. It emerged that the physician at the military hospital, who had been in charge when Joe was brought in by ambulance, and who had certified his death, had since been jailed as a supporter of the Shah. This meant we would not be able to obtain a death certificate.

What could we do without a death certificate? Before long I would learn how hard it is to deal with a bureaucracy, absent the proper documents.

"Please, try again to reach Arthur Higbee at the Intercontinental Hotel," I pleaded. "Or any of the other correspondents who were with Joe."

Arthur, the *UPI* man could not call out at all. We tried to reach him for three days. Phone connections from Greece to Iran were getting worse by the minute.

We finally reached Arthur on Tuesday. He came to the phone in tears. He was so shaken that he had a hard time answering my questions.

"Did anybody accompany Joe to the hospital?"

"I tried to get into the ambulance with him."

I could barely hear Arthur's shaky voice.

"But the ambulance driver refused. A second ambulance, which arrived a few minutes later, then took me to the military hospital."

Barely audible, Arthur nonetheless revealed some of the more unpleasant details I was asking for.

"Did Joe say anything before he died? "

"No."

Arthur struggled for a soft description of hard facts.

"No, no, he said nothing. I don't think he had time to say anything; all I heard was a groan and then he fell over."

"Was he still alive when he arrived at the hospital?"

"No, I don't believe so."

I found out later that Arthur had been almost hysterical when, after arriving at the hospital, he found Joe lying there on a stretcher, alone, no doctor in attendance. Arthur screamed for a doctor. When one finally arrived, he made Arthur feel the cold body to convince him that his friend was dead.

During my questioning, the team had fallen silent. Arthur was the first eyewitness I had had a chance to talk to. If there had been any lingering doubts in my mind, he wiped them away. We spoke for 15 or 20 minutes, Arthur struggling to be truthful, although undoubtedly he would have preferred not to have this conversation at all.

Ulla Morris-Carter

"I had to know," I told him. "Now I know."

Silence.

Had the line been cut? But Arthur was still on the other end.

"We send all our love, take good care of yourself, but please don't be so glum," I said, realizing how difficult it had been for him to discuss these dreadful details.

I had been struggling to accept the fact of Joe's death. When there is no physical or other convincing evidence, the finality of a death is difficult to grasp. That conversation with Arthur convinced me of the inevitability of the truth.

DAY FIVE—WEDNESDAY, FEBRUARY 14, VALENTINE'S DAY.

In the morning, Ann McCloskey, the charming wife of the U.S. ambassador, called to invite our journalistic household to lunch at the Embassy.

"You must get out of the house," she said. "I suggest we play a game of tennis before lunch."

"Tennis!" I almost screamed. "You can't be serious. There is no way I can play tennis."

"It'll be good for you. We'll play on our court at the Embassy. It's totally private, as you know."

Arguing would do me no good, I realized. Ann knew what she wanted. We were to play a game of doubles. Mary George would pick me up at the house. She was an excellent tennis player. I had played with her many times before. It seemed impossible to put on tennis clothes. What an outrageous idea!

Nonetheless, I managed to put on my tennis outfit. Not wanting to be seen in a short skirt, I covered it with a long coat. It was a sunny day, perfect for tennis. The American Embassy court was one of the best in Athens, a well-groomed red clay court, surrounded by graceful tall trees and gorgeous gardens. I remembered my countless tennis matches with Joe. He had been a spirited player. He never traveled without a racket.

We hit a few hard balls. It felt good to be outdoors, surrounded by nature. My turn to serve. I stood behind the base line, threw the ball into the air. Suddenly tears welled up in my eyes. I could hardly see the ball. All I could think was that Joe would never stand on the other side of the court again. He would never again come around the net and put his arm around me to console me when I had lost the game, which had happened frequently when I played him.

After a short pause, I managed to pull myself together, but I didn't play well. We changed clothes at the Embassy. I put on a blue wool dress.

"This is not a formal luncheon," Ann McCloskey had said. "Let's try and relax for a short time."

We, the three journalists, Randal, Schanche and Tuohy plus the *L.A. Times* foreign

Ulla Morris-Carter

Julia's poem

editor, Bob Gibson, Mary George and I sat around the attractively set lunch table, waiting for the Ambassador to join us. Virginia Papadopoulo arrived carrying a heart-shaped cake. It was Valentines Day, and also Jon Randal's birthday.

Anne McCloskey was called to the phone to speak to her husband, the Ambassador. He apologized for not being able to join us. Another violent event had occurred in a country even further away than Iran.

The U.S. Ambassador to Afghanistan, Adolph Dubs, had just been assassinated.

We sat in stunned silence. Then the natural curiosity characteristic of all journalists, interrupted the silence. They asked rapid-fire questions. Three of them, Randal, Tuohy and Schanche, had, like Joe, spent time in Afghanistan, including covering the Soviet invasion and occupation. Joe had last been in Kabul in 1978, less than a year earlier. He had returned with a precious old necklace made of antique silver, corals and shells, a present for me. Special permission had been needed from the Ministry of Culture to take it out of the country.

Now the U.S. Embassy in Greece was confronted with the death of two men, one of their own, plus one journalist, whose body was still missing. Both bodies would have to transit Athens. Although the luncheon was obviously not the uplifting experience Ann McCloskey had hoped for, she nonetheless proposed a toast to the *L.A. Times* team and its efforts. In reply, foreign editor Bob Gibson lifted his wine glass and said:

"Friends, I don't think it would be appropriate at this time for anyone of the *Los Angeles Times* to toast anything. Instead, let us express an appreciation for all the love at this table."

Back at the house the phone marathon continued. Two more *L.A. Times* foreign correspondents, Diall Torgerson and Charles Powers, had meanwhile arrived in Athens, hoping to fly into Iran. Don Schanche called the Royal Jordanian charter airline, Arab Wings, which until the outbreak of the revolution, had been able to fly in and out of Teheran ferrying crews and film for the three major American TV networks. All three networks promised to make it a priority to bring out Joe's body, if they could get in. But the first TV-chartered Arab Wings flight to Teheran was summarily turned back by the Iranian Air Force at Delzun airport, south of Teheran.

Despite this setback, Jon Randal and Bill Tuohy flew to Amman, Jordan, Wednesday night, accompanied by Diall Torgerson and Charles Powers, to stand by for a special *Los Angeles Times* charter of Arab Wings. Randal was to cover the events for *The Washington Post*, whose two Iran correspondents needed help. Tuohy was to bring out Joe's body, if it could be found. Torgerson and Powers were to help Ken Freed, who had valiantly tried to cover the chaotic events, in addition to trying to reach the military hospital, where Joe's body might possibly be.

Ulla Morris-Carter

DAY SIX—THURSDAY MORNING

After a night of little sleep and a talk with Karin and Julia, I knew that the time for a decision had come. I couldn't possibly sit and wait any longer in Athens. I was worried about Maria and Joe Sr. keeping their lonely vigil in Connecticut. Both of them were feeling left out of events, which I could only relay via telephone. The family should have been reunited long since in the United States. Given the increasing chaos in Iran, I decided to fly with Karin and Julia to Connecticut, to be together with family and to plan a memorial service.

From Amman, Arab Wings called to say they would attempt another flight to Teheran. The Bazargan government had given permission for one Arab Wings flight into Teheran, on humanitarian grounds, to bring Joe's body out.

Jon Randal's professional handling of the situation along with the efforts of Joe's *L.A. Times* colleague in Teheran seemed to be bearing fruit. Only Randal and Tuohy had permission to be on the plane. Teheran would allow only Tuohy to fly out with the body, no other journalists, no TV film, no tapes, no stories.

How to reach Ken Freed with no telephone lines open to Teheran?

UPI Athens correspondent John Rigos came to the rescue again. He volunteered to try telexing a message to Freed in Teheran via the extremely busy *UPI* telex. Miraculously it worked. Freed was alerted early in the morning. Somehow he managed to reach the shattered military hospital, where Joe's body might be. But to find the body in a mortuary literally filled with bodies, then to have it embalmed and ready for transport, was a near impossible mission. We knew we needed a miracle to have the body at the airport by that afternoon, when Arab Wings was hoping to arrive in Teheran.

Arab Wings did manage to land in Teheran, only to be held up by gun-wielding Khomeini irregular soldiers, who obviously had not been told that Arab Wings had special landing permission. Assuming that this was a CIA-managed operation, the revolutionary guards arrested the journalists. After heated discussions, Jon Randal was allowed one telephone call. He called the office of the Prime Minister. The journalists were released.

Then another crisis.

The ambulance with Joe's body did not arrive at the airport on time. Understandably nervous after their initial reception, Arab Wings flight crew wanted to leave Teheran as fast as possible, definitely before dark. Since the airport was officially closed, no landing lights or any other night facilities were functioning.

Just as the Arab Wings captain was about to start his engines, the ambulance with the body drove into the airport. Accompanied by Ken Freed and the *Washington Post* correspondents Bill Claiborne and Bill Brainigan, it had, miraculously, made it to the airport.

Then another delay.

Ulla Morris-Carter

Joe's passport with Iranian visas.

The Khomeini irregulars demanded to see Joe's bloodstained passport with the official entry visa. After searching for what seemed like an hour through the accordion folds of Joe's well-traveled passport, they found the entry visa and dutifully stamped Joe's last exit visa next to it.

Finally the body was released.

Bill Tuohy then realized with horror that the bulky, zinc-lined box holding the body would not fit through the small door of the executive jet. With the help of some soldiers, pushing and shoving, they managed to force the box through the door.

Just as darkness set in, the plane took off.

None of the Iranian officials suspected that, traveling with Joe's body, were some TV films and newspaper articles that reporters had managed to smuggle into the coffin.

Joe would have loved it.

In Jordan, where Arab Wings stopped to refuel, King Hussein's government waived all formalities normally required when a body passes through. King Hussein knew Joe well from discussions and interviews over the years.

By 11 p.m. Thursday night Bill Tuohy arrived in Athens with the body. I had wanted to go to the airport, but my well-meaning friends withheld the news from me. When I found out, too late, I was angry, frustrated and tired of the protection they continually accorded me. I wanted to be in charge of my life again, but now was not the time to quarrel. I had to pack for Karin, Julia and myself to fly to the United States the next morning, accompanying Joe's body on his last flight home.

Ulla Morris-Carter

Before we departed from Greece for the United States, a neighbor rang the doorbell carrying a light-blue envelope that she had found in the gutter near our house. The mailman must have dropped it by mistake. At that point we were receiving dozens and dozens of letters and Western Union mailgrams. The neighbor, a Greek lady I did not know, carried the letter carefully, using both hands as if she were delivering a valuable present. On closer inspection I understood why. The sender, The White House:

> I extend my deepest sympathy to you and your family in your great loss. I hope the prayers and good wishes of your family and friends will console and comfort you in the days ahead. Sincerely, Jimmy Carter.

It was signed, not stamped, by the President himself in dark blue ink.

After a sleepless night, Friday morning dawned with gray skies that gave way to cool, pale sunshine. Bob Gibson would fly with us. Ambassador McCloskey and some of his staff and a few friends were waiting at the airport when we arrived.

Greek widows are supposed to be dressed in black including a veil, but I was comfortably dressed for the long journey in gray corduroy trousers and a gray sweater. Ambassador and staff paid their respects. I thanked them for their care and tremendous help during the tumultuous past week. The Greek press photographed these farewells and published a photo showing me shaking the Ambassador's hand, smiling while thanking him.

Never known for accuracy or tact, the Greek press commented:

"This is how an American widow mourns her husband killed in Iran."

The blatant anti-Americanism of this was too much. The American Embassy demanded, and later received, an apology. I was glad to be out of the country when I heard about it.

The flight on Pan American Airlines was long and tiring. We were traveling first class. The children sat in front of me, Bob next to me. All I wanted was to close my eyes, sit back in silence, rest my raw nerves and regain my composure. Impossible. Details and funeral arrangements had to be discussed.

Somewhere below us, in cold storage, was the coffin with Joe's body.

After an eight-hour flight, I staggered down the stairway onto the runway in New York's Kennedy Airport, to be greeted by a barrage of television and press people. Barely managing condolences, they peppered me with questions.

"You are not carrying a photo of your husband?" they complained.

"What kind of person was your husband?"

"He was the kind of person I would have followed to the North Pole had he been posted there," I managed to answer, while trying to escape.

Ulla Morris-Carter

"What do you think of the situation in Iran?"

Who in the world cares what I think about the situation in Iran, I wondered.

So the questioning continued.

GUILFORD, CT.

Joe's sister Clare was waiting at the airport, as was my brother Hans who had flown in from Germany. Both of them were a welcome comforting presence.

A black limousine carried us to Guilford and the sad reunion with Joe Sr. and Maria. Though freezing cold outside, minus 5°F, Joe's house was warm and cozy, with a fire burning in the fireplace and the living room filled with brilliant late-afternoon winter sunshine and blooming branches of yellow forsythia on every window sill.

The flowers gave it the look of a spring day. I had always loved this house. It felt like home, and, of course, it had been home for all of us when we were on home leave. Even now it did not have the appearance of a house visited by death. Clare's four children, the cousins, had already arrived, and were keeping Maria company and preventing her from breaking down. But Joe Sr. was completely crushed. He held me in a long embrace, shaking ever so slightly, but trying to be strong, supportive and comforting.

"Why couldn't it have been me?" he asked quietly, looking at me with unspeakable sadness in his gentle eyes.

We sat down for a family dinner, prepared lovingly by Joe Sr. We were happy to be together finally after a week of longing for the closeness of family.

There was little time for rest. The service was to take place the next day, Saturday, at two p.m. Bob Gibson was staying with nearby friends of the Morris's. Early Saturday morning he went to the Guilford morgue to identify the body now, finally on U.S. soil. When I heard about it, I was extremely upset not to have been consulted yet again. Returning, he suggested that I come with him to the funeral home to choose a new coffin, the present one having been badly damaged when it was jammed through the narrow door of Arab Wings Learjet. I lost my composure once again.

"I don't care whether he lies in a blue, silver or gold box, damaged or polished," I burst out. "Who cares what box he lies in?"

I was no longer in control of my emotions. Not having been asked to go to the mortuary to view the body, I was determined not to go there now to choose a new coffin.

My brother Hans came to my rescue: "We'll cover the coffin with flowers and hide the damage," he said reassuringly.

He rushed off immediately with only a few hours to find flower shops in a small Connecticut town he knew nothing of. It was hard to find enough flowers in deep winter, and Hans spoke English haltingly. But somehow he succeeded admirably.

Ulla Morris-Carter

Braving severe weather conditions, icy roads and plane delays, more than a hundred journalists and friends managed to attend the service in Guilford on only a few hours notice. They came from Los Angeles; from Washington, DC; from Boston and Florida.

Entering the small non- denominational church in Guilford, with my three children, I felt completely detached. I had never been in this church before. There was nothing comforting or familiar. In front of us stood the coffin, covered from one end to the other with the most beautiful flowers.

GUILFORD, Conn., Feb.17-SERVICES FOR CORRESPONDENT - Rev. Edwin Lincoln leads a prayer from the pulpit at First Congregational Church in Guildord Saturday during funeral services for Joe Alex Morris Jr., a foreign correspondent for the LA Times. Morris was killed last week in Iran during the unrest there. Morris' wife, father, and three daughters occupy the front row in the church". AP

AP photos from the service.
Top: *The casket covered with flowers.* **Right:** *Joe Sr., myself, Julia, Karin, Maria.*

(NX3)GUILFORD,Conn.,Feb.17--CORRESPONDENT'S FAMILY AT SERVICES--The family of Joe Alex Morris Jr.,foreign correspondent for the Los Angeles Times who was killed in Iran last week listen during funeral services held for him in Guilford Saturday.In photo are: Morris' father,Joe Alex Morris Sr.;his wife,Ulla;daughter,Julia;Karin;Maria.(AP LASER-PHOTO) (rc71640stf/child) 1979

Ulla Morris-Carter

Bob Gibson gave the eulogy. But, overcome by emotion, he handed the poem Julia had written on the day her father was killed, to Larry Fellows, *New York Times* correspondent, to read. Larry was another long-time and trusted friend. Colleagues and friends related sad stories and funny incidents. Larry recalled a time when Joe had covered the strife between Greeks and Turks in Cyprus in the 1960s:

> During a lull in the fighting Joe decided to cross no-man's land to see what was happening in Nicosia, the capital of Cyprus. In an open convertible he led a line of cars containing foreign correspondents while the rifles of the Greeks and the Turks were trained on them. Halfway across no-man's land, a still functioning traffic light turned red. Joe stopped, halting the entire convoy, much to the other reporters consternation and to Joe's obvious amusement.

"In a group, other reporters tended to follow Joe's lead," wrote Ray Moseley in the *Chicago Tribune*. "Joe seemed to have a sure instinct of knowing what to do in a difficult situation."

Columnist Georgie Anne Geyer commented:

> "Those of us who knew the *Los Angeles Times* star correspondent loved him because he was the finest gentleman in the entire foreign press corps. While others flaunted their flamboyant non-abilities, this handsome, dark-haired, witty man quietly used his abilities."

After the service, those who could stay gathered at Joe Sr.'s house for food and drink. Though exhausted, I found comfort and solace in the presence of so many good friends and journalists who had loved and admired Joe. Mail was now pouring in, official condolences and letters from Joe's colleagues and friends that made me cry.

There were heart-warming letters from Iranians we had never met, and from a *Los Angeles Times* reader, evidently written before Joe's death:

> I particularly appreciated the article 'Fate of Iran Balanced on Khomeini's Shoulders,' for its lucid explanation of the history behind Khomeini's rise to power. It's a rare writer who can make such complicated issues . . . understandable.

Newspaper articles, some written by journalists who had been with Joe on that fateful day, arrived by mail or telex: "I Watched Joe Die" read the headline of the *Chicago Tribune* front page article by Ray Moseley, an article that brought tears to all our eyes:

> Of all the hundreds of foreign correspondents in Teheran, Joe was one of the most highly respected and easily the best loved . . . he was not only one of the finest reporters in the business, but a remarkable human being.

The *Teheran Journal* wrote:

> Among the press corps covering the Iranian Revolution . . . he was loved as a humorous and very human elder statesman.

Ulla Morris-Carter

Chicago Tribune

Sunday, February 11, 1979

Final Edition

60¢

'I watched Joe die Saturday'
Eyewitness report from Tehran

By Ray Moseley

Chicago Tribune Press Service.
© 1979 Chicago Tribune

TEHRAN—Joe Alex Morris Jr., a correspondent for the Los Angeles Times, was my friend for 15 years.

We covered two wars together. We also shared a great many pleasant experiences.

I watched Joe die Saturday in a photographer's studio where we had taken refuge from a battle between Iranian troops loyal to the government and air force cadets who support Ayatollah Ruhollah Khomeini.

A SHOT FIRED through a window took Joe's life. He was crouching before the window and was shot in the upper chest.

Of all the hundreds of foreign correspondents in Tehran, Joe was one of the most highly respected and easily the best loved. That is because he was not only one of the finest reporters in the business, but a remarkable human being.

In a group, other reporters tended to follow Joe's lead. He seemed to have a sure instinct of knowing what to do in a difficult situation.

In a career of some 30 years, he had survived the Indo-Pakistan War of 1965 and the Middle East's Six Day War of 1967. Later, he was to win a fight against cancer, and he became a reporting veteran of the Lebanese civil war.

IN ALL OF HIS wars, Joe was always to be found where the action was heaviest. Just two weeks ago, another reporter commented to me, "Joe doesn't know what fear means."

He was one of the people I most loved and admired. Being the man that he was, he was joking in his sardonic way almost to the end.

His death occurred on the second floor of a building a half block from the Air Training Command section of the Doshen Tappeh air base on the eastern out-

Continued on page 24, col. 1

Ray Moseley's first hand account ran in the Chicago Tribune *Sunday February 11, 1979.*

The next day, Sunday morning, the Guilford house was once again packed with people, even though Ruth and Larry Fellows had taken some of our relatives and friends to their house to spend the night. Where did everyone sleep? I only remember having to share my double bed with a lady friend.

I desperately wanted to be alone to try to pull myself together and then sleep.

Not a chance. Bob Gibson wanted me to travel with him to Los Angeles right away, where a mountain of paperwork awaited. The children would stay with Joe Sr. and Clare until my return. I found it hard to believe I had left Greece only on Friday, two days ago. Today, Sunday, I was on my way to Los Angeles. It seemed as if weeks had passed.

Not until we arrived at Los Angeles Airport had it even occurred to me that I would need a place to stay.

"You stay at my house, of course," said Bob.

I suddenly realized the awkwardness of the situation. Bob was the recently divorced foreign editor, whose ex-wife I had known well in New York in 1962. I was the new widow. I pleaded for a hotel room, but Bob wouldn't hear of it. In my current state, I didn't really care.

Los Angeles looked warm and sunny when I stuck my head out the window the next morning. I felt slighty better than the day before. But my body was reacting to eleven days of sleepnessless, jet-lag plus climate and time change. Heaviness spread through

Ulla Morris-Carter

my entire body. I could barely lift my feet off the ground. Emotionally I felt numb. But there was no time to linger. It was time to drive with Bob to the *Los Angeles Times*.

Wearing a light gray wool dress, I settled myself in the soft seats of Bob's American car. He was a tall man and loved big cars, those American-made cars that make you feel as if you were floating over the road.

"Prepare for the next ordeal!" I told myself. "Meet the publisher. Meet the editors. Meet the editorial staff. Show a brave face. Sign lots of papers. Then?"

Indeed, what then? I had simply pushed all thoughts of the future aside. Arriving in Los Angeles presented a new reality I was not quite ready for.

Los Angeles Times publisher Otis Chandler met me in the office of his editor-in-chief, Bill Thomas. Condolences, praise for Joe and his work, encouraging words and an offer of a job at the *Los Angeles Times*, either in Washington or Los Angeles. All within one hour!

I was called to the Personnel Department to sign off on their obligations to Joe's life in dollars and cents. Off to the accounting department to deal with Joe's expense accounts. How was I supposed to know how much money he had carried? How many traveler checks he had cashed? Promising to be diligent, to check the details once back in Athens after his belongings were returned, if indeed they were returned, I quietly cursed those bean counters.

Tony Day, editor of the editorial pages, and his wife, Lynn, gave a dinner party for me. They introduced me to parents with school-age children in the public high school in San Marino, a suburb northeast of Los Angeles, where they lived and where they suggested I might consider living.

"One of the best public schools," they assured me.

The Los Angeles visit was a whirlwind tour, two days dealing with paperwork and insurance questions, meeting too many people, whose names I couldn't retain, worrying about the children, wanting to return to Guilford as fast as possible.

Three days later I was back on a Pan Am flight to New York and Guilford. The gentleman sitting next to me asked whether I minded if he smoked a cigar.

"No problem, I rather like cigar smoke," I answered

He seemed pleased that he could indulge himself in his Cuban cigar. At the end of the flight he presented me with a small golden charm, a little airplane on a gold chain. Maybe he worked for Lockheed. I don't remember. Maybe he sensed my sadness. My children were impressed with this newest piece for their charm bracelet.

More painful decisions awaited me in Guilford. Joe Sr. took me aside to inquire, hesitantly, what I thought was to be done with Joe's ashes.

"Ashes," I said, "I have not even thought about ashes."

Ulla Morris-Carter

Ashes, I remembered are what one receives in a metal box, inside a small carton, from the crematorium, after cremation. Had I forgotten? I had never dealt with ashes.

"What did you do with Maxine's ashes?" I asked, feeling quite uncomfortable.

"I scattered them near our house on the hill, her favorite spot."

Twenty beautiful acres of rolling New England hills were part of Joe's property. No problem finding the perfect spot.

"Then let's spread Joe's ashes up on the hill," I heard myself say. "There where you planted that lovely maple tree for him years ago near the little pond. It's such a peaceful spot, very special, wild and windy, but open to the world."

Joe Sr. agreed. We decided not to consult the children. They had been through a horrendously traumatic two weeks. Externally they seemed to have recovered. They appeared close to their old selves. I hadn't thought about ashes, why should they?

On a gray, gloomy and cold February morning, the temperature was below zero, Joe Sr. and I donned our parkas and drove to the Guilford crematorium to pick up the ashes.

I felt sick to my stomach.

A somber-looking gentleman in an appropriately dark suit and tie, received us. Other than a mumbled message of sympathy, he hardly spoke. He disappeared, returned, bowed his head slightly, and handed us a nondescript paper carton containing a metal box.

Is that all that is left of that intelligent, joyous, beautiful and witty man, my husband, the father of our three children? It can't be possible, I mumbled to myself. I was going to be sick any moment.

After a few seconds the nausea passed. I pulled myself together. If Joe Sr. could deal with this situation I couldn't let him down now. The funeral director handed me an envelope containing cards of friends who had sent flowers. Moments later he pulled another smaller envelope out of his coat pocket. He seemed rather hesitant to present it.

He observed me carefully before explaining:

"This envelope contains Joe's wedding band," he said. "I had to cut it, because it wouldn't slip off his finger."

We left the box in the car when we returned to Joe Sr.'s house. Nobody in the family noticed our return. They were playing card games. This gave us an opportunity to complete our task. We took the box out of the car and walked slowly up the hill, holding hands, braving the biting winter winds. I was clutching the box. We were both shivering and shaking, from the cold, or from heartache? The weather suited our mood. It began to mist. We didn't speak, just clung to each other. The maple tree's bare branches formed a perfect canopy. With shaking hands we opened the box. Slowly we moved around the tree, alternating throwing out the ashes in a circle.

Ulla Morris-Carter

It was the saddest moment I have ever experienced.

We stood for a moment, overwhelmed by the pain that rolled over us like a giant wave, waiting for it to subside.

We walked back in silence.

The house was warm and full of life. With seven young people ranging from 12 to 20, there was no such thing as silence. It brought both Joe Sr. and me back to life and to reality. The cousins departed and Maria went back to Trinity College. After two more days in Guilford, Karin and Julia and I boarded a plane for Athens.

In my handbag I carried the little envelope with Joe's wedding band.

THE EVERGREEN CEMETERY ASSOCIATION
Non-Profit Organization
NEW HAVEN, CONNECTICUT

No. 11305   Date February 21, 1979

KNOW ALL MEN BY THESE PRESENTS, That

Joe Alex Morris, Jr.

has been cremated at Evergreen Crematory by authority of the cremation permit as issued by the local Board of Health.

New Haven, Connecticut

Evergreen Crematory

Superintendent.

Age: 51 yrs.
Date of Death: February 10, 1979
Cause of Death: Gunshot wound - Tehran, Iran
Place of Death: Tehran, Iran

Death certificate from the crematorium.

Ulla Morris-Carter

RIVERS OF MY LIFE

By WILLIAM BRANIGIN.

(c) 1979, The Washington Post

TEHRAN - It was a clear morning. We were cooped up in the room listening to machine gun exchanges. The sound of bullets smattering against the side of the building repeatedly sent us ducking away from the window.

Then the firing tapered off a bit, and we, again cautiously, approached the window to check through venetian blinds. As I turned away for a moment, we heard a loud crack and a groan. Everyone hit the floor again. I looked back and saw Joe Alex Norris slumping behind me.

A single shot, apparently a stray, had caught him full in the chest.

''Monsieur is dead,'' said an Iranian air force officer in broken French.

Thinking back on it now, Norris died in what may have been the first shots of the Iranian civil war.

It was shortly before dawn when we set off in a taxi from our hotel to Doshan Tapeh air base on the edge of Tehran to check reports of a clash there between the members of the Imperial Guard, the elite fighting force loyal to the Shah, and air force cadets supporting opposition leader Ayatollah Ruhollah

Telex copy from Washington Post *correspondent William Braningan who had taken shelter with Joe and others in the photo studio while covering the outbreak of fighting between members of the Imperial Guard and the Air Force cadets.*

Ulla Morris-Carter

x628

   R I ZCZCYNBYLRYR

BC-IRAN-BATTLE 1STADD 02-10....

(BRANIGIN; POST) (NEWS; FOREIGN)

XXX STREET.

WE SAW TWO SOLDIERS HIT IN THE LEG IN THE STREET JUST BELOW THE WINDOW. THEY WERE CARRIED OFF BY COMRADES.

THE SHOOTING, WHICH ERUPTED AT ABOUT 8:15 A.M., DROVE THE GUARDSMEN BACK; AND THE CADETS CAME RUNNING OUT OF THE COMPOUND AND SET FIRE TO AN ARMY JEEP. CIVILIANS, MOSTLY YOUTHS, JOINED THE CADETS.

THEN THE IMPERIAL GUARDSMEN BROUGHT A TRUCK WITH A HEAVY 50-CALIBRE MACHINE GUN MOUNTED AT THE REAR AND BACKED IT DOWN **THE** STREET TOWARDS THE MAIN GATE; FIRING ALL THE WAY. WE HAD BEEN WATCHING THE ACTION THROUGH VENETIAN BLINDS.

IT WAS AT THIS POINT THAT MORRIS WAS HIT. HIGBEE KNELT OVER HIM WHILE I CALLED FOR HELP AND TELEPHONED THE HOTEL TO SEND AN AMBULANCE.

USING A DOOR AS A STRETCHER, A COUPLE OF CADETS ARRIVED AN HELPED HIGBEE CARRY JOE'S BODY DOWN THE STAIRS AND BACK TO THE BASE WHERE HE WAS TAKEN TO THE AIR FORCE HOSPITAL, WE LEARNED LATER.

HE WAS PRONOUNCED DEAD ON ARRIVAL. INDEED, IT SEEMED THAT HE HAD BEEN KILLED INSTANTLY.

Ulla Morris-Carter

Los Angeles Times

Sunday
Final

1,332,875 SUNDAY   SUNDAY, FEBRUARY 11, 1979   CC† /532 PAGES/ Copyright 1979 Los Angeles Times / SUNDAY 60c / Designated Areas Higher

Heavy Tehran Fighting Puts Iran on Brink of Civil War

Loyalist Units Face Civilians, Rebel Troops

BY KENNETH FREED
Times Staff Writer

TEHRAN, Iran—Rebel military units joined by thousands of civilians battled progovernment troops for control of Tehran Saturday, leaving scores dead and Iran on the brink of a full-scale civil war.

Heavy fighting raged through the capital well into the night, and the sounds of machine guns, small arms and heavier weapons could be heard.

The fighting was touched off Friday night at the Doshan Tappeh air training base in the Farahabad district of the capital, about six miles southeast of the city's center.

A number of air force trainees began an antigovernment demonstration on the base, and a unit of the Imperial Guard moved in with tanks and machine guns to suppress the insurrection. According to one report, 12 persons were killed in the first round of fighting.

The air base was the scene of a major battle through the day Saturday with intense firing on both sides. The rebel forces used assault rifles, including types made by both the Soviet Union and the United States.

The government troops, made up of the elite Imperial Guard and members of the regular army, fought back with tanks, heavy machine guns and helicopter gunships.

An accurate casualty count was impossible, but hospitals reported more than 160 killed and many times that figure wounded.

Among the casualties was Joe Alex Morris Jr., 51, a Times correspondent in Iran, who was killed by a gunshot

WAITING—Iranians armed with rifles, Molotov cocktails ready at their feet, man a roadblock stretching across a street in Tehran.
AP Wirephoto

Los Angeles Times, Sunday February 11, 1979.

Left: *Front page featuring an article by Kenneth Freed, on his first foreign assignment with Joe, reporting on the impending Civil War and Joe's death.*

Below and Next Page: L.A. Times *journalists and long time colleagues, Paris Bureau Chief Don Cook and London Bureau Chief, William Tuohy, write an article about Joe's death and life.*

Slain Times Man Was Dean of Mideast Correspondents

BY WILLIAM TUOHY and DON COOK
Times Staff Writers

Joe Alex Morris Jr., the Times correspondent killed Saturday covering the violence in Tehran, earned a reputation second to none in a quarter-century as a front-line reporter in the Middle East.

He was the most experienced American newsman in that volatile region, universally respected for his integrity and professionalism. And he was the first U.S. reporter killed in the revolt against the rule of Shah Mohammed Reza Pahlavi in Iran.

From Beirut to Oman, from Athens to Aden, Morris knew the Middle East as no other American journalist.

As usual, he was at the center of events when he was shot in the chest while observing the fighting in Tehran early Saturday. Alerted by reports of a clash between troops loyal to the shah and dissident air force cadets, he had scrambled into his clothes and, with other American reporters, grabbed a taxi to get to the

scene at an air base in the Farahabad district on the outskirts of the capital. It was there that he was killed.

When Morris was on a story, he never stopped, never slowed. Fear simply had no part in his makeup, no place in his appetite for work.

Less than two weeks ago, just before returning to Tehran from his home in Athens, Morris wrote in a letter to Jack Nelson, chief of The Times Washington bureau:

"Life goes on here, most of it in Tehran, where I am due back Sunday after 10 days off—and after four straight weeks on the job. It's a strain, family-wise and otherwise, but one helluva story and a rare chance to participate in a classic revolutionary situation. In other words, I look forward to going back."

When he returned to Iran, he looked tanned and fit—he had squeezed in some European skiing in

Please Turn to Page 8, Col. 1

Ulla Morris-Carter

Slain Times Man Was Dean of Middle East Correspondents

Continued from First Page

his brief break away from the story—and he was off for his first appointment just two hours after he had checked into the Tehran Intercontinental Hotel. As usual, he was wearing his Basque beret and chomping on his Dunhill pipe.

Two correspondents who had worked with him on his last assignment testified to his reputation.

Jonathan C. Randal of the Washington Post said: "Joe . . . was simply the best guy in the Middle East. He kept at the job ceaselessly for a quarter of a century, he was enormously respected. . . ."

R. W. Apple Jr. of the New York Times noted: "When other reporters arrived in Iran or some other Middle East trouble spot, they turned first to Joe Alex Morris for help. He never failed them. He knew the region as few other Americans did, and he delighted in sharing his knowledge.

"In Tehran, typically he worked punishingly long hours. Even when he finished dictating a story to Los Angeles at 3 a.m., he would be down in the hotel lobby the next morning at 8 a.m. blue beret clamped on his head, ready for another interview or another tour of that tormented city."

In Los Angeles, Times Foreign Editor Robert W. Gibson said:

"The tragic death of Joe Alex Morris Jr. is a loss not only to his family, friends and colleagues but to the millions of readers with whom, over many years, he shared his insights into the Arab world and his unique knowledge of the Middle East. Joe never settled for less than the best information, regardless of personal risk or hardship. Ultimately, this determination for quality cost his life. Joe was proud of his profession; the profession is even more proud of Joe Alex Morris Jr. He set standards for us all."

William Branigan, a Washington Post correspondent, was one of three American newsmen with Morris when he died. The others were Arthur Higbee, Paris bureau chief of United Press International, and Ray Moseley of the Chicago Tribune.

They were watching the battle from a second-floor window of a photo shop near the air base.

"We saw two Imperial Guardsmen get wounded in the legs below the window," Branigan said. "Some shots appeared to hit the building near the window. We all ducked and then went back to the window to see what had happened. It was then Joe Alex got shot."

A single shot smashed through the window and the venetian blinds.

"I heard a groan and we all sort of tumbled down to the floor. When I looked again, Joe Alex was on the floor . . . face down. I think he was killed instantly.

"It was impossible to tell from which side the shot came," Branigan said. "I believe it was a stray bullet."

Higbee told The Times that Morris was the first of the four to go to the window after the initial shots hit the building.

"That was typical of Joe—always the first one," Higbee said.

Higbee and others took Morris through the crowded street to the hospital at the air base, where he was pronounced dead.

He was not the first Times reporter killed while covering a story. In 1944, Tom Treanor, a combat correspondent for The Times, was fatally injured when his jeep was struck by a tank in an accident in France. In 1970, Ruben Salazar, a Times columnist, former correspondent and news director for television station KMEX, was killed during an East Los Angeles riot when struck by a sheriff's deputy's tear-gas projectile.

Morris, 51, was born in Denver, the son of a noted journalist. The senior Morris was a former foreign editor of United Press (now United Press International) and of the old New York Herald Tribune.

Joe Alex Jr. served in the Army in Europe before being graduated from Harvard University in 1949.

His first writing job was with the Minneapolis Tribune in 1948-49. He later worked for the Hartford Times in Connecticut before joining the United Press, which gave him his first Middle East assignment.

He worked for UP in the Middle East from 1950 to 1957, covering the Suez war of 1956 among other stories.

In 1957, he joined the Herald Tribune as its Cairo correspondent, then moved to a job with Newsweek magazine in 1961. Four years later, he joined the foreign staff of The Times, establishing the newspaper's bureau in Beirut, Lebanon. From 1968 to 1975, he was The Times bureau chief in Bonn, returning to the Beirut bureau in 1975. He and his family stayed there until the severity of the Lebanese civil

Morris was in a hotel in Jerusalem's Arab sector when Israelis captured it.

war forced them to move to Athens, although Morris continued to concentrate on Middle Eastern coverage.

In 1959, he married Ursula Kirschbaum, a native of Dusseldorf, West Germany, whom he had met in Cairo. Ulla, as she is called, served as hostess not only to her husband's wide circle of friends but also to visiting journalists from around the world.

Their three daughters, Maria, Karin and Julia. grew up in Cairo, Beirut, Bonn and Athens. They grew accustomed to seeing their father leave the house on an hour's notice, lugging his typewriter to cover stories in far-flung places.

Morris covered nearly all the major Mideast stories.

In the Arab-Israeli war of 1967, he had driven from Amman, Jordan, to Jerusalem and was in a hotel in the Arab sector of the city when Israeli paratroopers captured it.

Morris was awarded the prestigious Overseas Press Club Award for international reporting for his coverage of the conflict. He also covered the 1973 Arab-Israeli war from the Egyptian side.

During the Lebanese civil war, the Morris apartment in Beirut became something of an oasis for journalists. Ulla Morris always managed to have a hot meal or a cold drink on hand for any visitor.

Reporters in those days remember Morris driving a sports car with a big white bed sheet flapping over its roof to identify himself as a noncombatant when he crossed front lines.

He and Ulla continued to reside in Beirut long after most other foreigners had evacuated the city. When artillery shells began exploding near their apartment building, ripping the plaster loose from the ceiling, they reluctantly decided to relocate to Athens.

He underwent surgery and radiation treatment for a period of several months, but went to his office in the Bonn bureau every day and continued to write.

He had no signs of cancer in recent years.

Joe was an inveterate sports enthusiast: he packed his tennis racket and jogging clothes on assignment in the hope that he might get in an early morning run in Beirut or Tehran or a set of tennis in Amman or Ankara. He even managed to get in a day's skiing in the mountains north of Tehran recently—although he was embarrassed to tell his friends because it had meant taking a day off work.

In Washington, State Department spokesman Ken Brown said:

"Mr. Morris was a respected member of his profession who had ably covered events in the Middle East for many years."

In Guilford, Conn., Morris' father told UPI:

"It was a very tough assignment. He was getting tired and hoped to get out before long. But he knew he couldn't get out until something went one way or another."

Morris is survived by his father, his wife and their three daughters. Plans for services were incomplete.

Ulla Morris-Carter

UPI Athens Bureau Chief John Rigos gave the eulogy at the memorial service in Athens after our return from the USA.

Joe Alex Morris

This is not a funeeal oration, not praise for a fallen warrior, although he deserved such a treatment, for he was a front-line fighter for the noble cause of freedom of expression, freedom of information and for people's right to know -- to know everything and to know correctly.

But if we can learn from his example and reaffirm our commitment to the cause he died for, if we make sure his untimely departure from life will not be only a loss, then I think we honor him enough.

He was not the first of our colleagues in Athens to die while performing his duty, and I am afraid he may not be the last: our fight, our struggle for news goes on, and one cannot exclude more the possibility of more casualties. But Joe Alex was a special case. He was a special colleague. He was a special friend, and his loss is felt more by those who knew him, by his colleagues, by us.

I am sure that even those of you who did not know him personally must by now have read his obituary, published in newspapers all over the world, and have known of his oustanding career in the Middle East, in Europe, Africa and in the United States.

He started working at the age of 21, in the Hartford Connecticut bureau of United Press, and from then on, he roamed the world for thirty years, reporting for Newsweek, the Herald Tribune and finally, for the Los Angeles Times. He covered almost every war and revolution of our times, including the various Arab-Israeli wars in the Middle East, the Bay of Pigs invasion of Cuba in 1962, the Indo-Pakistani war, the Lebanon landing by U.S. marines, the civil wars in Lebanon and the Yemen, and numerous other coups and revolutions, ending with the revolution in Iran -- his swansong.

But it was not because of his death, or because of his coverage of any specific situation, or for winning a prize for the best newspaper coverage of the Arab-Israeli war in 1967 that Joe Alex Morris was considered a distinguished reporter and a special colleague. It was everything about him, from A to Z.

Journalists are not like race horses, needing a pedigree as a pre-requisite for success. But it helps. Joe Alex Morris came from a family in journalism. His father, Joe Alex Morris Sr, was an oustanding correspondent, foreign news editor of the United Press, and a successful author. Family background is one thing: education makes for better journalists, and Joe Alex was educated for his job, graduating from Harvard University. And his education never stopped.

over/

Ulla Morris-Carter

He went on educating himself, every day of his life. I remember when
we were both based in Beirut, he had one of the best collections of
books on Middle East affairs. He had read them all, and was always
helpful, because he could tell his friends where to look for information
in his library.

He was also a sportsman. Not only because he kept in shape by jogging
or playing tennis, but by acting like a good athlete. His work was
honest work. What he wrote was true and proven. He never filled pages
because he had to write a story. He never made up stories. The stories
were there, and he discovered them and put them beautifully together,
without superfluous words, without pretension, but with a touch of
humor -- as if imprinting his perpetual smile on them.

One could spend hours reminiscing about time spent working together
in the hot sands of Aden, or the rocky mountains of the Yemen, or the
beaches of Lebanon. His instinct for news always took him there first,
to meet the rest of us. And one cannot forget the tricks fate played
on him, and how graciously he accepted them. Like when he took his wife
to Beirut for their honeymoon, and they were not allowed to stay in
the same hotel room, because they were travelling on passports of
different nationalities, and under different names.

Yes, Joe Alex took all these with grace, and although he was a top
journalist and one of the best foreign correspondents to cross the
Atlantic, he never lost his simplicity of manner, or his kindness. He
never talked down to his younger colleagues; he remained friendly and
unpretentious, always.

Most of those who wrote about his death mentioned his courage. Joe
Alex Morris was a brave man. He was not fearless, but he was brave. He
knew his job exposed him to dangers. He did not like it, but he knew
it was part of his job, and he accepted it.

In Greece, people say that an oil lamp burns in heaven for every man
and woman, and when the oil runs out, the person whose lamp it is, dies.
It is a colorful image of life and death, but I refuse to accept that
such a life as his depended on a heavenly lamp, and that a few more
drops of oil would have sufficed for him to be with us. And yet it was
a few ounces od lead, fired from an unknown weapon, that ended his life,
early in the morning of February 10, in Teheran.

Years ago, the quill pen was the symbol of journalism. Later the typewriter was more becoming. Tomorrow, the microphone or television camera
will be more representative of our job. But for foreign correspondents,
I believe that Joe Alex Morris, with his worn beret and his perpetual
smile, could be a much more appropriate and lasting symbol.

That peculiar start did not prevent his family life from blossoming,
and three beautiful daughters filled the Morris ranks.

Ulla Morris-Carter

Everyone is free,
Free to live, and
    Free to die,
But,
    In his freedom to kill,
He is killing someone
else's
    Freedom to live.

dedicated to my Dad
by Julia A. Morris

Joe Alex Morris jr.
Killed in Tehran on the 10th of February 1979

Commemorative card for Joe Alex Morris Jr., with Julia's poem on the inside.

REMEMBRANCES

Telegrams, telexes and testimonials arrived from friends and family, from ambassadors, ministers and Joe's colleagues—too many to list here. An overriding theme in all letters was the fact of Joe's fairness, his generous spirit, and his willingness to share and to listen.

THE WHITE HOUSE

WASHINGTON

February 13, 1979

To Ulla Morris

I extend my deepest sympathy to you
and your family in your great loss.
I hope the prayers and good wishes of
your family and friends will console
and comfort you in the days ahead.

Sincerely,

Jimmy Carter

Mrs. Joe Alex Morris
Athens-Psychico
Giza 5B
Greece

Ulla Morris-Carter

ROBERT CRICHTON

Dear Joe :

I've started this letter for almost a week now, over
and over. What does one say about a stray bullet that
shatters a window in a strife torn city and almost as
an afterthought takes a life ? It finally occured to
me that there isn't anything to say, nothing that is
meaningful and genuine and makes sense. Which, of course,
is exactly the deepest source of the sadness.

But I can say something else. Quite a few years ago I found
myself at a cocktail party in The Village. It was awful,
filled with fakes. By chance, Joey was there and we both
said , exactly at once : Come on, let's get the hell out
of here. We walked down to his place on King Street. Ulla
was away. He was just getting over a severe bout with
infectuous hepatitis and wasn't supposed to drink but he
had one drink, anyway, and it went to his head, and he
began to talk in the way of someone whose reticence has been
released by alcohol but who isn't drunk. He told me that
his work was a good deal more dangerous than he had ever
let you know or Ulla know. Now that he had children he
wondered if this was fair. He also wondered if he could ever
be as fearless as before. He told me about a number of
situations in which, if just one person decided to turn

Ulla Morris-Carter

ROBERT CRICHTON

about, that suddenly makes some sense out of that
bullets. Bullets were there, at every corner and across
every street there was some chance of injury or death.
Joe knew this, of course, this was the price and risk one
took to hold a job like the one he had mastered.

The death then is, in itself, senseless but the
fact of it is not. The fact of Joe's death is
the fact of where he was, when he was and the fact
that he could not have been anywhere else that day
in all the vastness of the Middle East. We used to
say in the infantry— somewhere out there was just one
bullet with your name on it. If you lasted long enough
it was bound to find you. I think, in the life he chose,
somewhere out there there was always a bullet waiting for
Joe and it finally found him. This is a terrible
thing but he was reporting on a terrible world
and I think there must be some semblance of solace in
allowing oneself to understand, that he wouldn't have
had it any other way, or could have had it any other
way.

Love :

One of Joe's longtime friends, author and writer Bob Crichton, wrote an eloquent touching letter to Joe Sr..

Ulla Morris-Carter

A newsman who gave his life

Joe Alex Morris Jr., killed by a stray bullet Feb. 9 in Tehran, died for you. He would have denied it, would have hated to see the words in print because he detested presumption, exaggeration and sentimentality and because he was a genuinely humble man.

But you are, in consequence of the fact that you are doing what you are doing, a newspaper reader. Joe was a serious man. He believed that a free people had a need and use for and a right to the truth and that its pursuit was simply the most worthwhile endeavor.

"Aw, come off it, Wilson," he would have said to that; and, if I could have persuaded him it was true he would have insisted that it was, nonetheless, unintentional.

We were at Harvard together, good, close friends, getting out, eager to have at the world, in 1949. That Spring we dated girls who knew each other, drank bock beer on the banks of the Charles, snuck off now and then to the Old How-

DAVID B. WILSON

ard and prowled joints like the Napoleon Club, the New Ritz, the Melody Lounge, the Silver Dollar and the 77, which was not yet The Sevens, attempting to convince each other of our extraordinary sophisitication.

Hemingway was our God and His Prophet the Robert Jordan of "For Whom the Bell Tolls." We proposed to equip ourselves with trench coats and .45's and wind up atop some mountain in Spain in sleeping bags with girls resembling Ingrid Bergman, prevailing, although hopelessly outnumbered, over hordes of Fascists.

Then we would, of course, write really good novels about the experience and become inordinately rich and powerful and famous and do good in the world, which the United States, at the time, bestrode colossally. It was all very boyish and innocent and not ignoble, and, in retrospect, I am glad we felt that way.

Joe got a lot closer to the dream than I did. Bored and spinning his wheels at the United Press in Hartford, he took a two-year job with Aramco in Saudi Arabia, which taught him, among other things, Arabic.

He went back to the UP in London, where his father had had the bureau in the glory days of the World War II blitz, and thence to Beirut as UP's first full-time man in the Levant.

He also worked for the old New York Herald Tribune, Newsweek and, finally, the Los Angeles Times, in the Near East and in Bonn and Moscow, always pressing, always straight, pursuing the facts and refusing to settle for less or to shade them.

His copy, which appeared frequently in The Globe, was a marvel of clarity, economy and precision. If a statement appeared in double quotes, you could be sure that it was exactly what the speaker had said. The work was rich with proper names, exact times, defensible numbers. You could rely on it.

in search of the truth

Self-deprecation was his style. In the 25th anniversary report of his Harvard class, there appears the following:

"For reasons difficult to divine, as they always are in these things, your correspondent received the Overseas Press Club's annual award for coverage of the 1967 Arab-Israeli War. The only apparent reason for the choice was that I was the only American correspondent caught in Arab Jerusalem by the outbreak, and had a picture window view of the whole Jordan campaign, something the usually helpful Israelis were denying to correspondents working from their side."

He covered the Yom Kippur War, too, and the revolution in Yemen. He was waiting on the beach when the Marines landed in Lebanon. He covered the Indo-Pakistan fighting in 1965. He had been operating in and out of Beirut the last two years.

He was, in sum, the real thing. He had report-

er's eyes (he would object to that), gray, unblinking, surveying chaos and arranging its details in communicable form.

He was not a media figure or a public personality because he was too shy and too busy. I am sure he had no patience with "news" designed to persuade, ingratiate, otherwise manipulate or coerce the reader or source. He did not think news was supposed to effectuate change or prevent disorder or reinforce ignorance or simply stroke people.

News is supposed to enlighten and inform people, to tell them what's happening, now. That is what Joe did, and for you, and it cost him his life, I suppose that if he had known he had to go, he would have chosen to go quickly, doing the work he respected enough to devote his life to it. I hope so.

David B. Wilson is a Globe columnist.

David Wilson, a close friend of Joe's from Harvard University days, and columnist for the Boston Globe.

Ulla Morris-Carter

Homer Metz, in The Providence Journal:

"It was early in the 1950's and it was his first trip to the Middle East. I was waiting for him at Beirut airport. He had been graduated from Harvard only a few months before and there were still traces of Cambridge fuzz on his pink cheeks. But he was bubbling over with enthusiasm and infectious good cheer. And he asked questions! .. For the next 20 years that part of the world was to be his main base of operations while he established himself as an outstanding authority on Middle Eastern affairs and people. ... One evening long after he has become a seasoned foreign correspondent hemma we had drinks and he was still asking questions. "Do you still believe being a foreign correspondent is important?" I asked. " Oh,yes," he replied. "More so that ever. I wouldn't want to do anything else." "But what about the dangers," I asked."You were taking a chance out there today in the street fighting in Beirut, covering fighting by a lot of madmen whom no one cares much about.' "The dangers aren't as great as those faced by -- say soldiers or combat pilots or police... And telling the people what is happening is important--very important."

"And fun?" I interjected.
"And fun," he acknowledged.

David B. Wilson, the Boston Globe columnist
"Joe Alex Morris Jr believed that a free people had a need and use for and a right to the truth and that its pursuit was simply the most worthwhile endeavor. We were at Harvard together, good, close friends, getting out, eager to have at the world. As a reporter, his copy was a marvel of clarity, economy and precision. You could rely on it. He was, in sum, the real thing. He had reporter's eyes -- gray, unblinking -- surveying chaos and arranging its details in communicable form. News is supposed to inform and enlighten. That is what Joe did and it cost him his life. I suppose that if he had known he had to go, he would have chosen to go quickly, doing the work he respected enough to devote his life to it."
--
Arthur Higbee, UPI
"Joe left many friends -- the reporters who knew and admired him during a long and distinguished career of covering the world. Those who worked with him become his friends He was a reporter's reporter who sought out both the historical and human sides of front page events, reporting them with understanding, depth and compassion. His dispatches made it all look easy. They rarely included the risks to his own life that he sometimes took to report them. He could never stay away from a big story. Perhaps that was why he never took the advice he once gave a younger colleague who covered the Lebanese civil war with him. 'Don't stay in the war corespondent business too long," he said. "There are only so many chances you can take and still stay lucky."

Left: *Homer Metz writing an obit in the* Providence Journal. **Right:** *David Wilson and Arthur Higbee, who was with Joe when he was shot, writing an obit for* UPI.

George Weller, another journalist friend, who resided for years on the island of Cyprus, and who invited us to use his small house and sailboat for our honeymoon in 1959, wrote:

I never had a colleague that I admired and loved more than Joe. His wonderful explosions of invention, his laughter, his pride in you, Ulla, and the girls will remain with me forever.

Good friends and admirers of Joe's work from our early Middle East days, Joe and May Kamalick telexed from Chicago:

We feel a personal loss, one extremely difficult to accept. Our lives were enriched by knowing so decent and gentle a man. Joe was that rare combination of cracker-jack journalist and perfect gentleman. Under pressures of deadline . . . many correspondents become short-tempered. But not Joe, never. Not once did I see or even hear of Joe treating anyone--telex operator or colleague, head of state or cab driver--with less than the most genial and considerate courtesy.

Ulla Morris-Carter

The Toronto Sun, Tuesday February 13, 1979 **11**

Death of a newsman

PETER WORTHINGTON

Journalists who make a specialty of covering wars, revolutions, crises believe there is a god who looks after them. They know there isn't, of course, but they like to pretend it is so.

"Nothing ever happens to journalists," they assure loved ones when they head into the unknown of another trouble spot they've been assigned to cover. And really, it is uncanny how rarely journalists are casualties, considering all the world troubles that are attended by the print and electronic media.

Yet every so often someone is killed which, while it may not mean much to millions who read the item on agency wires, stuns members of the media who knew the victim. So it was with the news that Joe Alex Morris of the Los Angeles Times had been killed by a stray bullet while covering events in Iran.

Joe Morris was one who had seemed indestructible. He had covered nigh every Mideast crisis for well over 20 years. He was something special.

Newsmen who cover crises are a unique clan. They only meet one another at crises, when things are tense and situations fluid. An unusual bond builds among those who share the experience of trouble spots, rather like the camaraderie that develops among front line soldiers who share the experience of battle, or fighters who've tested each other in the ring.

Joe Morris and I had been friends since 1958 when the U.S. Marines landed in Lebanon — the first of innumerable crises that eventually led to the chaos and misery that Lebanon has since become. Morris and I teamed up — I the learner, he the teacher. In those days he was with the now-defunct New York Herald Tribune. Ours was a relationship which benefitted me more than him. But like most in the foreign correspondent business, he was patient and generous with his knowledge and skills.

For 10 years we met at various crises and "ran" together, shared rented cars, covered for each other, tried to think of ways to steal a beat on colleagues and rivals. We met at crises in Lebanon, Syria, Iraq, Jordan, Egypt, Algiers, Cyprus, Pakistan. You can't be a loner covering a revolution. You need help. It's comfortable when you find someone like Joe Morris around.

Joe came by his journalistic credentials naturally. His father was one of the legendary names with United Press. Joe was unflappable, cool, imaginative. He had a wry sense of humor and an ear for anecdotes. He was the compleat foreign correspondent who had rarely lived in America. As much a part of his travelling equipment as his portable Olivetti was his tennis racquet. Joe had an unerring instinct for the nearest tennis court, no matter the crisis in question.

When the Herald Trib folded he went with Newsweek. But that didn't last. Morris was a writer of daily news, not a weekly summarizer of events. He went with the LA Times.

Back around 1959 when Joe was transferred from Beirut to Cairo he met and married a German girl, Ulla. The marriage ceremony was a classic newsman's fiasco. I wrote about in the Toronto Telegram. They were married on an Egyptian religious holiday and had to bribe a staff to serve at the reception. Liquor was forbidden so guests brought their own. At the mandatory civil ceremony preceding the religious one, they had to wait while a sobbing woman registered the death of her father and a woman registered her newborn babe and brought the wailing evidence with her. The commissioner of marriages got their names wrong so officially two other people were wed.

Police burst in on the church service and prevented the playing of Mendelssohn's Wedding March because the composer was a Jew. On their honeymoon in Beirut they still had separate passports and couldn't get a room together. "But we're married!" exclaimed Joe to the hotel clerk whom he knew from his Beirut days.

"Ah, Mr. Morris, things are tougher now, that doesn't work these days," apologized the clerk.

"But we really are married!"

"Naughty Mr. Morris — we can't do that any more." So the honeymoon had separate rooms.

In one of Jordan's recurring crises Joe and I talked our way into King Hussein's entourage (Joe knew the prime minister — later assassinated) and we flew with him to Aquaba where he received the homage of Bedouin shiekhs and we dined on sheeps' eyeballs. Another time in the Lebanese civil war we got into rebel leader (and later prime minister) Saab Salem's camp and interviewed the old rascal. Another time we got caught in a crossfire in the mountains where Kamal Jumblatt rebel stronghold was located.

We witnessed the hanging of a young man named Nabulsi at dawn in Beirut and found afterwards that a defective time-bomb was in the doorway where we watched the unpleasantness. In Algiers when the FLN were street fighting for independence Joe once got a group of us shot at in the old quarter while he hunted for a "fabulous restaurant" that specialized in couscous.

We were together in Cyprus in 1958 to file uncensored copy from Beirut when George Grivas was fighting the British, and nine years later were back and became mandatory "guests" of Turkish soldiers who thought we were Greeks. Joe knew the Turkish commander from an earlier assignment and we ended up eating roast quail.

When I was stationed in Moscow and my Russian translator defected in Beirut, it was Joe Morris I advised her to contact. There was a flurry of press interest in the case but he helped her and didn't write a word. A nice gesture.

Others have died while doing their job. Mostly they quickly become blurred memories. But Joe Morris was something special. He'd lasted so long, so cheerfully, was such a thorough professional who took calcuated risks but was never foolhardy. He had that most prized possession — the respect and friendship of his peers. There are a lot of newsmen who will shed a tear for the loss of one of the best — Joe Alex Morris, 51 foreign correspondent.

Obit by Peter Worthington of the Toronto Sun *who had known Joe since the late 1950's.*

Ulla Morris-Carter

February 10th, 1979

Dearest Ulla,
            Alot of friends and lovers of Joe Alex are
hurting this morning. And we will for a long time;
we will probably for as long as we live. He was
the nonpareil of the craft of foreign corresponding.
So many of us learned so much from him. I still remember, and try to practise, many of the guidelines
he told me in 1961 as I was heading off on my first
foreign assignment. He didn't lecture me; just spoke
like a big brother to one going off on a first love affair.
            I half laughed, half cried when I heard some
TV reporter say on the tube that Joe Alex was "the first
reporter killed in the Middle East...in 15 months."
            Joe Alex was no bloody reporter. He was a
foreign correspondent, a unique breed of noblemen
and knights pursuing truth under the most adverse
conditions. Joe Alex was the epitome of Hemingway's
phrase: "grace under pressure."

Above: *Letter from Jack Nugent, good friend, author and journalist with* Newsweek *amongst others.*

While we were in Guilford, Connecticut, for Joe's memorial service, I noticed that Joe Sr. picked up the mail, glanced at the many envelopes, and then, quickly, let one of the letters disappear under the cushion of the armchair he was sitting in.

"Why are you hiding that light-blue letter you just received?" I asked.

Joe looked somewhat sheepish, but a few minutes later produced the letter.

"I wasn't sure that you or anybody else in this room really wanted to see it," Joe answered.

"But here it is."

RICHARD NIXON

LA CASA PACIFICA
SAN CLEMENTE, CALIFORNIA

February 14, 1979

Dear Joe Alex,

When I read of your son's tragic death I thought back to those days when we first met in 1947.

In my estimation you were one of the best foreign correspondents of our generation. In this time of sadness you can be proud that your son gave his life in carrying on a great family tradition.

With deepest sympathy and warm regards,

Sincerely,

Right: *A letter from former president Richard Nixon to Joe Sr.*

Ulla Morris-Carter

TO MRS ULLA MORRIS
ATHENS

ON BEHALF OF THE BEIRUT PRESS CORPS, I EXPRESS OUR PROFOUND
GRIEF AT THE LOSS OF OUR RESPECTED AND LOVED
COLLEAGUE AND FRIEND, JOE. HIS PERSONAL INTEGRITY AND
HIS PROFESSIONALISM, FOR WHICH HE GAVE HIS LIFE,
WERE AN EXAMPLE TO ALL OF US, AND WE ARE PROUD
TO HAVE BEEN HIS COLLEAGUES. HIS FRIENDLINESS
AND KINDNESS MADE HIM ALWAYS A WELCOME VISITOR AMONG HIS
OLD AND NEW FRIENDS HERE IN BEIRUT. PLEASE ACCEPT OUR
MOST HEARTFELT CONDOLENCES AT THIS CRUEL LOSS.
JIM MUIR, SECRETACY, FOREIGN CORRESPONDENTS' CLUB IN
LEBANON.

1Q1Q2 RIGOS. WORDS ARE INADEQUATE, BUT PLEASE TELL ULLA
AT THE APPROPRIATE MOMENT THAT ALL OF US IN BEIRUT WHO KNEW
JOE, ADMIRED HIM AND TREASURED HIS FRIENDSHIP, WERE SHOCKED
AND SADDENED BY HIS DEATH. HE WAS AN EXAMPLE TO ALL OF US OF
EVERYTHING GOOD THIS PROFESSION STANDS FOR AND WE WILL MISS
HIM TERRIBLY. HEARTFELT CONDOLENCES.
    PEARCE TEMKO ZENIAN HAJJ

1Q11Q RIGOS. JOHN PLJASE ONPASS ULLA MORRIS. THE LOSS OF JOE
SADDENED AND SHOCKED EVERYONE WHO KNEW HIM IN LEBANON. WORDS
CANNOT REFLECT THE DEPTH OF OUR GRIEF AND HIS MEMORY WILL REMAIN
ALIVE WITH US. PLEASE ACCEPT OUR HEARTFELT CONDOLENCES.
ABDUL HAJJAJ
NEWSWEEK-BEIRUT

LOS ANGELES CA 90053

OLD FRIENDS OF JOE ALEX MORRIS, JR. ARE APPAULED BY THIS ANGUISHING

TURN OF EVENT. NO SECRET TO ANYONE, BUT HE WAS THE DEAN OF ALL OF US

IN THE MIDDLE EAST--RIGHT MAN, RIGHT TIME, AND IN THE END TRAGICALLY

AT THE WRONG LITTLE PLACE. MY FIRST REACTION IS BLIND ANGER, AND

THERE IS NOTHING MEANINGFUL TO SAY IN THE WAY OF CONDOLENCE ACCEPT

TO OBSERVE THAT HE WAS THE FINEST OF THE BREED. AND A STUPENDOUS

HUMAN BEING.

    GAVIN SCOTT, TIME MAGAZINE-SAN FRANCISCO

TERRIBLY SHOCKED BY NEWS OF JOE'S DEATH. HE WAS A JOURNALISTS'
JOURNALIST AND A DEAR AND RESPECTED FRIEND. IF THERE IS ANYTHING
I CAN DO TO HELP, PLEASE CABLE NEWSWEEK JERUSALEM OR CALL ME
AT (02) 228367 OR (02)-60914. I SHARE YOUR GRIEF AND THE
CHILDREN'S.
    MIKE KUBIC

Both Pages: *A small selection of the hundreds of personal and professional telexes that poured in to Athens and to the L.A. Times over the days following the news of Joe's death.*

Ulla Morris-Carter

To Otis Chandler, Los Angeles Times<

From Don Graham, Washington Post<

<

On behalf of all of us at the Post, please accept our heartfelt condolences on the death of Joe Alex Morris. He was a professional in the very best sense of the term, a journalist by whom many of his colleagues set the standard for their own work. Please also relay our sympathy to the Morris family.<

TERRIBLY SHOCKED TO HEAR YOUR TRAGIC NEWS. IT DEPRESSES US MORE THAN WE KNOW HOW TO SAY.

OUR DEEPEST SYMPATHIES,

MARIA AND CHRIS BYRON

TIME MAGAZINE

ALL OF US AT THE NEW YORK TIMES ARE DEVASTATED BY THE NEWS OF JOE ALEX MORRIS JR. S DEATH IN TEHERAN.

ON BEHALF OF THE PUBLISHER AND ALL HERE WE EXTEND OUR DEEPEST SYMPATHIES TO HIS FAMILY, FRIENDS AND COLLEAGUES.

MY GRIEF AT THE DEATH ON THE FIRING LINE OF BEAUTY *duty* OF MY LONG TIME FRIEND YOUR CORRESPONDENT JOE ALEX MORRIS JUNIOR HE WAS A BRAVE BRILLIANT AND HONEST MAN

CARLETON BEALS
KILLINGWORTH CT

DEAREST ULLE, OUR HEARTS AND PRAYERS ARE WITH YOU. THE SEARING QUESTION OF WHY IT HAPPENED TO YOU. YOU WHO WERE ALWAYS COURAGEOUS, SUCH A SUPPORT TO US ALL. WE WHIMPERED. YOU UNDERSTOOD THAT ADRENELIN, THAT COMPULSION TO ALWAYS BE ON THE ROAD: THAT ATTEMPT TO SEE THROUGH THE INJUSTICE, TO DISCIPHER THE INEXPLICABLE AND PROJECT AN ESSENCE OF TRUTH. YOU DEAR ULLE WHOM WE LOOKED TO AS AN EXAMPLE, HAD THAT INNER STRENGTH OF KNOWLEDGE, BORNE OF A LOVE THAT WAS CONSISTENT AND TRUE. EYE CAN COME TO ATHENS ON SUNDAY, OR LATER, WHENEVER EYE CAN BE OF MOST SUPPORT TO YOU. MYRKA CAN REACH ME EASILY. DEAN JOINS ME IN SENDING LOVE, REMEMBRANCE, AND SORROW, MARY ANNE.

Ulla Morris-Carter

February 29 1979

Dear Ulla,

Damn, damn, damn! It rang in my head on the Saturday
in question, a mere echo of the anger and sadness that
you must feel.
I was thinking a few days ago that there are some women
who on the death of their husbands receive letters
which surprise them. How little of the anger, sadness and
loss must have surprised you.

I think I only once ever saw Joe Alex express the
slightest sign of egocentricity. Walking with him, to
the Ayatollah's compound that week we noticed another
correspondent in front of us wearing a beret similar
to his.
" What's he doing?" I asked, " wearing that?" Joe Alex
gave me a look as if to suggest that the latest
poacher should be dealt with albeit gently.

Two things always struck me about him, the one his
modesty, the other, how much we who were greener
had to learn from him.
The third and in most ways the most important is the
vision of you both dancing the night away at Gleneagles
such a short while ago. Having so often sacrificed
my own personal life for the myth of a more exciting
professional pursuit I had a pang of envy - and learned
a lesson as well.
And what of you now? Will you remain in Athens, return
to Germany, go elsewhere? I'd like to know.
I'd also like to know if there is anything you need
done here though I suspect not. I spend at least two
days a week in Germany so if there is anything you
need there with which I can help please say so.
Not an easy letter to write - they must not be easy
to read either.

with affection

Above: *Condolence letter from Peter Jennings, ABC news anchor, journalist and personal friend.* **Below:** *A Letter from Jess Lukomski, good friend and tennis partner of Joe's, and journalist for the* Journal of Commerce.

It seems so hollow and almost sacrilegeous to say
that I have lost a true friend, a man I admired for his
courage in confronting adversities of life, a witty companion,
a respected colleague. But saying it puts in perspective
the enormity of your loss and my inadequacy to make it any
smaller. Yet I hope that sharing with you and the girls
your sorrow and desolation will help to make it more bear-
able.

"Le roi ist mort, vive le roi" - may Joe's
memory, his philosophy of life, and his zest to live it
fully, be both an inspiration and solace to all of you -
the king that is gone and yet lives.

I know dearest Ulla it will not be easy. But
like your mother, I also know that you are a very brave
girl indeed, a genuine human being with all those superior
qualities that it takes to come to terms with the senseless cruelty of fate, and to carve out for yourself and
the girls a life worth living.

Ulla Morris-Carter

Good-by, my friend

Georgie Anne Geyer

HUNDREDS of people have died in Iran. Every day these last tumultuous weeks, the ghastly toll went higher.

So why, one might ask, should we of the press care so much about one lone journalist, Joe Alex Morris Jr., who also died there? Is it professional chauvinism?

Those of us who knew the Los Angeles Times star correspondent loved him because he was the finest gentleman in the foreign press corps. While others flaunted their flamboyant nonabilities, this handsome, witty man quietly used his abilities.

He didn't want or need to "kill kings," a la Woodward and Bernstein, he just wanted to report on them. He was, indeed, reporting—brilliantly as always—on today's most violent killing of a king when he was shot in the heart last weekend and carried away over the heads of the mobs.

But there is a special reason why even those who did not know Joe Alex, a symbol now, should mourn and remember him. Unlike the Iranians—whose war it is, after all—he didn't have to be there.

He didn't have to, and yet he had seen them all. The '67 war in the Middle East, the Bay of Pigs, Cyprus. He and his wife stayed in Beirut through the last awful days. Three decades of war after war after war—and always he went, not for money, not for fame, not for kicks. For what, then? Why be the person who didn't have to be there?

Joe Alex felt as most of my colleagues feel. He knew that he was the person in between, playing a unique role. Neither for one side, nor the other, the clean sieve

JOE ALEX
MORRIS JR.

through which not only information but ultimately truth passes.

It takes a special kind of commitment —a kind not much in vogue these days.

He saw and communicated nearly three decades of the only truths we can really know—the truths we see with our own eyes—and he felt honored by the chance. He went to Tehran eager, he said, to study this "classical revolutionary situation."

But being this "person in between" means you often sow what others reap. Joe Alex sowed the mistakes of American diplomats and the shah and Savak and people he never dreamt of. And he was far more often right than any of them. And there is something else there today.

When Joe Alex started, being a foreign correspondent was a glamorous and respected business. You had special protection, much of it psychological, because you were recognized as a neutral. You had the protection of the then-power of your country.

It is enormously to his credit that he stayed in the profession, continuously risking his life in its genuine cause, while many others dropped out while and after it changed.

Today, the foreign correspondent is the target. The enemy. A threat. The representative of a nation no longer feared but often hated. The scapegoat for others' failings.

Saturday morning, early, he was the target. He got up at 6 and by 9 this reporter's reporter, this correspondent's correspondent, was dead. He had only arrived two hours before, and he told his friends "Maybe this one I should leave to the wires." But of course he didn't.

Good-by, my friend.

Fellow journalist, friend and syndicated columnist Georgie Anne Geyer's obit about Joe.

Ulla Morris-Carter

IN MEMORIAM

TEHRAN Jo

IT WAS an irony of the Iranian Revolution that the only journalist killed in action during the tumultuous events of the last year happened to be an American — Jec Alex Morris of the Los Angeles Times. Only a week before his colleague from the same paper Don Schanche had been injured while covering the bloody clashes in front of Tehran University which were the prelude to the final Battle of Tehran. As Schanche was wheeled on to a departing plane by his colleagues, he wheeped with delight. But for Morris who returned to replace him destiny reserved a more tragic ending.

Morris covered wars, riots and rebellions in every part of the world. With puzzling serenity, he never hesitated to go to the front line of the battle, whether it was in Yemen or Beirut. Having just passed the age of 50, one might have thought that caution would get the better of curiosity — and yet again it was his fearless curiosity which made him rush to the scene of the Farahabad Battle early Saturday morning. Though he could not have guessed it, he was watching the start of the momontous Battle of Tehran, the battle that in 24 hours was to stun the world and become a landmark in history. A stray bullet killed the veteran journalist and war correspondent and he never lived to see what surely would have delighted him, the final liberation of Iran. With great courage, he championed the Palestinian cause and his honest reporting of the Lebanese civil war aroused the instant enmity of the Falangist. Morris was respected for his fairness, his untiring quest for the truth, his willingness to listen, to learn, to observe. He exuded an aura of serenity — but he made short shrift of the cruel or the callous. Among the press corps covering the Iranian Revolution from the Intercontinental Hotel he was loved as a humorous and very human elder statesman.

THE TEHRAN JOURNAL TAKES THIS OPPORTUNITY TO CONVEY ITS CONDOLENCES TO THE WIFE AND CHILDREN OF JOE ALEX MORRIS AS WELL AS TO THE LOS ANGELES TIMES.

Memorial Missives from Iran.

Left: *Tehran Journal obit.*
Below: *Telex from the Shah's Imperial Embassy of Iran.*
Bottom: *Letter from the Secretary of the Ayatollah Khomeini-In-Exile, in Paris, to L.A.Times Paris Bureau Chief Don Schanche.*
Translation: Messieures,
It is with great regret that we received the news of the death of Joe Alex Morrison *(sic)*, your correspondent in Teheran, whom we regard as among the martyrs to liberty.
Believe, Messieurs that we share your sorrow and your pain.
Secretariat of the Ayatollah in Paris.

A   MRS JOE ALEX MORRIS JR   AHENS PSYCHICO

DIAMANTIDON 72

ON BEHALF OF HIS EXCELLENCY AMBASSADOR ZAHEDI MYSELF AND THE STAFF OF THE IMPERIAL EMBASSY OF IRAN I WISH TO CONVEY TO YOU AND YOUR FAMILY OUR HEARTFELT CONDLENCES FOR THE UNTIMELY AND UNEXPECTED DEATH OF YOU BELOVED HUSBAND WE SHARE TH GRIEF OF PASSING OF THIS COURAGEOUS JOURNALIST WITH ALL OF YOU   SINCERELY
ALI A.TABATABAI PRESS COUNSELOR   COL 72

Los Angeles Times
73,Ave. des Champs-Elysées
Paris

Paris ,le 12 Fév. 1979

Messieurs,
c'est avec beaucoup de regret que nous avons reçu la nouvelle du décés de Joe Alex Morisson,votre correspondant à Téhéran,que no us considérons parmi les martyrs de la liberté.

Croyez , Mes sieur ,à ce que nous partageons vos chagri ns et vos douleurs.

Secretariat de l'Ayatollah à
Pari s,

Ulla Morris-Carter

JOHN LAW   2-11-79pr0

TRIBUTE TO JOE ALEX MORRIS JR.

    Joe Alex Morris Jr. was the best foreign correspondent
I have ever known. I say this unreservedly, and I say this
on the basis of having watched him at work from close quarters
over a span of more than two decades--perhaps longer than any
other of his colleagues.

    Joe, however, was in a class by himself when the
performance of what is the basic job of a foreign correspondent:
finding out where the important news is likely to be; going and
getting it, whatever the obstacles; making sure his facts are
right; and putting them together quickly in a way that would
interest and inform his readers. Among the tools he brought to
his tasks were guts, persistence, curiosity, industry, shrewdness
and dedication.

    In Tehran, Joe ran out of luck. If he had been
a different person, he might be alive today. But he could
never have gotten himself to cover the story in any different
way than he did. I grieve for his family. But I also sorrow
for the fact that there will be no more new foreign correspondents
who will have a chance to watch Joe operate and see exactly how
the job ought to be done.

Selections from a letter written by John Law, U.S. News and World Report, *long-time journalist friend.*

Ulla Morris-Carter

Los Angeles Times

HARRISON GRAY OTIS, 1882-1917
HARRY CHANDLER, 1917-1944
NORMAN CHANDLER, 1944-1960

OTIS CHANDLER
Publisher and Chief Executive Officer

TOM JOHNSON
President and Chief Operating Officer
WILLIAM F. THOMAS
Executive Vice President and Editor

CHARLES C. CHASE, Vice President—Operations
ROBERT L. FLANNES, Vice President and Assistant to the Publisher
JAMES B. GRIDER, Vice President—Production
ROBERT C. LOBDELL, Vice President and General Counsel
DONALD S. MAXWELL, Vice President and Controller
VANCE L. STICKELL, Vice President—Sales

GEORGE J. COTLIAR, Managing Editor
ANTHONY DAY, Editor of the Editorial Pages
JEAN SHARLEY TAYLOR, Associate Editor

MONDAY, FEBRUARY 12, 1979

Joe Alex Morris Jr.

Joe Alex Morris Jr.'s reporting from the Middle East graced American journalism for 25 years, the last 14 of them for this newspaper. He was the most experienced American correspondent in that tumultuous stretch of land from the eastern Mediterranean to western Asia, and he was regarded by many of his colleagues as, quite simply, the best.

One reason he held that rank is that he was always there, at the front line of wars, revolutions, coups and upheavals; so it was that he died at 51 in the early morning hours Saturday outside an Iranian air base on the outskirts of Tehran, hit in the chest by a bullet as he was looking out of a window at the confused fighting outside. Those who watched him over the years put his life at hazard in the service of the story he was covering were awed by his almost jaunty personal courage, as were those

who knew of his successful battle against lymphatic cancer five years ago.

But it was not just being there, on the big story, that made Morris the foreign correspondent he was. He brought to his readers an understanding not only of what was happening, but also why, as far as he could discern it; he had a knowledge of the Arab and Moslem worlds rare in American journalism, and he shared that understanding with both his readers and his professional colleagues.

Joe Alex Morris Jr. had the best qualities of a professional newspaper man: a quick and sympathetic curiosity about the people, whoever they were, he was writing about; a wholly undogmatic view of men, ideas and events; and the ability to convey his understanding in clear, straightforward prose. His work and his life honored this newspaper and his profession.

Anthony Day, personal friend and editor of the L.A. Times' *editorial pages, wrote this touching piece a day after Joe's death.*

Letters to The Times

The Death of Joe Alex Morris Jr.

Joe Alex Morris Jr.'s death was a sad and shocking event. His reports from Iran filled a void for those who sought accurate and detailed news from that country. Now, once again, a bullet has put an end to the life of a man whose merits must be appreciated against a deep sense of loss.

Mr. Morris's death is a loss for The Times and to all of his readers—and in a very keen way that loss is registered on the Iranian readers in this country.

D. A. SHOJAI
La Jolla

A reader from Richmond, VA:

Rarely have I been as moved by any newspaper stories as I recently have been by the Middle East dispatches of Joe Alex Morris, Jr. The reporting has been superb and the writing truly first class, grabbing the reader by the arm and taking him on a guided tour of the land, showing the people and their problems in a clear and human way.

Ulla Morris-Carter

FEBRUARY, 1979

Joe Alex Morris had to be where the action was

Joe Alex Morris Jr.

Joe Alex Morris Jr. just could not stand to be away from the action, and it was to cost him his life early the morning of Feb. 10 while observing the fighting in the outskirts of Tehran.

He had had many close calls in the years of covering the wars and skirmishes in the Middle East, but the memory of those escapes did not ever deter him from getting up to the front row.

It was typical of Joe Morris to do as he did that fatal Saturday morning. Alerted to the outbreak of fighting at the airfield, he scrambled out of bed, and along with three other American reporters, took a taxi to the scene.

When bullets began to hit the building from which the newsmen were watching the fighting, they dropped to the floor, then got up and returned to the second-floor window. It was then that Morris was shot in the chest.

Arthur Higbee, chief of the Paris bureau of United Press International, who was one of the four, said that Morris was the first to return to the window. "It was typical of Joe —always the first one," he said.

Bill Tuohy, Times London bureau chief, and Don Cook, chief of the Paris bureau, who had been in Tehran a few days before Morris was killed, said in their story which appeared the day following his death, that "When Morris was on a story, he never stopped, never slowed. Fear simply had no part in his makeup, no place in his appetite for work."

Along with Bob Toth and Cook, who with him covered the 6-Day Israeli-Arab war in 1967, Morris had his share of close shaves.

In a piece written for Among Ourselves at that time, Bill Fox, assistant to the Foreign editor, told of Joe's arrest by Jordanians when he went to police headquarters to file his story in the first day of fighting. He was confined to a dank cell until being released after a Jordanian newsman interceded.

"Back at the hotel he tried to sleep that Monday night," Fox wrote. "But the noise of the battle was too much. So he went up on the roof to watch the war raging around the city that night and the next day. A sniper shot a light out over his head, so he said he tried to keep it down after that."

Then, a couple of days later, while driving east to the Jordan River with other

Continued from First Page

Joe and Ulla had been shot at while driving to the mountain resort of Brumanna, about 40 minutes out of Beirut, where their two younger daughters were attending a British boarding school. (The oldest girl, Maria, was in a boarding school in Switzerland.)

In April, Morris said, "Christian big guns up around Brumanna began shelling West Beirut, where we live, and the artillery down at the military beach, just below our house, was answering back.

correspondents, his car rounded a curve and was stopped by two Bedouins in full battle gear and automatic weapons. Credentials meant nothing to the illiterate tribesmen, but they finally took cognizance of the Jordanian license plates on the car and let the party go on its way.

During this period, because everyone on both sides was busy fighting, Morris took advantage of the situation to "move around the city and the countryside—violating the curfew and successfully avoiding getting shot."

In September of 1967, while on home leave, Morris appeared in the Harry Chandler Auditorium to assess the Mideast situation for Times employees.

He told the audience that his wife, Ulla, and three daughters, then 7, 3 and 1½, were still living in Beirut despite all of the turmoil. When a group of shouting demonstrators approached the area in which their apartment was situated, Ulla took the girls into the apartment and closed the shutters leading to the balcony.

Shortly, she missed the girls. They had opened the shutters and were strutting back and forth on the balcony, shouting, along with the demonstrators, "Nasser! Nasser! Nasser!" "I felt after that, that we were safe," Ulla said.

His coverage of that war earned him the 1968 Overseas Press Club Award for the best daily newspaper or wire service reporting of foreign affairs. (The hand-printed citation read "wine service.") In Joe's absence, his father, a renowned foreign correspondent in his own right, proudly accepted the award at the annual OPC dinner.

From 1968 to 1975, Morris headed the Bonn bureau, but returned to Beirut in time to get in on another war.

Writing in Among Ourselves in May of 1976, he told of moving his family to Athens as the fighting increased.

Please Turn to Page 6

"The shelling went on all week. That Thursday, Ulla and the kids were walking down Rue Bliss on their way back from shopping when they were caught in the open by a Christian salvo.

"One of the three shells hit a third-floor balcony just as Karin and Julia were walking under it. They were showered with concrete and dust but fortunately not hit by shrapnel. Karin was deafened for 10 minutes thereafter, the sound was so bad.

"For me, that was the last straw. We flew out to Athens the next week, just as soon as brother Jack Foisie arrived from Cairo."

(Joe maintained the bureau in Beirut for some time, but as things worsened, he packed up and moved everything to Athens, where he was headquartered at the time of his death.)

In their piece, Tuohy and Cook said that Morris "earned a reputation second to none in a quarter-century as a front-line reporter in the Middle East.

"He was the most experienced American in that volatile region, universally respected for his integrity and professionalism."

Their assessment of Morris was borne out by his colleagues from other American newspapers.

Jonathon C. Randal of the Washington Post said that "Joe . . . was simply the best guy in the Middle East. He kept at the job ceaselessly for a quarter of a century; he was enormously respected."

And R.W. Apple Jr. of the New York Times said, "When other reporters arrived in Iran or some other Middle East trouble spot, they first turned to Joe Alex Morris for help. He never failed them. He knew the region as few Americans did and he delighted in sharing his knowledge.

"In Tehran, typically he worked punishingly long hours. Even when he finished dictating a story to Los Angeles at 3 a.m., he would be down in the hotel lobby at 8, blue beret clamped on his head, ready for another interview or another tour of that tormented city."

It is ironic that Morris was the first U.S. reporter to be killed in the revolt against the rule of Shah Mohammed Reza Pahlavi, for it was he who made it possible for the late Jim Bassett, then associate editor of The Times, and then-Editor Nick Williams to be the first Western newsmen to enter the shah's new palace.

This happened early in 1967 when Bassett and Williams were traveling throughout the Mideast on a fact-finding tour.

Following their trip, Bassett wrote in Among Ourselves, "Joe was born a generation too late. He should have been Lawrence of Arabia.

"He doesn't cast sheep eyes, he eats them. He dotes on fermented yoghurt, seltzerized for drinking purposes. He travels light, disdains creature comfort, and is a whale of a good guide."

Morris joined The Times in 1965 after working in the Middle East for United Press, now United Press International, the New York Herald Tribune and Newsweek magazine from 1950.

Before he left for Athens to be with Joe's family, Foreign Editor Bob Gibson said:

"The tragic death of Joe Alex Morris Jr. is a loss not only to his family, friends and colleagues but to the millions of readers with whom, over many years, he shared his insights into the Arab world and his unique knowledge of the Middle East. Joe never settled for less than the best information, regardless of personal risk or hardship. Ultimately, his determination for quality cost his life. Joe was proud of his profession; the profession is even more proud of Joe Alex Morris Jr. He set standards for us all."

Obit from "Among Ourselves", the L.A. Times' internal paper.

Ulla Morris-Carter

WARNING: ALTERATION, ADDITION OR MUTILATION OF ENTRIES IS PROHIBITED.
ANY UNOFFICIAL CHANGE WILL RENDER THIS PASSPORT INVALID.

NAME
JOE ALEX MORRIS JR.

BIRTH DATE
JUNE 1, 1927

BIRTHPLACE
COLORADO, U.S.A.

HEIGHT
5 FEET 10 INCHES

HAIR
BROWN

EYES
BLUE

WIFE
X X X

ISSUE DATE
FEB. 5, 1975

MINORS
X X X

EXPIRATION DATE FEB. 4, 1980

SIGNATURE OF BEARER

IMPORTANT: THIS PASSPORT IS NOT VALID UNTIL SIGNED BY THE BEARER. PERSONS
INCLUDED HEREIN MAY NOT USE THIS PASSPORT FOR TRAVEL UNLESS
ACCOMPANIED BY THE BEARER.

PHOTOGRAPH ATTACHED

U. S. IMMIGRATION
020 BOS. 15

JUL 21 1975

ADMITTED_____
                              (Class)
UNTIL

Joe's passport, picture page, with the blood-stained edges from having it in his shirt pocket when he was shot.

LEAVING ATHENS

When I unlocked the door to our house on Gizi Street, I was greeted by a chilly orderliness more suitable to a hospital than to our normally warm and often messy house.

Why did everything look so unfamiliar? The house was the same, furniture stood where I was used to seeing it, the kitchen was clean, and the black and white concrete floor in the front hall was polished, but still ugly. Gone was the exuberant noise of children's voices that I was used to. Missing was the life that our house always exuded.

It seemed as if I had been away for an eternity. I felt weary and old and aimless. Before we had departed for the United States the scene had been hectic and chaotic, a house filled with people moving at rapid speed, making telephone calls, closing suitcases and helping Julia, Karin and me get to the airport on time. Now all this lay behind us. An eerie silence had settled over the house. Ireni, our indomitable Greek cleaning lady, had obviously cleared the house of all the debris we had left behind. It looked almost unoccupied. Though the sun was shining, the old house felt cold. It had not been heated since we left.

Karin and Julia raced upstairs, delighted to be home and to see their belongings and their treasures again. Unlike me, they resumed life where they had left off, calling their friends, gossiping about school projects and teenage problems. I was grateful when the house began to fill with noise again. Even the clutter of half-emptied suitcases was a welcome site. Anything to make the house look lived in.

I collapsed into a chair, jet-lagged, bone-tired and desperately wishing to turn back the clock. But before I had time to feel too sorry for myself, Ute and Ginny appeared in the door, flowers in hand, smiling and cheerfully welcoming me home.

Ulla Morris-Carter

"You have been spoiled long enough now!" Ute announced in no uncertain terms. "Time to move on!"

"Yes, yes, I'll try. But where do I start?"

How can they be so insensitive? How can I just restart where I left off three weeks ago? Nothing is the same, never will be the same, and nothing is normal. Do they not know that I feel rootless, that I feel like a feather blown around in the wind, that I have lost my anchor, my grounding?

"And where do we belong anyway?" I said aloud.

Of course, these two dear friends understood, all they wanted was to help me over the first hurdle. But there was no escaping the fact that sooner rather than later I had to make still more decisions. First, where were we going to live? Germany or America? And if America, Washington or Los Angeles?

Germany was a possibility. Günther van Well, long-time friend and then state secretary at the Foreign Office in Bonn, suggested I return to Germany and take on a job at the Foreign Office. I was grateful for the suggestion, but after days of weighing the pros and cons, decided against it. Schools were an issue for the children. Although they spoke German, they had never attended German schools and did not know the German school system. As for me, I had to consider job security and my future.

The *Los Angeles Times*, on the other hand, held a protective umbrella over my head, assuring me of their help and assistance. Joe was the first correspondent killed while covering a story for the *Times*. The *Times* felt a certain responsibility for my children and me. Karin had a suggestion.

"Why can't we move to Singapore?"

"Singapore? Why Singapore?" I asked. "We have no ties to Singapore at all."

"Well, my friend Susan is moving there," Karin replied. "Her father was just transferred there. It sounds much more interesting than America or Germany."

There were discussions with the U.S. Charge d'Affairs, Hawk Mills, who was from Berkeley. He favored California. There were discussions with Washington friends who felt that Washington would be just my cup of tea. I had a number of friends in Washington, but in the back of my head, there was always the question of how long I would be able to ride on the shirttails of my friends? In Los Angeles I knew practically nobody. How difficult would it be to start totally anew? Los Angeles and the *Times* were a contact with our past, but might it be helpful to pack away the past?

Three months after Joe's death, in May 1979, the *Los Angeles Times* asked me to return to the United States for a short, informational visit. The children, still in school until their summer break in June, remained in Athens with friends.

My first stop was New York, where the U.S. Immigration and Naturalization Services granted me a Green Card, a Resident Alien permit that allowed me to work in the

Ulla Morris-Carter

U.S. This represented a major achievement after only two months of intensive work, supported by Clair George, the U.S. Embassy Political Councilor, and a few other influential friends. I had never lived in the U.S. for any length of time and had no work permit. With Joe's death I had lost my only official sponsor. My children were all under 21 and could not sponsor me. Everybody around me was incredulous that after 20 years of marriage to an American, I had no American residence papers, no Green Card. The explanation was fairly simple. We had always lived abroad, and it hadn't seemed to be an important issue. I considered my German passport just as valuable as an American one. Now, however, the issue had become important.

How could I work in the U.S. or take on a job with the *Los Angeles Times* without a Green Card? Cokie and Steven Roberts, our friends and neighbors in Athens, were now back in Washington and offered help. Cokie's mother, Congresswoman Lindy Hale Boggs, the chairwoman of the National Democratic Convention in 1979, could put in a "private bill" for me, suggested Cokie. *Los Angeles Times* Publisher Otis Chandler offered to support it. In the end none of these somewhat drastic measures were needed.

While I was in New York, the Overseas Press Club of America invited me to their annual awards celebration. Bob Gibson, the *Los Angeles Times* foreign editor, flew in from Los Angeles and accompanied me. The Press Club celebrated the accomplishments of American journalists at its annual black-tie dinner, presenting awards for best reporting on foreign news, interpretation of foreign affairs, magazine writing, photography, news analysis and best book on foreign affairs.

This evening, the Overseas Press Club's President's Award was to be given posthumously to Joe.

When I arrived at the Press Club, Joe Sr. and Jane Condliffe, his long-time companion, plus a number of our closest friends were already there. I was so happy to see Joe Sr. again and to have him next to me as my great supporter and friend. Joe Sr. had been honored a number of times for his outstanding reporting and writing. Now he was to accept the award for his late son, one of his saddest moments, he told me later. He was proud to see his son honored, but the loss was still too new.

The President's Award was the last to be presented. The Master of Ceremonies read the citation:

> The Overseas Press Club of America Presents the President's Award posthumously to Joe Alex Morris, Jr. for his outstanding courage displayed under trying circumstances, who gave his life in the name of Freedom of the Press.

Only three months had passed since Joe had died in Teheran in February, 1979. It was not surprising to see Joe Sr. a little unsteady on his feet when he stood up and walked to the podium. He had barely begun to speak, thanking the Overseas Press Club for the honor, when he began to tremble and his voice faltered.

Ulla Morris-Carter

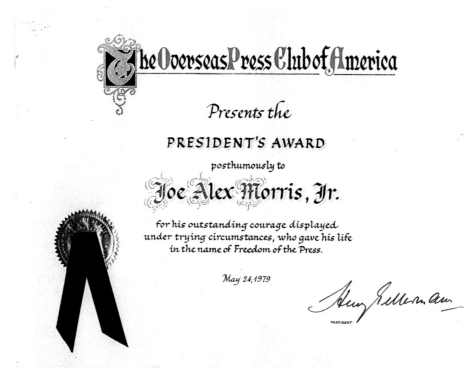

The Overseas Press Club of America

Presents the

PRESIDENT'S AWARD

posthumously to

Joe Alex Morris, Jr.

*for his outstanding courage displayed
under trying circumstances, who gave his life
in the name of Freedom of the Press.*

May 24, 1979

PRESIDENT

Overseas Press Club of America award, presently posthumously to Joe Alex Jr., accepted by Joe Sr..

Unable to continue, he broke down completely. Helpless, I looked around for someone to come to his rescue. When nobody moved, I stood up and walked to the podium, took Joe's hand, put my arm under his and held him tightly by my side. I don't quite remember what I said, but I can still see the sad moment. I thanked the Overseas Press Club on behalf of our family and ended by saying:

"Joe was a very special person, not only to his family, but also to his many friends and colleagues."

There was a moment of silence in this room filled with colleagues of both father and son. Then the room exploded with a standing ovation for both Joe Alex Morrises.

After this emotional event, I was off to Los Angeles.

This time I was invited to stay with the President of the *Los Angeles Times*, Tom Johnson, and his family in San Marino. Before I left New York, Tom Johnson called me at the hotel to inquire which of the following three events I would like to attend while in Los Angeles:

1. See the Los Angeles Rams play football.
2. See the Los Angeles Dodgers play baseball.
3. Attend a performance of the musical *Evita* at the Dorothy Chandler Pavillion.

Ulla Morris-Carter

I had never heard of either the Rams or the Dodgers, nor had I ever seen either sport being played, so I opted for "Evita," which turned out to be an exciting and excellent performance. More important, I was to visit the *Los Angeles Times* and interview with the Director of Public Relations, Gordon Phillips, for a possible job. The Public Relations Department was located on the third floor of the *Los Angeles Times* building on First and Spring Streets.

I walked up the stairs slowly, trying to gain a little time and self-confidence. The PR department was larger than I had anticipated. In a big well-lit room, 36 employees, ranging from advertising and radio promotion writers to graphic artists, tour guides and speechwriters, were working away on desks and drawing tables.

Gordon Phillips presided over his territory from a glassed-in office near the entrance. He was a grayish-looking man in his fifties with steel-rimmed glasses. He did not exude the joviality of some of his suntanned colleagues. He looked more like a bureaucrat. Under his critical gaze, I felt uncomfortable. There was no good chemistry between us. I realized that I was being forced down his throat by his bosses. He did not appear to be sympathetic to my plight.

At the end of a rather short conversation I asked him:

"Would you hire me if I were not the widow of Joe Alex Morris?"

His answer came quickly and precisely:

"An honest question requires an honest answer. No, I would not hire you. And why should I? I am used to hiring my own people. And beyond that, what qualifications do you have for Public Relations anyway?"

"None, I guess. I have never worked in public relations."

This ended my interview. We exchanged a few pleasantries, shook hands and parted company. Leaving his office I was near tears. So, this was going to be my future, I thought. How could I work in an office where I was not wanted?

What was I to do? How was I to survive? Where else could I go?

Too embarrassed to discuss this matter with Tom Johnson, I decided to say nothing. I did not want to begin my relationship with the *Los Angeles Times* by complaining.

Tom Johnson and his wife Edwina were warm and welcoming hosts during my three-day stay in Los Angeles. It felt good to be in a home rather than a hotel. My days were filled with bureaucratic matters, signing papers and dealing with insurance issues. Evenings I was invited to dinner by caring and helpful people, who introduced me to the pleasures of San Marino and San Gabriel, where, by general consensus, I was supposed to settle with my children. The public school was excellent, they all assured me, and San Marino was a safe place to live.

A lot of the conversation flew by me in a blur. There was simply too much to take in. I was particularly annoyed on the second day when the insurance company questioned

Ulla Morris-Carter

the way Joe died, obviously trying to avoid paying the double insurance due me because of "accidental or shooting death" on the job.

"Maybe he died of a heart attack out of fear," suggested an insurance agent, ignoring the fact that circumstances of Joe's death had been reported in almost every U.S. newspaper.

"Or possibly he died of cancer," he tried, in a second attempt.

I was furious. Yes, Joe had had cancer more than six years ago, but the required autopsy after his death showed that he was completely cancer-free when he died. Foreign Editor Bob Gibson came to the rescue and took over the conversation, threatening to cancel all contracts the *Los Angeles Times* had with the insurance company if they did not immediately stop harassing me. It might have been a small issue under normal circumstances, but for me nothing was normal. I felt vulnerable in a new world that was to be my future home. This is how immigrants or refugees must feel, I thought to myself. In effect, I was an immigrant entering a foreign country.

Whom could I trust, whom could I lean on for comfort, for advice, for counsel? All these charming people wanted to help me, but I had not yet developed a real relationship with any of them.

Tired and worried, I settled into the comfortable first-class seat of Pan American Airlines on my return trip from Los Angeles to Athens via London. I was glad to have a little time to myself.

How are the children doing? I wondered.

They did not look forward to living in the U.S. They loved being among their friends from many countries. Those thoughts floated through my head as I traveled home to Athens to pack up the house and Joe's office. It also meant saying goodbye to many friends.

The end of our life abroad was approaching.

I had to sell the car and wait for a new correspondent to arrive to replace Joe. In his office on the third floor, I sorted files and papers as best I could. I hoped the new correspondent would be patient with me. Often I had been the unpaid secretary of the *Los Angeles Times*, sending telexes and cables, clipping newspapers, taking telephone calls, booking flights and other necessary tasks. But in the months before his death Joe had been away so much and for so long that his office was a mess.

Looking around the house, I became aware of how fundamentally the rituals of our daily lives had already changed. Instead of eating dinner in the dining room, Karin, Julia and I would huddle in a corner of the living room around a small table. There was little, if any, laughter from Karin and Julia. They probably felt that this house could no longer tolerate laughter. And I was the cause of this sad state of affairs. I had not yet reached, and would take a long time to reach, any kind of what the Americans so glibly call "closure." In retrospect, I believe that leaving the house in Athens was probably the best thing that could have happened. But then, in 1979, I could not see it.

Cleaning out closets and giving away Joe's clothes was heartbreakingly difficult.

The packers arrived early in the morning, at least five of them. They spread out all over the house and packed so fast that I couldn't possibly supervise. A number of my friends had promised to help. Where are they, I wondered. I could really use some help, I mumbled to myself when I noticed a dustpan full of dirt being wrapped and packed into a box. By 11 a.m., still nobody. I called Virginia, no answer. And Mary didn't seem to be at home either. Strange, I thought. These loyal friends had been of immeasurable help to me during the past difficult weeks.

At noon Mary arrived, looking pale and tired.

"I am so sorry to be so late," she said breathlessly. "We just couldn't bring ourselves to phone you with this terrible news. But you do need to know," she finally managed to blurt out. "John died last night. All of us immediately rushed to John and Nicky's house to help Nicky."

I was speechless.

"John died? Impossible."

I had seen him and Nicky just two days ago, well and happy and looking healthy John was an American diplomat and a close friend. He and Nicky had been sailing the previous day. Tired from a day out in the open, John went to bed early. Nicky followed an hour later. Expecting him to be asleep, she quietly lay down next to him. He looked as if he were sleeping peacefully, but when she reached over to him, his body was already cold and rigid. John was dead. Nicky screamed for help. The ambulance arrived quickly, but there was nothing left to do other than confirm that he had died of a heart attack. Nicky was inconsolable. A religious woman and a strong believer in God and the church, Nicky had, after Joe's death, tried to console me by suggesting we pray a rosary together.

"You will see that it helps," Nicky had said.

When I visited her after John's death, the first thing she said was: "Ulla, it doesn't work, it doesn't help."

I knew instantly what she meant. One tragedy after another. I was reeling. In what kind of a star-crossed period were we living?

Meanwhile, the Greek packers continued working fast. I didn't realize until I unpacked in Los Angeles, that they had thrown our three precious, ancient Egyptian funerary masks from the Sakkara region in Egypt into the box with the vacuum cleaner, not even bothered to wrap them in paper, let alone individual boxes. Other things fell by the wayside as well.

Ulla Morris-Carter

Knowing that we would never again live in a house as large as this one, I had decided to ship half of our belongings to our old farmhouse in Italy and the other half to the United States. But I discovered that the packers were not paying attention to the stickers I had attached to each piece, yellow to the U.S., green to Italy.

Well, half the ping-pong table ended up in Italy and the other half in Los Angeles. Other items appeared in the wrong place. Garden chairs went to Los Angeles, but their cushions ended up in Italy. In truth, it really did not bother me that much. Too much had happened. Our lives were upside down anyway. Half a ping-pong table was not going to give me a sleepless night.

Doyle McManus, Joe's successor, arrived from Los Angeles. I remembered meeting him in the *UPI* office in Beirut a few years earlier. He had been hired recently by the *Los Angeles Times*. Younger than Joe, Doyle was highly intelligent with a quiet demeanor, and he knew the Middle East well.

Over the next few days, I learned how patient and sympathetic he was. Handing over the office to Doyle, actually our whole house, was the easy part. Handing over our car required the intervention of the Finance Minister of Greece. But shipping our furniture truly tested both of our patience, and my nerves.

"Only he, Joe Alex Morris, Jr., can take the furniture out of Greece. He brought them into this country," announced the Greek Customs official.

The official was a handsome, uniformed Greek, who knew what was required of an official. He showed off his importance in the Customs Office, and was not about to give in to a widow's request, a foreign widow to boot. The fact that I was not dressed in black with a black veil covering my head, probably did not help my case.

"Yes, I know HE brought the furniture in," I agreed, "but HE is no longer."

I tried to be patient, but exasperation grabbed hold of me.

I was nearly sick to my stomach having to watch in silence while this Customs official flipped through the pages of Joe's bloodstained passport, not once, but time and time again. Joe had carried this passport in his breast pocket when he was shot. His passport was a well-traveled document with many additional pages folded in accordion-fashion into the back.

"You see," insisted the Customs official, "it is stated clearly here that HE brought these items into this country. He signed by the side of the entry stamp. You cannot take them out. It is against the law. Only he can take them out," he repeated solemnly. "I don't even know whether your husband meant these items to go to you, or do you have a paper that shows clearly that you are to inherit these items?"

I was speechless. I feared I might break out in tears at any moment. Doyle and I had already spent most of the previous day in the Customs Office, only to be told to come back today to finish the matter. But day two brought no solution. Meanwhile I had

Ulla Morris-Carter

sent Julia and Karin to Germany to my brother's house, where they had the company of their two girl cousins, Nikola and Tanya. I was to follow the next day.

As day three in the Customs Office approached, my brother called to tell me that his wife had to undergo an emergency operation, and he urgently needed me to come to Düsseldorf to look after the four girls. My efficient Customs official remained unmoved. I pleaded with him to speed up the procedure. I knew that before departing, I had to have Joe's passport in my hands and needed the assurance that our belongings would be allowed to leave Greece. I was on the verge of screaming. This system was totally archaic.

Who had ever heard of an official insisting that a dead person was required to sign a paper of release? Sitting with me across from the official, Doyle realized that I was about to explode. Under the table he kicked my shin, gently.

He gave me an intent look that said, "Hang in, we are almost there, don't spoil it now!"

Indeed, on day three, in the afternoon, we finally managed, with help from some influential Greek friends, to receive permission to export our belongings to both Italy and the USA. I raced straight from the Customs Office to the airport to catch a flight to Germany to help my brother.

Joe's blood-stained passport with the Greek exit/entry stamps.

Ulla Morris-Carter

Top: *A promotional photo for an L.A.* Times *advertising campaign that appeared in the paper and all over Los Angeles on billboards and busses. We were all in different colors.* **Below:** *My L.A. Times ID card.*

AN OCEAN
OF UNCERTAINTY

Leaving Europe and the Middle East meant leaving behind the two rivers that had shaped my life. I faced an ocean of uncertainty on the Pacific Coast of America.

"Our new life and our future will start tomorrow," I said to myself, and repeated it to Karin and Julia, aged 14 ½ and 13, who were traveling with me from Greece to California.

It was a journey all of us wished we never had to make. I tried hard to convince myself that I had made the right decision—that moving to Los Angeles would work out in the long run—that living in Los Angeles would be exciting. Joe had been killed six months ago. What choices did I have? What else could I have done?

My oldest daughter, Maria, was already in the United States in her first year at Trinity College in Hartford, Connecticut. My two younger daughters were with me on that flight into our new world—a world we didn't know and that none of us had any desire to live in.

On this first day of September 1979, the temperature at the Los Angeles airport was 101 F. We had only visited Los Angeles twice before—for a few days on home leave from Joe's job as the Middle East Bureau Chief for the *Los Angeles Times*. Joe was not with us now—we were on our own. Los Angeles seemed at the end of the world. Still, we had some things to look forward to: a new job, a new silver-green Volkswagen station wagon, and a temporary home. Why complain?

A new country, a new life. The *Los Angeles Times* had offered me a job. Life goes on, children need to be fed, and college fees have to be paid. But I was neither a journalist

Ulla Morris-Carter

nor a writer, nor was English my mother tongue. So the *L.A. Times* decided I should work in the Public Relations department. I was to deal with foreign visitors, VIPs, education-related issues, seminars and presentations, speaking engagements and many other tasks. I was apprehensive. Having moved many times in my life, I knew that every move is traumatic. This change, however, beat all others. There was nobody to consult, nobody to commiserate with, and, worst, nobody who shared my past.

Bob Gibson, the foreign editor of the *Los Angeles Times*, picked us up at the airport. Trying to ease us gently into our new world, and hoping to make our entry into Los Angeles more exciting, he took us to dinner at a colorful Pasadena restaurant. If the temperature was 101°F at the airport, it felt more like 104°F in Pasadena. I knew about high temperatures and heat from the Middle East and also from Athens, where, in the summer, the asphalt would be so hot that ones heels sank into it.

Judging by the crowd of early diners, the restaurant was obviously a landmark, very well frequented. Its red roof, covered with fake snow, proudly showed off some Bavarian-style features. Was it a ski hut or a mountain cabin, I asked myself? The floor of the restaurant was covered wall-to-wall with peanut shells.

"I hope this will make you feel comfortable. No restrictions on the children—they can just join in and shell peanuts," Bob Gibson said encouragingly.

I was in a state of shock. I had never seen a place like this before.

"When is the next flight out of Los Angeles?" I asked myself, knowing full well that I was here to stay.

Our furniture and our personal belongings were floating on some ocean vessel, supposed to arrive soon at Long Beach Harbor. And the three of us also felt as if we were floating on an unknown ocean, drifting along, without a safe harbor in sight.

But we soon began our new life. I started my job in Public Relations at the *Los Angeles Times*. My two children registered reluctantly at the local public high school in San Marino. They never told their classmates why we had come to Los Angeles.

"We were transferred," they would say when asked.

Not even their teachers knew their story—as I only found out later. They never revealed their past.

My job was demanding. There was much to learn. I tried to do the right thing. A long commute made the day even longer. Leaving the house at 7:30 a.m., I hardly made it home before 7 p.m. For the first time my two teenaged daughters were totally dependent on themselves. Miserable without their trusted friends, they tried to fit into a clique of students who really didn't need new friends. The San Marino High kids all knew each other—some since Kindergarten or first grade. This was not Lebanon or Greece, where the community schools were full of foreign children whose parents had been transferred. Here, everybody belonged. Many children seemed to have lived here since they were born.

Ulla Morris-Carter

But most importantly, Karin and Julia silently grieved for their father. During the previous six months our life had been hectic and disruptive. We had been in Germany to see my family. We had been to Italy to sort out the unfinished old farmhouse we had worked on over the past five years. Joe had loved this place even more than we did. In fact, he told us that he wanted to be buried in the old cemetery of Ameno, where graves with photographs of the deceased went back to 1870. Before he was killed, we had already booked a ferry passage from Greece to Italy for Easter holidays. Emotionally, I had wondered whether I could handle returning to our place in Italy, where we had worked so hard and found so much joy creating our first family home.

My brother Hans knew only too well that I was having a hard time dealing with a place that had meant so much to Joe and me. But Hans, wisely, took a longer view and insisted that I keep this old house regardless of my feelings:

"You don't own anything," he reminded me. You must keep this house. At least it's a piece of real estate, if nothing else. It might come in handy one day in the future."

Now all this lay behind us. We needed to get settled. But in this tumultuous beginning a few things fell by the wayside. There never seemed to be enough time for a heart-to-heart talk with my daughters. There wasn't enough time to grieve together. The two youngest needed to be listened to and to be reassured after difficult and stressful school days. My middle daughter, Karin, self-sufficient and directed, was an excellent student, athlete and allround team player. But my youngest one, beautiful and silky, artistic, extremely vulnerable and less self-confident, needed more support and guidance. Frequently I was not there to give it. I had to assume that they would manage—and, mostly, to the outside world, they did.

Different from those immigrants who had desperately desired to make the New World their home, we, on the contrary, were involuntary immigrants, who did not yearn to live in the United States. I had loved living in the Middle East with all its ups and downs. I had loved the flow of life without the heavy structure imposed by rules and regulations I knew from Germany. In Egypt, restrictions pertained mostly to religious rules and traditions. In that part of the world I experienced some of my happiest and also some of my saddest days.

I worried that my previously varied and exciting life had come to an end. That was never entirely true. What was true was that after a long period of sadness and grieving, I would manage to start a new life—different, but fulfilling and interesting.

Within a few years I would be fortunate enough to experience the second half of my life on a new and positive note.

Ulla Morris-Carter

Addenda

Cleaning my father's grave plaque.

FINDING MY FATHER'S GRAVE

Bill came running when he heard me shout.

This was 2004. Bill Carter, a wonderful writer, photographer and clarinet player, was and is, my second husband. We lived then in northern California, on the peninsula south of San Francisco.

"What happened?"

He arrived breathless, a worried look on his face, fearing I might have had some kind of a mishap in the kitchen. Instead he found me sitting in front of my computer, staring at the screen.

"You won't believe what I just found. Look, look!"

On the screen in front of me a photograph of a a gravestone somewhere in Brittany, France, with my father's name on it, had appeared. It included his date of birth, confirming for me that, indeed, this was my father's grave.

"Unbelievable, after all those years of searching . . ." was all I could utter.

My father had died 60 years ago.

My excitement gave way to sudden grief.

Drafted into the German army in 1941, my father was killed near Brest, France, in January, 1944. Brest is a French coastal city at the northwestern tip of Brittany. Occupied by Germany for most of WWII, Brest saw many fierce battles. Its protected harbor, where many German submarines were based, made it a prime target for British aerial attacks. Many were killed there, French and Germans alike, and the city was largely destroyed. Not until the Allied landing in Normandy in the summer of 1944 was Brest freed by American troops.

Ulla Morris-Carter

Top: *The chaplain's photo of my father's first grave in Brittany.*
Bottom: *The German Soldier's name registry from 1968.*

In early 1944, in the middle of a very cold winter, a German military chaplain found my father, lying in a ditch badly wounded and barely alive. The Chaplain rushed him to the nearest hospital, but my father died on the way. We never found out exactly what happened. Wars hardly ever give away details important only to those who are left behind.

Some months later, the chaplain sent my mother a photo of my father's grave, a mound of earth with a simple wooden cross on which my father's name was painted in white. But we never knew the specific location.

In those terrifying months toward the end of the war with their daily bombardments, it hardly mattered whether we knew the location or not. Neither my mother nor I had any chance of traveling to Brittany, or, for that matter, to any place. We grieved, like so many others, without a body, without a grave to visit, without what some call "closure."

After the war, we heard through an organization called the German War Graves Commission, that the Americans had laid out a cemetery in the northwest of Brittany for all fallen German soldiers. Apparently my father's grave was there. Then in 1961, the German War Graves Commission announced that the graves of all German soldiers buried in Brittany had been moved to yet another site. Where the new cemetery was we didn't know for years.

My mother, who was blind for many years, was unable to follow up with the War Graves Commission. I, myself, busy bringing up three children in Lebanon and Greece, often without their father present, had no time to search for my father's grave. And even less so after Joe's death in Iran.

Computers entered our lives in the late 1980s, and many things changed. I began to research the site of the German War Graves Commission again, but without success.

In 2004, I glanced at the site once more and discovered that it had been updated. New information was available. Suddenly, the exact location of my father's grave and even a photo of it appeared on my computer screen. The German War Graves cemetery is located in a small town called Ploudaniel-Lesneven, 16 miles north of Brest.

Ulla Morris-Carter

I was stunned and emotionally undone. Bill immediately and generously decided that we should travel to France to find my father's grave. I studied the computer site intently. It revealed in detail the exact location of the grave, even mentioning the row and grave number.

We decided to travel right away. It was early May, 2004. Summer vacations hadn't started yet, and prices for a flight to France were relatively low. A week later we were ready to start. I was surprised by my emotional reaction. Never had it occurred to me that locating my father's grave would affect me so.

Twelve hours after departure from San Francisco, we arrived at Charles de Gaulle airport near Paris, where we boarded the TGV, Train Grande Vitesse, the rapid or bullet train, that took us in four-and-a-half hours to Brest. There, we rented a car and started off in search of Ploudaniel-Lesneven.

Even more than 60 years after the war, many of the French people whom we asked for directions to the German War cemetery, looked at us somewhat suspiciously and did not always seem particularly friendly. I could hardly blame them when I thought of the heavy damage the region had suffered during the war.

Eventually we found Ploudaniel, a small and quiet town, but we still couldn't find the cemetery. There were no signs to guide us, no arrows pointing toward a cemetery.

Finally, somewhere outside the town, we saw a long stone wall with the sign:

Deutscher Soldatenfriedhof *(German Soldiers Cemetary)*
Ploudaniel-Lesneven
Cimetière Militaire Allemand 1939-1945

This cemetery, amid wild flowers and grassy fields and surrounded by trees brought tears to my eyes. We did not encounter another living soul. It was a sunny day, totally quiet and totally peaceful.

A sign at the entrance hall reads:

Important Information about this Cemetery
This war cemetery was established by the Americans after the battles for the fortress of Brest and was later expanded by the French authorities. After the conclusion of the French-German War Graves Treaty of 1954, the Volksbund began in 1961 with the reburial in this cemetery of the German dead from the Finistére and Côte-du-Nord départments. With financial assistance from members and donors and with German Federal Government subsidies, the Volksbund expanded the cemetery. 5,831 soldiers are now buried there. On 7 September 1968 this war cemetery was publicly inaugurated.

A second sign explained the German War Graves Commission:

Our aim is to care for the graves of the victims of war and violence. We are a non-profit organization, which has been carrying out this work since 1919, when the state itself was unable to look after the dead from the 1914/18 War.

Ulla Morris-Carter

RIVERS OF MY LIFE

Left: *Sign pointing to the cemetary.* **Right:** *The German Soldier Cemetary,* Deutscher Soldatenfriedhof.

Today, on behalf of the government of the Federal Republic of Germany we look after 1.4 million German war graves from both World Wars in 30 countries in the Western World. Since 1990 we have also been working in the countries of Eastern Europe–a great challenge. War graves remind us of the horror of war. Everybody who wants to help is welcome to continue our work for peace.

The burial field was divided into 14 blocks. Two pathways led to the centrally located memorial. The memorial with its Comrades' Graves, the grave of the unknown soldiers, was a particularly powerful site, surrounded by a 23-meter circular wall resting on 12 reinforced concrete pillars.

In the middle of this circle was the Comrades' Grave, where 224 war dead were buried. Three tall granite crosses resembling obelisks, stood guard over this simple, serene memorial.

Sitting inside the circular memorial wall of the Comrades' Graves of the Unknown Soldiers.

Ulla Morris-Carter

The grass felt soft under our feet as we walked along row after row of well-kept graves. No flowers, no personal memorials. This cemetery brought back memories of that war, with all its losses and hardships. Every grave contained the bodies of four soldiers, their names and birth dates marked on bronze tablets placed on top of a flat concrete block.

We had had no problem finding my father's name, "Hans Kirschbaum." The instructions, provided in the entrance hall, were amazingly accurate. My father's name was hard to decipher at first. But after a primitive cleaning effort with the help of Kleenex and paper napkins, the name emerged, now polished and easily readable.

We spent a long time walking in silence through several connected areas of the large cemetery. It left me with a sense of peace and gratitude. My only regret was that my mother was never able to see her beloved husband's last resting place.

On the way out we passed a bench where a grandmother was sitting quietly, watching her little granddaughter playing in the dirt. This brought us back to reality, to the simple understanding that life goes on.

Finding my father's grave.

Ulla Morris-Carter

I have estimated the influence of Reason
upon Love and found that it is like that of
a raindrop upon the ocean, which makes
one little mark upon the water's face and
disappears.

~ Hafiz, a mystic Persian Sufi poet, 1320-1389

AFTERWORD

PERSIA—IRAN

The name Persia immediately evokes visions of the conquests of Alexander the Great, of Isfahan's glorious gardens, of the lyrical poetry of Hafiz of Shiraz, and the magnificent ruins of Persepolis.

In more recent times, in the 1960s and 70s, we remember Shah Reza Pahlavi of Iran for his pro-Western orientation, but also for his extremely autocratic rule. The West, particularly the United States, had heavily supported the Shah because of the Cold War with the Soviet Union. But by 1977–78 there was growing dissatisfaction within Iran over the Shah's tight political control. As a journalist for the *New York Herald Tribune*, for *Newsweek*, and later for the *Los Angeles Times*, Joe covered Iran under Shah Reza Pahlavi from the mid-1950s up to the Iranian revolution in 1979, when Joe was killed.

Twenty years later, in 1998, my husband Bill and I (I remarried in 1985), had a chance to travel to Iran. The Santa Barbara Museum of Art organized a tour for a small group of mostly architects and their spouses or partners, to visit Iran and Uzbekistan. We were invited to join. Then, as now, it was difficult to visit Iran as a tourist. In 1998 visas had to be obtained via the Pakistani Embassy—a lengthy and arduous process.

Fabled Persian cities, such as Shiraz, Bishapur, Persepolis, Yazd and Isfahan were part of our travel program. Instructions on the dress code for women had to be strictly followed. Obeying Islamic rule, women had to wear long dresses or coats and socks, heads had to be covered at all times with a head scarf. No hair should be showing. When visiting holy places, a black chador had to be added. Make-up and jewelry were strictly forbidden. One of our first hotels greeted us with a banner headline "Death to the USA." Yet the Iranian people were extremely warm and welcoming, even excited

Ulla Morris-Carter

to see American tourists. Only groups, but not single individuals, were allowed to travel to Iran. Bill and I had flown four days ahead of our group, after receiving special permission. We stayed at the Laleh Hotel in Teheran—the former Intercontinental—where Joe and most of the foreign press had roomed in 1979. The new, young concierge was very surprised to see an American tourist, accompanied by a German lady, arrive at the hotel. Of course he wanted to know how we had managed to be there and why.

I was hesitant to answer on the first day, but relented on the second. When I told him that my late husband had stayed at the Intercontinental Hotel during the revolution, and had been killed in Teheran in 1979, the new concierge immediately mentioned the old night concierge, Ahmed, who apparently had been working at the Hotel during the time of the revolution.

"Ahmed knew all the journalists who stayed in this hotel very well. He is still alive and, as a matter of fact, helps out here occasionally and takes on the night shift. I will call you as soon as I am able to talk to him," the concierge promised.

An Iranian "tour guide" had been assigned as Bill and my minder. Ali turned out to be not only a terrific guide, but also a well-informed and very helpful person. He accompanied Bill and me on a flight to Mashad, some 500 miles northeast of Teheran—an important holy place we wanted to visit, which was not included in our travel itinerary. Mashad is considered Iran's holiest city, where the tomb of the 8th Imam, the Shiite Imam Reza, is located. Reza, we were told, was poisoned and martyred in Mashad in 818. He is considered, by some, the Imam of all Moslems. Thousands—some say millions—of pilgrims visit the holy shrine and the nearby golden-domed mosque every year. Foreigners like us were only allowed into the holy shrine as far as the outer circle. However, our wonderful guide Ali went to his sister's house in Mashad and borrowed an all-covering chador for me to wear inside the shrine. It allowed me to become an unrecognizable visitor as long as I did not lift my face to show my blue eyes.

It was an amazing feeling, at the age of 65, to do something totally forbidden. It reminded me of long-past school days when disobeying a school rule gave us great pleasure. Covered in three layers of clothing, I now could move closer to the most elaborate and beautiful inner sanctum of the shrine. It was not enough to wear scarves covering our heads and loose dresses to hide the shape of our bodies, but also long socks, to make sure not a piece of bare skin was visible. Thank God, it happened to be a cool day. I struggled with my chador—this shroud-like garment—that covers all but the face. The only way to secure it was by using one hand to hold it tightly under the chin.

When we returned to our hotel in Teheran, our American group of ten had arrived. Led by the former British Ambassador to Iran, Paul Bergne, who spoke fluent Farsi, Arabic and German, we had a most knowledgable and fantastic docent. We were fortunate to travel through Teheran's terrifying traffic in an extremely comfortable

Ulla Morris-Carter

bus. This bus had that same year been used by Iran's reformist President Mohammad Khatami during his successful national campaign in 1998. In the back of the bus was a conference room that could be curtained off, if desired.

Equipped with little tables, decorated with plastic flowers in small vases, our bus displayed large photos of President Khatami on two side windows and on the back of the bus. Frequently, Iranians would stop, looking startled and surprised to see a group of foreigners stepping off the presidential campaign bus.

On our return to the Laleh Hotel from one of our tours, the concierge excitedly called me to the front desk. The old concierge Ahmed, standing behing the desk, was waiting for me. With tears in his eyes he told me how unbelievably shocked and saddened he, and all the journalists staying at the Intercontinental in 1979, had been when they heard of Joe's death.

"Mrs. Morris, we all loved and admired your husband. I was assigned to go to his room and pack up his belongings to be sent back to America with the *New York Times* correspondent. I even still remember your American address."

While I was standing in the lobby, feeling quite shaky and jittery by this encounter, Ahmed called out to a gentleman who had just entered the lobby.

Ahmed introduced me to him and explained: "Mohamed was the head of the hotel taxi drivers in 1979."

Mohamed, extending his condolences, looking ever so sad and upset, said haltingly, "And I drove Mr. Morris to the airbase that fateful morning. As a matter of fact, I drove him to most of his appointments."

Mohamed spoke excellent English.

He continued: "My father's best friend was the commander of the airbase. It was he who called Mr. Morris at four a.m. to tell him of the trouble and the shootings at the base. My father is dead now, but the commander is still alive. He is a dear family friend. You must come and meet him at my house—I know he would love to see you."

What an unbelievable coincidence! Almost 20 years after Joe's death I was lucky enough to meet people who had known Joe on his last day alive. How could I not accept this invitation? Alas, I had to decline. Our group was leaving that same evening on the once-a-week flight to Tashkent, Uzbekistan. I had no way of catching up with them later.

Even today, in 2017, almost 37 years after Joe's death, I think of this extraordinary encounter in the lobby of the Laleh Hotel in Teheran—a time out of time, insulated from the present, in a capsule of bitter amazement, pain and joy so close and so far, not unlike a mystical moment in the poetry of ancient Persia.

Ulla Morris-Carter

REFERENCES AND SOURCES

Nikos Kazantzakis (1883-1957); Greek writer, poet and philosopher. Author of *Zorba the Greek*.

Pierre Nora (1931); French Historian.

William Manchester (1922-2004); American author, biographer.

Cecil Day-Lewis (1904-1972); Anglo-Irish poet and writer.

Erich Kästner (1899-1974); German author, poet, screenwriter and satirist.

Wolfgang Borchert (1921-1947); German author and playwright.

W. Ph. Davison; *The Berlin Blockade*.

Pope Pius XII. (1876-1958); reigned as Pope 1939-1958.

Khalil Gibran (1883-1931); Lebanese-American poet, writer and artist.

E. M. Forster (1879-1930); English novelist, short story writer.

Virginia Woolf (1882-1941); English writer, journalist, modernist.

Thomas Mann (1875-1955); German novelist, social critic, essayist, 1929 Nobel Price in Literature.

Harvey Overesh (1893-1973); Vice Admiral US Navy.

Herbert Hoover; 31st president of the United States, *The Memoirs of Herbert Hoover*.

David Roberts (1796-1764); Scottish Painter, known for lithographs and prints of the Middle East.

Amr ibn el As; seventh century Arab commander.

Francois-Rene de Chateaubriand (1768-1848); French writer, diplomat, historian.

Karl Dietrich Bracher (1922-2016); German historian of Weimar Republic and Nazi Germany.

Margarita Papandreou (1923-); *Nightmare in Athens*, former First Lady of Greece.

Hafiz (1315-1390) ;Persian lyric poet.

Ulla Morris-Carter